'Brave and brilliant. Guy Shrubsole tackles a subject as crucial as it is neglected, and succeeds magnificently'   George Monbiot

'No one writes about land ownership and governance with greater knowledge and passion than Guy Shrubsole. Urgent and essential, this forensic and compelling account should be required reading for all government ministers and for anyone who recognises that the fate of our land is far too important to be left to the few who own it'
                    Caroline Lucas

'The unjust impositions of historic land ownership blight all our lives – here Guy shows why'   Chris Packham

'Guy's book is dynamite that will explode – calmly, and with facts and reason – our comfortable myths about land ownership. Unlike earlier revolutionaries, this Guy has a smart, peaceful and practical plan for how we can turn this land into our land'   Patrick Barkham

'Guy Shrubsole has done it again. Exhilarating, insightful and bristling with rightful indignation, this is a book that will ignite the debate about our broken relationship with the land like never before'
                    Lee Schofield, author of *Wild Fell*

'This book beautifully subverts the central orthodoxy of England, that owning land is the only way to care for it. Rather than being against landowners, its message is one of hope and inclusion for every one of us'
                    Nick Hayes, author of *The Book of Trespass*

'Extraordinary. An affirmation of another kind of rural life that exists within this lie, and all the possibilities that are open to us if we defy it. It gives me so much strength'
                    Nicola Chester, author of *On Gallows Down*

'The land we love is ailing. Guy Shrubsole makes clear why and how the healing can begin. This unflinching, illuminating book manages to be both dynamite and medicine'   Amy-Jane Beer, author of *The Flow*

'A rousing call to action that proposes practical interventions for how management of the countryside could – and should – be improved for the benefit of both people and environment'
                    Claire Ratinon, author of *Unearthed*

'Who really cares for the countryside? Guy does. His articulate fervour, seasoned with humour, shouts from every page. He throws down a timely gauntlet to centuries of tradition'   Tom Heap, author of *Land Smart*

'A heartfelt, historically resonant call to reject the myth that private landownership delivers good stewardship of nature ... asks nature lovers to act now before it's too late'
Professor Corinne Fowler, author *of Our Island Stories: Country Walks Through Colonial Britain*

'Shrubsole sets out a bold new social contract between landowner and landless. Authoritative and well-researched, this is a most important book, essential reading for anyone who cares about the future of an environment we must – somehow – all share'
Marion Shoard, author of *This Land Is Our Land*

'Guy expertly guides us through the murky waters of land ownership in Britain with timely clarity, wisdom and insight. A book on this subject shouldn't be so readable. It's essential dynamite. A triumph'
Sophie Pavelle, author of *Forget Me Not*

'A groundplan to recover England's green and pleasant land'
Professor Alastair McIntosh, author of *Soil and Soul*

'Comprehensively researched, beautifully written and brilliantly argued ... it provides insightful and often novel solutions to deliver a better, more sustainable world. If you care about our environment, read this book'
Professor Sir John Lawton CBE FRS, Chair of Making Space for Nature

'Shrubsole has the belly fire of a campaigner but the precision of a historian. This book should be on the reading list of any new secretary of state thinking about land use'
Roger Mortlock, Chief Executive of CPRE, the Countryside Charity

'Essential reading for everyone who cares for our countryside and loves our National Parks. Radical and urgent, measured and considered ... If the Labour government is serious about wilder National Parks, *The Lie of the Land* is the place to start'
Dr Rose O'Neill, Chief Executive, Campaign for National Parks

THE LIE OF THE LAND

Who Really Cares for
the Countryside?

GUY SHRUBSOLE

**WILLIAM
COLLINS**

William Collins
An imprint of HarperCollins*Publishers*
1 London Bridge Street
London SE1 9GF

WilliamCollinsBooks.com

HarperCollins*Publishers*
Macken House,
39/40 Mayor Street Upper,
Dublin 1, D01 C9W8, Ireland

First published in Great Britain in 2024 by William Collins

1

A catalogue record for this book is available from the British Library

ISBN 978-0-00-865177-0

This book is set in Adobe Garamond Pro by HarperCollins*Publishers* India

Printed and bound in the UK using 100% renewable electricity at CPI Group (UK) Ltd

This book contains FSC™ certified paper and other controlled sources to ensure responsible forest management.

For more information visit: www.harpercollins.co.uk/green

For Amy, Dan, Harry, Jess, Jon,
Lewis, Maria, Nadia, Nick & Paul:
the best team I've ever been part of

'Land needs to be owned if it's to be looked after.'

— Matthew Parris, BBC Radio 4, 10 January 2023[1]

'The earth . . . shall become a common treasury for all.'

— Gerrard Winstanley, 1649[2]

CONTENTS

Introduction:
The Lies of the Land

Let me begin with the parable of the landowner who destroyed a river.

In 2023, John Price, a multimillionaire landowner and farmer, was jailed for destroying part of the River Lugg in Herefordshire. The Lugg, whose name means 'bright stream' in Welsh, rises in the Radnorshire Hills before flowing down through the small town of Presteigne and into England.[1] Its banks abound in willow trees and alders; dragonflies dance among the yellow irises and sprays of cow parsley lining its edges; Atlantic salmon thread their way through viridian mats of water crowfoot.

To own a stretch of this river is to possess a small slice of paradise. Yet to John Price, owner of over a kilometre of the Lugg and the lands either side, it needed work. Sometimes, after a downpour, the river would breach its banks and nearby fields would flood. So Price set about it with diggers and chainsaws.

After he had finished, the river no longer resembled the bright stream of its etymology. Photos of Price's tract of the Lugg look like a First World War battlefield: a morass of mud crisscrossed with tyre tracks and piled with sawn-up branches. The landowner ripped up seventy trees, drove a bulldozer along the river to dredge its bed, and used an 18-tonne digger to scour its banks of all vegetation.

Price's actions sparked a huge outcry. Large stretches of the Lugg are designated a Site of Special Scientific Interest (SSSI), or

1

'triple-S-I', for their unique habitat. Herefordshire Wildlife Trust called the incident 'a crime against the environment'.[2] Its chief executive, Jamie Audsley, bemoaned the 'immense harm' done to the site, saying: 'Landowners have a clear and vital responsibility to look after the rivers in their care.'[3] The government's green watchdog, Natural England, said that the damage to the SSSI had been 'devastating', and proceeded to press charges.[4] Presiding over the case, Judge Cole stated that John Price had displayed 'outrageous behaviour', and had engaged in 'vandalism of the environment on a grand scale'.[5]

In Price's view, he was simply being a custodian of the land. 'I have always looked after the river,' he claimed, in comments reported by the press. 'I was asked to stop the erosion because I'm the landowner so I'm responsible for the river.'[6] By re-profiling the meandering Lugg, Price had effectively turned it into a sterile and lifeless canal, down which any floodwaters could now flow faster. Future flooding had not been prevented: it had just moved further downstream, displaced from fields into front rooms.

Price's defenders, however, did not let these facts trouble them. 'He always says the farmers are the country's gardeners. We look after our land,' Price's partner told the press. 'He was trying to do the best and look after it in the way that they've done it for years and years, as he always says, like his father and like his grandfather.' In the wake of Price's conviction, other landowners and farmers circled the wagons, proclaiming him to be 'a very good farmer' who should be 'freed immediately and compensated'.[7] After Price was sentenced to twelve months in the clink, the *Telegraph* ran an extraordinary article defending him, claiming the government relied on landowners like him to be 'stewards of the land'.[8]

Not everyone agreed, of course. Ben Goldsmith, a prominent Conservative environmentalist and landowner himself, observed that 'many "custodians" of the countryside aren't quite the custodians they like us to think they are'.[9] The environmental campaigner George Monbiot concurred: 'It's bad enough that the extreme concentration of landholding in the UK means an extreme concentration of daily decision-making . . . It's worse still when they insist on being treated as the "guardians of the countryside".'[10]

We are constantly told by politicians and the press that landowners and farmers are the 'custodians of the countryside', its trusted stewards; yet the fate of the River Lugg stands as a clear refutation of that idea. Stewardship, though a noble ideal, is too often greenwash – deployed as a PR term by groups like the Country Land and Business Association (CLA) and National Farmers Union (NFU) to deflect attention away from the many landowners who are doing the opposite. One might conclude that the parable of John Price is a classic tale of hubris: from self-proclaimed custodian, to custodial sentence.

But if we see Price as an aberration, a lone 'bad apple' spoiling the barrel, we are missing the true lesson of his example. What's truly disturbing about the story of John Price is that his actions were wholly consistent with how private property rights normally operate. Price was merely giving full expression to a time-honoured right of all landowners: the *jus abutendi*, or right to destroy.

Land ownership comprises a 'bundle of rights' – such as the right to enjoy the fruits of the land, and the right to exclude others from it (which is where trespass laws originate). One of the rights included in this happy bundle is the right to destroy or abuse the land. As the legal thinker John Sprankling puts it, 'The right to destroy is an inherent component of the right to property . . . Today major legal systems implicitly recognize that an owner is entitled to consume or transform the thing that is the object of property rights.'[11] The right of landowners to destroy and waste their property has been settled law for centuries. As the eighteenth-century legal scholar William Blackstone stated, 'if a man be the absolute tenant in fee simple* . . . he may commit whatever waste his own indiscretion may prompt him to, without being impeachable or accountable for it to anyone.'[12]

Without being accountable for it to anyone. You and I, as members of the public, have very little say over how land is used and abused by its owners. In England, just 1 per cent of the population own half the land, and we are told they can be trusted to steward it on our behalf. So what happens when they fail to

---

* In other words, a freehold owner.

look after the land? To whom are the self-proclaimed stewards accountable, but themselves?

The only reason that John Price was held to account was because his land happened to fall within the 8 per cent of England that's designated as Sites of Special Scientific Interest. These comprise some of our best remaining habitats, from gorgeous chalk streams and lichen-clad ancient woodlands to windswept moorlands. Over this small fraction of the countryside, the landowner's 'right to destroy' has been qualified and curtailed by the government, following decades of campaigning by environmental groups.

Yet even here, all is not well for nature. Between 2006 and 2021, Natural England issued just fourteen prosecutions for damage to SSSIs.[13] The true extent of the degradation is far greater: less than half of English SSSIs are judged to be in favourable condition.[14] Many others are declining, thanks to overgrazing, burning, ploughing and other forms of neglect and abuse. It's possible to prosecute a landowner for actively destroying a nature reserve, but far more difficult to hold them accountable for ongoing damage. The government, meanwhile, has pledged to protect 30 per cent of England for nature by the year 2030 – a UN-backed commitment known as '30x30'. This would require far more landowners and farmers to get involved in nature recovery than just those who own SSSIs. Yet conservation groups reckon that only 3 per cent of England is properly protected and managed for nature at present.[15]

Some have argued for property rights to be changed to remove the right to destroy and replace it with a legal duty of stewardship. The academic Christopher Rodgers, for example, makes the case for the introduction of 'a general duty of environmental stewardship as an attribute of property ownership in the law of England and Wales'.[16] But such ideas remain politically taboo, occupying the fringes of intellectual discourse.

Instead, it remains the assumption of most politicians and commentators that – in the words of former Tory MP Matthew Parris – 'land needs to be owned if it's to be looked after.' Yet the actions of landowners like John Price remind us that ownership confers many more rights than it does responsibilities; even the right to destroy. Most 'responsibilities' that come with land ownership are ethical rather than legal duties – exercised voluntarily, if at all. It is often only where the public has pushed for laws to override such private property rights, like legal protections for nature reserves, that landowners start to act in the public interest.

The idea that you need to own land in order to care for it is being challenged from another direction, too. Just downstream from where a landowner destroyed a river, there are groups of landless people doing a far better job of stewardship.

The Lugg is a tributary of the River Wye: a watercourse which has become a symbol of the dire state of Britain's rivers. In the eighteenth century, the landscape writer William Gilpin could recommend drinking 'a draught of pure water from the fountains of the Wye'.[17] Anyone taking Gilpin's advice today would risk contracting a serious stomach bug. The waters of the Wye have been described as now resembling pea soup, due to increasingly vast algal blooms triggered by nitrogen pollution. Salmon numbers in the river have declined by some 94 per cent since the 1960s.[18] And in 2023, Natural England downgraded the ecological status of the Wye, declaring it to be in declining condition.[19] Everyone agrees on the main cause of this catastrophe: the giant chicken farms that have spread like a rash over the river's watershed, pumping the Wye full of chicken shit. *Nearly* everyone, that is. Characteristically, the NFU has protested that farming is not to blame for the pollution in the Wye – despite studies showing that up to 70 per cent of the phosphate load in the river stems from agriculture.[20]

But the River Wye has also become a byword for something else: citizen campaigning. The cause of caring for the Wye has fallen not to its landowners, but rather to a huge panoply of community groups who swim, fish and kayak along the river – very few of whom actually own the land they're trying to protect.

In 2021, the Save the Wye campaign – a coalition of local residents – staged a month-long pilgrimage along the full length of the river, from its source in Wales to where it flows into the Severn Estuary. Pure springwater was gathered from the headwaters of the Wye at Pumlumon, and carried downstream by a succession of walkers, canoeists and paddleboarders. 'Our connection to the river Wye is strong,' declares the campaign's website. 'We live, work, play and are inspired by it . . . We are passionate about defending it and all life that depends on it – for ourselves and for the future. If the river dies, we die.'[21] Another community group, the Friends of the Upper Wye, runs citizen science projects to monitor water pollution along the river. They describe their purpose as being 'to defend and champion our local river' and to 'restore the ecological health of the river for local communities, for visitors to the region and for all the invertebrates, fish, mammals and birds that also call it home'.[22]

Elsewhere in England, some river campaigners have gone still further – by declaring that rivers are not mere property to own, but have rights themselves. On Midsummer's Day in 2021, a group of Cambridge residents gathered to solemnly declare the rights of the River Cam, including the 'right to be free from pollution' and the 'right to flow'.[23] The barrister Paul Powlesland, who helped initiate the declaration, has pioneered the idea in the UK that nature should have rights – as it has among many indigenous cultures around the world, such as the Maori people of New Zealand. Equally at home in smart legal attire or a pink jumpsuit, Powlesland lives in a canal boat on the River Roding in London, and at weekends can usually be found picking up rubbish along its length or reporting pollution incidents to the authorities. 'I relate to the river as a sacred entity,' he says, 'and I'm doing whatever I can to uphold those rights, through law, campaigning or direct action.'[24]

Such a philosophy is underpinned by the idea that if rivers can be deemed 'alive', and granted legal personhood, then no one can truly own them – as we would nowadays shudder at the concept of one person owning another as goods and chattels. The sense that *no one* can own land – that we belong to the Earth, rather than the Earth belonging to us – is a revolutionary one. But dispensing with ideas of ownership and giving rights to nature seems alien in a country like England, which essentially invented private property rights. 'The UK is one of the hardest nuts to crack,' Powlesland says. 'We are where the idea of nature as a resource originated.'[25]

None of these activists own huge estates or great tracts of land, yet they care for land and water that they do not own. They love these rivers because they live beside them, use them, take pleasure in being near them. Still, if one is to develop such a deep love for a particular place, it helps to have access to it. Most of England's rivers are off-limits to the public: 96 per cent of waterways in England and Wales have no clear rights of navigation for kayakers and canoeists, and the laws surrounding wild swimming are as murky as the waters its enthusiasts swim in.[26] The Wye is one of the few rivers to have clear access rights along its full length (in England, at least),[27] so it's no coincidence that this is where some of the most vocal campaigns against river pollution have arisen. Of course, this flies in the face of conventional wisdom, which argues that the public has to be kept out of the countryside for fear that they will mess it up, with discarded crisp packets and dogs let off leads.

As the nature writer and enthusiastic wild swimmer Amy-Jane Beer writes in *The Flow*, her elegiac love-letter to rivers: 'In every access debate you come across the entrenched idea that people who don't own land cannot be trusted to treat it well. This overlooks both the countless individual and community actions that actively benefit the environment, and the fact that plenty of people who do own land mistreat it appallingly.'[28] The idea that we should allow the public to have greater access to nature, *precisely in order to care for it more*, stands the whole access debate on its head.

At this point, you might reasonably be thinking that not all landowners are as bad as all that. Aren't there some really green farmers too?

Yes – there absolutely are. I could easily write a book praising the efforts of enlightened landowners, drawing on my own anecdotal experiences. It would certainly cause me less grief to do so, and perhaps even win me praise from the landowning establishment.

I could tell you that my grandparents farmed in Cornwall all their lives, and that my mum grew up on the family farm. I could recount my memories of visiting the farm growing up, and talking to my nature-loving Nan about the cuckoos she used to hear in the area when she was younger, whose song had since fallen silent. I could regale you with stories of the amazing farmers I've come to call friends since moving to Devon three years ago: like Naomi Oakley, whose tenanted farm on Duchy of Cornwall land is awash with orchids each spring. Or the landowner John Howell, whose work to regenerate the temperate rainforest of Piles Copse on Dartmoor is little short of heroic. Or Rebecca Hosking, a regenerative farmer in the South Hams who is pushing back against the trend in the region to intensify dairy production. Or Will Watson, an energetic young farmer near Totnes who's following in the footsteps of his uncle, the organic pioneer Guy Singh-Watson.

But the plural of anecdote is not data.

After all, there have been many books written about – and by – green farmers and landowners already. I'm in awe of the work of rewilding pioneers Isabella Tree and Charlie Burrell on their Knepp Estate in Sussex, for example, whose efforts are recounted in Tree's bestselling book *Wilding*. One summer, I spent a joyous day at Knepp searching for Purple Emperor butterflies gliding majestically amidst the veteran oaks, and lost my way ambling through the fields of regenerating scrub and vibrant ragwort. I also hugely admire the work of Jake Fiennes, manager of the huge Holkham Estate in Norfolk and author of the book *Land Healer*, who succeeds in balancing ecological restoration with food production and public access. And the example set by James Rebanks, Lakeland shepherd and author of *English Pastoral*, in returning nature to his farm, deserves replication across the uplands.

The trouble is, the work of these heroes remains too small to turn the tide of destruction on its own. The combined acreage of land owned or managed by Issy, Charlie, Jake and James runs to just 0.09 per cent of England.[29] There's no doubt, of course, that the example they've set has inspired others to follow in their footsteps. But a handful of enlightened landowners, farmers and land managers does not negate the ongoing damage done by the majority. And the groups that claim to represent the sector – the National Farmers Union, the Moorland Association, the Countryside Alliance and others – continue to lobby vociferously for what are evidently ecologically destructive practices, for profit over people and planet, and for the defence of private property rights at all costs. All whilst blithely assuring us that all is well, and that their members can be trusted to care for the countryside.

When we turn from anecdotal evidence to hard data, we see that something is rotten in the state of Britain. We have lost half of all farmland birds since 1970. Ninety-seven per cent of lowland hay meadows, once bursting with wildflowers, have been destroyed since the 1930s. Half of our ancient woodland was cut down in just three decades in the middle of the twentieth century, lost to modern plantation forestry and intensive agriculture. Thousands of miles of hedgerows were grubbed up over the same period. More recently, once-common species like hedgehogs have started to see their populations go into freefall. Insect numbers are in terrifying decline. Even earthworms, crucial to soil formation, are threatened: UK populations of them may have fallen by about a third in the past twenty-five years.[30] Expressed as cold statistics, the temptation may be to shrug; what can be done? But as the folk singer Utah Phillips once said, 'The Earth is not dying. It is being killed, and the people killing it have names and addresses.'

So yes: not *all* landowners are destroying the environment – in the same way that not all men are sexist, and not all white people are racist. The problem is that *some* are, and they are propped up by a system of entrenched power. Unsustainable land use is embedded in government policies, defended by landed interests, even woven into the legal tapestry of private property rights. And none of that is resolved by simply praising the farmers and landowners doing good things. We wouldn't absolve the fossil fuel company Shell for their crimes against the planet by pointing to the wind farms and solar panels installed by a green start-up like Ecotricity. Every sector of the economy has progressive pioneers doing good, but every sector also has its laggards and, sometimes, downright reactionaries who resist all change. That's just as true among landowners and farmers. The only difference is our peculiarly British (and particularly English) reticence in talking about who owns land, who has a say over how it's used, and who's responsible for screwing it up – because for centuries, these subjects have been taboo. Defence of landed property has ensured that even mild proposals for land reform are often dismissed as the 'politics of envy'.[31]

'The main British conservation groups have routinely praised the good in farming and ignored the bad,' argues the veteran environmental campaigner Chris Rose. For decades, Rose contends, nature conservationists hoped to inspire landowners and farmers to become greener by promoting examples of 'good farming'. 'It made some progress,' he concludes, 'but was ultimately a failed strategy. It recruited perhaps 2–5% of farmers.'[32] There's little point in lavishing attention on a few rewilded fields if the engine of destruction continues apace just down the road. If we're to make progress towards fixing habitats and restoring species in these dewilded isles, we also have to be prepared to call out bad practice.

And if we hold up a few individuals as examples of good stewards, we should really also be pointing out that it's a small handful of landowners who've had a disproportionately negative impact on the ecosystems of this country. I was inspired to investigate this by a line in John McNeill's environmental history of the twentieth century, *Something New Under the Sun*. McNeill recounts that it was one man, the chemist Thomas Midgley, who invented both leaded petrol and ozone-depleting CFCs – whose subsequent use resulted, respectively, in millions of people breathing poisoned air, and a vast hole being ripped in the Earth's ozone layer. McNeill says Midgley 'had more impact on the atmosphere than any other single organism in earth history'.[33]

Later chapters will introduce you to a cast of characters who have had similarly outsize impacts on the landscapes and ecosystems of Britain.* We have, for example, Queen Victoria

---

*This is a book primarily about England, and what the Westminster government needs to do to change how land is used and abused. At points, it strays into Wales and Scotland – both to illustrate how the Scottish Highlands became a playground for England's aristocracy, and how Scotland's more recent experience of land reform should be a model for the rest of Britain to follow.

and Prince Albert to thank for sparking the fashion for driven grouse moors, which has transformed millions of acres of our uplands in the past century and a half. Decades of moorland burning and drainage, to make conditions favourable for grouse, has tipped these peat bogs from being vast carbon sinks into active sources of greenhouse gases, fuelling the climate crisis. The Fens of Cambridgeshire, meanwhile, used to be one of the largest wetlands in Europe: yet all it took to drain them was thirteen Stuart-era venture capitalists, led by the landowning 4th Earl of Bedford. And it was due to the misguided foibles of the Earl's descendant, the 11th Duke of Bedford, that we now have grey squirrels in this country – an invasive species that's wreaked havoc on England's native red squirrels.

But though I point to these individuals as examples, the problem of unsustainable land use is a systemic one. And the solution has to be systemic, too. We have to make the self-appointed custodians of the countryside answerable to the rest of us.

This book is about how we use our land – but it's also about exposing the lies we tell about our countryside.

There are many such myths in need of busting. One such popular misconception is the idea that England is now mostly concreted over. Coupled to this is the idea that the onward march of bricks and mortar is the main cause of declining species and habitats. Neither assertion is true. Just 8.8 per cent of England is built on; 73 per cent is farmland, and 10 per cent forestry.[34] The biggest drivers of biodiversity loss in this country are modern agriculture, forestry and shooting.[35] All of these take up far more land than our urban areas. That's not to say that new roads, infrastructure and housing developments don't threaten wildlife: but when assessing the threats to nature, we remain in thrall to the Victorian idea that our supposedly 'green and pleasant land' is threatened only by the 'dark satanic mills' of urban industry. In fact, the greatest threat to the countryside comes from within it.

Related to this is the myth of the 'rural–urban divide': the idea that the people who live in towns are utterly different from those who live in the countryside. It's a myth that groups like the Countryside Alliance and landowning *Telegraph* columnists love to stoke, stirring up fears about townies invading rural areas, dropping litter and fuelling crime. The reason for spreading this lie is to get the public to butt out of rural affairs: *you have no authority here, Jackie Weaver.* Unless you're born and bred in the countryside, so the narrative goes, you have no say over how we do things. Never mind the billions of pounds of taxpayers' money that prop up England's farmers and landowners. Never mind the fact that pretty much everyone in England lived on the land, up until the enclosure movement kicked people off it, as we'll see in the next chapter. Now, when the public seeks a greater right to roam in the countryside, beyond the 8 per cent of England in which it's currently legal, they are rebuffed by the large landowners whose ancestors did the enclosing. The accompanying retort – *would you like it if I came and trespassed in your garden?* – is a testament to how distorted our understanding of land has become. By conflating all land in England with someone's veg plot, we ignore the fact that private homes and gardens take up just 5 per cent of the country. The reality is that we all have a legitimate interest in how the other 95 per cent of our land is used, because we all depend upon it.

Coupled with this is the idea that 'this country is full'. Those were the words used in 2012 by Tory MP Richard Drax, owner of the 14,000-acre Charborough Estate in Dorset, which is bounded by one of the longest walls in the country – presumably to keep the rest of us out.[36] If only landowners like Drax would share a little more of their extensive estates with us plebs, perhaps living conditions in our cities wouldn't feel so crowded. England is certainly a densely populated nation, though no more so than the Netherlands.[37] But such arguments are usually wheeled out to attack immigration, rather than to debate how we might make best use of our limited supply of land. What we consume, rather than how many people live here, is a much more important determinant of how we use our land. Various studies have been done on the question of 'can Britain feed itself?' The answer is always 'yes – by eating less meat and dairy.'[38] But the anti-immigrant voices would rather blame someone else for the country's woes before changing their diets or altering land use.

Then there's the myth that we need every scrap of land in England to grow food. Not so. There are large swathes of the country where, for reasons of geography, climate and poor soil quality, food production has always been marginal. In fact, as the independent National Food Strategy concluded in 2021, England could essentially cease farming on 21 per cent of its least productive land, and only make a 3 per cent dent in food production.[39] That tiny reduction could be more than made up for by eating less meat and dairy, diverting fewer crops to feed livestock and biomass power stations, and wasting less food. Most of the landscapes I discuss in this book are extremely marginal for agriculture – from upland peat bogs to chalk downland – and have only been yoked into efforts to eke food from them in the past hundred years. In the twenty-first century, we ought to be prioritising these places for nature restoration, carbon storage and flood mitigation, rather than try to squeeze a few calories from them.

Another myth is the notion that all landowners are farmers. In fact, this wasn't even true at the time of the Norman Conquest. The two hundred Norman barons who were handed half of England as spoils of war by William the Conqueror didn't sully themselves with tilling the fields: they left that to their serfs.[40] Today, parts of England are still owned by descendants of those Norman barons. Plenty of these landowners have very little to do with their land: they lease it to farmers, and have their estates run by land agents and gamekeepers. Many are absentee landlords, flitting between town house and country manor. England's uplands are often depicted as the preserve of small-scale sheep farmers, but they are actually *owned* by a tiny elite of aristocrats and City bankers, who occasionally visit their vast estates to shoot grouse. But because being a farmer is rightly seen as hard, honest work, lots of big landowners like to claim they're the salt of the earth. Alexander and Diana Darwall, who famously brought a court case to contest the right to wild camp on Dartmoor, were often described in fawning press articles as a 'farming couple'.[41] In reality, Alexander Darwall is a hedge fund manager, who employs other people to do the actual work of managing hedges, and whose 4,000-acre estate is devoted to pheasant shooting and deer stalking.[42]

But the greatest lie of the land is the idea that you have to own land to care for it. That private property ownership is the only way that people come to steward and look after land for the long term. This is frequently not the case – whether it's grouse moor owners setting fire to our biggest carbon store, or institutional landowners like the Church letting our fertile Fenland soils blow into the sea, or dukes who've unleashed invasive species into our countryside. And there are many alternative ways to repair our wounded land, rather than relying on voluntary efforts by private landowners.

Voluntarism, after all, is not working. Land use remains one of the most weakly regulated parts of the economy, despite accounting for 11 per cent of UK greenhouse gas emissions.[43] As the government's climate adviser, the Climate Change Committee (CCC), has pointed out, 'the agriculture and land use sectors do not have a dedicated Net Zero delivery plan or strategy.'[44] The CCC has warned that 'in agriculture and land use, emissions are essentially unchanged from a decade ago'; yet 'the land use sector must become a net [carbon] sink by the mid-2030s.'[45] To achieve this, there need to be major increases in peatland restoration and woodland creation. Instead, progress has been sluggish. Just 10,000 acres of peat was rewetted in England in 2022, well off course to meet the government's own target of restoring 35,000 acres annually by 2025; and only 7,000 acres of trees planted, versus a target of 18,000 acres per year by the end of this parliament.[46] As for turning sterile conifer plantations back into wildlife-rich deciduous woodlands: the area of Plantations on Ancient Woodland Sites restored by all private landowners in England in 2022 was a pathetic 2.5 acres.[47]

Paying landowners and farmers to be good stewards is not delivering either. The government has set much store by Environmental Land Management schemes (ELMs), its post-Brexit system of farm payments. Within this, the lowest-ambition tier of payments, the Sustainable Farming Incentive, has been allocated the lion's share of the budget. But as one recent analysis put it, this scheme will 'deliver only 2.6 per cent of the UK-wide emissions cuts needed from the farming sector from 2023 to 2027'.[48] The more ambitious Landscape Recovery scheme, meanwhile, has been starved of cash.[49]

We don't treat any other sector of the economy with such kid gloves. Energy companies are not relied upon to *voluntarily* cut their emissions: they are regulated. A decade ago, legal limits were placed on power plant emissions, and firms forced to pay a Carbon Floor Price to wean them off polluting fuels. As a result, power sector emissions have plummeted, with reliance on coal collapsing from 28 per cent of the electricity mix in 2010 to just 2 per cent in 2022.[50] Our deference to landed power, however, means no similar transition has yet occurred in how we treat our land.

Yet there are plenty of alternatives to relying on the 'custodians of the countryside' to wake up and smell the coffee. Why does England not take lessons from Scotland, and empower communities to buy more land for nature restoration? Why doesn't the state spend less money paying landowners who fail to deliver, and more on buying land itself, creating a new Public Nature Estate in the process? Why are our national parks not, in fact, owned by the nation – and why do we not give national park authorities the powers to make these precious places wilder? This book will make the case for a series of radical new policies that would transform nature conservation in England and put the country on a path to restoring its lost wildlife.

Most of all, we have to find ways of making the governance of our land more democratic. Owning land, particularly large swathes of it, ought to come with serious responsibilities to society and to the rest of the natural world. And to be meaningful, those responsibilities can't just be answerable to your own conscience, or to abstract notions of future generations. Those claiming to be stewards of the land have to be made accountable to the public in the here and now.

1

Stewards of the Earth

What would it mean to be a steward or custodian of the land, as landowners often claim to be? The dictionary definition of 'stewardship' is 'the careful and responsible management of something entrusted to one's care'.[1] Its etymology dates back to the Middle Ages, when a 'sty-ward' was the ward of a lord's pigsty: he looked after the swine for his master. To be a 'custodian' is similarly defined as someone 'entrusted with guarding and keeping property'.[2] The essence of stewardship, therefore, is to care for something on behalf of someone else.

But who are landowners stewarding the land for? And why are the public at large not regarded as being capable stewards of the land? These questions are seldom asked, let alone answered by those who repeat the mantra of stewardship.

'British landowners and farmers are among the most progressive stewards of the natural environment found anywhere in the world,' asserts Mark Tufnell, President of the Country Land and Business Association[3] – whose members own around a third of the land of England and Wales.[4] 'Moorland managers are the stewards of these precious places for the benefit of all,' declares the Moorland Association, a lobby group that represents grouse shooting interests.[5]

Britain's aristocracy also make regular reference to themselves as stewards of the land. There are, for example, twenty-two dukes in the British Isles today who own land, together possessing

16

around a million acres.[6] I took a look at the websites for each of these vast ducal estates: over half of them boast of their 'stewardship' of the countryside.[7] 'The Estate is responsible for the long-term stewardship of almost 100,000 acres of agricultural land,' proclaims the website of Northumberland Estates, the landholdings of the Duke of Northumberland.[8] Many of the ducal families have owned land in this country for centuries, and want us to know that this inherited privilege makes them excellent custodians of the land for the future. 'As current stewards of the Belvoir Estate,' says the website of the Duke of Rutland, 'following in the footsteps of our ancestors here over the past thousand years, we are very conscious of our responsibilities in nurturing this land in the best way possible for future generations.'[9]

Our political leaders are also in thrall to the idea of stewardship. The then Environment Secretary, Thérèse Coffey, told the annual conference of the National Farmers Union in February 2023: 'I do believe our farmers are true custodians – of the natural environment, of food production, and our countryside.'[10] Her predecessor, the climate sceptic Owen Paterson – by general consensus one of the worst Secretaries of State for the Environment ever – similarly praised private owners' 'environmental stewardship, in which people are prompted naturally and without compulsion to fulfil their social obligations'.[11]

Not everyone is convinced by such declarations of stewardship: not even all landowners or farmers. The Lake District shepherd James Rebanks, author of several bestselling books, puts it most pithily. 'I'm a very proud defender of good farming,' he posted on Twitter in 2021, 'but the "custodians of the countryside" argument only washes if we are genuinely doing that – otherwise it's self serving bullshit.'[12]

I'm with James Rebanks on this one. It's the argument of this chapter – and this book – that while stewardship of the land is a noble ideal, too often it's deployed by landowners as self-serving bullshit. It has become a way of justifying the continued ownership of land by a small elite, and a form of greenwash – a

PR tool to look like you're doing good deeds for the environment, without actually doing them.

More insidiously, these unchallenged assertions of custodianship have been deployed to avoid the public looking too closely at what actually goes on in the countryside. Politicians wedded to the ideology of a small state, austerity and 'cutting red tape' have invoked the supposedly inherent desire of all landowners to be good stewards of their land, in order to justify environmental deregulation and rely instead on 'voluntary initiatives' by estates. While the public sector has been starved of cash, huge amounts of taxpayers' money has continued to be handed out to private landowners in the form of farm subsidies.

How did stewardship become a term with such currency amongst the landowning classes? And when it's invoked, what other interests might it serve? To answer these questions, we need to turn back the clock to a time in certain ways strangely similar to our own, a time of escalating energy crises, rampant inequality, war and revolution. Back to when King Charles was on the throne, land reform was in the air, and commentators were urging landowners to plant more trees. Back, of course, to the seventeenth century.

In the seventeenth century, anyone looking for guidance on how the Earth's riches should best be managed and shared would naturally turn first to the Bible. In 1611, the King James Version was published – one of the first translations of the Bible into English, rather than Latin, meaning it reached a far wider readership. In Genesis, the biblical account of the creation of the world, readers could now discover how God gave humanity 'dominion over the fish of the sea, and over the fowl of the air, and over the cattle, and over all the earth, and over every creeping thing that creepeth upon the earth'.[13] A later verse in Genesis also referred to God placing Adam in the Garden of Eden 'to dress it and to keep it'.[14] The Edenic paradise was a picture of abundance, with the world a well-stocked larder created for humanity to feast upon.

Some environmental thinkers have seen in these injunctions the root of humanity's ecological destructiveness. Historian Lynn White, for example, blamed Christianity's anthropocentrism for causing the environmental crisis: 'no item in the physical creation had any purpose save to serve man's purposes.'[15]

But there was another interpretation, most eloquently put forward by the influential English barrister Matthew Hale, Chief Justice of the King's Bench under Charles II. In his essay 'The Great Audit, with the Account of the Good Steward', published in 1679, Hale asserted that God had only given humanity temporary stewardship over nature. In Hale's own life, 'I received and used thy Creatures as committed to me under a Trust', he wrote, 'and as a Steward and Accomptant [accountant] for them; and therefore I was always careful to use them according to those limits . . . with Temperance and Moderation.'[16] After all, as the book of Psalms stated, 'The Earth is the Lord's, and the fulness thereof.'[17] If the Earth belonged to God, humanity could only hope to be its stewards on God's behalf.

Hale's ideas about good stewardship had powerful resonance in the seventeenth century, because it was becoming obvious that Britain was already exhausting some of its natural resources. In particular, the reign of the Stuart monarchs was beset by an energy crisis. The nation was fast running out of wood.

Britain's forests were being decimated for fuel – both for domestic hearths, and for the fires of industry. Timber, meanwhile, was essential for constructing the ships of the British Navy. Writer Michael Drayton, in his epic poem *Poly-Olbion*, bemoaned the destruction of the ancient woodlands of the Weald for iron smelting, writing how 'mans devouring hand . . . Hath hew'd her timber downe'.[18] Drayton imagined even the dryads – the tree-spirits of classical mythology – being driven from England's woods as a result of deforestation.[19] The agriculturalist Arthur Standish wrote several pamphlets advocating 'the increasing of Woods, the decay whereof in this Realme is universally complained of'.[20] There was little sign of these God-given resources being used with the 'temperance and moderation' demanded by Hale.

The energy crisis of the Stuart era gave rise to one of the earliest examples of environmental advocacy. In 1664, the celebrated diarist John Evelyn published *Sylva, or A Discourse of Forest-Trees*, urging landowners to replenish the nation's woods. Evelyn raged against the iron industry which had 'wasted our stately woods', and implored the aristocratic landowners of great estates to get planting: 'How goodly a sight were it, if most of the demesnes of our countrey gentlemen were crown'd and incircl'd with . . . shady and venerable trees.'[21] He called on King Charles II to become the nation's '*nemorum vindix & instaurator magnus*', or 'great protector and restorer of woodlands'.[22] This was an accolade that would surely appeal to Charles Stuart, whose dynasty derived their family name from their title 'High Steward of Scotland'. Evelyn hoped to conjure up a 'new spirit of industry in the nobility and gentry of the whole nation . . . for the repairing of our wooden walls' – by which he meant the timber trees that were so essential to the British Navy's defence of the realm.[23] The environmentalism of *Sylva* was a groundbreaking appeal to private landowners to act in the long-term public interest.

Some progressive landowners heeded Evelyn's clarion call, and restocked their estates with trees. But many ignored the warnings, and the nation's woods became still further depleted over the following two centuries. By 1919, the UK's forest cover had fallen to an all-time low, clothing just 5 per cent of the country.[24]

The trouble was, most landowners in the seventeenth century had other things on their minds than being good stewards. They were far more interested in using their extensive landholdings to get rich quick, and then defend this wealth from the land-hungry and increasingly rebellious lower classes. Owning land had meant big bucks for the gentry and peerage since the Tudor period, when the lucrative wool trade had taken off. Since then, landowners had been acquiring ever more acres to run their sheep ranches, through enclosing the commons.

A common is an area of land which may be privately owned, but over which various other people – known as commoners – have usage rights, such as the right to graze livestock or collect firewood. Commons acted as a kind of medieval welfare state, a social safety net for the poor who could draw sustenance from them. Common land still comprised some 30 per cent of England around the year 1600, but by then it was shrinking thanks to the process of enclosure: the fencing off of commons by the gentry for their profitable sheep.[25] Thomas More had attacked this land-grab in his satire *Utopia*, blaming the landowners who 'enclose grounds that they may lodge their sheep in them' for causing poverty and destitution: 'sheep … may be said now to devour men and unpeople, not only villages, but towns'.[26]

Those thrown off the land formed a growing population of itinerant workers, landless squatters and 'masterless men', who roamed the countryside in search of work and bread.[27] Land hunger became particularly acute in the 1640s, when a series of disastrous harvests combined with the upheaval of the Civil War to cause a spike in food prices. Desperate times led men to embrace previously heretical ideas. The defeat and eventual beheading of Charles I in 1649 seemed to some to mark a millenarian moment, when the world had truly been turned upside down. In those feverish years, radical movements arose, expressing a yearning for equality, democracy, and a more equitable sharing of the Earth's riches.

One such faction was known as the Levellers, who – far ahead of their time – called for universal male suffrage. Many of the footsoldiers in Oliver Cromwell's New Model Army had sympathy with the Levellers: they had, after all, just fought for their country, and now wanted a say in how it was governed. In the Putney Debates of 1647, Colonel Thomas Rainsborough made the Levellers' case to the army generals for giving all men the vote. But the landed officer class was horrified. The aptly named Colonel Nathaniel Rich, inheritor of a large estate, fretted that if landless men were given equal voting rights, 'there may be a law enacted, that there shall be equality of goods and estate.' General Ireton, rejecting the Levellers' demands, retorted that 'no person hath a right to an interest or share in disposing of the affairs of the kingdom . . . that hath not a permanent fixed interest in this kingdom'.[28] Or in other words, you only get a say on the laws of the land if you own a chunk of land. The right to vote in Britain remained confined to men of property for over two centuries after the Putney Debates.

Still more radical were the Diggers, who sought to overturn ideas about landed property outright. Their most vocal leader, Gerrard Winstanley, railed against the 'Norman yoke' that had enslaved England since the time of William the Conqueror. 'The power of enclosing land and owning property was brought into the creation by your ancestors by the sword,' he wrote in one of his many pamphlets.[29] But Winstanley did not merely fulminate against enclosure and landed wealth in print; he also took direct action. In April 1649, Winstanley and a band of landless men and women went to dig upon St George's Hill in Surrey, an area of common land formerly owned by the Crown. They began to cultivate land that was not their own, to provide food for hungry mouths in a time of poor harvests and civil strife. The Diggers' vision was for a world 'set free from intanglements of lords and landlords', in which the public had a say over how the land was used: 'the earth . . . shall become a common treasury for all'.[30]

Both the Levellers and Diggers met with ignominious defeat. The Levellers were marginalised by the army generals – who, instead of instigating a democratic republic, installed Cromwell as military dictator. The Diggers were driven off St George's Hill, their crops trashed by gangs organised by the lord of the manor; their leaders were tried in court, and other groups of Diggers across the country were similarly dispersed. And though the Levellers' demands for political democracy were eventually met centuries later, we still have not democratised the governance of land in the way that Winstanley envisaged.

In fact, the outcome of the Civil War cemented the power of landed wealth more firmly than ever before. Even after the restoration of the monarchy in 1660, Parliament remained powerful; and because you had to own a considerable amount of property to vote, the MPs that got voted in spoke for the landowners' interests. The rise of newly moneyed wealth from trade and commerce presented a momentary challenge to the old landed aristocracy and gentry, but that was soon seen off: an Act of 1711 forbade anyone from even standing as an MP unless they owned land, too.

Landowners were increasingly portrayed as the guardians of the nation, through dint of them owning a chunk of it. In the eighteenth century, the Tory landed interest argued that land alone guaranteed patriotic commitment, since those with their wealth in stocks and shares could abscond overseas with their cash.[31] As the historian H.T. Dickinson has put it, 'most Tories remained convinced that the natural rulers of society were the men of landed estates . . . only men of substantial property possessed the qualities necessary to sit in Parliament'.[32] What was good for the wealthy landowner, they argued, was good for the nation.[33]

With the rise of the 'Great Estates' of the Georgian period, landowners styled themselves more and more as benign stewards of the landscape. It helped, of course, that they owned most of it: the process of enclosure gathered pace through the eighteenth century, enabling dukes and earls to accrue vast estates spanning tens of thousands of acres. Arguments for enclosure usually rested on claims of agricultural 'improvement', to boost food production (and profits). But landowners also now fancied themselves as guardians of the countryside, shaping it to meet their ideals of beauty. This was the great age of landscape gardening: when aristocrats thought nothing of moving entire villages just to improve the view from their mansions. Aristocratic patronage enabled the landscape gardener Lancelot 'Capability' Brown to leave his mark on some half a million acres of parkland, remodelling hillsides and altering the course of rivers to create the perfect vista.[34]

This period also gave rise to the English pastoral myth, which has buttressed landowners' claims of stewardship ever since. In essence, English pastoralism was a philosophy that rural was good and urban was bad – encapsulated by the poet William Cowper in 1783: 'God made the country and man made the town'.[35] Cities were manmade and hence flawed, sinful places; by extension, so were the people who lived in them – the 'great unwashed', who had to be kept out of the countryside at all costs. The English countryside, by contrast, was seen as natural, bucolic, beautiful – fashioned by God and now cared for by his stewards. 'Townies' needed restraining from messing up the countryside, but landowners and farmers could be trusted to look after the land, without the need for any oversight by the government. The industrial revolution certainly did transform the nation's cities and scar the landscape with its factories. But the fact that rural England was being profoundly changed by its landowners at the same time – as we will see in ensuing chapters – was largely overlooked.

With the coming of the French Revolution at the close of the eighteenth century, the defenders of landed interests once again reached for the language of stewardship. Terrified that the uprising might spread to England, MP Edmund Burke mounted a vigorous defence of what he called the 'natural landed interest of the country' against the 'swinish multitude'.[36] The French revolutionaries, after all, had not just overthrown the King of France, but also deposed the aristocratic order and redistributed their lands. Burke's *Reflections on the Revolution in France* (1790) venerated 'the partnership . . . between those who are living, those who are dead, and those who are to be born'.[37] To him, this contract between generations was epitomised by the continuity of the landed estate, with earls and viscounts passing on their lands to their first-born sons. As one social scientist notes, 'Burke . . . conceived of landed property in terms of stewardship.'[38]

Burke's arguments, however, highlight a key conceptual flaw in claims of stewardship. Who, exactly, are landowners stewarding the land *for*? To whom are they accountable, should their actions fall short of the ideals of stewardship? To devout Christians like Matthew Hale, the answer was God. Yet you were only answerable to God after you died, in the Last Judgement at the end of all time – the 'Great Audit' referred to by Hale. For Edmund Burke, landowners were accountable to future generations. Such an idea, at least, has the benefit of reminding us to think long term. But future generations, by definition, do not yet exist, so conveniently can exercise no judgement or protest over one's actions in the present.

Surely any meaningful duty of land stewardship should involve accountability towards the living public. In other words, decisions about how land is used should be made more democratic. In a country where 1 per cent of the population owns half of all England, such decisions are currently made by a tiny elite.

Claims of stewardship have also diverted attention away from this vast concentration of landed power. By claiming to be merely the stewards, guardians or custodians of their land, some landowners seek to occlude the advantages and degree of control brought through ownership. As the sociologist Howard Newby has written: 'stewardship . . . is a self-deprecation which attempts to deflect a recognition of the benefits which derive from ownership towards an emphasis on altruism and service . . . The notion that the landowner is in effect merely a life-tenant continues to be constantly invoked in order to defend the existing pattern of landownership against any radical changes.'[39] I'm reminded of a BBC interview given by the Duke of Northumberland, owner today of over 100,000 acres of land. 'It doesn't feel to me as if I'm sitting here and owning vast tracts of land,' remarked the Duke laconically, 'because I obviously share it with hundreds and thousands of people.' 'Yes – but you're the *owner*,' pointed out the incredulous interviewer. 'I am the ultimate owner, I suppose,' the Duke reluctantly admitted.[40]

Having started out as Hale's noble religious ideal in the seventeenth century, stewardship increasingly became a convenient way of buttressing the power of the landed classes. Britain's emerging ecological crises, such as the decline of its forests, went unresolved by the nation's supposed stewards. And the wider public remained shut out of debates about how best to manage the land. Worse, however, was to come.

The language of stewardship was deliberately revived in the late twentieth century by landowners and farming unions to defend themselves against accusations of environmental destruction.

Three decades of industrialised farming had put a huge dent in the idea that landowners and farmers could be trusted to steward nature. Between 1950 and 1980, around a third of Britain's ancient woodlands were cut down.[41] Tens of thousands of kilometres of hedgerows had been grubbed up since the Second World War, and 97 per cent of wildflower meadows lost to the plough.[42] By the late 1970s, environmental pressure groups like Friends of the Earth were sounding the alarm about the destruction of the British countryside, and public disquiet was growing. As the campaigning author Marion Shoard put it in her seminal book *The Theft of the Countryside*, 'the English landscape is under sentence of death . . . The executioner is not the industrialist or the property speculator . . . Instead it is the figure traditionally viewed as the custodian of the rural scene – the farmer.'[43] Both Shoard and Friends of the Earth campaigned for an extension of planning controls over agriculture and forestry, arguing that self-regulation by landowners was no longer working.

Terrified by the prospect of the public suddenly taking an unwanted interest in their affairs, the landed lobby staged a fightback. In 1977, the Country Landowners' Association (CLA) and National Farmers Union (NFU) published a joint statement entitled *Caring for the Countryside*. In the words of rural policy expert Michael Winter, it 'represented the beginning of a high-profile and sustained publicity campaign to promote farmers and landowners as the natural custodians and stewards of the countryside'.[44] 'Farmers had to reassert their self-image as the countryside's trusted custodian,' argues academic Robert Burton, because they were 'coming under increasing threat from the environmental lobby as a result of the damage caused by intensive farming practices'.[45] By resurrecting the language of stewardship, landowning groups were able to draw on what linguist George Lakoff calls a 'deep frame' – a concept deeply embedded in public consciousness through dint of history and repeated use.

The phrase 'custodians of the countryside' owes its popular currency to constant repetition by the NFU. It began in 1971, when then NFU president Henry Plumb first used it in a speech. 'I speak as a farmer for farmers, as one of the custodians of our countryside,' he declared.[46] Ever since, repeating this slogan has become a rite of passage for successive NFU presidents. In 1998, president Ben Gill spoke of farmers' 'awareness of their responsibilities as custodians of the countryside'.[47] The next NFU president Tim Bennett said that 'farmers play an important role as custodians of the countryside', shortly after he launched a 'a new long-term campaign to make sure the public knows what farmers do to protect and enhance the environment'.[48] His successor Peter Kendall spoke in 2007 of the need to 'promote our work as custodians of the countryside through the national media'.[49] Minette Batters, NFU president from 2018 until early 2024, made repeated use of the phrase, such as in a letter to the *Guardian* pushing back on the need for a lower-meat diet because 'farmers are the original custodians of the countryside.'[50] Yet in the half-century since an NFU president first uttered this soundbite, the UK has lost half of all its farmland birds, like corn buntings and starlings – many of them due to the agricultural intensification that the NFU lobbied for over those decades.[51]

For a time at the start of the 1980s, it appeared that the landowning and agribusiness lobbies had been wrongfooted. Landowners were forced to accept some constraints on their property rights when the Wildlife and Countryside Act was passed in 1981, leading to Sites of Special Scientific Interest (SSSIs) being given legal protections for the first time (although this didn't stop some owners from ploughing up SSSIs before they were formally notified). But SSSIs only covered a small percentage of the nation; and when environmentalists sought to address the mismanagement of the wider countryside, they found they were up against an indomitable defender of private property rights: Margaret Thatcher.

Thatcher's surprising embrace of environmental politics in the late Eighties led to her wholeheartedly adopting the language of stewardship. 'It's we Conservatives who are not merely friends of the Earth – we are its guardians and trustees for generations to come,' she told delegates at the 1988 Conservative Party Conference. 'No generation has a freehold on this earth.

All we have is a life tenancy – with a full repairing lease.'[52] Ostensibly, this was strikingly radical language, particularly for a politician who had done more than most to encourage Britons to become freehold owners of property through the sale of council housing. 'There is no prouder word in our history than freeholder,' Thatcher had told the 1982 Tory conference.[53] No doubt electoral necessity compelled Thatcher to espouse environmental rhetoric, with the Green Party riding a wave of public concern that propelled them to 15 per cent of the vote in the 1989 European elections. Yet Thatcher almost certainly believed in environmental stewardship: if not as a Burkean one-nation conservative, then as a committed Christian.

What Margaret Thatcher also believed in, of course, was limited government and the sacred nature of private property. Her government went on to publish the first ever White Paper on the Environment, *This Common Inheritance*, which stated boldly: 'The starting point for this Government is the ethical imperative of stewardship which must underlie all environmental policies.'[54] But what this meant in terms of practical policy for managing land seemed rather less bold. 'The Government's policies for the countryside are based on sound stewardship of the heritage,' it stated. 'Most of the countryside is privately owned. Wherever possible, the Government works in partnership with its owners and managers to protect it through voluntary effort.'[55]

Sound stewardship of the land, therefore, seemed to lie once again in the hands of its traditional custodians – the landowners and farmers – who could be relied upon to enter into voluntary initiatives. Michael Winter observed in 1991 that, faced with calls for more planning controls and regulation, the Conservative government responded by 'championing the voluntary approach . . . as the best means to secure environmental objectives throughout the farmed countryside'.

Outside of the 8 per cent of England protected as SSSIs, Thatcher's administration continued to assert 'a philosophy of voluntarism' which generously allowed landowners 'maximum freedom . . . to interpret regulations'. There was no obligation on farmers and landowners to participate in official schemes to reduce nitrate pollution, set aside land from food production, or increase the amount of woodland on farms. As Winter noted with astonishment, 'participation . . . is voluntary in each case, in spite of the fact that the Government maintains that each provides an essential plank for the re-orientation of agricultural and environmental policies in the United Kingdom.'[56]

Where voluntary action wasn't forthcoming, the main form of intervention by the government wouldn't be to regulate, but rather to incentivise good behaviour. *This Common Inheritance* had expressed concern about the 'shortcomings' of regulation to control pollution, with its attendant 'compliance costs'. Instead, it expressed enthusiasm for 'market mechanisms', which offered 'the prospect of a more efficient and flexible approach to environmental issues'.[57]

Since agriculture was already heavily subsidised by the government, via the European Common Agricultural Policy (CAP), it made sense to start by tweaking farm subsidies to incentivise greener land management practices. In 1991, the government launched the first England-wide grant scheme for greener farming. They gave it a name they knew would resonate with landowners and farming unions: Countryside Stewardship.

The greening of farm payments was undoubtedly a positive development. Up until that point, the CAP had essentially been a subsidy for environmental destruction: its overarching emphasis on producing cheap food had contributed to a massive intensification of agriculture. So-called 'headage' payments had rewarded farmers based on the headcount of livestock they owned, thus driving up sheep and cattle numbers massively and leading to chronic overgrazing. From the 1990s, however, CAP payments were progressively decoupled from food production. From 2005, 'Pillar I' payments were based on the amount of land you farmed, essentially becoming a subsidy for the privilege of owning large swathes of land. But an increasing proportion of farm subsidies was also going towards 'Pillar II' payments for greener farming. In England, these grants have gone through various iterations over the years, but have all been called Countryside or Environmental Stewardship.[58]

This emphasis on complex packages of voluntary incentives has crowded out discussion of alternative policy measures, from tougher environmental regulation to different models of ownership. To find out more about the intricacies of farm subsidies, I spoke to agricultural policy expert Tom Lancaster, who's worked on the design of green farm payments for years.

'We do limit ourselves in this country to focusing on stewardship schemes, versus other policies on conservation,' Tom told me. '"Stewardship" is a very Anglo-centric term, based on an English cultural concept – it's not used even by the other UK nations for their agri-environment schemes. And stewardship payments are a much bigger part of our conservation policy toolkit than other countries.' The situation is very different in New Zealand, for example, where the government's Department of Conservation owns roughly a third of the entire country, managing those areas directly as nature reserves.[59] By contrast, only about 8.5 per cent of England is owned by the public sector.[60] We remain far more deferential to private landowners, transferring them vast sums of public money to manage the land.

Tom and I decided to take a look at the sheer scale of taxpayers' money handed to landowners and farmers through stewardship payments over the past thirty years. Surprisingly, no official body or select committee appears to have scrutinised this before. The data is not easy to come by for England, particularly for the earliest years. But by trawling back through old reports buried on the National Archives website, we pieced together a figure. Between 1992 and 2022, the public paid a staggering £9.2 billion to landowners and farmers through environmental stewardship schemes, when measured in cash terms – or £12.5 billion when adjusted for inflation.[61]

This narrow focus on paying farmers and landowners to be good stewards wouldn't necessarily be a problem if it worked. But in too many cases, huge amounts of money have been spent with little discernible result. When Countryside Stewardship was first set up, Tom tells me, it was essentially a 'new social contract' brokered between landowners and farmers on the one hand, and the British public on the other. For their part, landowners would accept certain constraints on their private property rights, and stop damaging SSSIs – but if the public wanted landowners to actively *restore* nature, it had to give them money in the form of stewardship payments. 'The problem is, that social contract has been broken,' says Tom. 'Many SSSIs, despite receiving public funding under various stewardship schemes over the decades, are *not* in good condition. In fact many are still declining.'

Yet the emphasis on voluntary action by landowners has only become more acute under the most recent Conservative government. Since 2010, environmental regulators have become ever weaker. Years of austerity have cut the government's green watchdogs to the bone: the budget for Natural England was slashed from £265 million in 2008–09 to just £85.6 million a decade later.[62] Funding for environmental protection services provided by the Environment Agency over the same period was cut in half.[63] The result has been a collapse in basic regulatory functions. Natural England has struggled to even monitor the nation's network of SSSIs properly over the past decade, let alone put in place measures to get them recovering. And the Environment Agency's failure to clean up the shit in our rivers speaks for itself. If we could trust the 'custodians of the countryside' to prevent nitrate run-off into our waterways and nurture our nature reserves, we wouldn't need such regulators. But decades of damage and neglect would suggest we can't.

Brexit has supercharged the impetus for environmental deregulation, whilst also tying up enormous amounts of civil service time. Egged on by free-market think tanks like the Taxpayers' Alliance and Institute of Economic Affairs (IEA) clamouring to slash 'red tape' and light a 'bonfire of the quangos', successive Tory administrations have done their best to render their environmental regulators toothless, and itched to rip up residual EU law. Leaving the European Common Agricultural Policy, meanwhile, has led to the UK government redesigning its system of farm payments, and has at last led to an improved system of Environmental Land Management schemes. But the new schemes have only recently started after seven years of debate, and the time spent developing the details has overshadowed discussion of any alternative policies. The focus of government land use policy has remained squarely on how we best reward landowners and farmers by paying them billions of pounds of public money to do the right thing.

Recently, I was contacted by a former policy adviser for the Country Land and Business Association. Speaking to me on condition of anonymity, the adviser told me: 'the idea of inherent good stewardship by landowners is so pervasive . . . to the extent that no one in government or even NGOs can afford not to preface discussions on policy with some version of "of course farmers and landowners know best how to manage their land", even if this is clearly not true.' My source related that this had 'clear consequences' for policymaking, 'as the premise was that those who currently manage the land have to continue doing so, and if they're not willing to change, then policy must adapt to their desires, not vice versa'.

But perhaps now there is a chance for a different conversation. As I write, a new government has just taken power. Change is in the air. As the social scientist Howard Newby has written: 'Occasionally the ideology of stewardship may rebound – such as when . . . the nation decides it would like a say in how the land which is being looked after on its behalf should be cared for.'[64]

That time has now arrived. It is time to hold the self-proclaimed stewards of the land to account for what they have done to it.

2

The Ultimate Trophy Asset

It was one of the bleakest landscapes I had ever seen. Drab expanses of lank brown heather stretched for miles around, interspersed with jaundiced yellow clumps of moor grass. Sheets of rain descended over a vista bleached of colour. The land looked like a wounded animal, huddled beneath a lowering sky, its vital signs slowly draining away.

In front of me, the belly of the land had been opened up, exposing its innards. Peat had been forming here beneath the surface for thousands of years: black as midnight, black as coal, a fossil fuel in the making – but now dangerously exposed to the air, causing it to oxidise and leach carbon into the atmosphere. Carbon that would only add to the cycle of heating and extreme weather and destruction playing out across the world. A collection of peat hags – eroding, decomposing banks of peat – lay before me. With a mixture of helplessness and disgust, I watched them bleed out into the nearby clough. The stream that frothed and cascaded down the hillside was so clogged with dissolved peat, the waters had turned the caramel-brown colour of Coca-Cola.

It wasn't hard to see how the land had got into this state. Climbing higher to gain perspective, I looked back. Below me, the moor had a chequerboard pattern, bearing the scars of repeated heather burning carried out over the years. And scoring the moorland like the scratchmarks of a cat were drainage ditches, into which the degraded peat ebbed with every rainstorm. Everywhere I saw reminders that this was a habitat managed to within an inch of its life. Following the polluted stream into the hills, I found animal traps set by a gamekeeper every ten metres, lashed to wooden poles laid across a ravine. This was a sick landscape, clinging to life. Or, to put it another way, this was a grouse moor.

Grouse moors exist for one purpose only: to maximise the numbers of a particular bird, the red grouse, for wealthy men and women to shoot. Theirs is an entirely artificial, intensively managed environment. Moorland heather is regularly burned to encourage the fresh shoots eaten by young grouse. Many grouse moors were drained historically, because it was thought this would improve the otherwise damp conditions for both sheep and gamebirds. Gamekeepers lace the moors with traps to kill animals that predate on grouse: stoats, weasels, foxes and birds of prey. It's illegal to kill birds of prey, but that doesn't stop it happening: the unlawful persecution of raptors is endemic on Britain's grouse moors. And if you want to own a grouse moor, you have to be rich: even the *Spectator* says that owning one is 'screamingly elitist' and 'the ultimate trophy asset'.[1]

The moor where I stood belonged to the 7th Duke of Westminster, Hugh Grosvenor, one of the richest men in Britain – owner of a £9.8-billion fortune, according to the latest *Sunday Times* Rich List.[2] The Grosvenor family traces its ancestry back to the Norman Conquest. The late 6th Duke of Westminster, when once asked for his advice for young entrepreneurs, replied laconically: 'Make sure they have an ancestor who was a very close friend of William the Conqueror.'[3] The family have owned land in Cheshire since 1066. But the grouse moor I had visited, the 23,000-acre Abbeystead Estate in Lancashire's Forest of Bowland, was a more recent acquisition: bought by the Duke of Westminster's Trust in 1980, reportedly for £2.5 million.[4] The Grosvenors acquired it knowing it was good for sport. It holds the accolade for the most grouse shot in a single day – a staggering 2,929 birds. This grisly record was set on 12 August 1915, the so-called 'Glorious Twelfth' that marks the start of the grouse shooting season each summer.[5]

But, as a sign erected by the Grosvenor Estate proudly proclaimed, this moorland was also a 'Conservation Area'. Since 1951, the majority of the Abbeystead Estate has been part of the Bowland Fells Site of Special Scientific Interest.[6] One might hope that a family as wealthy as the Grosvenors would invest plenty of money in the upkeep of a nature reserve like this, to speed nature's recovery on the high moors. After all, the Grosvenor Estate, which manages the Duke's landholdings, boasts that it 'is responsible for the long-term stewardship of three rural estates in the United Kingdom'.[7] So what condition is the moorland in today, three decades on from the Dukes of Westminster acquiring it?

Surprise: it's not looking great. The government's official environmental watchdog, Natural England, divides SSSIs into 'units' to assess their condition. Out of twenty-one SSSI units covering the Abbeystead Estate, eighteen are considered by Natural England to be in 'unfavourable condition', with just three judged 'favourable'. In fact, the two units covering the area I visited are deemed to be in 'unfavourable *declining*' condition. Natural England's most recent site checks from 2021–2 note the same problems that I did: that despite some peatland restoration works, there was 'exposed peat' and 'limited' moss cover. Officials also noted regular burning of the moor, which was keeping the floral diversity low and allowing heather to dominate.[8]

So much for habitats; things aren't looking too good on the wildlife front, either. The symbol of the Forest of Bowland Area of Outstanding Natural Beauty is the hen harrier, a rare bird of prey. Yet as the conservation group Wild Justice notes, 'driven grouse moors in the Forest of Bowland . . . owned by the likes of the Duke of Westminster, have been curiously lacking in hen harriers for most of the last two decades.'[9] There *are* breeding hen harriers on the neighbouring moorland owned by the water company United Utilities, which recently decided to end grouse shooting on its estates.[10]

That's not to say nothing's being done to improve things: there has been some work to restore peat bogs on the moor in recent years, some of it funded by the Abbeystead Estate themselves.[11]

But the poor condition of this incredibly important carbon sink is despite millions of pounds of public money being handed to the estate and its tenants, for the express purpose of bringing the SSSI into favourable condition. Just under the latest iteration of Environmental Stewardship schemes, lasting from the 2010s into the early 2020s, the estate and its farm tenants were handed £5.5 million of taxpayers' money.[12] (This figure doesn't include the additional public subsidies handed out as Basic Payments, nor the earlier iteration of Countryside Stewardship grants which ran during the 1990s and early 2000s – data for which is no longer publicly accessible.) Despite all this public money, the majority of the Duke's estate is still in unfavourable condition – and even, in some places, declining.

For the same amount of taxpayers' money that it's handed to the Duke and his tenant farmers, the government could have bought the Abbeystead Estate back in 1980 at the reported sales price of £2.5 million – *and still had £3 million to spare.* I've spoken to numerous civil servants and policy analysts who make this same point about the way we've paid large landowners to be good stewards. In many cases, they say, the taxpayer would've been better off if the government had simply acquired the land outright, rather than wasting millions of pounds paying private landowners for environmental outcomes that they failed to deliver.

Nor is this a problem confined to one or two estates. Grouse moors dominate our uplands, covering over half a million acres of England: that's an area the size of Greater London.[13] Much of this land consists of rare blanket bog habitat, notionally protected as SSSIs, whilst the deep peat soils of the moors comprise our single most important carbon store. Yet we have handed over this crucial resource to around 150 aristocrats, oligarchs and City bankers to use for sport. Despite their wealth, and despite the millions of pounds of public money they have swallowed in the name of environmental stewardship, they have wrecked this land. It has been turned from a carbon sink into a huge carbon source, emitting millions of tonnes of CO_2 every year: transformed from a critical national resource into the ultimate trophy asset.

So why on earth did we let this happen? How did we get to this point of crisis?

The history of grouse moors begins, like many things in Britain, with the Crown. But it begins earlier than you might expect: with the Duke of Westminster's very close friend, William the Conqueror.

The Norman kings established patterns of ownership and land use that continue to resonate even now. First, it was King William who imposed a feudal system of land tenure on England, creating the highly unequal distribution of land ownership that persists to this day. By vesting all land in the Crown and then parcelling some of it out to his two hundred barons, the Conqueror established a system in which a small aristocratic elite owned most of the land. And second, the hunting habits of the Norman kings set trends that were copied by the aristocracy down through the ages. It was William who established the New Forest as a royal hunting ground – where kings and their court favourites, armed with bows and arrows, would hunt deer and wild boar. The creation of numerous Royal Forests sparked a fashion amongst the barons to set up deer parks of their own. Bound together by patronage and courtly customs, and in possession of vast acres of land, both monarchy and aristocracy have held huge sway over the way we use land for a very long time.

For centuries, the hunting traditions of the English Crown and aristocracy arguably went hand-in-hand with conservation. Nobles mainly hunted wild game, rather than introduced species,* and you ate what you caught. Moreover, hunting secured the preservation of large areas of woodland and wooded parkland for game, sparing these places from the axe. The New Forest, for example, is widely considered by woodland experts to be the 'finest ancient forest remaining on the lowland plains of northwest Europe'.[14] And we have the Norman aristocracy's

---

* Although the Normans did introduce fallow deer, a species not native to Britain, unlike red and roe deer.

taste for venison to thank for England's astonishing number of ancient trees, many of them preserved in old deer parks.

All this changed in the Victorian period. Though some nobles had always shot red grouse, a bird native to the English and Scottish uplands, it had remained a fringe pursuit: grouse were too fast and too few in number to make the trek over difficult moorland terrain worthwhile.* But in the Peak District, a landowner called Sir William Spencer-Stanhope pioneered what became known as 'driven' grouse shooting, involving the intensive management of moorland to artificially boost the numbers of grouse. Heather was burned on rotation, speeding up the growth of fresh heather shoots, and thereby increasing grouse populations. Men were employed to drive the grouse out of the undergrowth and towards the waiting guns – hence the phrase 'driven shooting'. The invention of the breech-loading shotgun also made it easier to shoot lots of game quickly. Yet Spencer-Stanhope was merely one of the lesser gentry, and as he bitterly recounted, his new-fangled methods were looked down on by his social superiors as 'unsportsmanlike'.[15]

But then, in 1852, Queen Victoria and Prince Albert purchased the Balmoral Estate in Scotland. 'Albert returned at twenty minutes to three,' read one of the Queen's diary entries from their first visit to Scotland, 'having had very hard work on the moors, wading up to his knees in bogs every now and then, and had killed nine brace of grouse.'[16] Victoria and Albert's passion for driven grouse shooting and deer-stalking over this 60,000-acre expanse of the Cairngorms sparked a fashion amongst the Victorian aristocracy that continues to this day. Anybody who was anybody was seized by the 'Balmorality' – the need to buy an upland estate, the bigger the better, and manage it to maximise the number of grouse. Britain's uplands, from the Scottish Highlands to the North York Moors, were transformed. The Crown's enthusiasm for driven grouse shooting popularised it to the point where it became a major industry amongst the aristocracy and the newly wealthy industrialists who aspired to join their ranks.

---

* This is known as 'walked-up shooting'.

British hunting fundamentally changed. Where previously the hunting pastimes of royals and aristocrats had helped conserve semi-natural habitats, the Victorian upper classes oversaw huge ecological changes, transforming whole landscapes in the name of bloodsports. Victorian landowners became obsessed with the sheer number of living things they could kill for sport. Moorland estates were renowned for the size of the 'bag' they could offer, a measure of the number of grouse one could expect to shoot on an average day. Where once it had been enough just to bring home a brace of wildfowl for the table, now dukes and earls competed to shoot the most gamebirds, setting obscene records. Lord Walsingham, for example, killed a thousand grouse in one day, whilst Lord de Grey clocked up a lifetime shooting tally of half a million birds.[17] The competition culminated, as we've seen, at Abbeystead Estate in 1915.

This Victorian cult of death spread to the gamekeepers employed by each estate, who sought to trap, shoot and poison every natural predator of the red grouse. They scoured the uplands to remove anything that might reduce gamebird numbers, waging a savage war against stoats, weasels, foxes, pine martens, rooks, crows, hen harriers, buzzards, falcons, kestrels – even various species of owl. The polecat, a slinky mustelid whose black-and-white facial fur makes it look like a bandit, was so severely persecuted by gamekeepers that it became virtually extinct in England by the early twentieth century.[18] An arsenal of modern snares, poisons and traps were deployed by Victorian estates to industrialise the uplands, creating a system that the conservationist Benedict Macdonald terms 'canned hunting'[19] – one that demanded little skill on the part of the hunter, prizing quantity over quality.

The fad for grouse moors also spurred on the enclosure of England's upland commons by the aristocracy. As the historian Tom Williamson recounts, because 'greater numbers of birds were now required . . . systematic rearing and preservation were rendered easier by enclosure and the consolidation of ownership.'[20] Commoners who had once used the moors for grazing found themselves dispossessed. 'In the huge parishes that straddled the Pennines,' writes the local historian David Hey, 'lords opted to receive large stretches of the "wastes", tracts of little value that could be converted into grouse moors.'[21] The Peak District, for example, lost virtually all its upland commons, as it was carved up into huge grouse shooting estates: the Duke of Rutland at Longshaw and Moscar Moors, the Duke of Norfolk in the upper Derwent Valley, the Duke of Devonshire at Kinder Scout.[22] And as the moors became increasingly managed for grouse, so their owners became ever more hostile to the public walking over them and disturbing the game. This led to battles between gamekeepers and ramblers for access to the moors, culminating in the Kinder Scout mass trespass of 1932, when four hundred hikers trespassed on the Duke of Devonshire's grouse moor.

Most significant of all for the ecology of the uplands was the intensification of moorland burning. The regular burning of heather was 'adopted in a more systematic form in the 1850s', and soon became standard practice.[23] A parliamentary inquiry into grouse shooting in 1912 reported that landowners were 'doubling and trebling the bag of grouse by burning tracts of ground'.[24] Astonishingly, the inquiry even recommended that 'peat hags should be burned when the ground is not too dry', and that 'wet "flow" ground should be burned in big stretches outside the ordinary rotation'.[25] As we shall see shortly, the impact of such practices on the ecology and carbon stocks of moorland peat has been disastrous.

Victoria and Albert's purchase of Balmoral precipitated the transformation of several million acres of Britain's uplands. What royals and aristocrats started in the nineteenth century has more recently been taken up with gusto by City bankers, Saudi princes and newly minted businessmen, all looking to buy into the lifestyle of the 'country gent'. Today, around 150 grouse moor estates cover 550,000 acres of England's uplands. There are another 300 or so grouse shooting estates in the Scottish Highlands, covering around 2.5 million acres.[26] This tiny elite of landowners possess not merely millions of acres of land, but also one of the most important carbon stores in the country: a habitat they have progressively trashed in the past century and a half. Let's now examine the scale of these ecological impacts.

If you listened to some folks in the grouse shooting industry, you'd think that the existence of Britain's moorlands was entirely down to them. 'Grouse moor management has played a key role in creating and maintaining our upland landscapes,' claims a briefing by the Countryside Alliance.[27] It has certainly played a key role in modifying them. But the truth is that peat bogs and heathlands have existed for thousands of years, getting on just fine before their current owners came along. In reality, it's the past century and a half of mismanagement which has disrupted the natural functioning of these ecosystems.

If they were in a healthy state, our moors would be dominated by 'blanket bog'. This is an ecosystem that formed across Britain's uplands some 5,000 years ago, in the wake of climatic shifts and upland forest clearances. Blanket bog supports a range of weird and wonderful plants, like the insect-eating sundews, yellow-flowering bog asphodel and white-tufted cottongrass. But it gets its name from the blanket of mosses that dominate it: in particular, sphagnum moss, a group of colourful bryophytes which range in colour from cherry red to acid green. Sphagnum moss thrives in the high rainfall conditions of Britain's uplands, soaking up water and acting like a giant sponge. Stand on a thriving blanket bog and, if you're lucky, it'll bounce and undulate beneath your feet. If you're unlucky, you'll puncture the blanket of moss and fall into several feet of peaty ooze. But it's what's happening beneath the surface that's really important.

Blanket bogs consist of a thin layer of living sphagnum moss – the 'acrotelm' – beneath which is a much thicker layer of dead plant matter, sometimes several metres deep: the 'catotelm'. Because healthy blanket bog is saturated with water, oxygen can't reach the catotelm layer. This means that when sphagnum mosses die and are replaced by a new layer of living moss, they don't fully decompose. Much of the carbon they contain isn't oxidised, but instead is stored safely in the anaerobic environment of the bog. It's these anaerobic conditions that explain why archaeologists sometimes discover 'bog bodies' – human remains perfectly preserved from thousands of years ago, sacrifices to watery gods. But still more miraculous is what happens to the dead moss. It forms peat, an extraordinarily carbon-rich form of soil – a fossil fuel in the making. Peat bogs are, by far, the UK's most important carbon store, containing some 3 billion tonnes of carbon.[28]

Forming a natural halo around these blanket bogs is upland heath. Because the peat lying beneath them tends to be shallower and less saturated in water, it supports a different plant community – 'dwarf shrub heath'. Nowadays we think of heathland as being dominated by purple swathes of heather, but historically these places would have been more varied: home to bilberry, lingonberry, gorse, bracken, even scattered trees like birch and rowan. Heathland is a largely artificial habitat, held in arrested succession by grazing and burning, which prevents trees and scrub from reclaiming it. But intensive management for grouse shooting has sought to turn our heathlands into heather monocultures. In the process, the shallow peat soils beneath them have been damaged, just like the deeper peat lying under the blanket bogs.

Since the 1850s, landowners have degraded both blanket bog and heathland habitats in two main ways: through drainage and repeated burning. Draining moorlands involves digging drainage channels (called 'grips') through the peat, into which the surrounding water runs out and off the hillsides. By lowering the water table, drainage kills the sphagnum mosses, stops peat from forming, and causes terrible damage to the underlying peat by drying it out. Exposed to the air, the carbon in the peat starts to oxidise, releasing carbon dioxide into the atmosphere. And by gouging holes in the blanket bog, it loses its sponge-like capacity to hold water, sending it downstream to cause floods.

Nowadays, pro-shooting groups like the Game and Wildlife Conservation Trust (GWCT) like to blame moorland drainage on historic state subsidies aimed at improving grazing for sheep.[29] There *is* some sheep grazing on grouse moors, though in low densities; too many and they start to eat the heather. Mainly the sheep are there to be 'tick mops' – mopping up the ticks that can spread disease to grouse.[30] And it's certainly true that misguided government grants for hill farm drainage were doled out between the 1950s and 1980s.

But grouse moor owners were draining their moors for many decades before this, for the express purpose of improving conditions for grouse. As the historian Tom Williamson notes, 'drains were often dug into the wetter areas, in order to encourage the growth of heather at the expense of purple moor-grass, cotton grass and bog-moss, something which deprived birds such as snipe and redshank of suitable nesting areas.'[31] In his history of the Peak District moors, David Hey describes a nineteenth-century drain called the Black Dyke, which 'the Duke of Devonshire ordered to be cut across the moor for 1½ miles between two cloughs'.[32]

Indeed, moorland drainage was repeatedly recommended to grouse moor owners, from the Edwardian period through to the 1950s. As the editor of *The Field*, a shooting magazine, advised readers in 1904: 'There can be little doubt that where surface drainage is properly carried out on a grouse moor, not only the sheep but also the grouse are thereby benefited . . . As regards grouse, excess of moisture impoverishes the heather, and makes it unhealthy for the birds to feed upon.'[33] That same year, an article in *Country Life* on 'The Management of Grouse Moors' instructed its audience: 'in order to be the happy possessor or lessee of a really satisfactory grouse moor, the following axioms are essential, viz . . . careful and systematic heather-burning . . . Vermin mercilessly destroyed . . . [and] drainage operations carried out with an eye to the welfare of the grouse, as well as the sheep.'[34] The conclusions of Parliament's inquiry into grouse disease in 1912 also stated: 'it can be urged with confidence that a well-drained moor is less liable to dangerous infection . . . than a moor with stagnant pools . . . On most moors money would be well expended in draining, for not only would the risk of infection be thereby lessened, but the total yield of heather would be increased.'[35]

As late as 1958, the author Richard Waddington expounded draining in an influential book on grouse moor management:

'Neither the grouse bird nor the heather plant likes wet feet and a large area of wet boggy ground is a dead loss on a grouse moor.'[36] And landowners continued to heed such advice. As an academic article on moorland management from 1977 reported, 'land managers frequently drain wet moors in an attempt to increase grouse stocks.'[37] A survey carried out in 1979 by the Game Conservancy – which later became the Game and Wildlife Conservation Trust – found that 'in the north of England, 28 of 51 grouse moor owners (55%) had drained parts of their moorland estates in recent years'.[38] As recently as 1993, the management plan drawn up for the Duke of Devonshire's huge Bolton Abbey Estate included the 'cleaning of grips, ditches and drains' as one of the stated duties of their gamekeepers.[39]

So much for drainage; what about burning? I've witnessed moorland burning on some of England's grouse moors. The surreal shock of seeing a moor being deliberately torched by a gamekeeper; the vast plumes of smoke choking the air. The awful aftermath: a charred landscape, the blackened remnants of heather, dead mosses left bleached and bone dry, the tiny skeletons of frogs and mice that got caught in the inferno. Kevin Walker, the head of science at the Botanical Society of Britain and Ireland, compares moorland burning to 'burning down forest cover every few decades, and losing all the specialists that microclimate supports. That's mosses, lichens, Lesser Twayblades, Wintergreens and much more.'[40]

But not only is repeated burning devastating to the botanical diversity of our uplands, it's also bad for air quality and flood risk. Acrid smoke belches from a moor in a video posted online by the environmentalist Bob Berzins in October 2023. 'A lot of anger from Sheffield residents about appalling moorland burning,' he wrote. 'Suburbs of Crosspool, Hillsborough and more full of health damaging smoke.'[41] After the smoke clears and the winter rains start, a different risk emerges for communities that neighbour grouse moors: flooding. The EMBER study carried out by Leeds University in 2014 concluded that 'river flow in catchments where burning has taken place appear to be slightly more prone to higher flow peaks during heavy rain.'[42] It's galling that wealthy grouse moor owners are allowed to dump smoke and floods on those living downstream.

What about the wisdom of lighting fires on one of Britain's most important carbon stores? As a review by Natural England found, 'there is strong evidence that managed burning affects various components of the carbon cycle of upland peatlands.'[43] Advocates of burning are keen to point out that they're only intending to burn the heather growing on peat soils, not the peat itself. But burning can reduce the rate of peat accumulation and below-ground carbon storage. If the layer of living sphagnum moss is scorched, peat formation slows. And burning can expose and dry out the underlying peat soil, causing it to oxidise and erode. This also leads to more peat running off into streams as dissolved organic carbon – the cause of the caramel-brown discolouration of the brook I'd witnessed on the Duke of Westminster's estate – some of which is later released as CO_2. And sometimes, when moorland burning gets out of control, it can set fire to the peat itself, releasing huge amounts of carbon.[44]

The science of burning is complex and contested – not least by the grouse moor industry themselves. Some, for instance, try to claim that by having 'controlled burns' of heather, grouse moor owners are reducing the risk of wildfires and the resulting pulse of carbon emissions.[45] Old woody heather is dry and highly flammable. By periodically removing the old heather, goes the argument, burning actually reduces the 'fuel load' of the moor. The grouse moor lobby would like us to believe that we have to fight fire with fire.

But you don't fight fire with fire: you fight it with water. By rewetting peat bogs, we not only make them less flammable, but also reboot their ability to soak up carbon and reduce flooding. We do that by stopping moorland burning, which dries out the peat. We do it by filling in drainage ditches (called 'grip-blocking'), which allows water to be retained on the high moors and enables sphagnum moss to grow again, restarting the creation of peat. The high 'fuel load' of heather moorlands is also a result of driven grouse moor management creating a heather monoculture. Through draining and burning, it's created conditions ideal for heather to flourish in. But a more diverse heathland flora, full of green shrubs like bilberry and cranberry, would already be less flammable. And if the moors were rewetted, heather's dominance would be further reduced, giving way to moisture-laden bog plants. Restored blanket bog doesn't burn. We need, in other words, to make Britain wet again.

Grouse moor owners have utterly failed to steward the vast carbon store in their possession. Instead of being a carbon sink, our upland peat is now a net source of greenhouse gas emissions, exacerbating climate breakdown. The most definitive stats on this are in a government-commissioned report by the Centre for Ecology and Hydrology from 2017, which sets out the way peat emissions are accounted for in the UK's official greenhouse gas inventory. Whilst the report doesn't give a figure for emissions specifically from grouse moor management, it does give a total for the 3 million acres of UK peat that's been 'affected to varying degrees by human activities including drainage, burn-management, and livestock grazing' – a colossal 3.4 million tonnes of CO_2e (CO_2-equivalent) per year.[46]

Even the GWCT, in a 2020 report based on some questionable assumptions, claim that English grouse moors are responsible for slightly over half a million tonnes of CO_2e per year. They also state that grouse moors in England cover around 697,000 acres, meaning an average of 0.75 tonnes of CO_2e per acre per year.[47] Extrapolating this approach to include the 2.5 million acres of grouse moors in Scotland would mean total emissions from UK grouse moors of around 2.4 million tonnes of CO_2e annually.

So what might be the *cumulative* amount of carbon pumped into the air by grouse moor owners since Victoria and Albert bought Balmoral? Let's take the more solid government-backed figure of 3.4 million tonnes of CO_2e per year as our basis for this. But let's be reasonable, and assume that emissions took a while to ramp up from zero as the driven grouse shooting industry developed during the Victorian period, before reaching their current level around the start of the twentieth century, and plateauing down to the present. Between 1850 and 2023, I estimate that Britain's grouse moors were responsible for

504 megatons of CO_2e emissions. That's half a billion tonnes of carbon dioxide, spewed into the atmosphere by a few hundred aristocratic estates, all for sport.[48]

And all of this is before we even talk about how many mammals and birds of prey are still killed on grouse moors. Gamekeepers continue to litter the uplands with poisons, traps and snares to snuff out any and all creatures that might predate on grouse. Crows, foxes, stoats, weasels: you name it – if it affects gamebird numbers, it has to die. Even beautiful mountain hares, their winter fur white as snow, are not spared death. Because they carry a tick that spreads disease to grouse, they have been culled in vast numbers on grouse moors. A 2018 study found that mountain hare numbers on some Scottish grouse moors had fallen by 99 per cent since the 1950s.[49]

Grouse moor owners like to defend themselves by pointing to the work they're doing to protect the endangered curlew. It has become their shield: as a staff member at the Wildfowl and Wetlands Trust once confided to me, the grouse moor lobby have 'weaponised curlews'. Their reasons for doing so are entirely self-serving, and incidental to their main business. Obviously, when you remove all natural predators in the uplands, this also benefits some other ground-nesting birds. But this is at the expense of culling hundreds of thousands of other animals to produce a wholly artificial environment, in which natural food webs have been abolished.[50] Curlews existed for millennia before the Victorians invented driven grouse shooting: what's changed has been the loss of their habitat. As the columnist Rod Liddle – not exactly a bleeding-heart liberal – points out, 'The game lobby . . . cling to the curlew as a spider clings to the side of a bath as the water rises beneath it.'[51]

Though much of the slaughter is entirely legal, wildlife crime is also endemic within the grouse shooting industry. Since 1990, fifty-six gamekeepers have been convicted of illegally persecuting birds of prey in Scotland alone, and that's just the tip of an iceberg.[52] Because raptors like hen harriers and goshawks predate on grouse, they are frequently found shot or poisoned by gamekeepers – despite it being against the law to do so. Over a hundred hen harriers have gone 'missing' or been found illegally killed in the UK since 2018, most of them on or close to grouse moor estates.[53] This isn't just a few rotten apples spoiling the barrel: this is an epidemic. And it goes to the very top. In 2020, film footage emerged of a gamekeeper killing a protected goshawk on the Queen's grouse moor in North Yorkshire.[54] Victoria and Albert started the trend for driven grouse shooting, and what takes place on the sovereign's land continues to influence what other estates do. The fish rots from the head. There is something rotten in the state of our uplands, and it stems from this archaic bloodsport.

So why hasn't this been stopped already? If grouse moors are so detrimental to the public interest, how come they still exist? The answer is simple: because they are the preserve of the elite, and landed wealth remains deeply entwined with political power. It's not just the royals, aristocracy and billionaires who prop up grouse moors: it's also our political class.

From the Victorian period to the 1960s, it was completely normal for prime ministers to enjoy a day's shooting on a grouse moor. Disraeli shot at Balmoral; Chamberlain shot elsewhere in the Cairngorms; Churchill went shooting on the Duke of Westminster's Welsh grouse moor.[55] But the classic example is Harold Macmillan, Conservative prime minister between 1957 and 1963. Each August, photographs would appear in the newspapers of Macmillan dressed in tweedy plus-fours with a shotgun resting on his arm. 'PREMIER ON GROUSE SHOOT', ran one headline. 'Mr Harold Macmillan (right) strides out across the rain-swept moors at Masham, Yorkshire . . . With him are Lord Swinton (centre) and the Home Secretary, Mr R A Butler . . .'[56] The vast Swinton Estate was a favourite haunt of Macmillan's. At other times, he would go shooting with the Duke of Devonshire – who happened to be his nephew.[57]

As for Macmillan's Foreign Secretary, Alec Douglas-Home – well, he *owned* a grouse moor. But when Home took over as PM in 1963 in the wake of the Profumo scandal, the shine had started to come off such elite pastimes. Whilst the newly launched

Private Eye excoriated the peccadillos of the Tory establishment, the new working-class Labour leader, Harold Wilson, offered voters 'a chance to sweep away the grouse-moor conception of Tory leadership and refit Britain with a new image'.[58]

For some decades, shooting went out of fashion amongst the political class. Ted Heath preferred yachting; Jim Callaghan pottered about on his farm; Margaret Thatcher famously didn't understand the concept of relaxation. Grouse moors no longer had the same cachet and their owners could no longer hobnob with cabinet ministers in the shooting butts. And with the rise of modern ideas of nature conservation, grouse moor estates faced growing questions about their sustainability. To survive, grouse shooting would have to reinvent itself. It started by setting up a new lobbying group: the Moorland Association.

Of course, a panoply of organisations already existed to loudly beat the drum for shooting: the Country Landowners' Association, the Gamekeepers' Association, the Game Conservancy. But what was new about the Moorland Association was how it sought to rebrand grouse shooting as an act of conservation. It was founded in 1986 by a baronet, Sir Anthony Milbank: a keen grouse shooter on the 7,000-acre estate he owned in North Yorkshire, but also someone who genuinely cared for wildlife and was respected by conservationists.[59] The Moorland Association sought to ditch the industry's image as a sport for toffs by focusing on something with clear public appeal: preserving the purple heather of the moors.[60]

But the Moorland Association was clear from the outset that there were limits to what it wanted to conserve. 'There is no doubt in my mind that too many birds of prey, like all other predators, can seriously damage the management of a grouse moor,' admitted Milbank.[61] And whilst the grouse moor owners craved good public relations, they didn't actually want the public traipsing about their land. During the 1987 election, the Conservatives had, somewhat surprisingly, promised to enact a long-standing demand of the Ramblers to create more access over upland commons.[62] One of the Moorland Association's first big campaign wins was to get the government to drop this manifesto pledge. 'There is not and never has been a right to roam across the moors,' Milbank wrote, citing concerns about public disturbance to ground-nesting birds.[63] As one disappointed rambler wrote to a newspaper letters page, this U-turn had been brought about due to a 'tiny clique of grouse moor owners' who, having formed the Moorland Association, 'began a heavyweight campaign of lobbying both Parliament and the Civil Service'.[64]

But the Moorland Association's biggest win was the public money it helped secure for grouse moors in the form of greener farm subsidies. Many of the first wave of stewardship grants, trialled in the late 1980s and early 1990s, were spent in the uplands.[65] In 2019, I investigated farm subsidies going to grouse moor owners, and found that sixty-one estates raked in over £10 million in just one year.[66] The RSPB, analysing data supplied by Natural England, found that over a ten-year period more than £105 million of environmental stewardship payments had gone to grouse moors.[67]

Of course, the grouse shooting lobby disavows the idea that it is propped up by public money. As the newspaper columnist and notorious climate sceptic Matt Ridley claimed in 2016, writing about moorland: 'Grouse shooting has saved this special habitat . . . while making very little demand on the taxpayer.'[68] That would have shocked one Matt Ridley, who when employed as a young reporter on the *Newcastle Journal* in 1994, wrote in consternation that 'landowners, landlords and even grouse shooters will be claiming some of the money' from the then-novel environmental stewardship schemes.[69] But since he penned those words, Matt Ridley has inherited the title of viscount, acquired a 6,000-acre grouse moor in the North Pennines, and become president of the Moorland Association.[70]

One might have expected grouse moors to get short shrift under the 1997 New Labour government. But in at least one respect, they did very well. A raft of grouse moor estates signed up to a payments scheme called 'Higher Level Stewardship', and as a result, the SSSIs on their land were automatically graded as being in 'recovering' condition. As Kate Jennings of the Royal Society for the Protection of Birds says: 'Many of these "recovering" sites are not recovering at all. Natural England put many SSSIs into this category a decade ago because it assumed that entering into a plan or agreement with the landowner would automatically lead to the restoration of the site . . . A decade on, the evidence clearly shows that this was a mistake . . . This is despite large amounts of public money being spent on agreements which were never going to drive recovery, including some which allow moorland burning to continue and so perpetuate damage to these precious places.'[71]

And then, with the Coalition government in 2010, came the return of the Old Etonians – and with them, a more favourable attitude to grouse shooting than the industry had known for decades. Admittedly, David Cameron was more partial to shooting pheasants than grouse, but as one journalist noted, 'there is the whiff of the grouse moor about "Dave"'.[72] Cameron soon appointed the grouse moor owner Lord Benyon as environment minister, who despite his vested interests failed to recuse himself from decisions over shooting. When Benyon took office, Natural England was in the process of prosecuting the owners of a grouse moor, the Walshaw Moor Estate, for damaging protected blanket bog habitat. But then, suddenly and without explanation, the case was dropped. A series of chummy emails between the minister and the Moorland Association emerged, thanks to Freedom of Information requests by campaigners. But Benyon 'maintained an aloof silence on the matter', and the Walshaw Moor Estate was later awarded a new £2.5-million stewardship scheme.[73]

It only got chummier from there on in. Whilst Mayor of London, Boris Johnson was reported to have gone grouse shooting on an estate owned by hedge fund manager Jeremy Herrmann, whose wife Edwina happened to be a major Tory party donor.[74] And as Prime Minister, Johnson became close pals with David Ross, multimillionaire founder of Carphone Warehouse and owner of two grouse moors in North Yorkshire. Ross was another major donor to the Tories; he once offered a day's shooting on his moors at a Tory fundraising party.[75] Later that year, during the Covid-19 pandemic, Johnson exempted grouse shooting parties from the 'Rule of Six' that then restricted outdoor gatherings to no more than six people.[76]

And then came Rishi Sunak. His constituency of Richmond in Yorkshire contains, by my reckoning, no fewer than fifteen grouse moor estates.[77] Sunak was soon delivering for his constituents – or at least the tiny percentage of them who owned these grouse moors. In 2016, during a parliamentary debate on grouse shooting sparked by a petition calling for it to be banned, Sunak argued strongly against. 'Banning grouse shooting would undermine the balanced ecosystem of our countryside,' he claimed.[78] In 2018, Sunak visited Bolton Castle grouse moor in his constituency, accompanied by the Moorland Association, who bragged afterwards they had been 'delighted' to join him and 'show the many benefits of moorland [management] for grouse'.[79] When Sunak became PM, the grouse shooting lobby was ecstatic.[80] He did, at least, claim during the Tory leadership campaign that his 'pet project' was peat restoration.[81] But this has turned out to be marsh gas. The latest official stats show that landowners' efforts at peat restoration are falling far short of even the government's pitiful targets.[82]

The extremely cosy relationship between wealthy grouse moor owners and our political class has meant the industry has avoided any serious regulation for decades. Politicians have treated these lords of the uplands with kid gloves, trusting them to take voluntary action – backed by substantial sums of public money. One recent debacle shows why we simply can't rely on the grouse moor-owning clique to keep their pledges of stewardship: the battle to control moorland burning.

After the government dropped its legal case against the Walshaw Moor Estate over blanket bog burning, residents of the flood-prone Calder Valley downstream of the estate started a campaign called Ban the Burn. They were joined by the RSPB, who lodged a complaint about the landowner's burning practices and those of other grouse moor estates – with the European Court of Justice. The European Commission then opened infraction proceedings against the UK government, suspecting it to be in breach of the Habitats Regulations, a key piece of European law. As these lengthy investigations rumbled on, Britain voted to leave the EU: would the whole case now be null and void? But with Brexit also proving to be a protracted affair, public pressure about moorland burning continued to build, and the then Environment Secretary Michael Gove felt he had to act. He invited grouse moor owners to a meeting in Whitehall, hosted by the Department for the Environment, Food and Rural Affairs (DEFRA). But the meeting took place behind closed doors, with no environmental groups in attendance. So I decided to submit a Freedom of Information (FOI) request for the minutes.

I discovered that Gove's meeting had been attended by some of the largest landowners in the country – from the Duke of Northumberland, a Tory party donor, to Jeremy Herrmann, who had hosted Boris Johnson on his moor a few years previously. Gove pleaded with them to 'help the Government demonstrate its intent to the Commission to cease rotational burning on blanket bog'. If the Commission were to press charges, the UK government could face a hefty fine, not to mention political embarrassment. Rather than regulate the landowners doing the damage, Gove offered them a softer solution – a voluntary ban.[83] This was something the Moorland Association was very keen on. In emails sent to Gove, which I eventually prised out of DEFRA under FOI laws, they stated that a voluntary burning ban was 'a big prize . . . it can be used to demonstrate to Europe that this sea-change is underway voluntarily and there is no need to regulate'.[84]

I later obtained a list of the grouse moor estates who had signed up to the voluntary burning ban. At the time I worked for Friends of the Earth, and with my colleague Alastair Cameron, we decided to hold the landowners to their word. At the start of the burning season that October, we hired a car and drove around the Yorkshire Dales, visiting several of the estates that had agreed to cease burning on blanket bog. For two days, the weather was awful, with no sign of any burning. But as the rains abated on the third day, we spotted a plume of smoke rising from the hills, and headed towards it. Sure enough, it was a fire deliberately started by a gamekeeper, and it was taking place on an estate that had signed up to the ban – and in breach of the conditions they had agreed to. The film footage we obtained was shown on BBC *Countryfile*.[85]

Ours was but one of numerous examples of grouse moor estates flouting the burning ban they had willingly signed up to, with evidence collected by groups like the RSPB, Wild Moors and volunteer 'moorland monitors' across the country. It's worth noting that this citizen science was only possible because the public have finally regained a right of access to moorlands. In the year 2000, the Countryside and Rights of Way Act gave people the right to roam over England's moors and commons, centuries after they were enclosed by aristocratic estates for grouse shooting, long after the Kinder Scout mass trespassers did battle with the Duke of Devonshire's gamekeepers, and despite the best efforts of the Moorland Association. Practices hidden from the public for a long time are now becoming subject to public scrutiny.

Facing a barrage of evidence that voluntary measures weren't working, Gove was forced to act. He announced a statutory ban on moorland burning. It was a significant victory, particularly given the government's closeness to the grouse lobby. But when the legislation was published, it was full of loopholes. Burning was only banned on peat deeper than 40cm, which I thought was a curiously precise figure; when I asked DEFRA for a map of peat deeper than 40cm, they said they didn't have one. Such loopholes, I assume, were lobbied for by the grouse moor industry, to make enforcement harder. And despite the law coming into effect, plenty of estates continued to flout it. An investigation by Greenpeace Unearthed found over two hundred and fifty peatland burning incidents during the first burning season after the legislation came into force, fifty of them on deep peat.[86] Gradually, Natural England has begun bringing prosecutions. The rot goes right to the top. In October 2023, one of the Moorland Association's directors, Ben Ramsden, was convicted for burning on deep peat on his estate.[87]

Private finance is the grouse shooting lobby's new wizard wheeze to save itself. Not content with swallowing vast sums of public money over the past few decades in the name of 'environmental stewardship', grouse moor owners are now keen to profit from burgeoning markets in carbon offsets and biodiversity credits. The push is being spearheaded by an outfit called Tellus Natural Capital, founded in 2021.[88] Its website claims it 'helps investors and the landowning community to contribute to the natural capital policy debate'.[89] It certainly has good political access: in January 2022, Tellus Natural Capital held a lobbying meeting with Environment Minister and grouse moor owner Lord Benyon, and later that year met with Rishi Sunak whilst he was Chancellor.[90]

So who's behind it? It turns out that the organisation's directors all have very close links with grouse moor estates. Director Andrew Stone, for instance, is the son of the late Michael Stone, who owned thousands of acres of grouse moors in the North Pennines.[91] One of the company's shareholders is Richard Bannister, the owner of the Walshaw Moor Estate.[92] At the launch party for Tellus Natural Capital, speakers included the Moorland Association's president Matt Ridley, and the former chair of the GWCT, Ian Coghill. A video from the launch event shows Coghill informing viewers that 'grouse actually are the natural capital on the land. From that cascades all the other benefits.'[93] There is no sense from Tellus' public pronouncements that it foresees moorland owners giving up grouse shooting or fundamentally changing what they're doing. It appears, in my opinion, to be little more than a front group for grouse moor owners to protect their interests.

I used to think that the owners of our uplands might reform themselves. There's a perfectly viable alternative business model for upland estates, practised for decades in Norway and called *fjelljakt* or 'mountain hunting'. 'Fjelljakt has a lot to teach us about how Britain's uplands could one day look,' writes the conservationist Benedict Macdonald. 'Large broken woodlands – dominated by pine, willow and birch – mingle with open mires, heather and grasslands. But this varied wilderness is hunted too.'[94] Adopting this Scandi model in Britain would require moorland owners to dispense with their outdated Victorian methods of managing land and obsession with maximising the number of gamebirds. But it would still allow for some hunting – just practised at a lower intensity, and perhaps requiring a little more skill.

So why isn't it happening here? Some of the most prominent advocates of rewilding, after all, have been private aristocratic estates, from Knepp in Sussex to Wild Ken Hill in Norfolk. But these pioneers have mainly been in the English lowlands: none seems prepared to challenge their peers to follow suit in the uplands. It's true that recent years have seen some positive developments: United Utilities has announced an end to grouse shooting on its land, Yorkshire Water is reviewing its shooting tenancies, and the National Trust is slowly reducing the area of its upland estate where intensive grouse shooting is permitted.[95] Yet it's the corporate and charitable landowners making changes, responding to pressure from customers and members. No grouse moor-owning aristocrat or billionaire seems prepared to do the same.

Given how Victoria and Albert started the fashion for intensive grouse moor management, perhaps the royal family could also bring it to an end. As the Scottish environmental campaigner Nick Kempe recently wrote: 'The royal family is at the apex of sporting estate owners . . . If they were to stop muirburn [moorland burning] then other Scottish grouse estates might follow.'[96] But there is currently no sign of the royal family abandoning its Victorian traditions. Prince William continues to shoot on the royal grouse moors – and even takes his young son Prince George along to school him in the ritual.[97]

It's clear that we now need to ban *all* forms of moorland burning, close the ludicrous loopholes in the law, and ban driven grouse shooting outright. The industry is beyond reform. It has already been given hundreds of millions of pounds in public money to improve things, only for the nature reserves and vast carbon store under its stewardship to decline further. Endemic wildlife crime and flouting of the current partial burning ban in England only underscores how many of these estates believe themselves to be above the law. The Scottish government has started down this road, recently tightening rules on muirburn and introducing the licensing of grouse shooting, in an effort to curb raptor persecution. But the time for half measures is over. The incoming government at Westminster must end this Victorian practice for ever.

Properly enforced legislation of this sort by a new government would likely spark a wave of sales of grouse moor estates in coming years, as landowners realise the game is up. There is a risk, however, that they will be snapped up by carbon offsetting cowboys and plantation forestry firms, swapping one form of environmental destruction for another.[98] So we need a safety net. The next two chapters will outline how both communities and the government should be given the tools to acquire this land themselves.

Enough is enough. The tiny elite who own grouse moors have taken the rest of us for fools for too long. Through their reckless failure to steward this land, they've forfeited their right to own it. The huge carbon store they possess is clearly a critical national resource, one that needs managing in the common interest. It's time for this so-called 'ultimate trophy asset' – privatised, enclosed, commodified and despoiled – to be turned back into a public asset. It's time to return this land to the people.

3

The Land for the People

The horse stamped and snorted, flecks of foam flying from its mouth as it chewed on its bit. A troupe of flautists had just finished playing 'Auld Lang Syne'. Screaming swifts slid beneath the multicoloured bunting that hung across the high street, lit by the weak rays of early morning sunshine. It's not every day that you find thousands of people thronging the streets of the Scottish town of Langholm; still less likely that you'll find many of them dressed in suits, clutching pints of ale before breakfast. But this was no ordinary day. This was the day of the Common Riding, Langholm's ancient celebration of its land rights.

Suddenly, the crowd fell silent. A man had climbed on to the back of the horse, steadying himself as he stood bolt upright on the saddle: the Crier of the Fair. And then, in a loud, clear voice, he began to recite a proclamation of the town's centuries-old rights over nearby land:

> *'Now, Gentlemen, we're gan' frae the Toun,*
> *An' first of all the Kil'green we gan' roun',*
> *It is an ancient place where clay is got,*
> *And it belongs tae us by Right and Lot . . .'**

---

* Anglicised version: 'Now, Gentlemen, we're going from the Town, / And first of all the Kilngreen we go around, / It is an ancient place where clay is got, / and it belongs to us by Right and Lot'.

The people of Langholm, the Crier explained, held common rights to gather stone for building and bracken for livestock bedding from land neighbouring the town. 'Now, Gentlemen,' he concluded, 'it is expected that everyone who has occasion for Peats, Breckons, Flacks, Stanes or Clay will go out in defence of their property, and they shall hear the Proclamation of the Langholm Fair upon the Castle Craigs.'

As Langholm erupted in cheers, I stood listening to these words in fascination, sipping my own beer from a plastic pint glass: hair of the dog, I'd reasoned, after staying up late on previous nights to hear the town's pipe band perform in packed-out pubs. I'd come to Langholm to meet up with my friend Nadia – fellow Right to Roam campaigner, Geordie, and resident of the Isle of Bute – to scope out an action we were organising along the Scottish-English border. Langholm lies just fifteen minutes' drive north of England and, hearing about the Common Riding, we'd decided to stay for the festivities.

The Common Riding originates in an eighteenth-century dispute over land. In 1759, the town won the rights of common over the Kilngreen and Common Moss in a legal case involving the landowner, the Duke of Buccleuch – then, as now, one of the largest private landowners in Scotland.[1] But as a condition of holding these rights, each year the people of Langholm would have to mark the boundaries of the lands to which they applied. At first, this was done by merely walking the perimeter, rather like the old English custom of beating the bounds of a local parish. Then the townsfolk began to mark it by riding the area on horseback.

Like all good traditions, the Common Riding has accumulated a raft of symbols, at first mysterious to outsiders, but each of them speaking to the Langholm community's connection to its land, plants and soils. Schoolchildren hold aloft besom brooms they've made out of heather cut from the moor. A giant thistle tied to a pole is paraded through town: an emblem of Scotland, obviously, but one which the Common Riding's official guidebook suggests may have been adopted 'on account of its "jags", as a warning to anyone who contemplated interfering with the Fair'.[2] Most important of all is the ceremonial spade used to mark the boundaries of the Common Moss by digging a sod of turf. Originally, the townsfolk's rights included cutting peat from the moorland to burn as fuel, a custom no longer practised.

The ritual draws in thousands of people from miles around. Nadia and I watched in bemusement as a cavalcade of men and women on horseback cantered through Langholm's streets, kitted out in tweed and jodhpurs. A bowler-hatted man with an impressive ginger beard sat astride a sleek brown charger, its mane and tail neatly braided. Many wore orange and blue rosettes. 'Sponsored by Irn Bru?' suggested Nadia – although it turned out they were the colours of that year's Derby winner. Some of the horses, startled by the crowds, turned skittish; the scent of the rain began to mingle with the reek of fresh horseshit. But then they were off, galloping up the hill towards the Common Moss.

In English rural towns and villages, when you see people wearing silly outfits riding horses, you think 'fox hunt'. But no animals are harmed in the making of the Common Riding, and there's none of the class dimensions of a hunt: this is a festival that the whole town takes part in. It's a rite of passage each year for the young man – always a man – who plays the part of Cornet, who leads the Riding and carries aloft the Town Standard – a beautiful flag resembling an old trade union banner. This year the honour had fallen upon 22-year-old boiler engineer Christopher Tait. Shop windows throughout the town bore posters wishing him well: *Good luck Cornet Tait*. Flanked by his predecessors and wearing his ceremonial gold chains, Langholm's acting provost addressed the lad from a podium in the town square: 'You have carried out your duties with distinction; I suspect you will remember this day for the rest of your life.'

As we drank our pints and watched, Nadia and I talked about how rarely we'd felt rooted in communities in England. Partly, we thought, this was the result of renting – insecurity of tenure means young people move around a lot and don't stay long enough to get involved in the affairs of a local area. But also, we decided, it was down to how much ritual in modern-day England is bound up in hierarchy and nation rather than place and nature. Our civic ceremonies revolve around the monarchy (coronations), the flag (Remembrance Day) or mass consumerism (Christmas). They tend not to celebrate locality, and still less land rights. Here in Langholm, by contrast, was a tradition about people's shared rights over a piece of land. It was at once a story of resistance – the townsfolk against the landowning Duke – and of unity: the town coming together to celebrate, and, of course, to get pissed.

For 250 years, the people of Langholm have had rights over the common land in their vicinity. For some time, however, there remained uncertainty over who owned the freehold to the land itself.[3] In 2019, all that changed, when the Duke of Buccleuch put his Langholm Estate up for sale.

'Everything you can see, from here to the horizon,' said Jenny, 'is now owned by the community.'

I gazed out across mile after mile of moorland, drinking in the glorious sight. Over 10,000 acres of purple heather and peat bog, ancient wood pasture and windswept hills, bisected by the clear waters of the River Tarras. This land used to be the Duke of Buccleuch's grouse moor, but following a review of his vast property portfolio, the Duke decided to dispose of it. Between 2020 and 2022 it was bought out by the Langholm community, to become the Tarras Valley Nature Reserve. I'd been driven up to this vantage point by Jenny Barlow, estate manager for the reserve, and Kat Mayer, its project officer; and I've got to admit that I was pretty excited. Back home in England, I'd visited plenty of community-owned pubs and village halls, but nothing on a scale like this. Jenny agreed, laughing. 'It's bloody massive!'

Langholm Moor still bears the scars of its life as a former grouse moor. A huge area of the moorland had been drained, its fells crisscrossed with drainage channels as if scraped by a rake. Rotational burning has degraded the peat further, and I could see the far hillside bore the characteristic chequerboard pattern left by past burns.

But shooting has now ceased, there's no longer any moorland burning, and the community plans to block up the drains next and start rewetting the peat. What really excited me was how fluid the landscape felt. I was elated to see so many young trees naturally regenerating up the hillside. The high moor was exploding with heather and bilberries, scattered birch saplings and scrub. A savannah-like landscape, all too rare in our uplands these days. Released from its stasis as a heavily managed shooting estate, it's a landscape alive with possibilities.

The plan, Jenny told me, was to keep the landscape evolving as a 'dynamic habitat'. There had been no grazing over this area for some years, save for a few wild goats and occasional roe deer. But Jenny explained that they intended to reintroduce a small number of grazing animals at some point, so the hillside wouldn't simply become closed-canopy woodland, but rather a rich mosaic of scrub, woods and open habitats. Cattle would help trample the bracken and leggy heather and reduce fire risk, and the community were interested to trial putting pigs or ponies on the moor to see if they could break up the tussocky areas of purple moor grass. Restoring the peat bogs will also change the growing conditions and likely put a brake on the amount of tree regeneration on the higher moorland. 'Once the hydrology has been restored through rewetting the peat, let's see what the land wants to do,' said Jenny.

Jenny's interest in communities owning land came from trying to defend English towns and villages against flooding. She grew up in Sunderland and used to live in Leeds, where she worked for the Environment Agency to reduce flooding through natural means – such as by restoring peat and planting trees, to retain more water upstream. In her job, Jenny had to negotiate with lots of private landowners, to try to get them to change how they managed their land, but felt 'really limited by land not belonging to the public or communities . . . Imagine the number of communities in England who could benefit from buying their own natural flood defences.' In Scotland, where communities have far greater powers to acquire land, Jenny didn't have to imagine.

Bird species on the moor are also thriving. Kat reeled off a list of the bird species they have on the reserve: hen harriers, goshawks, short-eared owls, skylarks, meadow pipits, curlews, red grouse, black grouse; even eagles, she said, come to visit from time to time. Kat studied ecology at university but, after doing a teacher training course, prefers the job description of 'environmental educator', and clearly loves enthusing people about nature. Jenny pointed out to me what's known as 'hen harrier corner', where birdwatchers come for the view.

Gone is the apparatus of traps and poisons deployed on so many grouse moors for controlling predator numbers. We discussed how traditional grouse moor management is obsessed by killing. 'It's so controlled, many moors are managed to within an inch of their lives,' Kat agreed. In the 1990s and 2000s, when it still belonged to the Duke, Langholm Moor underwent a series of laudable experiments to see if it was possible for driven grouse shooting to coexist with high numbers of hen harriers. To cut a long story short, it isn't. Take out the raptor persecution and you get lots more birds of prey, but the grouse populations don't reach the unnaturally high numbers that would make shooting economic.[4] To me, it's further confirmation that driven grouse moors are artificial environments, reliant on suppressing food webs and natural processes to satisfy a Victorian sport. Better to let the moor 'find its own balance', concurs Jenny.

The size of the buyout also gives the community the chance to restore nature at a landscape scale. The reserve covers almost the entire catchment of the Tarras Water, from its headwaters down to where it joins the Esk below Langholm.[5] Down the valley from the moor, we visited the rich alder carr woodland that grows along the banks of the Tarras. A gorgeous stretch of wood pasture boasted some of the oldest alder trees I'd ever seen, their gnarled and knotted boles providing plentiful anchor points for 'air trees' – young rowan saplings growing epiphytically out of their trunks. Marsh orchids sprouted in profusion alongside reeds and yellow flag irises; in the drier meadow, we found yellow rattle, purple knapweed, betony, hemp agrimony, and tonnes of water mint, filling the air with its fresh scent as we brushed past it. A sea of meadowsweet hugged the banks of the river itself, its flowers frothing like bubbling champagne. The aim is to now let this glorious woodland spread further up the Tarras.

So how did the community of Langholm come to possess such treasures?

When the Duke of Buccleuch dropped the bombshell news that the moor was up for sale, Kevin Cumming, an employee of local community development trust the Langholm Initiative, was trying to relax in his caravan. 'It was the first day of a one-week holiday, and from then on my phone never stopped ringing,' he says.[6] At the time, Kevin was working on a project to bring more income into Langholm through eco-tourism. The small town had been hit badly by the recent closure of a local woollen mill and the loss of two hundred jobs. Kevin saw immediately that if Langholm acquired this land, it could be a huge shot in the arm for community regeneration. And as an environmentalist, he saw the opportunity for this to be achieved in tandem with ecological restoration.

Kevin wrote a proposal for a community buyout of the moorland estate and its transformation into a nature reserve. It was a bold plan; unprecedented, even. As one fundraising pamphlet put it: 'If the plan comes to fruition, it would be the biggest community buy-out ever seen in Scotland south of the Great Glen, and the most extensive ecological restoration project outside of the Cairngorms.'[7]

Another motivating factor was fear of who might buy the land if the community *didn't*. There were concerns that a new private owner might be hostile to the town's traditions, preventing the Common Riding from continuing; might not share their vision of ecological recovery; or even worse, might turn it into a forestry plantation or another grouse moor. On my visit, I met Margaret Pool, former chair of the board of the Langholm Initiative, and something of a local legend. For decades, Margaret has worked tirelessly to instil pride in the town, organising litter-picks and supporting community regeneration projects.[8] I found her, characteristically, on her hands and knees weeding the planters outside the Langholm Initiative offices. We talked about how a huge area of land to the other side of Langholm had recently been sold by Buccleuch to a forestry firm, who planned to clear off the tenant farmers and carpet-bomb the area with conifer plantations. 'The Highlands have already suffered from one Clearance,' said Margaret in her broad Falkirk accent. 'People cleared for sheep. This time, is it to be for trees?'

There was widespread feeling, therefore, that the community had to try to acquire Langholm Moor. After Kevin, Margaret and others approached the government-run Scottish Land Fund to register the community's interest, they were given just a fortnight to gauge local opinion. A team of volunteers went door-to-door around town, conducting a survey of residents, and ended up with eight hundred signatures of support – nearly a third of the entire population.[9] This helped unlock a grant from the Land Fund, which exists to support community buyouts, and enabled a full business proposal to be written. Then it was a matter of raising the money to buy the land: the whole 10,500-acre estate had been valued for Buccleuch at a cool £6.4 million. The Duke was gracious enough to recognise this was a tall order for the community to raise in one go, and divided the land into two halves, holding one back from sale. Even so, this still meant raising over £3.8 million – and the clock was ticking.

The public crowdfunder went live in May 2020, and quickly developed into what Richard Bunting, the team's press officer, called 'a rollercoaster – and one of the most inspiring, uplifting projects of hope I have been involved in'.[10] Launching the appeal in the midst of the Covid-19 pandemic, Jenny recalled, provided some 'hope in a dark time'. She remembered reading a note that somebody had sent attached to a donation, which made her well up: '"Here's £5, I'd love to give more, I believe in this so much but I'm on Universal Credit."' Clearly the appeal had touched a public nerve, because some 4,000 people donated in total. Conservation groups and philanthropic trusts gave generously as well. And crucially, the community was also able to draw on a £1 million grant from the Scottish Land Fund. As the sales deadline approached – ominously set for Hallowe'en – the crowdfunder smashed through its target, and took the bid over the line. 'A new era begins for this special land with which our community has such a deep and long-standing connection,' wrote Margaret at the time.[11] Then, a year later, the community did it all over again to successfully buy the second half of the estate.

Raising this much money was clearly a deeply impressive achievement. But how does a community-owned nature reserve make ends meet? I asked. 'We're never going to be loaded!' laughed Jenny. But the reserve could count on a number of income streams in future, she explained: farm payments (which, post-Brexit, are shifting towards paying land managers for environmental services); the sale of timber from old plantations as they're felled and replaced with native trees; rents from the various buildings on the estate; and income from paid courses and eco-tourism, as more people hear about Langholm and visit to see the burgeoning wildlife.

Jenny was keen to emphasise that community ownership, in her words, 'isn't a utopia . . . it can be messy, there are disagreements. If someone says, "everyone agrees with us", you probably haven't done your engagement right!' One such point of disagreement is over the future of sheep farming on Langholm Moor. There are still 1,300 sheep on the northern half of the moor, which perhaps sits uneasily with the reserve's reputation as a community rewilding initiative. On my visit, we were greeted by William the shepherd, who'd agreed to transfer his employment from the Buccleuch Estate to the new community-owned venture. The reserve still needs some grazing animals to achieve its objectives, but it's hard not to be struck by how overgrazed its northern reaches remain. I'm curious as to how this will eventually be resolved. 'William knows that the government aren't going to subsidise sheep for ever,' Jenny tells me, 'so he's open-minded, we'll work together to shape what comes next.' This is a transition playing out over the entirety of the uplands of Britain. In Scotland, with its still-raw memories of the Highland Clearances, throwing farmers off the land doesn't go down too well. If we're to effect a 'just transition' away from ecologically destructive agriculture, we need better ways of managing such inevitable conflicts; and perhaps community ownership offers a more mature way of resolving them through dialogue and acceptance.

As for now, the only real opposition to the buyout appears to come from those who think the community shouldn't have had to buy the land at all. I discovered this when I popped into the Langholm newsagents to buy a map of the local area, and found myself greeted by a group of men standing around a table drinking whisky and gin. Festivities ahead of the Common Riding had begun; I'd managed to walk in on a gathering of Cornets past and present.

'D'ye want a drink?' asked the newsagent, a silver-haired man called Billy, who had been Cornet in 1984. Soon I was merrily downing a bottle of beer and chatting about the upcoming festival, the town's traditions and how beautiful the Tarras Valley was. Emboldened by booze and the kindness of strangers, I decided to ask the main question on my mind. 'So what does everyone think about the community buying the land from the Duke?'

There was a deathly silence. 'Controversial topic?' I said nervously.

'Aye, you could say that,' said Billy. 'Some of us think we should never have had to pay for the land, particularly the Common Moss. It always belonged to the people.'

'And the Duke isn't exactly short of cash,' muttered another man.

Laughter broke the silence, and we drank to the success of the Common Riding.

Even if Langholm's buyout were a unique experiment, it would still be inspiring. But it isn't: it's part of a widespread and growing movement for community land ownership in Scotland.

As of 2023, there are some 711 assets in community ownership across Scotland, owned by 484 community groups, and covering slightly over half a million acres of land.[12] 'Today,' writes the historian James Hunter, 'you can stand on any one of more than 500,000 acres in the Highlands and Islands and, on asking some local person who owns that acre, get the answer, "Us".'[13] The land reform campaigner Andy Wightman calls the growth in community buyouts 'the single most significant change in landownership in Scotland'.[14] So how has this transformation come about?

There is a misconception that Scotland is in some ways an inherently more communitarian, left-wing society than England. It is true that Scotland has a keen memory of the injustice of the Highland Clearances, the century following 1750 when tens of thousands of Scots were evicted from the land by their aristocratic landlords – although England shares a very similar history with the enclosures, just one we have been taught to forget. And some Scottish communities intentionally keep alive a popular understanding of common rights over land, as I had witnessed at Langholm's Common Riding. But as Andy Wightman asserts, with the exception of the Isle of Lewis, gifted to its inhabitants by the enlightened Lord Leverhulme in 1919, 'there was no thought given to community-based solutions [to land management] for the best part of the twentieth century'.[15]

Indeed, when land reform movements arise, there is just as much likelihood that they will push for individualist outcomes as community-focused ones. Many modern efforts at land reform in western societies have sought to turn subsistence peasants into capitalist farmers by gifting them land. In Ireland, for example, the Wyndham Land Act of 1903 was enacted by the British government to break up large estates, but only in order to create a new class of owner-occupier yeomen farmers.[16] Yet since the 1990s, Scotland has taken a dramatically different turn, with its land reform movement pushing for collective ownership of land.

This communitarian turn in Scottish land politics has also made it particularly alert to ecological sustainability. Scotland's community ownership movement has asked searching questions about what land is *for*, whose interests it serves, and how to manage land for the common good. Sustainable development and democracy are written into the legal underpinnings for community right to buy in Scotland. And though it is not a panacea, the movement has created a new framework, unique in Britain, to hold landowners accountable for how they use land. For that, we have to thank some of the pioneers of community ownership in the late twentieth century.

Community buyouts arose as a genuine grassroots uprising against landed power in pre-devolution Scotland. John Major's unexpected victory in the 1992 UK general election, the Tories' fourth consecutive win, dashed hopes that Scotland would soon achieve some measure of greater independence and generated intense frustration north of the border. In despair, a number of Highland and island communities decided to take matters into their own hands.[17] Prominent amongst them were the inhabitants of the Isle of Eigg.

In the booming 1990s, Scottish islands were treated as tradeable commodities for the super-rich: a piece of marketing spiel from the time described them as 'Van Goghs on the international island market, masterpieces of mother nature'.[18] The Isle of Eigg was owned by Keith Schellenberg, an absentee laird and multimillionaire businessman from Yorkshire – who had allowed the island's housing stock to fall into disrepair, evicted tenants at short notice, drove around the island in his Rolls-Royce like Toad of Toad Hall, and whose daughter once hung a swastika flag from the balcony of their family lodge ('a bit of a joke', he said).[19] In 1994, persistent rumours started circulating that Schellenberg would soon have to sell Eigg to settle an expensive divorce bill. But when some of the islanders suggested he sell it to its resident population, Schellenberg scoffed. The islanders, he intimated in a radio interview, were not responsible enough to run their own affairs.[20]

This triggered a predictable backlash, and Eigg's residents sought out the help of one Alastair McIntosh. To Schellenberg, McIntosh must have seemed an eccentric and ill-matched opponent: a bearded, woolly-jumpered academic, who lectured in human ecology at Edinburgh University, and whose political philosophy was an eclectic mix of Celtic Christianity, Latin American liberation theology, deep ecology and a Saul Alinsky-esque approach to community organising. But this warm-hearted sage and the community of Eigg were soon to launch a revolution in Scotland's approach to land use and ownership.

The islanders set up the Isle of Eigg Trust as a community-run body for the anticipated future purchase and ownership of Eigg.

McIntosh, aware of his 'outsider' status, insisted on a vote; he was elected to the board alongside residents who had lived on Eigg for decades. The Trust's founding document declared its purposes to be: 'To secure the Island for Scottish and global heritage, to be run in the interests of the community . . . whilst conserving the ecology of this unique and beautiful island so that it may be enjoyed and shared by all.'[21] Of course, the community's most immediate ambitions were to overthrow their terrible landlord, repair their homes and rebuild their local economy. 'Just help us to get rid of that man,' one elderly resident implored the Trust.[22] But from the outset, McIntosh also foresaw that what the people of Eigg pioneered could have far wider ramifications. The Trust, he wrote in his account of its founding, 'had to kick-start a process that would break the spell of consent that landlordism had enjoyed. It had to create a new constellation of possibility.'[23]

The community's acquisition of Eigg was not intended to be merely the transfer of private property rights from one owner to another. It was, to McIntosh, simultaneously a 'seriously legitimate' challenge to 'landed power'[24] and 'a third way approach to land holding: "communitarian" rather than capitalist or communist'.[25] Indeed, through unmooring the land from the anchor of private property rights, McIntosh asserted that 'title over the island of Eigg had to be set free . . . You can't own the land; the land owns you.'[26]

This 'deep green' philosophy was central to the DNA of Scotland's community ownership movement. It emerged at the same time as anti-roads protestors were climbing trees across Britain, as Swampy was becoming a household name, and as the Scottish charity Trees for Life was getting set up with the aim of resurrecting the lost Caledonian pine forests. Community land trusts seemed to enable people, in McIntosh's words, to 'live in a more authentic relationship *with* the land, even if not necessarily *from* the land'.[27] This was not back-to-the-land in the sense of returning to a peasant way of life, but rather about bringing modern lifestyles more in tune with ecological limits. To this end, Eigg's community partnered with the Scottish Wildlife Trust for help with their buyout plans. The Trust's wildlife officer had himself been threatened with eviction by Schellenberg, and together they sought 'security of tenure for themselves and the island's wildlife'.[28]

At that time, there were no laws in Scotland supporting community buyouts, and no specific government funding to assist such efforts. Eigg's residents would have to rely on their own advocacy and fundraising. 'We would have to work with market forces to keep within the law,' accepted McIntosh. 'We would be trying to buy back what was, in effect property stolen simply by having been declared property under historically lurid circumstances.'[29] The islanders, however, did have one trick up their sleeve. They could attempt to force Schellenberg to lower the asking price for Eigg through a process of 'market spoiling'.[30] The mere existence of a trust agitating for greater community say in how the island was run would, they reasoned, make the land less desirable to wannabe investors. This, in turn, would mean having to raise less money to eventually buy it – that was, if Schellenberg ever agreed to sell it to them.

Schellenberg, however, had no intention of losing face to the islanders, and Eigg woke up one morning to discover it suddenly had a new owner – an eccentric German artist who called himself Maruma. Schellenberg had quietly sold it to him off-market. But it soon emerged that Maruma was under investigation for fraud with a string of unpaid debts.[31] In financial deep water, he agreed to sell Eigg to the Trust. A frantic fundraising sprint netted an astonishing £600,000 from 10,000 small donations, plus a £1 million gift from a mystery donor.[32] On 12 June 1997, the Isle of Eigg was bought by its residents, for considerably less than Schellenberg's original asking price: the first Scottish community to clear a laird from his land, rather than the other way around.

Eigg's inspiring victory was part of a wave of community buyouts in the late 1990s. The parallel work of the Assynt crofters, and the residents of Knoydart and the Isle of Gigha, to acquire land for their communities helped push land rights up the political agenda. And after Tony Blair's government enacted devolution, land reform was high on the list of priorities of the new Labour-led Scottish Executive. The newly created Scottish

Parliament was unicameral – possessing no equivalent to Westminster's House of Lords, with its aristocratic landowners eager to block land reform measures. A Scottish Land Fund was established in 2000: at first with National Lottery funding, and then, in a later incarnation, backed by taxpayers' money. The area of land under community ownership almost trebled between the start of the new millennium and 2010.[33] And a new Land Reform Policy Group was set up to make recommendations for legislation.

In 2003, the Scottish Parliament passed the Land Reform (Scotland) Act, Part 2 of which created a Community Right to Buy.* This gave community bodies the right to register an interest in rural land, and then a right of first refusal to buy that land when the current owner put it up for sale. To qualify, a 'community body' has to be a registered company, charity or community benefit society, the majority of whose members must be residents of a defined geographical locale.[34] The normal sales process is then paused, giving the community eight months to raise the funds to buy the land.[35] These provisions alone represent a striking departure from the ordinary exercise of private property rights. Usually, when a landowner decides to sell their land, they sell it to whomsoever they choose, normally the highest bidder. But Community Right to Buy means that landowners must give communities first refusal over the land being sold, providing they have formally registered their interest in it.

Later legislation has gone further still. The Community Empowerment Act 2015 and second Land Reform (Scotland) Act 2016 extended Community Right to Buy to land in towns and cities, and created new rights for communities to *compulsorily purchase* land in certain circumstances. Previously, compulsory purchase powers – the ability to force the sale of land – had been wielded only by the state. But now community

---

*Part 3 of the Land Reform (Scotland) Act 2003 also created a right for crofting communities to compulsorily acquire crofting land in certain circumstances.

bodies in Scotland have also been given this chance: first, where land has been abandoned or neglected, or whose use by the current landowner is deemed to be harming the 'environmental wellbeing' of a community; and second, where the community wishes to purchase land for the purpose of 'furthering sustainable development'.[36]

Of course, such laws were not introduced without a backlash. The unsubtle front-page headline of the *Scottish Daily Mail* on the day the first Land Reform Act was passed was 'LET THE GRAB BEGIN' – complete with a photo of Zimbabwean dictator Robert Mugabe.[37] But no such 'grab' has occurred. The right to private property in the UK is protected under the European Convention on Human Rights (ECHR). Article 1, Paragraph 1 of the ECHR states that 'every natural or legal person is entitled to the peaceful enjoyment of his possessions.' But whilst it makes clear that 'no one shall be deprived of his possessions', the ECHR follows this with a qualifying statement: 'except in the public interest and subject to the conditions provided for by law'. It is this qualification that legitimises the careful compulsory purchase of land by states and, in Scotland, by communities – providing a clear legal process is followed, and that the former owners are compensated. Community Right to Buy laws have been subjected to legal challenge on ECHR grounds, and have withstood the test.[38]

Taken together, Scotland's Community Right to Buy laws and funding schemes offer a radical new way of creating accountability over the use of land. In the first instance, they begin to democratise how land is owned and used. To obtain grants from the Scottish Land Fund, applicants have to demonstrate that there is community support for the land purchase, for example by undertaking a community survey – and the community group has to be properly constituted with democratic elections for positions.[39] To exercise the legal Community Right to Buy powers granted by the three Acts, a still more exacting democratic process has to be followed. Community bodies must organise a ballot of their community (defined by postcode unit) on the question of whether they should acquire the land – and, for the vote to be valid, they have to ensure turnout is at least 50 per cent. Anyone who's done any campaigning will know that getting this level of engagement is a tough ask and requires a *lot* of work – lots of door-knocking, leafleting, and conversations in pubs and village halls.

Nor is the community ballot merely a rubber-stamping exercise: communities can and do vote down proposals for land purchases. I spoke to Sam Firth, co-owner of a tiny croft on Morvern in Argyll, who helped organise an attempted community buyout of the Killundine Estate on the peninsula in 2020. Sam, her partner Alasdair and a group of other residents put in a huge amount of work preparing the bid and raising all the funds needed for the purchase. But when it came to the all-important ballot, the community voted against it proceeding.

'I was obviously in favour of the buyout happening,' Sam told me, 'but there clearly were some genuine concerns locally about how to practically manage such a large area of land . . . some people worried that it would be a drain on the local community, a burden to deal with.' Sam's past experience of living and working on the community-owned Knoydart Estate had convinced her it was achievable, but some communities can't yet imagine taking the leap to large-scale ownership. It didn't help that the vote had to be held in the midst of the Covid-19 lockdowns, making door-to-door campaigning virtually impossible. But Sam was also philosophical about the disappointing outcome. When I put it to her that the democratic nature of community ownership is part of its strength – that people really can say no and not just wave something through – she agreed. 'Community ownership is definitely more democratic than private ownership,' she told me. There are no such checks and balances over the acquisition and use of land by private landowners.

What's more, a commitment to sustainable development is written into the legal underpinnings to community ownership laws. In order to approve a community buyout, Scottish ministers have to be satisfied that the community body and the land being acquired are both 'compatible with furthering the achievement of sustainable development' – with some applications being turned down for failing to meet these criteria.[40] The academic Andrea Ross argues that the embedding of sustainable development as a primary objective of Scotland's Community Right to Buy laws makes them 'exceptional in UK and global terms', with 'real potential to deliver transformational change'.[41] Indeed, some community buyouts have been at the forefront of Scotland's transition away from fossil fuels. After the Isle of Eigg was acquired by its residents, it went on to create a pioneering renewable energy system, long before such solutions became mainstream.

Even so, 'sustainable development' – a buzzword of late-1990s-to-early-2000s environmentalism – is a pretty vague and baggy concept, which isn't clearly defined in Scottish law or really anywhere else.* It revolves around creating 'balance' between the three priorities of economy, society and the environment – when in reality, it's the environment that's invariably been deprioritised for decades and needs to be given greater weight in decision-making. Some of Scotland's community buyouts have clearly been motivated more by priorities of economic regeneration and rural repopulation than by nature restoration or climate mitigation. I would favour community buyouts today being subject to clearer obligations on meeting net zero and regenerating nature on their land. That being said, we have to remember that there are *no* such legal obligations on private landowners, *at all.* Community ownership in Scotland is far more democratically accountable and far more legally bound to care for our environment than private landowners with their vague pledges of stewardship.

What also makes Scotland's community ownership movement inspiring is activists' openness about its shortcomings, and their willingness to engage in a vibrant debate on how to improve imperfect policies. The half million acres of land owned by communities still only comprises around 2.6 per cent of Scotland –

---

*The most frequently cited definition is that of the Brundtland Report of 1987: 'Development that meets the needs of the present without compromising the ability of future generations to meet their own needs.'

a figure that falls far short of the Scottish government's target of reaching a million acres in community ownership by 2020.[42] Land reform campaigners have criticised the complexity of the rules surrounding Community Right to Buy powers, which deters some communities from making use of them. Figures assembled by Andy Wightman show that most community buyouts have taken place *outside* of the legal framework laid down by the three Acts to date, and that access to funding from the Scottish Land Fund has been more important to the spread of buyouts.[43] An investigation by *The Ferret* in 2023 found that only two communities have applied to force the sale of neglected land since these powers came into operation five years ago. Community Land Scotland, the representative body for community buyouts, says that the legislation sets 'too high a bar' for most communities.[44] Yet the fact that Scotland is even having this public debate, in a way that just isn't happening in England, speaks volumes. The independent Scottish Land Commission, set up in 2017, stimulates public discussion about land reform through its frequent reports, and the Scottish government has been consulting on proposals for a third Land Reform Act.

Perhaps the most intractable issue for community ownership is the price of land. Large upland estates, such as grouse moors and deer-stalking estates, are so expensive that few communities can realistically afford to buy them in their entirety. It took two marathon fundraising efforts, coupled with two hefty grants from the Scottish Land Fund, for the Langholm community to buy out the Duke of Buccleuch's grouse moor, and such large purchases remain the exception rather than the rule. The recent sale of the Tayvallich Estate in Argyll has brought spiralling land prices to the fore. Valued at £10 million, there was clearly no way the local community would have been able to afford it, even if supported by public grants: the *entire* annual budget of the Scottish Land Fund, after all, is around £10 million.[45] So what's the solution?

Some – like the Langholm residents I met at the Common Riding – baulk at the idea of having to pay wealthy landowners for land that was arguably stolen from the people in the first place. But short of armed insurrection, this stance offers few practical fixes.

Other campaigners propose a land value tax to bring down the price of land, with the proceeds recycled into a larger Scottish Land Fund.[46] Taxing land certainly has merits, and I'll explore this further in a later chapter. But whilst such measures could *reduce* land prices, it cannot (and should not) remove the need to compensate existing landowners when buying their land, because such property rights are protected by the ECHR and a large body of case law.

Of course, one could keep increasing the size of the public fund to assist community buyouts. But at a certain point, the question inevitably arises: why doesn't the public sector simply use such money to buy the land in question directly? After all, if community buyouts offer one way of increasing democratic control over the way land is owned and used, then greater ownership of land by a democratically elected government offers another. The radical potential of public sector land ownership for driving nature restoration will be picked up in the next chapter.

These drawbacks aside, community ownership offers a radical new approach to managing land for nature, operating within a framework that fosters democratic accountability. England ought to be eagerly following Scotland's example, and applying lessons from its experiments with community ownership south of the border. Instead, as usual, England lags far behind.

There is far, *far* less community ownership of land in England than there is in Scotland. After reading about the encouraging half million acres of Scottish land owned by community groups, I asked Tom Chance, director of the Community Land Trust Network, what he thought the equivalent area was in England. 'It's very hard to say, I'm afraid – it's less well-defined here,' he said, 'but a wild stab might be around 100 hectares [250 acres], all told.' That's roughly 0.0007 per cent of the country.[47]

One of the reasons for this pitifully small figure is that our politicians have much more interest in telling us to 'take back control' than actually handing us the powers to do so. In 2010, as he embarked on swingeing cuts to the public sector, David Cameron tried to sugar-coat the pill of austerity by talking a lot about the 'Big Society'. Communities, he purred, would willingly take on the public services that the state could no longer provide. The government passed the Localism Act 2011, which created a 'Community Right to Bid'. Whilst this sounded similar to Scotland's Community Right to Buy, there the resemblance ended.

England's Community Right to Bid does give communities the power to designate land or property, such as a local library, as being an 'asset of community value'. And if the property comes up for sale, it gives the community group six months to raise the money to buy it (rather than the eight months allowed in Scotland). But there is no obligation on the owner to sell to the community: no right of first refusal. A community can raise the funds, and then still be gazumped by another buyer offering more after the six months are up. It is all mouth and no trousers: a bit like the prime minister who brought it in.

Since 2021, England has also had a Community Ownership Fund. Though its total budget is actually bigger than its Scottish counterpart, it has been considerably less generous in the grants it hands out, with the expectation that communities raise more of the money themselves. For its first two funding rounds, applicants could only bid for a maximum of 50 per cent of the capital funds they sought; for the Scottish Land Fund, the figure is 80 per cent.[48]

It's not like England is short of communities crying out to take on the running of land. In my home town of Totnes, the community has been trying for the last fifteen years to build affordable housing and create a nature reserve on the site of a derelict factory next to the train station. But the 'Atmos Totnes' project, as it's known, has foundered because the powers granted to communities under the Localism Act remain so weak. Despite years of work piecing together planning permissions, raising funds and winning a local referendum for its plans, the community group had the rug pulled out from under them when the landowner sold the site to a private developer.[49]

England's inadequate community ownership laws and grant schemes mean that it's mostly pubs and village halls that get bought up by communities at present, rather than significant amounts of land more generally. Tom Chance tells me that there are only two community land trusts in England to date who have nature conservation as their core purpose: the Middle Marches Community Land Trust in Shropshire, which wants to buy land to create a wildlife corridor between two existing nature reserves, and the Ore Valley group near Hastings, who are hoping to buy an ancient woodland to protect it.[50]

Yet across England, communities dream of buying up land for nature and amenity. In 2014, the iconic mountain of Blencathra in the Lake District was put up for sale by its owner, the Earl of Lonsdale, who said he hoped that 'some daft Russian' would buy it 'to show off'. This didn't go down well with locals, who formed a Friends of Blencathra group and raised £250,000 in donations – a figure, however, that fell far short of the £1.75 million asking price. Following the public outcry, the Earl ended up taking Blencathra off the market. But for a short while, the audacious idea of an English community owning a mountain seemed to open a portal to a different way of doing things.[51]

The allure of community ownership reared its head again more recently in Northumberland, when the huge Rothbury Estate was put up for sale by the son of the Duke of Northumberland. Steven Bridgett, an independent councillor for the area, tried to galvanise a community buyout. 'We don't have the legislation in place like they do in Scotland nor the funding that the Scottish government offers towards those kind of community buyouts,' he said. 'But if we don't try, as a community, I think we may regret it.'[52] With the Rothbury Estate's asking price standing at £35 million, however, there's sadly not a chance in hell that the locals will be able to afford it.

Just think of the possibilities if ordinary people in England could take control of more land locally. A community could buy their own stretch of river, for example – not only ensuring access for local wild swimming groups, but also taking responsibility for its care. The more communities that have a stake in rivers, the more pressure there will be on water companies and farmers to clean up their act and reduce pollution. Or imagine what community ownership could do for an English town like Hebden Bridge in West Yorkshire, currently at the mercy of a huge grouse moor upstream that periodically sends floodwaters crashing into residents' front rooms. A community buyout could end the sorts of mismanagement we saw in the previous chapter – restoring the moor's damaged blanket bog to become a natural flood defence and carbon sink.

Change may be coming. The Labour Party has pledged to introduce a Scottish-style Community Right to Buy in England. In a speech in 2022, Lisa Nandy, then shadow Levelling Up Secretary, promised 'first refusal on assets of community value . . . with the right to force a sale of land or buildings in a state of significant disrepair'. Nandy declared her intention of 'following in the footsteps of the last Labour government in Scotland, which ensured land could be taken back into community hands to be used for the good of all the people'.[53] Angela Rayner, who took on the shadow Levelling Up brief in late 2023, has reaffirmed Labour's commitment to a 'strengthened Community Right to Buy' – a pledge also set out in the party's 'five missions for Britain'.[54] A report commissioned by the party on community ownership recently recommended adopting the same laws as Scotland has pioneered.[55]

It's clear from Scotland's example that having a right of first refusal for communities is vital, with a sufficiently long pause in the sales process to raise money, and that generous funding is just as important as new laws. And the fact that Scotland has been getting on with community ownership for twenty years already means England should learn from it, even improve upon it – for example, changing vague legal requirements to 'further sustainable development' to refer precisely instead to delivering net zero and nature recovery targets.

Community ownership offers a strikingly different way to own and manage land more democratically than merely trusting in the benevolence of large private landowners. 'Democracy is the worst form of Government,' famously declared Winston Churchill, 'except for all those other forms that have been tried from time to time.'[56] When it comes to governing society, we trust in democracy, rather than benign dictatorship. Why not try something similar for the governance of land?

4

A Public
Nature Estate

Instead of paying landowners to be good stewards, why doesn't the state simply buy up more land for nature?

We used to think this way, back in the time of the Second World War. To the pioneering ecologists and conservationists of the 1940s, it was obvious that the state had a vital role to play in protecting the natural world. Professor Arthur Tansley, the 'father of British ecology', called in a 1945 treatise for 'the formal placing of wild life under State protection'.[1] Tansley was no ideologue: he was the most eminent botanist of his day, whose extensive studies of British vegetation became the standard textbooks for a generation. It's thanks to him that we have the concept of an ecosystem.[2] 'What is wanted', Tansley wrote, 'is unequivocal public recognition of nature conservation as a national interest.' This could only come, he argued, from a national authority.[3]

British nature conservation up until that point had been the preserve of charitable endeavours. Organisations like the National Trust and the Royal Society for the Protection of Birds were rooted in Victorian philanthropy, from an age when the state remained small, undemocratic and unwilling to solve pressing social problems. The first wildlife sanctuaries in the UK were set up by voluntary organisations, like the Society for the Promotion of Nature Reserves (SPNR), founded in 1912 – the predecessor of today's Wildlife Trusts.

But in 1943, a seminal report instigated by the SPNR recommended a seismic change. 'The Government should take formal responsibility for the conservation of native wild life, both plant and animal,' it concluded.[4] Two years later, the British Ecological Society similarly declared that 'the native plants and animals of Britain are a national asset for which the nation, through its Government, should be responsible.'[5]

Already in the interwar period, some local government authorities had spearheaded the acquisition of land for nature and amenity. Two decades before maintaining a 'Green Belt' became part of planning rules, London councils had started buying up chunks of countryside on the edge of the metropolis to protect it from development and preserve it for city-dwellers to enjoy. The city of Sheffield bought part of the Peak District in 1927 so that residents could take day trips there to ramble in the open air, whilst in the same era Eastbourne Council acquired downland at Beachy Head to save it from urban sprawl.[6] The free-market, laissez-faire approach of nineteenth-century governments was giving way to a new generation of politicians – spanning Radical Tories through New Liberals to Labour's 'municipal socialists' – who saw protecting natural beauty for public enjoyment as a key role for the public sector.

The Second World War meant an inevitable increase in the power of the state. From directing industry to make Spitfires and munitions, to implementing food rationing, central government suddenly found itself responsible for all manner of new activities. And as the war progressed, so did the public's confidence that more government, rather than less, was the answer to a whole series of entrenched social problems. In the aftermath of the Blitz and with the Allies ascendant, people started to dream of building a better world once the war ended. The 1942 Beveridge Report – the blueprint for the welfare state – became a surprise instant bestseller, eagerly read by millions who had suffered sickness and unemployment in the 1930s. Public opinion swung sharply to the left during the course of the war. As the historian Paul Addison put it, 'when Labour swept to victory in 1945 the new consensus fell, like a branch of ripe plums, into the lap of Mr Attlee.'[7] It was this newfound belief in the state's power to do good that enabled Clement Attlee's government to create the NHS and nationalise some 20 per cent of the British economy, from railways to gas.[8]

The novel appetite for government intervention extended to the use of land, in the creation of the planning system, and the setting up of national parks – both of which will be examined in more detail in later chapters. Alongside this push to preserve Britain's landscapes, the government commissioned a group of leading ecologists to report on how best to protect wildlife and their natural habitats. The Huxley Report of 1947, chaired by the popular public scientist Dr Julian Huxley, agreed with Tansley and the SPNR: 'the Government should take a general responsibility . . . for the conservation and control of the flora and fauna of this country'.[9]

Attlee's administration promptly passed a law in response in 1949 that created the world's first public conservation body, the Nature Conservancy, and gave it wide-ranging powers.[10] Not only would the new body be able to designate nature reserves; the Nature Conservancy also possessed the power to acquire land of its own – even compulsorily, if need be. This far-reaching legislation essentially laid down the basis of all subsequent nature conservation law and institutions in Britain.

The story of how the modern welfare state was born out of Britain's wartime ashes is a familiar one, but we've forgotten nowadays that the era also gave birth to what historian Matthew Kelly calls the 'Nature State'. Kelly sees the Nature State as a parallel development to the welfare state – and warfare state – which operated as a similar set of new institutions and regulations. Where the welfare state looked after people's health and quality of life, the Nature State sought to care for their environment. It extended the mandate of the state to cover environmental issues. Most modern countries possess some form of Nature State, Kelly argues, but its strength varies from nation to nation.[11]

There are striking parallels between the birth of Britain's Nature State and the present moment. It was forged in the heat of an international emergency, when the British government had mobilised to take swift action, and was established through farsighted laws and institutions that still exist now. Today we face an even more existential threat than invasion: the climate crisis and the unravelling of the very web of life that we all depend upon. Yet, after decades in which governments have been in thrall to an ideology of free markets, voluntary action and big business, our confidence in the state's powers has been sapped. It's time for Britain's Nature State to be rejuvenated. But to understand the political challenges in doing so, we need to take a closer look at how it began.

The Nature Conservancy was the forerunner of Britain's official environmental watchdogs, now known by their devolved titles: Natural England, NatureScot and Natural Resources Wales. (This account will mainly focus on its English branch.) Looking back at its early history, it's striking how much power, budget and independence the Nature Conservancy had compared to its successors. With every reorganisation of the machinery of government since, the voice of nature conservation has become weaker and easier to ignore.

A key aspect of the Nature Conservancy's relative autonomy was that it was answerable directly to the Lord President of the Privy Council: an obscure but high-up role within Whitehall. It was treated as an independent scientific advisor, giving expert advice on ecological matters to those at the top of government. The Conservancy was not, therefore, the creature of a particular government department. Today, Natural England is a 'quango', or arm's-length body, of DEFRA. That may sound sensible on paper, but in practice it means the organisation is beholden to a secretary of state who in turn has to answer to farming and landowning bodies – and you can guess who wins in that tug-of-war.

From the outset, the powers granted to the Nature Conservancy were extensive. It had the mandate to designate land as National Nature Reserves (NNRs) – intended to be the 'jewels in the crown' of nature sites in Britain. It also had a remit to notify landowners that their land contained habitats and species of scientific interest – the origins of Sites of Special Scientific Interest. Moreover, it had the power to acquire land itself, to protect it for nature. Most land purchases were assumed to be done on the free market, but the Conservancy also had the power to *compel* landowners to sell if they were unwilling.

The National Parks and Access to the Countryside Act 1949 gave the Nature Conservancy authority that for 'any land that it is expedient in the national interest that it should be managed as a nature reserve, they may acquire the land compulsorily'.[12] This was seen as a clear necessity by leading ecologists of the era. Dr Julian Huxley had even recommended that 'all shooting rights over any part of a National Reserve should be acquired' by the Conservancy[13] – so that shooting could be managed or banned if contrary to nature conservation. Yet his recommendation was ignored. Huxley would revolve in his grave if he knew how some landowners continue to operate pheasant shoots over what are meant to be the best-protected wildlife sites in Britain.[14]

In its early years, the Nature Conservancy snapped up tens of thousands of acres of land across Britain. As the historian John Sheail puts it, 'the Conservancy was impatient to acquire . . . extensive tracts of countryside and coast as rapidly as possible.'[15] The first tranche of NNRs purchased in England in 1952 included Yarner Wood in Devon, a fragment of Atlantic oakwood, today recognised as temperate rainforest; the ancient yew forest of Kingley Vale in Sussex; and Moor House – a former grouse moor in the North Pennines.

Of course, it was not all plain sailing for the fledgling Conservancy. First, it had to see off rival bids for land by those seeking to develop it. At the auction for Yarner Wood, for example, the Nature Conservancy made the highest offer; but the property was mysteriously withdrawn from sale. An old document in the National Archives relates how the Conservancy 'discovered afterwards that the whole estate had been purchased before the auction by a London Investments Company for whom the auctioneers were selling, no doubt on a speculative basis'.[16] After trying to fleece the Nature Conservancy for more money, the investment firm eventually relented. Had the Conservancy not stood firm, Yarner Wood could have ended up being sold for timber – the fate of so many Atlantic oakwoods at that time.[17]

Second, it had to contend with the watchful eye of the Treasury. Because the land being acquired for nature reserves was mostly marginal for agriculture and 'of little economic value', the cost to the taxpayer was low.[18] That didn't stop penny-pinching Treasury officials from being wary, particularly at a time when rationing was still in effect and budgets tight. What the Exchequer had not reckoned with, however, was the determination and charisma of the Conservancy's second director-general, the legendary Max Nicholson.

Nicholson was a visionary, fearless and assertive in his dealings with Whitehall colleagues. A childhood spent birdwatching perhaps equipped Nicholson with the patience needed to stare down obstructive civil servants. He had contracted polio prior to his appointment to head the Conservancy in 1952, and 'only through sheer will-power was he able again to walk and take up his new post.'[19] Nicholson's approach seems to have been to ask for forgiveness, not permission. Leafing through the musty records of the Nature Conservancy in the National Archives, I found a typewritten letter from Nicholson to a Treasury apparatchik. 'I am sorry to learn that we have apparently failed to comply with a Treasury instruction,' he wrote mischievously. The gist of the subsequent admission goes something like (and I paraphrase only slightly): *whoops, sorry old chap, we've managed to buy six properties without getting your approval. Terribly sorry, what can be done?* You can almost hear the tut-tutting as the Treasury civil servants discuss how to respond, one writing peevishly: 'so far as the past is concerned, there is nothing to do but give them covering sanction.'

Unabashed, Nicholson was soon making bold suggestions to the Treasury for new ways of raising funds for nature conservation. He proposed 'increasing the tax on gun licences and appropriating the revenue to assist the finances of the Conservancy' – essentially a nature tax on the shooting lobby.[20] It was, Nicholson pointed out, something that already operated in the USA, where wildfowlers chipped in to habitat preservation through a gun licence levy. The Treasury officials smiled wanly and brushed the proposal under the carpet. Still, it's impossible to imagine Nicholson's successors in Natural England nowadays even broaching such an idea: the *Daily Telegraph* would be calling for their heads before the day was out.

But the biggest conflict of the Conservancy's early years was between the ecologists and the landowners. The 1951 election had seen Labour booted out of office, and the incoming Conservative administration contained rather more landowning aristocrats than its socialist predecessor. The new Lord President of the Council, to whom the Nature Conservancy was answerable, was none other than the Marquess of Salisbury, Robert Cecil – owner of 10,000 acres of estates in Hertfordshire and Dorset.[21] Cecil – or 'Bobbety' to his friends – seems at first to have looked favourably on the work of the Conservancy, praising its efforts to protect the Scottish Highlands. But then Bobbety got wind of Max Nicholson's new list of proposed Sites of Special Scientific Interest.

'I see . . . that you are interested in Lord Salisbury's troubles about the Nature Conservancy,' begins one internal Treasury document, ominously, from late 1955. The 'troubles' had begun with the Conservancy daring to designate part of a Tory MP's estate as an SSSI, without the landowner's permission. At this point in time, designating SSSIs merely meant sending the landowner a polite note that they possessed land of scientific interest – there were no legal repercussions or constraints on what they could do with it. Yet even this had been enough to spark a 'very angry letter' from the MP, Major John Morrison – owner of the vast Fonthill Estate in Wiltshire – to the Lord President. Worse still, Nicholson had produced a list of future SSSIs the Conservancy wished to name, which the Treasury described – in an extraordinarily revealing sentence – as a 'document of enormous and quite tactless length . . . the general impression given is that they are going to spatter the whole of the United Kingdom with living museums.'[22]

Lord Salisbury was furious. 'He felt that the mere publication of all these names would reduce the value of the land to the owners,' related the Treasury official, 'and that the whole thing was being done on an unreasonable scale.'[23] Never mind protecting nature: the important thing was to protect the value of private property. The Tory party had long been the party of the landed classes, and it was now starting to dawn on them that the Nature Conservancy represented, in John Sheail's words, an 'intrusion of the State into the ownership and management of land' – no matter how mild its intrusion was.[24] Salisbury, according to the Treasury's florid briefing, had originally intended to 'summon a meeting of Ministers instantly and, like Cronos, to devour his own child at the banquet'. But though he was talked down from such rash action, he nevertheless got what he wanted: Max Nicholson 'agreed to suppress' the list of proposed nature sites.[25]

This clash was merely an early straw in the wind for future battles between government conservationists and those representing landed interests. Though the original designation process for SSSIs was extremely light-touch, there was no getting away from the fact that, at some point, protecting nature would require intervention in property rights. If the landowner wanted to preserve the habitats and species on their land, there was no problem. But if the landowner had no such qualms, and instead damaged or even destroyed the site's scientific interest – whether through overgrazing, ploughing, spraying it with pesticides, or whatever – then the state would have to find some way of intervening. Having accepted that the country's natural heritage was a 'national asset' in which there was a legitimate public interest, the government could not simply stand by whilst it was destroyed.

Despite hostility from landowners, these were the golden years of the Nature Conservancy. Within fifteen years of its creation, the Conservancy had acquired more than a hundred National Nature Reserves.[26] As the tweed-clad Fifties gave way to the Swinging Sixties, Britain swapped a government of landowners for an administration of technocrats: out went the grouse-shooting laird Alec Douglas-Home, in came Harold Wilson with his passion for science and the 'white heat' of technology. And by the early 1970s, many more members of the British public were becoming concerned about pollution and ecology, turned on to the matter by Rachel Carson's *Silent Spring* and the first images of the Earth from outer space. When the Conservancy had started out, nature conservation had been a fringe issue. Now the whole world was waking up to what Max Nicholson called the 'Environmental Revolution'.

But the inevitable consequence of technological progress in the years since the war had been a vast expansion of industrial agriculture and forestry. The Conservancy's efforts to preserve small fragments of habitat as nature reserves was swimming against a stronger tide of destruction. 'We desired a paradise to care for,' bemoaned Nicholson, 'but what we found called rather for the improvisation of a field hospital.'[27]

Nicholson's successors increasingly found themselves having to launch rescue missions for habitats before they succumbed to the depredations of their owners. In 1978, the vast salt marshes of the Ribble Estuary in Lancashire were put up for sale. The RSPB and the Conservancy – now called the Nature Conservancy Council (NCC), and an offshoot of the Department for the Environment – tried jointly to buy the site. But it was sold to a wealthy Dutch businessman, Piet Hereema, who planned to drain the wetlands for intensive agriculture. The resulting tussle demonstrated some of the levers that Britain's Nature State could pull, but also the limits of its powers.

On the one hand, there were no real constraints on a landowner doing this. Planning controls only applied to the built environment, and not to farming and forestry. The Ministry of Agriculture could withhold farm subsidies, but had no control over a landowner if they chose to go without such payments. When the Conservancy beseeched Hereema to sell voluntarily, he demanded almost three times the price he had bought it for. On the other hand, the NCC still had an ace up its sleeve. It now threatened compulsory purchase. Eventually, the political furore persuaded the landowner to sell, and the salt marshes were saved.[28]

But many thousands of acres of habitats were not as lucky as the Ribble, and were not saved: they were designated as SSSIs, and their landowners damaged or destroyed them anyway. Up until this point, SSSI notification had conferred no real legal protections. There had, after all, been an assumption that most landowners were 'custodians of the countryside', and that informing them of the scientific value of the land they owned would deter them from causing harm. Alas: the intensification of farming methods, subsidies for food and timber production, and pursuit of profits lured many farmers and landowners to lay waste to SSSIs in the thirty years after the war.

Rising public disquiet about the destruction of the countryside helped the NCC champion a partial solution: the laws governing SSSIs should be strengthened, so that they afforded proper protections. The resulting Wildlife and Countryside Act 1981 gave the NCC new powers: landowners would have to give them advance notice before carrying out activities that might damage an SSSI. Even winning this small advance had been an uphill political battle, particularly under Margaret Thatcher's new Conservative government, in which over three-quarters of the cabinet were landowners.[29] Landowners at large were outraged about the potential lowering of their land value, and the restriction of their freedom to farm as they wished.[30] So in order to alert landowners about this change to their property rights, the NCC had to renotify each and every Site of Special Scientific Interest.

A loophole in the renotification process gave some unscrupulous landowners the time they needed to destroy the SSSIs on their land, to get ahead of future constraints. A golf club in Northamptonshire stripped the species-rich turf from the land it owned; a Welsh farmer spent several days ploughing up a bog.[31] Angry farmers on the Somerset Levels made a bonfire of their notification papers, and literally burned effigies of conservationists. In scenes reminiscent of *The Wicker Man*, a straw figure depicting the head of the NCC, Sir Ralph Verney, was hanged from a makeshift gallows and set alight.[32]

The landowners and free-marketeers would eventually get their revenge on the NCC when their man in the cabinet, Nicholas Ridley, was appointed Environment Secretary in 1986. Ridley was the second son of a viscount, scion of a wealthy landowning Northumberland family, and president of the Selsdon Group, a free-market think tank. When in opposition, he had dreamt up the 'Ridley Plan' for defeating the miners, and helped put it into effect in government as one of Thatcher's most trusted ministers. Compared to beating the unions, swatting away the ecologists was merely a diverting pastime for this architect of Thatcherism. In 1988, Ridley summarily placed a two-year freeze on the NCC buying any land for nature reserves.[33] 'I do not believe that the Nature Conservancy Council should be a way of achieving the nationalisation of land,' he told the House of Commons.[34] Ridley also presided over the dismemberment of the NCC into separate bodies for England, Scotland and Wales. Whilst this might now seem like a reasonable reform, the Thatcher government was not known for its support for devolution, and a more likely explanation lies in their desire to reduce central government expenditure and weaken the power of the Nature State.[35]

Ridley's ideas had much longer-term ramifications for the future of the Nature State. He was one of the earliest proponents of 'privatisation' – the sale of public sector bodies and industries to private companies. This was a highly unpopular position to take prior to the mid-1970s, when both Labour and the Conservatives broadly accepted the postwar consensus laid down by Clement Attlee, of a mixed economy with a significant role for the public sector. But that consensus had started to break down in the economic travails of the Seventies, and Ridley was one of a new breed of 'neoliberal' Tories pushing for a radically different approach. Privatisation was attempted only fitfully in Thatcher's early years, but taken up with gusto after her 1983 landslide election victory. By the time Ridley got his hands on the Environment Department, he set about producing a Bill to privatise the water industry. 'I am absolutely delighted that this Bill achieves the privatisation of nearly 500,000 acres of land,' he salivated to the Commons in 1989, referring to the extensive watersheds owned by the utilities. We can today see the fruits of Ridley's privatisations in the torrent of sewage that enters England's rivers each year, following decades of underinvestment by the water companies.

Still more fundamentally, the small-state ethos of Thatcher, Ridley and co. successfully closed down debate about the public ownership of land for a generation. The focus of policymaking on nature conservation swung towards how best to pay private landowners and farmers to be good stewards of the land. Meanwhile, successive governments, both Tory and New Labour, presided over the sell-off of some 5 million acres of public sector land – around 10 per cent of the entire British landmass – according to calculations by the academic Brett Christophers.[36]

When the Conservatives returned to power in 2010, they had unfinished business from their last time in office. Thatcher had considered selling off the Forestry Commission's public forest estate, but thought better of it; and Ridley had tried and failed to get the NCC to consider privatising its public nature reserves.[37] So now it fell to the so-called 'children of Thatcher',

David Cameron and his Chancellor George Osborne, to try again. Luckily for them, this time they had some surprising allies within the charitable conservation sector.

David Cameron's foiled attempt to privatise the Public Forest Estate is well-known, thanks to the strength of public feeling against it – but less appreciated was his secret effort to also flog off the publicly owned National Nature Reserves. Extraordinarily, it would appear that this effort was set to be facilitated by the then head of the Wildlife Trusts. I spoke to Rosie Wood, former policy principal at Natural England, who was privy to the political wranglings over the mooted transfer of the public nature reserves in 2010 and 2011. 'It was a deal with the Wildlife Trusts,' she told me. The chief executive of the Wildlife Trusts' central body at that time was Stephanie Hilborne, who was 'very well connected' with Conservative ministers. 'She persuaded them to transfer NNRs from Natural England to the Wildlife Trusts,' said Rosie, who accused the NGO of 'empire building'. 'However, once the Coalition came into government and the deal unfolded, she realised just how little money went with NNRs, and therefore how very hard it is to care for them on Natural England's stretched budgets.' As a result, the Wildlife Trusts pulled out of the deal. 'DEFRA was very pissed off,' Rosie recalled.[38]

I relate this story not to have a go at the Wildlife Trusts, who do great work for conservation, but rather to illustrate how far the political pendulum has swung away from recognising the central role the public sector has in nature conservation. It was, after all, the Wildlife Trusts' predecessor body, the Society for the Promotion of Nature Reserves, who were the first to call for the government to take the lead on conserving wildlife back in 1943. Yet since the 1980s, even some environmental NGOs seem to have bought into the neoliberal model of nature conservation: acquiescing to the shrinking of the state, lobbying for 'biodiversity offsetting' policies that financialise nature,* and sometimes cheerleading for the privatisation of public land.

---

*Such as 'Biodiversity Net Gain', a change to the planning system brought in in 2021 that allows builders to offset the impact of their developments by paying for nature restoration elsewhere.

Whilst the sale of the public nature reserves failed once again, Natural England was still cut to ribbons by a decade of austerity. Osborne's axe slashed the organisation's already insufficient budget by two-thirds.[39] Between 2010 and 2019, no new NNRs were acquired or designated at all.[40] Though its finances have recovered slightly since the veteran environmental campaigner Tony Juniper became its chair, Natural England has been rendered incapable of carrying out even basic functions. By 2018, almost half of England's SSSIs had not even been monitored by government ecologists in the past six years.[41] And although Natural England still retains the compulsory purchase powers of the old Nature Conservancy, they are seldom used these days. As of 2023, just 0.37 per cent of the country belonged to Natural England.[42]

For the past seventy years, England's fragile Nature State has weathered attacks from free-marketeers, battled with landowners, and grappled with collapsing ecosystems. Yet it has endured. The chequered history of its central institution is a good guide to the challenges faced by any government or public body trying to prioritise nature conservation. There have always been some landowners who resist any curbs on their property rights, even when these involve protecting small fragments of habitat. And there have been repeated efforts by politicians representing those vested interests to weaken the Nature State's powers, whether through sapping its ability to regulate, cutting its budgets or privatising its assets. As we face down the existential ecological crises of the twenty-first century, can the Nature State be revived?

As the scale of the climate and biodiversity crises escalate, environmentalists are waking up again to the need for a proactive Nature State. 'It is bizarre that government opts out of land ownership as a means of delivering wildlife recovery,' argues the veteran ornithologist Mark Avery, former Conservation Director at the RSPB. 'Wildlife is a public good,' he contends, 'and yet we aim to stem a long-term and continuing loss of wildlife through exhortation of private landowners to do more . . . Why don't we just buy up land ourselves and manage it for wildlife?'[43]

Why indeed? There are many reasons why public sector land ownership is an excellent tool for aiding nature recovery. The first is the government's ability to move fast when it is forced to. When I was a civil servant, we used to joke that the UK state had two speeds – 'treacle and lightning'. We might reasonably despair at the competence of recent governments to get things done, but there is no question that the state can move like lightning in times of crisis: look at how the British economy was turned around on a sixpence to produce guns rather than butter during the Second World War. The new Westminster government will have just five short years if it's to meet an official UN pledge to protect 30 per cent of England's land for nature by 2030. Currently, about 3 per cent of England is properly protected and managed, so it's going to have to get a shimmy on. The government could faff around with tweaking farm payments, or it could buy more land itself and get on with it.

Second, owning land yourself rather than renting it is cost-effective. It is, after all, why people who can afford to do so buy a house rather than renting all their lives. The current system of environmental stewardship payments essentially amounts to the taxpayer renting environmental outcomes from private farmers and landowners. That's great when it delivers. But in many cases, as we've seen, those environmental outcomes have *not* been delivered: SSSIs remain in unfavourable condition, biodiversity continues to decline. In many cases, it would be cheaper for the state to simply buy the land outright and manage it better itself, than keep paying landowners millions of pounds in rent.

Third, the state has deep pockets – the deepest pockets of any investor. It alone has the power to levy taxes, and it can usually borrow at very low interest rates. We might prefer nature reserves to be managed by conservation charities, or by community groups – and we certainly should make it easier for such groups to acquire more land. But there's a limit to how much communities can raise through crowdfunding, as we saw in the previous chapter. And even an organisation like the National Trust, with its 6 million fee-paying members, can struggle to muster the capital needed to acquire large areas of land. In some cases, it would just be easier for the state to step in and acquire the land, and then lease it to a conservation charity or community group to manage. And in terms of value for money for the public finances, investing in land means the state acquires one of the safest assets there is.

Fourth, the public sector is far more accountable and democratic than private landowners. If you don't like the way the government is managing its nature reserves, you can vote them out every five years. In the meantime, you can berate your MP, subject government departments to a barrage of Freedom of Information requests, or lobby your local councillor. Ministers can be held to account by Parliament, and civil servants are politically impartial and obliged to serve the public interest. We may feel cynical about the public sector after years of being lied to by politicians. But at least we can do something about it. The same cannot be said about the local Lord of the Manor when he decides to trash his moor for the sake of the grouse. Public land ownership is subject to all kinds of checks and balances that private landowners are not.

Fifth, the public sector is a necessary backstop to the private. You don't have to believe that all land should suddenly be nationalised to see the value of a government willing to take on the ownership of land if private landowners refuse their responsibilities. Where landowners are manifestly failing to be good stewards, we need the state to be able to intervene. That can be through regulation, and it can also be through a change of ownership – or the threat to do so. Imagine if landowners took seriously the possibility that Natural England might buy out their land if they didn't manage it properly for nature: the fear that it could happen would be a sharp spur to better stewardship, even without much land changing hands. When schools fail, they're taken over by their local council; when councils fail, they're taken over by central government. Why not follow a similar procedure with failing landowners?

Lastly, lots of other countries have stronger and better-equipped Nature States than we do. The US federal government owns around 28 per cent of the land of the United States, managing much of it as national parks and forests.[44] In New Zealand, the Department of Conservation (DOC) owns and manages around a third of the landmass of the country.[45] Of course, there are plenty of issues with how these countries manage their public lands: the US federal government leases large tracts of its landholdings for fossil fuel extraction. And, as countries colonised by Europeans, there are big questions about the legitimacy of how these states acquired their landholdings: the history of national parks in the US is deeply intertwined with the expulsion of Native Americans, whilst the Crown in New Zealand expropriated land from the Maori peoples. The same cannot be said, however, of Germany, where half the country's forests are owned by municipalities, states and the federal government.[46] Or Japan, where the state owns roughly half the land in all its national parks.[47] It's time for England to move towards this model of public nature conservation too.

In 2023, I worked with Wildlife and Countryside Link – a coalition of over sixty UK conservation charities – on a report that called for the creation of a Public Nature Estate in England. Frustrated by the government's slow progress towards its '30x30' pledge – to protect 30 per cent of land for nature by 2030 – the coalition proposed a fresh approach. Their vision of a Public Nature Estate would be the biggest change to nature conservation since the 1940s. The idea takes inspiration from the pioneering ecologists of that era, like Arthur Tansley and Max Nicholson, who first harnessed the state to the cause of saving our wildlife.

A Public Nature Estate would have two main functions: to transform how existing public sector land is managed, and to acquire more land for nature's recovery.

At the heart of a Public Nature Estate should be a reinvigorated green watchdog. Natural England should have its budget restored, so that it can carry out its functions properly. Ministers should also give the agency back its independence. Ecological expertise needs to be able to speak truth to power, yet Natural England has been muzzled for too long. The organisation needs to be freed from the shackles of DEFRA, and made an advisor to those at the top of government – as its predecessor, the Nature

Conservancy, once was. Perhaps it could become an agency of the Cabinet Office, sitting at the heart of Whitehall. From there, it would be able to have proper oversight over the landholdings of all government departments, and advise on their management.[48]

A new Public Nature Estate would encompass the large swathes of public sector land that could and should be better managed for nature. The Forestry Commission, Ministry of Defence, local authorities and other public bodies between them still own millions of acres, despite decades of land sales and privatisations. Collectively, the public sector owns around 8.5 per cent of England, which is a paltry amount, but still makes it the biggest single landowner in the country. Some of this land is built on, or earmarked for development. But vast amounts of it comprise moorlands, forests and farmland – all of which could be doing more to aid nature's recovery and combat climate change. Not all of this land currently contains the wealth of species and habitats that merit designation as National Nature Reserves, or even SSSIs; but far more of it could be devoted to ecological restoration.

The Forestry Commission's English arm, Forestry England, owns a 489,000-acre estate.[49] Yet much of it comprises monoculture plantations of conifers, doing very little for biodiversity – and sometimes actively harming it. The FC was set up in the aftermath of the First World War, with the explicit remit of tackling the nation's dire shortage of timber. That was the pressing national need a century ago; today, the climate and ecological emergencies should take precedence.

Forestry England's landholdings include, for example, some 105,000 acres of Plantations on Ancient Woodland Sites (PAWS).[50] This means that they used to be ancient woodlands – defined as being at least 400 years old – but were unforgivably cut down in the twentieth century for conifer plantations. To their credit, Forestry England have committed to eventually restoring all these PAWS woods, by removing the conifers and replanting with deciduous tree species. But the pace of change is slow: under 5,000 acres were restored in 2022–3.[51] By bringing Forestry England's landholdings under the ambit of the Public Nature Estate, and updating their legal duties to prioritise nature recovery, this process should be sped up. So too should the work of the 'Forest Wilding' team, a recently formed unit within the organisation,[52] which seeks to restore natural processes to publicly owned forests – like reintroducing pine martens to control grey squirrels, and deploying wild boar and beaver to create glades and wetlands.

The Ministry of Defence (MOD) owns around 397,000 acres in England,[53] containing some incredible sites for wildlife: from the butterfly-rich chalk grasslands of Porton Down and Salisbury Plain in Wiltshire, to the rapidly rewilding scrub and heath of the Pirbright Ranges in Surrey. But it also possesses various sites in need of decontamination, such as the former atomic weapons testing sites on the island of Foulness in Essex, whose toxic payloads risk leaching out into the Thames Estuary as sea levels rise. And the MOD's land disposals process leaves a lot to be desired when it comes to valuing nature – such as when the old training camp of Lodge Hill in Kent, the UK's premier site for nightingales, was almost sold off for development before an outcry by environmentalists halted the sale.[54]

English councils, too, own large swathes of land – from the metropolitan boroughs who bought up green fields in the 1930s in order to protect them from development prior to the creation of Green Belt, to the many county councils who still possess County Farms. Bringing these landholdings under the aegis of a Public Nature Estate, too, would add some 1.3 million acres of land across England.[55] Yet much of it is not currently managed with nature in mind. Indeed, for the past decade, local authorities have been beholden to a mantra of outsourcing services, cutting budgets and shrinking their asset base. The unthinking sale of public land has seen councils flog off half of the nation's County Farms Estate since the late 1970s, depriving first-time farmers who lack capital of a vital way into farming.[56] Instead, such farms ought to become beacons of sustainable agriculture, let out on tenancies that encourage the use of agro-ecological methods. (As we'll see in the next chapter, some council-owned farms have a particularly important role to play in retaining Fenland carbon.) Tired and neglected country parks could similarly be revived as pioneers of municipal rewilding – like the London councils currently trying to reintroduce beavers in the Green Belt.[57]

A bold government would actively add to this Public Nature Estate through acquiring more land. There are plenty of English landscapes in dire need of rescuing for the public interest. Right at the top of the list should be our upland peat bogs, which as we've seen desperately need saving from their current owners. Burned, drained and blasted, these moorlands are currently treated as a rich man's playground. Yet if England's peatland – with its vast store of biological carbon and huge potential to soak up more CO_2 – isn't a public asset, then what is?

At the close of the Second World War, the British Ecological Society posited that 'the native plants and animals of Britain are a national asset for which the nation, through its Government, should be responsible.' What was true then is now even more true in the context of the climate crisis. Our natural carbon sinks are national assets that need managing in the national interest. If the current landowners won't do this, the public sector has to step in to do so. One of the very first National Nature Reserves acquired by the Nature Conservancy as long ago as 1952 was Moor House, a former grouse moor in Teesdale. Why not safeguard more of our upland peat and the carbon it contains by purchasing more grouse moors and vesting them in the Public Nature Estate?

A proper ban on moorland burning, coupled with banning or licensing driven grouse shooting, might result in some upland landowners selling up voluntarily. But for any who don't sell, and who persist in damaging this national asset, there is a strong case for the government to make use of compulsory purchase powers. Natural England miraculously still has these powers, after they were first granted to the Nature Conservancy back in 1949. Anyone who is concerned about an overmighty state should be wary of governments deploying such powers too readily. But we accept the principle of the public sector being able to buy land compulsorily when it builds infrastructure; why not for nature? If the government can buy land for roads, railways and energy, why not for vital carbon sinks and the ecosystems we all depend on?

The compulsory purchase of land for infrastructure projects is guided by documents called National Policy Statements. Yet, as the Wildlife and Countryside Link coalition say, 'green infrastructure is not considered to be nationally significant . . . and there is no similar approach for nature.' So, let's put in place a new National Policy Statement for Nature, that defines and governs when it is appropriate for public bodies like Natural England to step in and acquire land for ecological restoration. Functioning ecosystems and carbon sinks are essential green infrastructure for the twenty-first century, and deserve the state's backing just as much as built infrastructure, if not more so.

Where should the money for such land purchases come from? The Labour Party has pledged to invest £15 billion per year during the next parliament under its 'Green Prosperity Plan'.[58] Whilst most of this is rightly intended to pay for decarbonising the energy system, it's essential that a proportion of it also goes towards restoring natural carbon sinks and repairing habitats. As the promised money is being borrowed, it's intended as capital investment, rather than day-to-day revenue spending – so that the government sees returns on its investment and can pay back the debt. Some of this money should certainly, therefore, be invested in public sector land purchase, as land is a capital asset that will increase in value over time – particularly when it's delivering valuable additional services, such as preventing floods and accumulating carbon.

The foundations of Britain's Nature State were laid down over seventy years ago. Four decades of neoliberalism have wrecked our faith in the power of the state to do good, seen large parts of it privatised, and made even talking about public ownership something of a taboo. But it is high time we broached the subject again. As the historian Matthew Kelly says, these are 'not new ideas'; the idea that 'the state should be empowered – or should use existing powers – to bring valuable natural habitat into state ownership when landowners fail in their custodial duties, resurfaces periodically.'[59] And there is nothing as unstoppable as an idea whose time has come.

5

The Great Draining

Travelling in the unendingly flat countryside of the Fens, an odd thing happens to your sense of perspective. At first, your eye is drawn to the profound blackness of the freshly tilled Fenland soils: a rich, obsidian-coloured peat. But the featureless fields soon become monotonous, and your gaze is drawn up to the skyline, where the only details in view appear narrowly sandwiched between Earth and the heavens. A fringe of trees; the occasional farmstead – these are among the only vertical disruptions to a fundamentally horizontal landscape.

Yet something was amiss as I drove around this prairie-like part of Cambridgeshire. For such a flat landscape, its roads were terrible. They rolled and undulated like the surface of the sea. These were no mere potholes, scourge of all country lanes. The roads themselves are cracking and buckling as the peat soils of the Fens subside.

There's a simple explanation for this. The Fens were once underwater, but they were drained for agriculture around four hundred years ago. This centuries-long process – the 'Great Draining' – transformed a vast expanse of saturated marshes into some of Britain's most fertile farmland. The peat soils in the Fens are classified as Grade 1, signifying the most fecund and versatile type of land. That puts them at the opposite end of the scale to the peat bogs of the uplands, where steep slopes, harsh winds and high rainfall makes it hard to grow anything at scale. The Fens, by contrast, are flat and get plenty of sunshine – perfect for cultivation. This 330,000-acre region now supplies a third of England's fresh veg: the fields are full of carrots, potatoes and peas.[1] Growing these popular 'cash crops' is very profitable for those who farm here.

But the ecological impact of farming the Fens is also huge. This is a profoundly extractive form of agriculture. Peat takes thousands of years to build up. Draining it – etching the Fens with ditches like the wounds left by a barbed-wire fence – means the peat ceases to form. Worse, it is actively destroyed. As the water has drained out, the ground level in the Fens has dropped dramatically, like a deflated balloon. The peat then starts to dry out and break apart: the millennia of fertility locked up in it is leaching out to sea and into the atmosphere. Soil carbon oxidises with the air to form carbon dioxide in vast quantities. Lowland peat on which crops are grown emits around 7.6 million tonnes of CO_2-equivalent per year, about twice as much as even the upland bogs.[2] We are essentially mining the Fenland peat to grow food, a short-term win for a long-term loss.

Thirty minutes' drive outside Peterborough, I parked in a layby, miles from any major settlement. A line of electricity pylons running through one field leaned at different crazy angles, like a procession of drunks: another sign of the restless earth. The land I had come to see belongs to the Church Commissioners, part of their 5,000-acre Fenland estate. One of the five core missions of the Church of England is to 'safeguard the integrity of creation'.[3] I wanted to see how well they were stewarding this vast expanse of peat.

The entire landscape here was crisscrossed with drainage ditches. The water they contained, ebbing slowly but inexorably towards the Wash, was a liquid mirror to the wide Fenland skies. Grassy banks bordering each ditch presented thin veins of green cutting through the dark black fields. In one grew a crop of sugar beet; in another, the remnants of recently harvested maize. Hedgerows were few and far between, providing shelter mainly for discarded tractor tyres and drinks cans thrown from passing cars. The bark of each hedgerow tree, I noticed, was coated with a vibrant yellow lichen, *Xanthoria*, that thrives in places polluted by nitrogen fertiliser. Nature was not wholly absent: overwintering geese honked loudly as they soared overhead. But most life had been pushed to the margins. At one point I thought I glimpsed a bird of prey. But on closer inspection, it was merely a plastic bird scarer, fluttering in the breeze on a wire fixed to a pole.

By a bend in the road, I found a sad shrine to someone who had died in a car accident. Fenland roads are full of right-angle turns, treacherous in icy conditions and the thick fogs that often wreath the Fens. This poor person's passing was now marked only by bunches of dead dahlias, propped up in a cluster of Stella Artois bottles. My eyes were drawn to the drainage ditch flowing below the makeshift memorial. Amidst the reeds, long tendrils of grey sewage fungus writhed in the current. I recoiled in disgust. These bacterial blooms thrive in polluted water, where levels of nitrogen fertiliser are high. Sewage fungus smothers fish eggs and sucks the oxygen out of water, killing most of the plants and animals that depend on it.[4] The huge amounts of excess fertiliser running off the fenland fields means it's not just the carbon cycle that's out of joint here: it's the nitrogen cycle, too. Fertility begets death.

So much for 'safeguarding creation'. Cold, tired and thoroughly depressed, I trudged back to my car. None of what I'd seen was unique to the Church's estate, of course. It's a feature of nearly all land in the Fens today. But if even landowners supposedly motivated by moral causes are keeping it in this state, what hope for those motivated solely by profit?

As I warmed up with flask tea, I reflected that my decision to visit in winter meant I'd missed one of the most dramatic signs of fenland decline. During the dry summer months, Cambridgeshire plays host to a phenomenon called the 'Fen Blow'. Videos posted online show the Fens engulfed in great dust storms, the air filled with a choking brown haze.[5] The peat soils, dried out by hot temperatures and with no moisture to bind them together, are blown high into the air by the winds that whip across the Fenlands. The Fen Blow is East Anglia's equivalent of the dustbowl that afflicted Midwestern America in the 1930s. Smaller in scale, of course, but more insidious – because the carbon that the Fen Blow throws into the air is fuel for the worsening heatwaves that cause it in the first place.

The best illustration of the slow-motion crisis afflicting the Fens, however, was still ahead of me, twenty minutes' drive south of Peterborough. Holme Fen is a nature reserve, a fragment of birch wood and willow carr growing in damp, boggy soils. But even this haven for nature is not immune from the wider forces transforming the landscape.

When I visited, Holme Fen was drenched in a wintry mist. The frozen grass crunched beneath my boots, and each frond of bracken was outlined with silver hoarfrost. There, on the edge of the wood, stood an iron pole: oddly incongruous, like the lamp-post in the forest in *The Lion, the Witch and the Wardrobe*. But the Holme Fen Post, as it's known, doesn't light the way home: it tells us how far down we've sunk. It was driven into the earth in the year 1851, when the sinking land was already evident, and its pinnacle marks the level of the ground back then. Now four metres of the pole have been exposed, a terrifying measure of how suddenly and dramatically the peat here has collapsed. Holme Fen today lies 2¾ metres below sea level, the lowest point in Britain: and it's still sinking.[6]

Craning my neck to look up at the post, one hand on the peeling green paint covering its rusty surface, I tried to imagine what the Fens would have looked like before they were drained. I closed my eyes and imagined myself underground, entombed in a swamp, surrounded by darkness. Around and above me lay metre upon metre of rich peat. For thousands of years, nature had added to this treasure trove of black gold, patiently sequestering carbon and storing up fertility. And then, suddenly, it was gone.

But the natural wealth of the Fens didn't just disappear: it was stolen. The story of how the Fens were plundered is a tale worthy of any heist movie. To tell it, we must return to a time when the fenland was much, much wetter.

The Fens were once one of the largest wetlands in western Europe. They were a 'vast wet wilderness', writes the ecologist Benedict Macdonald, comparable in size to the Danube Delta in Romania: 'We can hardly imagine the scale of these places or the exuberant chaos of areas where rivers are in charge.'[7]

From the few remaining scraps of semi-natural fenland, and from surviving fens in other European countries, we can start to reconstruct what this lost ecosystem may have looked like. It was in all probability a rich mosaic of habitats, with varying degrees of wetness: from great inland lakes and meres, through marshes thick with sedges and flag irises, to waterlogged meadows. The ecological historian Oliver Rackham suggests that 'the natural vegetation of fenland was probably a complexity of pools, reedbeds, grassland, bog-myrtle thickets, and woods, full of wonderful birds and fishes'.[8] The air would have teemed with insects, providing sustenance for vast numbers of wetland birds like moorhens, lapwings and bitterns. Beavers would likely have been found everywhere.[9]

Clues to the natural abundance of the fenland come from historical accounts. An eighth-century monk called Felix wrote about a 'fen of immense size' lying not far from Cambridge, filled with 'many islands and groves, and interrupted by the braiding of meandering streams'.[10] The medieval chronicler William of Malmesbury described the Fens as 'a very paradise and a heaven for the beauty and delight thereof, the very marshes bearing goodly trees'. He related how they were home to 'plentiful' wildfowl, and such an 'abundance of fish as to cause astonishment to strangers, while natives laugh at their surprise'.[11]

Indeed, the undrained Fens did not just boast a wealth of wildlife, but also, crucially, a surfeit of food for people to eat. The cathedral city of Ely, built on an island in the midst of the Fens, gets its name from what the Venerable Bede described as the 'great plenty of eels' that once inhabited the surrounding marshes.[12] The European eel is nowadays classified as critically endangered, but in the fenland of the Middle Ages it was so common as to be used as a de facto currency. In one such transaction, Ely Cathedral paid Thorney Abbey 26,275 eels to rent an area of fen.[13] As the historian James Boyce argues, 'The medieval prosperity of the Fens thus occurred not *in spite* of the survival of a vast undrained marshland but *because* of it.'[14]

The problem was, this prosperity was hard for any one person to *own*. Apart from the abbeys founded upon the few areas of higher ground, permanent settlement was impossible over large swathes of the Fens. 'Even those portions that escaped winter flooding', wrote the historian H. C. Darby, 'were subject to an annual heaving motion as the swelling peat absorbed more and more water.'[15] The undrained Fens were thus for the most part a giant, wet common. Commoners grazed their cattle upon the communal meadows after the winter floods receded, and ventured out onto the marshes to catch fish, eels and wildfowl. As a result of this natural wealth shared in common, the Fenlands boasted 'a higher proportion of small farmers and a lower proportion of very wealthy ones'.[16]

Life in the Fens was no idyll: for one thing, the marshes were infested with malarial mosquitoes. But the landscape and its egalitarian peasants were increasingly vilified by outsiders, who looked down upon it as a wasteland populated by savages. The seventeenth-century scholar William Dugdale described the fenland air as being 'for the most part cloudy, gross, and full of rotten harrs [fogs]; the water putrid and muddy, yea full of loathsome vermin'.[17] Another observer of the time castigated the fenland peoples as 'half fishe, half fleshe'.[18] Later, the Victorian historian Lord Macaulay succumbed to the 'enormous condescension of posterity' in his descriptions of the Fennish folk of the past. 'In that dreary region,' he wrote, 'covered by vast flights of wild-fowl, a half-savage population, known by the name of Breedlings, then led an amphibious life, sometimes wading, and sometimes rowing, from one islet of firm ground to another.'[19] Macaulay's caricature lived on in the *Narnia* books of C.S. Lewis, in which Puddleglum the Marsh-wiggle resides in the marshlands, living off eels. Even today, inhabitants of East Anglia are disparaged as being inbred or having webbed feet.

The point of these tall tales was to justify the colonisation of the Fens. According to certain onlookers, the land needed 'improving' for agriculture, and its denizens required civilising. After Henry VIII's dissolution of the monasteries in the 1530s, formerly monastic land on the edges of the Fens had been handed out to court favourites. These nouveau-riche landowners looked upon the neighbouring common lands of the Fens with avaricious eyes. If they could drain the Fens of water, making them suitable for cultivation, they would be richer still. The General Draining Act of 1600 had already granted landowners powers to suppress common rights in pursuit of 'improving' land for agriculture. As Oliver Rackham puts it, the incentive to drain the Fens arose not from local dissatisfaction but from the desire of 'outside landowners . . . to make easy money out of arable crops and improved grassland'.[20]

One such landowner was the 4th Earl of Bedford, Francis Russell, whose family had been gifted the fenland estates of Thorney Abbey.[21] Hugely wealthy and with powerful sway in the royal court, the Earl of Bedford had the capital and connections to embark on grand projects. In 1631, Bedford joined with a dozen other 'Adventurers' – a seventeenth-century word for someone who ventured their money for risky undertakings – to propose a suitably ambitious scheme: the draining of the Fens.

Up until that point, some areas of the Fens had been drained by the monasteries and some by the Romans before them, but these works had been piecemeal and small in scale. Bedford and his Company of Adventurers had something entirely new in mind, and contracted the Dutch engineer Cornelius Vermuyden to help them. With his experience of land reclamation in the low-lying Netherlands, Vermuyden proposed cutting two gigantic drainage channels through the Fens, later to be named the Old and New Bedford Rivers in honour of their chief sponsor. These colossal incisions into the peat, each 21 miles long, would empty the waters from the southernmost third of the fenlands into the Wash, 'reclaiming' some 95,000 acres of land. What the Earl and his gang of venture capitalists were advocating was nothing less than the destruction of an entire ecosystem.

Draining the Fens was arguably an early expression of reckless 'frontier capitalism', mirroring the other colonial frontiers that England was then opening up in the Americas and via the slave trade. And just as ventures like the East India Company and later the Royal African Company received backing from the Crown, so Bedford's Company of Adventurers obtained enthusiastic support from King Charles I. The cash-strapped Stuart kings were always looking for new ways to raise revenue, and fenland drainage promised rich rewards to those in on the game. Anyone who bought shares in the Company of Adventurers was promised swathes of reclaimed land once the drainage was complete. A single share in this undertaking was worth 4,000 reclaimed acres. The Earl of Bedford owned two shares, so stood to gain 8,000 acres; likewise his son and heir, William Russell. Other investors included the Earl of Bolingbroke and several Members of Parliament. Charles I stood to gain 12,000 acres.[22] In this respect, the Earl and his mates were rather like the gang of thieves in *Ocean's Eleven*, who set out to rob a casino and agree to divvy up the spoils between them.

But, as in all heist movies, the gang's plan started to go awry. Their scheme met far stiffer resistance than they had expected. Even some aristocratic landowners were dubious about the vaunted benefits of fenland drainage. One, Lord Willoughby, had opined some years previously that 'instead of helping the gennerall pore, it would undo them and make those that are allreddye ritch farr more ritch'.[23] As for the 'gennerall pore' of the Fens, they began mobilising for a campaign of resistance. One of the investors in the company, the landowner Sir Miles Sandys, was alarmed by a 'great riot' that broke out in 1638 in protest at the 'Lord of Bedford's works'. 'If order be not taken,' Sandys wrote frantically in a letter to his son, 'it will turn out to be a general rebellion in all the Fen towns.'[24]

Commoners formed guerrilla bands that became known as the 'Fen Tigers', who hid amongst the reeds to launch surprise assaults against drainage works. Fen Tigers filled in drainage ditches, beat up workmen employed by the Company of Adventurers and threw them into rivers. On one occasion, rebellious villagers gathered under the pretext of holding a community football match – which in Stuart times was a game played by hundreds of participants – only to lead the crowd to sabotage local drainage ditches.[25] A glorious poem of the time, *Powte's Complaint*, voices the resistance to fenland drainage from the perspective of a burbot: a freshwater species of cod that lived in the Fens but is now extinct in England. The rallying cry of this fishy Che Guevara went as follows:

Come, Brethren of the water, and let us all assemble
To treat upon this matter, which makes us quake and tremble;
For we shall rue it if't be true that Fenns be undertaken,
And where we feed in Fen and Reed, they'll feed both Beef
and Bacon.[26]

The company also met resistance from the land itself. Whilst at first the drainage ditches seemed to be working, Bedford and Vermuyden had not anticipated how quickly the peat would subside as the waters bled out of it. As the ground level dropped, the floodwaters rushed back in. As the historian Eric Ash argues, draining the Fens had 'unintended ecological consequences that created at least as many problems as it solved'.[27] Landowners responded by building windmills to pump away the excess water, but the fenland was to be plagued by seasonal flooding for centuries. Only with the advent of steam-powered pumps in the Victorian period was the drainage project finally completed. The last of the big inland lakes to be drained was Whittlesey Mere, just to the north of Holme Fen, in 1851. That same year, the Holme Fen post was driven into the ground to monitor the collapsing peat. The demise of Whittlesey marked what James Boyce calls the 'final conquest of the Fens'.[28]

As the last water drained away, so the Fens emptied of their once bountiful wildlife. The celebrated botanist Derek Ratcliffe would later write: 'probably the biggest single loss [of British habitat] up to 1940 occurred through the draining of the East Anglian Fenland, causing the extinction in Britain of a group of wetland plants and animals, and replacement of a once rich ecosystem by one of singularly low diversity.'[29] The beautiful Large Copper butterfly, which relies on wet fenland for its habitat, became extinct in Britain in the same year that Whittlesey Mere was destroyed.[30] A staggering 99 per cent of the original swampy fenland has been eradicated.[31]

Despite uprisings of water and of commoners, the landowning venture capitalists had emerged triumphant. The Company of Adventurers went on to claim the lands of the Fens as their own. Some of the original investors continued to own this land for centuries: the descendants of the 4th Earl of Bedford, for example, kept hold of their 18,000-acre Thorney Estate until 1910.

Two old maps of the Fens graphically illustrate the scale of the transformation. One, drawn up in the early 1630s, shows the fenland prior to drainage.[32] It's a wild and untamed landscape, the huge marshes etched with wavy lines that make them look like a vast inland sea. A second map from 1658 shows the Fens shortly after they were first drained.[33] The picture has changed utterly: now the fenland is torn up with drainage channels and scored with straight-edged field boundaries. Zoom in, and you can see that the whole landscape has been divvied up into lots for auction; a habitat commodified. A once-thriving wetland ecosystem had been totally destroyed, and all it had taken was thirteen unscrupulous landowners to set the process in motion.

So who owns the Fens today, and how well are they stewarding it?

The venture capitalists have left, but the institutional investors have moved in. Gone are the days when the fenland was a frontier, carrying high risks for those willing to sink their capital into expensive drainage works. Freed from the threat of floods and Fen Tigers, the black gold of the fenland soils has been transmuted into over a billion pounds' worth of fresh vegetables sold annually.[34] That makes for profitable rents and high land values. Nowadays, owning a chunk of the Fens is seen as a safe investment, guaranteed to pay out over the long term.

That's attracted organisations like pension funds, Oxbridge colleges and private schools to snap up large expanses of fenland. One of the largest landowners in the Fens is – rather incongruously – the South Yorkshire Pension Authority, which owns some 12,000 acres of prime agricultural land. The British Steel Pension Fund possesses around 1,500 acres, whilst Winchester College – the elite boarding school where Rishi Sunak was a student – lays claim to some 3,700 acres.[35] The Wellcome Trust, a medical charity founded by a pharmaceutical magnate and with an investment portfolio of £37 billion, also owns a big chunk of fenland peat.[36] Many of these landowners lease their land to tenant farmers, but it's the landlords who benefit from the high rents harvested from intensive agriculture.

Today's fenland landowners represent capital from around the world, looking for a good return on investment. Around 4,000 acres of the Fens belongs to an agribusiness firm registered in Germany called Eaubrink Farm GmbH. The Utah-based Mormon Church, meanwhile, has bought up over 7,600 acres of land in the Fens since the 1990s: its UK holding company traces its ultimate ownership back to Salt Lake City.[37] When a journalist visited one of their farms shortly after morning prayers, she spotted a mission statement pinned to an office wall that read: 'Our business is farmland. Profit motivated: No Excuses.'[38]

The problem is, whilst these landowners are enjoying big private profits, they're generating ecological risks that affect us all. By continuing to farm the Fens intensively, they're fuelling the climate crisis, contributing to the 7.6 million tonnes of CO_2e emitted from arable peat soils in the UK every year. The huge carbon footprint of farming on lowland peat sits uneasily with the green claims made by some fenland landowners. The South Yorkshire Pension Authority, for example, has set a goal of reaching carbon neutrality by 2030.[39] They'd better get a move on, then: they have just a few years to work out how to stop their huge fenland estate leaking carbon.

And with the Fens sinking ever lower as the peat degrades, they become ever more at risk from the *impacts* of climate change, in a catastrophic loop. With much of the land now below sea level, and with sea levels rising and torrential rainfall increasing, fenland owners are hugely dependent on the upkeep of pumps and sea defences. Inundation from the sea would be devastating: quite apart from the damage done by flooding directly, the saline water would salt the land for years afterwards, affecting crop production.[40]

Indeed, these landowners are not only worsening the climate crisis through their pursuit of short-term profit: they're jeopardising the UK's food security, too. Intensive use of the peat soils is causing them to lose their precious fertility – blown away in the dust storms that sweep the Fens in summer, or washed out to sea with the rains in winter. As a report commissioned by Natural England in 2010 warned, 'While peat soils have been the foundation of [the Fens'] productive capacity, there are clear signs that the soils themselves are being rapidly "farmed out".'[41] The report went on: 'Continued arable production will degrade the remaining peat soils, at the annual rate of about 10mm to 30mm . . . At current rates, the bulk of the remaining peats will become "wasted" over the next 30 to 100 years.'[42]

The natural wealth of the Fens, built up over thousands of years, is being squandered by its present owners. It is a supreme irony that the current ownership of the fenland is dominated by pension funds and institutional investors who pride themselves on making risk-averse long-term investment decisions. Yet the way they and their tenant farmers are treating the Fens is short-sighted to the point of being foolhardy. Fossil fuel divestment campaigns have had some success in persuading pension funds and institutions to ditch their investments in coal, oil and gas, by pointing out to them that fossil fuel infrastructure will be a 'stranded asset' in a net zero world. When it comes to owning land that's fast sinking below sea level, the Fens are not so much a stranded asset as a marooned one.

It's hard to hold any landowner to account for their lacklustre stewardship. But one fenland landowner shows this particularly starkly; one of the largest landowners in the UK – the Church of England. There's a great gulf between what the Church of England claims to be its environmental values, and its ownership of large swathes of degrading peat in the Fens. 'The Earth has been and continues to be abused, raped, objectified and exploited,' states the C of E in an official document discussing its 'five Marks of Mission'. 'As a landowner, the Church is well placed to take a lead in ecologically sensitive land management.'[43] So how does the C of E square these strong words with the way it's managing its land?

I decided to ask them. I teamed up with the Anglican ordinand Hannah Malcolm and the botanist Tim Harris to investigate how the Church treats its land. To get started, we had to grapple with the C of E's byzantine organisational structure. It's led by bishops, some of whom – like the Archbishop of Canterbury – sit in the House of Lords, but it's notionally governed by a democratic body called the General Synod. In terms of landholdings, the Church's forty-two dioceses own approximately 70,000 acres between them. But still more significant is the 105,000-acre estate owned by the Church Commissioners, a separate body that administers the C of E's £9-billion investment portfolio and pays priests' pensions.[44] Some of this land has been owned by the Church for centuries, while other areas are relatively recent acquisitions. Five thousand acres of their estate comprises Fenland peat – the land I visited at the start of this chapter.

Hannah, Tim and I sought to grill the Church Commissioners on how they use their land. But we soon discovered that they weren't so keen on public scrutiny. 'We do not give out plans of the Commissioners' land,' we were told bluntly when we asked the organisation for maps. Despite being the established national church with representation in Parliament, the C of E isn't considered a public body, so is exempt from Freedom of Information requests. Fortunately, however, I was able to build up a picture of the Church Commissioners' landholdings from an obscure source. Under section 31 (subsection 6) of the otherwise extremely dull Highways Act 1980, landowners can guard their land against rights of way claims by depositing a map of their estate with the local authority. So with geekish glee, I tracked down all the maps the Church Commissioners had deposited with councils across England, and stitched them together to reveal what they own.[45]

Next, we sought to get questions raised in Parliament. One of the oddities of the way church and state are intertwined in England is that the Church Commissioners always have an MP who represents them in the House of Commons, holding the arcane post of Second Church Estates Commissioner. At the time we were investigating it was the Tory MP Andrew Selous. We worked with Labour MP Kerry McCarthy, who doggedly asked question after question about the Commissioners' management of their land. Eventually, Selous relayed that the Church Commissioners were working on a new 'natural capital audit' of their landholdings, and 'the Church does want to be an exemplar in this area'.[46] A few months later, the Commissioners announced they were developing a 'net zero carbon strategy for [their] land investments'.[47]

We then went through the time-consuming process of getting questions asked at the Church's General Synod meetings. Hannah persuaded various vicars and canons to table questions for us, and together we drafted the wording. During the November 2021 Synod, the Reverend Canon Anne Brown referred to the Church Commissioners' net zero aspirations, and asked: 'can the Commissioners state what will happen to the approximately 5,000 acres of deep peat soils they own in the Cambridgeshire Fens, and how it will be managed to reduce carbon emissions from the eroding peat soils?'

The response was vague and non-committal. 'We continue to work on understanding the extent of the Commissioners' ownership of deep peat soils,' said Alan Smith, the First Church Estates Commissioner. 'The holdings around the Fens may be areas of focus,' he went on, stating they were 'seeking to find ways of encouraging more carbon-friendly farming practices including cultivation methods that particularly benefit peaty soils to prevent erosion.' Though it felt good to push the Commissioners to concede there was a problem, they didn't seem to be in any rush to tackle it.[48]

Worse, it transpired that the Church Commissioners didn't feel bound by net zero targets that the C of E's governing body had agreed to. In 2020, General Synod had voted for all parts of the Church to reach net zero by 2030 – twenty years ahead of the government's net zero target for the UK as a whole. It was an ambitious commitment, to be sure – as we've heard, the C of E says it wants to 'take a lead' and 'be an exemplar' on environmental challenges. But then, the Church Commissioners announced the 2030 goal didn't apply to them, and that they were aiming to reach net zero twenty years later.[49] As a landowner, they appear to be unaccountable – even to the Church's own democratic bodies.

Other groups have now picked up the baton of holding the Church Commissioners to account. An excellent report in 2022 by Operation Noah – a Christian-led climate campaign – urged the Commissioners to actually identify all the peat habitats they owned, and to 'protect and restore the peat to a rewetted, healthy state'.[50] But progress remains frustratingly slow. In a glossy brochure published in 2023, the Church Commissioners trumpet their 'sustainable stewardship' and 'ethical policies'. The small matter of the carbon bomb exploding in their Fenland estate is relegated to a pull-out box. Beneath a photo of eroding Fenland peat, the Commissioners ponderously state: 'We engage with and understand the legitimate debates and concerns relating to land use and soil emissions that are not easily resolved.'[51]

Meanwhile, with every passing year, the Fens emit more carbon and sink lower. I'm forced to conclude that what really motivates the Church Commissioners is not ethics, but profits.

How do you fix a problem like the Fens? Well, a few Fenland landowners and farmers are charting a different course.

There are just four fragments of semi-natural fenland left in the Fens, all of them owned by conservation charities.[52] Indeed, the idea of setting aside land as a 'nature reserve' originates from the Fens, the brainchild of the banker and early conservationist Charles Rothschild. Passionate about butterflies, and a world expert on fleas, Rothschild differed from other Victorian entomologists in seeing the need to protect habitats rather than just collect specimens.[53] In 1899, recognising the importance of the last areas of undrained Fenland for insect life, he purchased part of Wicken Fen near Ely, and donated it to the fledgling National Trust. In 1910, Rothschild also bought Woodwalton Fen, to the south of Peterborough. The organisation he subsequently set up – the Society for the Promotion of Nature Reserves, which we met in the previous chapter – is today known as the Wildlife Trusts.[54]

Today the Wildlife Trusts own both Woodwalton Fen and Holme Fen, home to the famous iron post. We have the far-sighted Rothschild to thank for the survival of these tiny fragments of fenland. But the Wildlife Trusts have hatched a scheme to do more than simply conserve what's left. The Great Fen Project, as it's called, is a bold plan to reconnect these two surviving remnants by buying the intervening farmland and rewetting it.

Visiting Woodwalton Fen, I got an inkling of what this might look like. The contrast with the surrounding flat black fields is striking. A tangle of willows, alders and birches greeted me at the entrance gate. Old drainage channels had been stopped up with wooden 'leaky dams', allowing them to flood and spill over into the surrounding land. Reeds and bulrushes murmured in the wind. In the wildest part of the reserve, a huge reedbed stretched as far as the eye could see; peering through the wintry mist, I spotted a Chinese water deer grazing in the middle distance. A grey heron passed overhead, honking. On the site notice board, somebody had scrawled a list of some of the species sighted here over the summer: *kingfisher, hobby, marsh harrier, coot, kite.* To which someone else had added, at the end: *I saw a crocodile.*

Crocodiles are not yet on the agenda for this rewilding project. But the Wildlife Trusts have been purchasing neighbouring fields and beginning the gradual process of fenland restoration. Ponds and scrapes are being put back in, arable fields are reverting to wet pasture, wildflower meadows are being sown. Rymes Reedbed and Kesters Docking are two areas of recently acquired land to the east of Holme Fen, close to where Whittlesey Mere once existed. An artist's impression of the vision for the Great Fen Project shows these areas becoming open water again.[55]

Eventually, the Great Fen is intended to comprise some 9,000 acres of rewetted fenland. That will be a huge increase compared to the tiny amounts of natural fen left after centuries of drainage. But, compared to the 330,000-acre expanse of Fenland peat, it's still just a drop in the marsh. Given the high price tag for farmland in the Fens, there's a limit on how much conservation charities can afford to buy (and a limited number of existing landowners willing to sell). And since it's Grade 1 farmland, producing a high yield of vegetables each year in a country that imports almost half of its food, there's a debate to be had about how much we should be taking this land out of production entirely.[56] That's led the Wildlife Trusts and others to explore the question: can you rewet land and still grow food on it?

This is the idea behind 'swamp-farming' – the art of growing crops half-submerged in water. Or, to give it its more formal name, 'paludiculture' – from the Latin *palus*, meaning swamp. 'Perhaps because agriculture began on the arid soils of the Middle East, we've come to believe that the only route to productive land is to drain it,' writes wetland expert Olly Watts. But paludiculture is in use across the world – just think of rice paddies in China, for instance.[57] Unfortunately, as a DEFRA-sponsored review states, there are 'no varieties of rice that could be grown under existing climatic conditions in the UK'.[58] So the hunt is on for other crops that can be grown in rewetted fenland soils.

Some are obvious: watercress (eaten in salads) and water mint (used in herbal teas) both thrive in waterlogged conditions – the clue's in the name. Both, however, are rather niche markets. Some small-scale swamp-farming trials up and running in the Fens involve growing common bulrushes to burn in bioenergy plants, reeds for thatching, and sphagnum mosses for compost.[59] But useful though this is, you can't eat rushes, reeds or mosses. Bilberries, cranberries and other members of the *Vaccinium* family, however, grow naturally in peat soils, and there is a multimillion-pound global industry in producing cranberry juice and berries for breakfast.[60] Celery, already grown in the Fens, also tolerates growing in wetter conditions.[61] Perhaps the most promising crop in the running is floating sweet-grass (*Glyceria fluitans*): its edible grains used to be widely eaten up until the nineteenth century, and it can be ground into flour and made into flatbread. The Wildlife Trusts are trialling its production as part of their Great Fen Project.[62]

Paludiculture, therefore, offers a route for some of the Fens to be rewetted without losing all of its productive capacity. There are clearly limits on what crops can be successfully grown in fully saturated soils: popular vegetables like potatoes, carrots and peas would all rot. But paludiculture is promising enough for it to be getting official backing from the UK government. In 2021, DEFRA set up the Lowland Agricultural Peat Taskforce, which submitted its report two years later. 'I want to see paludiculture become a mainstream option for farming on lowland peat,' wrote its chair, the fenland farmer Robert Caudwell. 'I do not believe that wetter farming on peat will pose a threat to our national food security; I am more concerned that in future our food security will be threatened . . . by the loss of our fertile peat soils.'[63]

Various private estates and farmers' groups are starting to trial paludiculture in the Fens and beyond. But the government is currently missing a trick by not roping in more public sector landowners to such trials. The largest single landowner in the Fens is in fact Cambridgeshire County Council, which owns some 20,000 acres of lowland peat through its network of County Farms.

County Farms were first set up in the late nineteenth century as a way for poor rural labourers to get into farming. They were the product of a now-forgotten land reform movement that arose in the midst of a long agricultural depression, and as part of the late-Victorian reaction against the enclosure of the commons. Local authorities bought land from local owners and built up an estate of County Farms covering over 400,000 acres of England, leasing them to first-time farmers at low rents. But since 1979, the extent of County Farms has halved in size. Repeated bouts of austerity and a Thatcherite zeal for paring back the state has forced many councils to flog them off.[64]

Cambridgeshire Council, however, is one of the few authorities to retain a County Farms estate of serious scale. It's also supportive of its tenant farmers innovating with new forms of agriculture. Stephen Briggs, for example, has been pioneering the use of agroforestry on his farm on the edge of the Fens. 'When we took this farm on in 2007, it soon became quite apparent that these very fertile Fen soils are prone to wind erosion,' he says.[65] Stephen decided to try planting rows of apple trees between his lines of organic wheat. The tree roots help to keep the soils in place, whilst the apples provide a supplementary source of income. Agroforestry is unlikely to work in deeper peat soils, but paludiculture might – and the Cambridgeshire County Farms estate is well placed to trial it at scale. Instead of forcing local authorities to sell off their remaining County Farms, the government should be incentivising councils to rejuvenate them for the twenty-first century, with tenants supported to adopt new ecological farming methods.

Given how quickly Fenland soils are eroding and sinking, however, we also need to be considering more drastic measures.

One option is to move some types of food production off the Fens entirely. Whilst the high fertility of Fenland peat makes it ideally suited to growing veg in the present climate, that fertility clearly isn't going to be available in a few decades' time if the Fens continue to be farmed the way they are. And the carbon cost of producing food here is rapidly outweighing the benefits. As farmer Robert Caudwell says, 'it is right to make society aware of the significant carbon footprint of vegetables, grains, meat, sugar and dairy products produced in drained lowland peat landscapes'.[66] The think tank Green Alliance has calculated that wheat grown on Fenland has a carbon footprint *seven times larger* than soya grown in the Brazilian Amazon.[67]

When I speak to Green Alliance's Dustin Benton about this, he points out that quite a lot of the Fens is used for producing food that could be grown elsewhere. Grains like wheat and barley, for example, are cropped extensively in the Fens – yet they also grow perfectly well on non-peat soils found across the rest of dry and sunny East Anglia. Much of the Fenland cereal crop doesn't even go into making bread, but is fed to livestock instead. The key flaw in the government's approach, says Dustin, is that it wants to retain all the food production on lowland peat that we have today. But there is a hard trade-off, he argues, between 'flogging the land for food' and allowing it to become a natural carbon sink again. 'We've got to be radical about peat,' he says, 'because it's such a stonkingly big source of carbon.'

Shifting cereal production off the Fens is clearly possible, where horticulture would be harder to give up. Yet it would surely be a positive change if we could grow our vegetables across the country, rather than rely so heavily on one carbon-emitting area that may soon be reclaimed by the sea. Britain has, after all, seen a big decline in domestic horticulture over the past fifty years, as we've switched to imports from countries like Spain. The Lea Valley in London, for instance, used to have over 1,000 acres of greenhouses producing fresh veg for the capital. Today it has fewer than 200 acres of them.[68] The government seems to have no interest in the issue: in 2023, it abandoned its promised Horticulture Strategy for England.[69]

Whether it's shifting wasteful types of production off the Fenland, switching to paludiculture, or restoring areas of wild swamp as a carbon sink, any efforts to fix the Fens will have to contend with the profit-driven mindset of its landowners. Predictably, the government's solution to date has been to offer them more money. One of the key demands of the Lowland Agricultural Peat Task Force was for 'public money for wetter modes of farming on lowland peat'.[70] In January 2023, ministers duly obliged, offering to pay Fenland farmers and landowners who rewet their peat soils at premium rates of £1,409 per hectare.[71]

If the Church Commissioners took advantage of these new Countryside Stewardship payments to rewet their entire Fenland estate, they could stand to benefit from £3 million in public funding each year.[72] Were the South Yorkshire Pension Authority similarly minded to raise water levels across its 12,000 acres in the Fens, it could bring in nearly £7 million annually.[73] Payments would go in the first instance to the tenant farmers, but these landlords would stand to gain in terms of increased rents. If it incentivises the restoration of lowland peat, great. But do we really want to be handing millions of pounds of public money to already wealthy institutional investors? These investors have, after all, already profited greatly from the natural wealth of the Fens, and presided over its degradation as an ecosystem. In environmental policy, a key principle is that the polluter pays to clean up the mess they've made. But, as Dustin Benton tells me, 'all land use policy in Britain to date has been to *pay the polluter*.' Is there really no alternative?

Well, it turns out there is. If we want to fix the Fens, we shouldn't just be talking about carrots, but also about sticks. The major landowners in the Fens are institutional investors with plenty of capital: do we really need to pay them even more money to be good stewards? Why, instead, are we not *taxing* them when they do bad things? Under the 'polluter pays' principle, we impose carbon taxes on some forms of fossil fuel pollution in Britain – the Carbon Price Floor, for instance, has been levied on electricity companies for the past decade and has swiftly driven dirty coal power off the grid. Why not introduce a Carbon Land Tax on landowners who continue to degrade fenland peat?

Defining which landowners would be liable to pay is easy enough: just use Natural England's official maps of peat, and Land Registry data to map the owners and their landholdings. If the landowners continue to degrade the peat soils they own through conventional intensive agriculture, they would pay the Carbon Land Tax. If they switch to paludiculture or choose to rewild areas as semi-natural fenland, they'd be exempted from paying the tax.

Let's be fair, and give landowners in the Fens two years, say, in which to change their business models and take advantage of the new Countryside Stewardship grants to rewet peat. If they've not done so by then, the Carbon Land Tax would kick in. Levying the tax at the same rate as the payments currently on offer could generate up to £188 million in revenues across the 330,000 acres of Fenland peat.[74] Ah, you might ask, but wouldn't this lead to higher prices for fresh vegetables? Well, the Treasury could ringfence the proceeds from the Carbon Land Tax, give some of it to the County Farms pioneering paludiculture, and hand out the rest of it as subsidies for horticulture *outside* the Fens.[75]

Four centuries ago, a small band of venture capitalists sought to profit from the Fens by draining them of water. In doing so, they destroyed one of the largest wetland ecosystems in western Europe, upended the livelihoods of the commoners who depended on the Fens for fish and wildfowl, and triggered the collapse of this vast carbon sink. The institutional investors who have come to own this land today are still benefiting from that ecological disaster. Yet as we've seen, even those Fenland owners notionally most motivated by ethical considerations – like the Church Commissioners – seem unwilling to be held accountable, and in no hurry to change their ways. We should be telling these landowners in no uncertain terms: if you continue to drain the Fens, we will drain your wallets.

6

A Plague upon the Land

Barely anyone noticed when the outbreak started. A few escaped specimens were discovered; a few enquiries made. But at the time, no one had any inkling of the scale of devastation that was about to be unleashed. I'm not talking here about a viral pandemic, or the start of a zombie movie. I'm talking, of course, about England's plague of grey squirrels.

Before the late nineteenth century, few people in England had even seen a grey squirrel. English woods and gardens abounded instead with red squirrels, native to these shores since the last Ice Age, fondly depicted in countless stories – from the mythological figure of Ratatoskr in Norse legend, scampering up the world-tree Yggdrasil, through to Beatrix Potter's character Squirrel Nutkin. North America had the Eastern grey squirrel, a much larger, heavier creature than its Eurasian cousin. For millennia, the two relatives never met. But then a few aristocratic landowners decided to shake things up.

As the historian Dan Eatherley writes, 'the procurement, display and release of non-native species is a pursuit long favoured by Britain's elites.'[1] So-called 'acclimatisation societies' became all the rage during the Victorian period – set up by colonial explorers and collectors to import exotic species from abroad and try to 'acclimatise' them to conditions back home in Blighty. But it was 'left to individual landowners . . . to make the real running'.[2] And aristocratic landowners in particular had the money, time and above all the acreage over which to conduct such experiments.

The Earl of Derby, for instance, pioneered the captive breeding of Hawaiian geese at his Knowsley Hall estate near Liverpool. The naturalist Charles Waterton, meanwhile, released little owls at Walton Hall in Yorkshire. But nothing would come close to the 'scale and scope of the extraordinary collection' which the 11th Duke of Bedford, Herbrand Russell, began amassing when he inherited the family's ancestral estate at Woburn Abbey, soon to become 'the largest of all experiments in animal acclimatisation in this country'.[3]

The 11th Duke – a descendant of the 4th Earl of Bedford, whom we met in the previous chapter busily draining the Fens – managed to outstrip even his ancestor's record for damaging the wildlife and habitats of England. Herbrand Russell was not an especially pleasant character: he 'reputedly suffered from pathological shyness, manifesting itself in an autocratic exterior'.[4] Prior to inheriting the title of duke, Russell had leased a shooting estate in Dumfries and Galloway, burned most of the moorland to maximise numbers of grouse, and begun 'casting about for exotic animal species to populate it'.[5] With the 12,000-acre Woburn Estate in Bedfordshire, the Duke had the perfect site for his menagerie.

Woburn became a vast zoo, boasting species from around the world. Visitors reported walking through the sprawling parkland and watching European bison charge around, as Saiga antelopes grazed alongside zebras, llamas, camels and ostriches.[6] Most of the species were unable to vault the walls bounding the estate, so could do little harm elsewhere. But the real problems started when the Duke took a delivery of ten grey squirrels from New Jersey.

'You won't find "Squirrel Spreader-in-Chief" amid his undoubtedly voluminous entry in *Debretts*,' says Eatherley, 'yet the duke has one of the better claims for the title.'[7] Other landowners also brought grey squirrels to England, but the Duke of Bedford was 'one of the worst offenders', according to Dr Lisa Signorile of Imperial College London. After compiling a DNA database of grey squirrels across England, she concluded that 'the only way greys could have travelled so far was by human intervention.'[8] The Duke loved to 'gift' grey squirrels to other estates, from which they promptly escaped.

We can track the rapid spread of grey squirrels across England through old newspaper archives. The *Leighton Buzzard Observer* recorded sweetly in January 1904 that 'a very rare kind of squirrel has been introduced into the Duke of Bedford's woods'.[9] But just three years later, in summer 1907, the *Luton Times and Advertiser* was reporting that 'the grey squirrels that are so numerous on the Woburn estate are a great nuisance in the gardens, as they are too fond of green apples and ripe strawberries.'[10]

By 1910, a local fruit-grower wrote to the *Luton Reporter* to complain about the 'rapidly multiplying' grey squirrels in the area and admitted that 'summary justice has been administered to several of the robbers'.[11] Another account has it that the landlord of a local pub, upon finding seven grey squirrels eating his garden peas, shot them all – and that the Duke 'was much incensed at what he regarded as an outrageous act'.[12] Most ominous of all was mounting evidence from Woburn, recorded in another gazette in 1906, that the grey squirrels 'have expelled or exterminated the common English red species'.[13]

Despite such warning signs flashing in his back yard, all this time the Duke carried on handing out grey squirrels like candy. In 1906, he 'gifted' some to Regent's Park in north London, home to the Zoological Gardens. 'SQUIRRELS LET LOOSE' ran one jolly headline, which recounted how two young visitors to the park mistook the grey squirrels for rats. Speaking to the park attendant, the reporter was told emphatically that the grey squirrels would not survive for long: 'There isn't any food in the park for them.'[14] More fool him, because just a few months later, newspapers were reporting that 'the Duke of Bedford's experiment in introducing American grey squirrels into the London parks has met with complete success', with a nest discovered in Regent's Park. The greys had found plentiful food, it appeared, since visitors freely fed them with 'monkey nuts, biscuits, or toffee'.[15]

Some ninety-one grey squirrels were released in Regent's Park between 1905 and 1907;[16] and as late as 1908, the Duke was still doling out greys to Kew Gardens.[17] 'Herbrand saw to it that deliberate releases of Woburn squirrels ensued at estates up and down the country,' recounts Eatherley. 'With an aristocratic tailwind . . . there would be no stopping the species.'[18]

The Duke seemed intensely relaxed about the havoc he had just unleashed on English ecosystems. Even his family motto seems suitably insouciant: *'Che sara sara'* – 'Whatever will be, will be'.[19] Yet even he eventually felt the dawning of an 'oh, shit' moment, when complaints from his Woburn neighbours about squirrel damage to trees and crops became too frequent to ignore. The Duke's gamekeepers were instructed 'to kill as many as possible' and start to wage a 'war against squirrels'.[20] But by then it was too late.

By 1930, when the ecologist A.D. Middleton made the first extensive survey of grey squirrel distribution, the species was 'well entrenched in a substantial slice of south-eastern England'.[21] Middleton's study named Woburn as the 'most important mother-colony' of grey squirrels, and warned that their rapid spread over such a wide area 'now made the colonisation of the whole country merely a matter of time'.[22]

Over the coming years, the authorities engaged in a set of increasingly desperate efforts to shut the stable door after the squirrel had bolted. In 1937, Parliament belatedly passed a law forbidding the deliberate release of grey squirrels.[23] Newspapers ceased treating greys as novel curiosities and started referring to them in ever more bellicose terms: 'pests', 'little grey killers', 'North American invaders', even 'public enemies'.[24] The Board of Works in London ordered the extermination of the species from Kensington Gardens.[25] A National Anti-Grey Squirrel Campaign was launched, with posters distributed around the country warning of the encroaching menace. At a meeting held to discuss the campaign, one councillor rose to declare, amidst laughter: 'I should like one of those posters sent to the Duke of Bedford.'[26]

Meanwhile, evidence of the devastation caused by invasive grey squirrels continued to grow. The Forestry Commission, set up after the First World War to address the UK's chronic shortage of timber, suddenly found itself in a war with this tiny enemy. Greys, it discovered, were seriously damaging and even killing trees by stripping the bark from their trunks; and whilst red squirrels had been known to do the same, their grey cousins lived in higher numbers together in the woods, so had a greater impact.[27] To address the threat, the Forestry Commission offered a bounty on grey squirrels – paid out at the price of two shillings for every squirrel tail presented to the authorities. But even this grisly incentive did little to stem the tide, and the bounty was abandoned in 1958.[28] The grey squirrels were officially out of control.

Worst of all was how the invasive greys triggered a collapse in the population of red squirrels, extirpating them from most of England in a matter of decades. Competition for food was one factor, but the main cause was that grey squirrels spread a deadly disease called 'squirrel pox'. Greys had evolved immunity to this disease in North America – but red squirrels, previously unexposed to it, died in their droves. Today, there are around 2.7 million grey squirrels in England, whilst reds have been vanquished – surviving only in a few remote locations where greys have not yet reached.[29] And all because of the careless actions of a handful of aristocratic landowners who thought they knew better.

An 'invasive species' is defined by the government as 'any non-native animal or plant that has the ability to spread, causing damage to the environment, our economy, human health and the way we live'.[30] Not all non-native species are harmful: down through the centuries, around 2,000 non-native plants and animals have found their way to Britain, many of which are benign, like slender speedwell or the mandarin duck, or fail to spread.[31] We should also, of course, be wary of how some of the narrative around non-native species veers towards xenophobia: *bloody squirrels, comin' over here, taking our jobs.* But a small percentage of invasive species, whether through destructive habits or sheer weight of numbers, have ended up causing immense damage to Britain's ecosystems.

England's large landowners have played an outsize role in releasing invasive and non-native species into our ecosystems. Humanity has, of course, always aided the spread of other species – from the rodents that accompanied seventeenth-century Dutch sailors to Mauritius, spelling doom for the dodo, to the introduction of rabbits from Britain to Australia, with devastating consequences for the continent's vegetation. But England in the Victorian and Edwardian periods was a particularly fertile Petri dish for the spread of invasive species. First, its far-flung empire meant naturalists and traders were forever bringing back seemingly exotic wildlife from every corner of the globe. And second, it was governed by a landed aristocracy whose parks, gardens and estates covered half the country,[32] and who arrogantly believed themselves to be stewards of creation.

England's outbreak of grey squirrels was just one of the ecological disasters unleashed by this powerful combination of imperial ego and landed power. Some of the worst impacts came from the importation of exotic plants. *Rhododendron ponticum* was brought back from the Iberian peninsula in the late 1700s, planted in estate gardens and as game cover in woods, and from thence has spread to choke the country's last remaining fragments of temperate rainforest. It is now estimated to cover an area of Britain four times the size of Birmingham.[33]

Japanese knotweed, too, owes its spread to large estates. Practically unkillable and capable of growing through tarmac, knotweed is today reviled as the scourge of property-owning Middle England. It is thought to infest some 5 per cent of UK homes, potentially cutting £20 billion off their collective value, because it is so difficult to eradicate.[34] But in the nineteenth century, Japanese knotweed was considered a pretty addition to gardens. A study by biologists at the University of Leicester examined knotweed hotspots in Britain and found clear correlations with 'private gardens extensive enough to accommodate such large plants . . . By far the largest cluster [of knotweed] in the British Isles is in West Surrey . . . with its numerous large estates and expensive country houses.'[35] Many of these estates had been landscaped by the garden designer

Gertrude Jekyll, who had a particular penchant for knotweed. But it was landowning patronage that helped turn Jekyll into Hyde.

Time and again, the same names keep cropping up with invasive species. As if the grey squirrels aren't bad enough, we also have the Duke of Bedford to thank for our muntjac deer, introduced from China. After the initial release of muntjac to Woburn in 1894, they escaped into the wild and spread across the south-east, perhaps aided by further introductions at the Earl of Iveagh's Elveden Estate in Norfolk.[36] The UK's population of muntjac deer is now somewhere north of 50,000 animals.[37] Since muntjac, like other deer, love to browse on tree saplings, their exploding population is only adding to pressures on our woodlands. A DEFRA-funded study in 2023 found that invasive non-native species overall may be costing the UK a staggering £4 billion annually.[38]

'Surely,' you may be thinking, 'that sort of thing could never happen nowadays.' Well, up to a point, Lord Copper. There *are* now stricter controls governing landowners' release of some invasive species. But the country is still dealing with a massive backlog of foolhardy introductions from a century or more ago. And landowners are still releasing non-native species into the countryside, some with potentially huge ecological ramifications. In terms of sheer numbers, there is no other species released with such wanton abandon into the British countryside than the common pheasant.

Pheasants, originally from Asia, are now omnipresent in the modern British landscape. Male pheasants, with their striking red wattles and iridescent blue-green heads, are unmistakeable; and even if you've never seen one close up, you'll certainly have heard their crowing *tuk-tuk* call whilst out on country walks. Female pheasants, with their muted brown feathers, are less conspicuous; but you may have been startled by one erupting out of the undergrowth, or sworn at their unerring ability to leap from hedgerows into the path of cars.

Pheasants have probably been present in Britain since Roman times, and certainly since the Norman Conquest, yet their numbers remained small up until the Victorian period. Their increase since then is thanks to the sporting tastes of the upper classes. It was reputedly the 2nd Earl of Malmesbury who, on a Grand Tour of Europe at the close of the eighteenth century, discovered the continental fashion for driven or 'battue' hunting, which employed beaters to flush out pheasants from the undergrowth and drive them towards the guns. As with grouse shooting in the uplands, Victorian aristocrats developed driven pheasant shoots in the lowlands, releasing ever more birds to produce bigger 'bags' on shoot days.[39] Today, they are everywhere. And that's because, every year, landowners release close to 50 million pheasants into the British countryside.[40]

Yes, you read that right: *50 million*. Almost one pheasant per person. A quantity that makes them easily the commonest bird in Britain during the September release season. For comparison, the UK wintering population of blackbirds is around 10–15 million individuals.[41] Or, to put it another way: the weight of pheasants released each autumn is greater than the total breeding biomass of the *entire* British wild bird population.[42] What's more, this vast influx occurs each year with barely any governmental regulation. The ubiquity of pheasants in the landscape is yet another example of how landowners get to play the stewardship card: keep on doing what you've done, it's a sporting tradition, no questions asked.

The chance that this huge influx of pheasants is having no untoward impact on the countryside is close to zero. Unlike grey squirrels and muntjac deer, pheasants are normally referred to as being 'non-native' rather than 'invasive'. But in British conservation policy, 'invasive' simply means that the introduced species is causing detrimental impacts on other wildlife or habitats.[43] And in that regard, the evidence for pheasants' negative effects has been mounting for some time.

Not all of the evidence cuts one way. Some deciduous woods may have been spared the axe during the timber-hungry twentieth century because they were used for pheasant shoots instead. Shooting estates have also planted thousands of acres of copses and hedgerows for pheasants to shelter in, creating space for other wildlife in the process. And the cover crops that many estates grow for pheasants – like maize and kale – may also provide food for wild bird populations.[44]

But this giant uncontrolled experiment is having negative ramifications, too. The Game and Wildlife Conservation Trust – who, as their name suggests, are generally supportive of game shooting – estimates that one in twelve of all English woodlands contains a pheasant release pen, where pheasants are placed prior to general release for shooting.[45] Studies by the GWCT have shown that high densities of pheasants in such release pens have detrimental effects on woodland ground flora, reducing plant diversity and boosting 'weed' species,[46] and that woods can take decades to recover from these impacts.[47] Another GWCT-sponsored study found that pheasants can alter the structure of hedgerows, leading to 'more bare ground, fewer stable perennial plant species, more weeds and fewer tree and shrub seedlings in hedges near to release sites'.[48]

A study of seven large pheasant shoots on Exmoor, meanwhile, discovered that 'there was less moss, lichen and similar species on trees in pheasant release pens, and in the surrounding woodland'.[49] Exmoor lies within Britain's temperate rainforest zone, the defining characteristic of which is the rare lichens and mosses that thrive in the damp climate – raising the possibility that pheasants may be feasting upon our last rainforests.

But pheasants don't just eat plants: they're omnivorous, and also eat insects, earthworms, snails, slugs, field mice, lizards, and even small birds and young snakes.[50] Yet another GWCT study has found that releasing pheasants causes 'significant changes' in the types of beetles present in release pens, and 'alters woodland invertebrate communities'.[51] There has been much debate about whether pheasants are behind the ongoing decline in British populations of adders. Shooting advocates dispute the link. But Nigel Hand, a trustee of Amphibian and Reptile Groups of the UK, who has been studying adders for twenty years, has publicly stated: 'The adder is on the brink of extinction in many sites across Britain . . . and it is the uncontrolled release of millions of pheasants by shooting estates which is pushing it over the brink.'[52]

The food that shooting estates provide for pheasants also creates as many problems as it resolves. You may have seen a pheasant feeder whilst on a woodland walk: they're the blue barrels on little stilts, dispensing grain to gamebirds. But though the shooting industry claims these also help songbirds get through the winter, a study has shown they're just as likely to be feeding rats and crows – whose bolstered numbers may then be predating the nests of rarer bird species.[53] And the grains and legumes used in pheasant feeders? There are social and ecological costs here, too. Around 2 per cent of the UK's entire annual wheat production is used to rear pheasants: a crazy waste of a cereal that could be used to feed people.[54] Worse still, some pheasant feeds contain soy, a key driver of Amazon deforestation. Even if game feed companies claim to only source from responsible suppliers,[55] anyone who's investigated Brazilian supply chains will tell you that such guarantees are murky, to say the least.

It's not like many pheasants actually make it to the dinner table, after all: most of those released aren't even shot. The most recent GWCT data shows that just 13 million pheasants are shot in a year.[56] There is a self-sustaining 'feral' population of around 4 million that survive each winter to breed again the following spring.[57] So that means roughly 33 million pheasants aren't shot, but perish from other causes: some from disease, some as roadkill – and some as food for other animals like foxes, stoats and crows. As the conservationist Mark Avery comments: 'it is difficult to imagine that this amount of "free" meat does not affect the numbers of predators able to survive the winter in rural areas.'[58]

A glut of pheasants, in other words, may be distorting food webs and boosting predator numbers. The shooting industry is notoriously obsessed with controlling predators, littering the countryside with a panoply of traps and snares. Its primary goal, of course, is to minimise predation of gamebirds, but it often makes the case for predator control by pointing to the co-benefits for native bird species. Yet it seems likely that the sheer scale of modern pheasant shooting is itself helping to boost populations of foxes, mustelids and corvids. These, in turn, may be having negative repercussions on other, rarer species of birds. As Mark Avery says, the huge numbers of pheasants released by landowners 'will undoubtedly influence the ecological balance in the countryside . . . Could pheasant releases have a deleterious impact on species of conservation concern through increased populations of generalist predators?'[59] In answer to this question, one recent study by the British Trust for Ornithology found that *yes*, 'gamebird releases have a significant, positive effect on the abundance and population growth rate of several avian generalist predators.'[60] The solution to this problem is surely not to pepper the landscape with even more traps, but rather to reduce the number of pheasants.

Perhaps the biggest risk associated with the uncontrolled release of millions of pheasants is how they may be helping spread avian flu. In 2021, avian flu erupted around the globe, devastating populations of wild birds. It likely originated in intensive poultry farms, where millions of chickens are crammed together in unsanitary conditions: the perfect breeding-ground for mutating viruses. But in 2022, bird flu was found in seventy pheasants in Britain.[61] Battery farms, repugnant though they are, are at least hard to escape: the birds in them can be regularly tested and their movement tightly controlled. Pheasant release pens, by contrast, are designed to let pheasants move in and out. And shoots are very weakly regulated: as we'll see, there isn't even good monitoring of the numbers of pheasants kept by each shooting estate. The government belatedly recognised this in its avian flu risk assessment, when it concluded: 'the release of several millions of captive pheasants . . . has a very high likelihood of infecting one or more wild birds.'[62] This led to some temporary restrictions being placed on pheasant releases in disease control zones, although not the full moratorium that the RSPB had called for.[63]

But it's not just the scale of pheasant releases that poses problems: it's the speed with which it's happened. To better understand how we got here, we need to turn to the books of Roald Dahl.

* * *

Most people's knowledge of pheasant shooting starts and ends with Roald Dahl's wonderful novel, *Danny the Champion of the World*. In it, the eponymous Danny and his father live in poverty in an old caravan in rural England, and run a petrol station with bright red pumps. In the woods nearby, Mr Hazell – a newly rich landowner and 'roaring snob' who drives around in his Rolls-Royce and whose 'property stretched for miles' – runs a pheasant shoot: 'the best pheasant shoot in the South of England'. When the shooting season starts on 1 October every year, the great and the good descend from miles around: 'Dukes and lords, barons and baronets, wealthy businessmen and all the fancy folk in the county . . . all day long the noise of shooting rolls across the valley.'[64]

To put food on the table, Danny's father begins poaching some of the pheasants. But one night, he is snared in a trap, injuring his leg. To take revenge, Danny hatches a cunning plan to drug the landowner's flock of pheasants using raisins doped with sleeping pills. They do so, poaching 120 stunned pheasants, hiding them in their filling station, and ruining the odious Mr Hazell's shoot. When the drugs wear off, most of the pheasants fly away.

Though most of Dahl's plotlines spring from his fertile imagination, some of them also draw upon real life. So I decided to pay a visit to the village of Great Missenden, where Dahl lived and wrote for thirty years, to see if I could track down some of his inspirations.

Great Missenden lies nestled in the rolling hills and ancient woods of the Chilterns. This pretty village of wisteria-festooned cottages and rambling roses is full of rather twee homages to Dahl. The bistro café was called Matilda's, and in the churchyard where Dahl is buried, the path to his grave was marked by 'Big Friendly Giant' footprints cast in concrete. But I also saw evidence of the things that inspired his writing: there was, for instance, an old filling station in the high street complete with red pumps. And at the Roald Dahl Museum in the centre of town, a walking guide claimed that local woods 'provide the setting for the pheasant poaching scenes in *Danny the Champion of the World*'.[65]

In fact, just a few miles down the road from Great Missenden lies a famous pheasant shoot, the Hampden Shoot. Like Mr Hazell's, it is acclaimed in the shooting world: it was named as one of the top twenty shoots in the country by *The Field* magazine in 2015.[66] The land over which the shoot takes place is the 3,000-acre Hampden Estate owned by the Earl of Buckinghamshire.[67] There's an oblique reference to this in *Danny the Champion of the World*, too: at one point, Danny's father recalls poaching in his youth in 'the big forest the other side of Little Hampden which used to belong to the Duke of Buckingham'.[68] The *Earl* of Buckingham*shire* still very much owns the woods on the other side of Little Hampden. So I set out to explore the area.

Walking along country lanes down which 4x4s careened with alarming speed, I passed hedges thick with blackberries and drifts of rosebay willowherb. Red kites wheeled overhead in the golden autumn sunshine. Following a footpath past the crenellated splendour of Hampden House, I made for a section of woodland labelled 'Pheasant Pond Plantation' on my old Ordnance Survey map. There was little sign of pheasants in the wood at the time I visited: still too early in the season for them to have been released. But outside the village pub, the Hampden Arms – its sign emblazoned with the crest of the Earls of Buckinghamshire – I found a noticeboard erected by the estate. 'The Hampden Shoot', read a notice pinned to the board: 'Shooting takes place on the Hampden Estate between the months of October–January inclusive. Please be aware of this activity and take reasonable precautions when requested by shoot staff.'

So where were all the pheasants currently, I wondered, if they weren't in the wood? After a refreshing pint, I didn't have to walk far to find them. Just to the south of the Hampden Estate, I came across a field containing what looked like a prisoner-of-war camp.

Long lines of sheds with corrugated iron roofs; an outer perimeter with electric fencing; row after row of pens, each of them covered with netting on all sides. And scuttling around inside the pens were thousands upon thousands of pheasants. The inmates in this avian Colditz scurried around their compounds, pecking at their grain feeders; the air was filled with a constant cheeping and the sound of ruffled feathers. It wasn't so much Mr Hazell's pheasant shoot as Boggis' chicken farm from *Fantastic Mr Fox*.

This, I realised, was a game farm: a place for rearing pheasants prior to release. I later discovered it belonged to the Davis family, who have been breeding gamebirds here for the past four generations. The Davises' game farm, in fact, is 'the oldest in the country', according to a local historian.[69] It transpired that the current owner, George Davis, is now the chairman of the Game Farmers Association. In a blog post looking back on the development of his family's business, he observed how 'it was the start of the 1980s that saw the rise of the commercial shoots . . . more and more Syndicate shoots started to form all over the country and shooting has flourished over these last 40 years. We have been living the dream.'[70]

What may be a dream for game farmers is, however, a nightmare for the ecological balance of the countryside. Pheasant shooting has long since ceased to be about bagging a few birds for the pot; it has become a massive industry. Pheasant eggs are imported from France, and young birds reared in vast farms like the one I'd stumbled across, before being sold to estates and shooting syndicates. All of this gobbles up resources: grain, water supplies, gas heating for the pheasant coops when it's cold. In an adjacent field I found the detritus of a former set of rearing pens: a giant mound of discarded wire-mesh fencing and old plastic pheasant feed bags.

Danny the Champion of the World was written as pheasant shooting started to get out of control. Published in 1975, it's a snapshot of the countryside on the brink of change, as newly moneyed landowners like the fictional Mr Hazell began driving a massive expansion in game shoots, farms and pheasant releases. Since Roald Dahl wrote the novel, the number of 'feral' pheasants living in the British countryside has almost doubled, the number of pheasants shot has increased five-fold, and the number of pheasants released has grown ten-fold.[71] Even just returning pheasant numbers to what they were in Danny's day could make a big difference to the habitats and wildlife they're disrupting.

* * *

Surely an industry of such vast scale, expanding so dramatically in such a short space of time, would be being carefully monitored and regulated by our government? Funnily enough, no. In fact, the government barely has a handle on where pheasants are being let loose.

Pheasants have a truly bizarre legal status. When they're kept in rearing or release pens, they're classed as livestock, granting their owners some tax benefits and exemptions from certain planning controls.[72] Yet when pheasants are released into the wider countryside, they magically become wild birds, meaning they can be lawfully shot. Such legal gymnastics suit the shooting industry. But pheasants' temporary status as livestock does at least mean that owners are obliged to register the number of birds they keep with the government's Animal and Plant Health Agency (APHA), who manage the spread of animal diseases. Given how the government have recently realised that uncontrolled pheasant releases are a potential vector for avian flu, you'd have thought this would be a civic duty. Unfortunately, as I discovered, many landowners could not care less.

I uncovered this when I sent APHA a Freedom of Information request, asking them to disclose data for how many pheasants were on their register, broken down by postcode district. At first, APHA refused my request, arguing that publishing such information could allow individual estates to be identified and be in breach of data protection laws. But when I pointed out that aggregating the figures by postcode district, as I'd asked, would involve no release of personal data, they relented. What I hadn't expected was the scale of under-reporting by shooting estates. APHA's register suggested there were just 20 million pheasants being reared and released in England, an implausibly low figure given that we know some 50 million are released annually across Britain, and that most shoots are in lowland England.[73] As the government's green watchdog Natural England has since complained, the state of the official database suggests that less than a quarter of shooting estates are actually registering their birds.[74]

This is another example of how landowners don't consider themselves accountable to the public; some even consider themselves above the law. Widespread failure to register gamebird numbers has led George Davis, chair of the Game Farmers' Association, to publicly beg his industry colleagues: 'please, please register . . . Laws can be seen as a burden but [they are] there to help.'[75] Yet whilst those with an eye on the industry's future are starting to panic about law-breaking, it seems that many of the owners of pheasant shoots just don't care.

Still, the government's data did at least suggest some clear hotspots for pheasant numbers – Exmoor, North Yorkshire and the Cotswolds. A single postcode district in the North York Moors reported a staggering 1 million registered pheasants.[76] However, from the stats I'd been sent, it wasn't possible to differentiate between pheasants being *reared* on game farms and those being *released* by shooting estates. Arguably, a high number of pheasants concentrated in one Boggis-style farm is having less extensive impact on the wider countryside than big shoots where they're being unleashed en masse. Having been tipped off by a land agent that the southern edge of Exmoor National Park is a hotbed of pheasant shoots, I decided to focus on this region, and see if I could uncover more about these estates than the government cares to know.

I'm a big fan of 'Open Source Intelligence' (or 'OSINT') methods of investigative journalism, in which journalists make use of the wealth of digital data now in the public domain. Thinking along these lines, I realised that it might be feasible to locate large pheasant shoots just by using Google Earth. Grouse moors are obvious from above: their chequerboard pattern of burn scars means they show up easily in aerial imagery. Pheasant shoots are less dramatic, but once you know what you're looking for, they start to leap out of the landscape. Scrolling around Google's aerial photos of Exmoor, some tell-tale patterns started to emerge: I kept spotting rectangular blocks of fencing, each containing a structure like a hen coop. Pheasant release pens, it turns out, are visible from outer space – as are the game crops planted nearby as supplementary feed.

Using this method, I was able to pinpoint no fewer than 180 pheasant release pens and 91 plantations of game cover crops in the Exmoor region, the majority of them within the boundaries of the national park itself. Doing this by eye alone, I'll undoubtedly have missed a lot – no doubt more could be uncovered through 'machine learning', by training a computer program to sift through aerial imagery looking for these patterns. What this approach also misses is what *can't* be seen from above: all the release pens hidden from plain sight under the canopies of woods, not to mention all the invasive rhododendron and cherry laurel planted in these forests as game cover. One study suggests pheasant release pens have enclosed a staggering 1 per cent of all the woodland in England.[77] Nevertheless, zooming out to view my map of Exmoor in its entirety, a clear picture emerged of a landscape littered with pheasant shoots.[78]

A GWCT report noted a decade ago that there are sixty-three game shoots on and around Exmoor, covering almost 100,000 acres of land.[79] The Exmoor Society, a charity devoted to the preservation of the national park, has expressed concern that game shooting has 'grown significantly on Exmoor over the last 20 years', meaning that 'greater ecological impact is inevitable'. It criticises the increasing impact of shoots on the beauty of Exmoor's landscapes, alongside the plastic litter from expended shotgun cartridges, and the 'infantry battle noise' of shoot days.[80]

The Exmoor National Park Authority has recently mapped the extent of shooting estates within its boundaries, finding far more shooting infrastructure than my own amateur efforts. Its maps show over *seven hundred* pheasant rearing and release sheds and shelters, and a similar number of fields planted with game crops.[81] Its report concludes that 'pheasant rearing and shooting takes place over about one third of the National Park', warning that 'high numbers of bird releases in commercial shoots leads to significant impact in localised areas' – from damaging woodland flora to destabilising riverbanks. But as the national park authority notes, there are few sanctions that can be brought to bear: 'there are currently no regulations to ensure land managers avoid, minimise, restore or compensate for negative environmental impacts of intensive game bird shooting.'[82]

Spoiled for choice, I decided to visit one of Exmoor's shooting hotspots: an area that one local estate boasts as being Devon's 'famous shooting triangle'.[83] The drive took me along narrow country lanes, fringed with beech trees, to Exmoor's southern edge. Here the terrain rises steeply from the in-bye farmland up to the moorland edge, its slopes bisected by deep coombes thronged with damp woodland. This is temperate rainforest country, but it's prized by the shooting fraternity for another reason: it's the perfect topography for high-flying pheasants, which supposedly make for a more exciting and challenging shoot.

I'd come to the 6,000-acre Molland Estate, having identified it in my mapping analysis as having a high concentration of pheasants. The land here belonged to the Throckmorton baronets for eight hundred years, and most recently to Elizabeth Throckmorton up until her death in 2017; since then, the estate has been run by the family trust. In a delicious twist of fate, Elizabeth's sister Felicity married Roald Dahl.[84]

I parked in the village of Molland, where every house is painted in the estate's green colour scheme, and the village pub has as its emblem – you guessed it – a proudly strutting pheasant. A family of sparrows chirruped loudly from the eaves of a thatched cottage; a swallow's nest clung to the porch roof of the ancient church, three tiny beaks poking out the top. But as I ventured out into the wider countryside, one bird species above all made its presence known. The surrounding coombes reverberated, continually and insistently, with the *tuk-tuk-tuk* of male pheasants.

Wending my way up the valleys, I was struck by just how many areas had been fenced off for gamebirds; how many fields had been planted with feed crops like maize. Entire pastures scattered with plastic pheasant feeders. Electric fencing. Discarded game feed bags. Pheasant feathers, disembodied pheasant wings, the corpse of an unlucky bird caught in netting. And descending into the valley woodlands, I was dismayed to find the understorey being choked by rhododendron, clearly planted as game cover.

The company that markets the Molland Shoot calls this area 'unspoiled'.[85] But this was a landscape designed and built for shooting – a landscape wrecked by it.

Yet this is also a landscape that, until recently, was propped up with a tax break from the government. The Molland Estate is listed in the HM Revenue & Customs 'tax-exempt heritage assets' scheme.[86] Set up in the 1980s, it's designed to free the owners of so-called 'heritage assets' from paying inheritance tax. Around three hundred landowners currently benefit from it: some have entered their art collections, some their stately homes, others their entire estates. In return for the tax break, the owners have to do two things. First, they have to grant the public some degree of access. That makes sense when it's a private house or art collection not normally on public display. But for many of the large landholdings entered into the scheme, access is now a legal obligation anyway: the moors that comprise a large chunk of the Molland Estate have been subject to a public right to roam for the last twenty years. Second, the owners have to promise to 'look after' the land. To qualify as a heritage asset it must be 'land of outstanding natural beauty and spectacular views', or be of 'outstanding scientific interest, including special areas for the conservation of wildlife, plants and trees'.[87] So how come sprawling pheasant shoots get to qualify for this tax break?

A raft of shooting estates appear to be benefiting from this wizard wheeze: from the Hampden Estate near Dahl's Great Missenden, to the Newburgh Priory Estate in Yorkshire, famed for its pheasants; to half a dozen grouse moors in the north of England.[88] It may be, of course, that these estates *are* delivering good value to the taxpayer, in return for not paying inheritance tax. The trouble is, the taxpayer will struggle to find out. Hardly anyone has even heard of the scheme; and the 'Undertakings' and 'Management Plans' that estates have to draw up to prove to the taxman that they're looking after the land are not published anywhere. Nor do HMRC publish any reports on the scheme's effectiveness.

I contacted the Molland Estate to ask them for these documents. A land agent replied on behalf of the estate, explaining that following the death of Mrs Throckmorton in 2017, her executors were still negotiating a renewal of the deal with HMRC. Fair enough; but what had the estate been doing to qualify for this tax break in the first place? I was sent a three-page document listing the agreed undertakings, but these pertained mostly to things like footpath maintenance, rather than habitat conservation. Did the estate have a management plan, I asked? 'We do indeed have a management plan,' came the reply. 'Please can you explain your interest in the plan as it is not a document that the Estate normally circulate outside the people involved in the management for the Estate?'

We all have an interest in how the countryside is managed, not least when it's being supported through tax relief. The government should make the publication of these plans mandatory, so that landowners can be held accountable if they fail to keep their promises. They should also attach more exacting rules to the tax breaks, obliging landowners to genuinely enhance biodiversity and store carbon. If it turns out that landowners have been exploiting these tax breaks to prop up large pheasant shoots and other environmentally questionable enterprises, the scheme should be abolished. Inheritance tax, after all, is only paid by the wealthiest 4 per cent of society.[89] Surely the least we should expect from the self-appointed custodians of the countryside is some transparency about what they're doing in return for generous tax breaks.

In recent years, a few champions of the world have tried to take on the pheasant plague. In 2019, conservationists Chris Packham, Ruth Tingay and Mark Avery set up Wild Justice, a group dedicated to using the legal system to fight for nature. One of their first cases was about pheasants.

In particular, the founders of Wild Justice were concerned about the effect that massive pheasant releases were having on the country's most important nature reserves. Under the Habitats Regulations – a piece of EU law that has been preserved post-Brexit and remains in force – many of Britain's best wildlife sites are protected as Special Areas of Conservation (SACs).

In practice, this means pretty much the same habitats as are protected as SSSIs. The law requires that any 'plan or project' that could affect these protected sites – such as building a road or housing nearby – has to be rigorously assessed by the UK government. But, as Wild Justice discovered, no such assessment had been made for the huge numbers of pheasants disgorged annually in the vicinity of these nature reserves.

Wild Justice promptly took the government to court to demand they properly monitor and regulate pheasant releases. As Chris Packham said at the time: 'What is blindingly obvious to anyone with even a basic understanding of natural sciences is that dumping at least 50 million non-native birds into the UK countryside will have a profound effect on its ecology – it's about time we measured what that effect is.'[90] The government squirmed, realising it had been caught with its pants down. But it was forced to carry out an analysis confirming that some 50 million pheasants were released each year, and that *yes*, this could be having a detrimental impact on protected nature sites.[91] Landowners, it turned out, could not simply be trusted to be good stewards: in these circumstances, they would have to be regulated.

As a result of Wild Justice's successful legal challenges, the government put in place a new system of regulation for pheasant releases in and around nature reserves. Pheasants were added to Schedule 9 of the Wildlife and Countryside Act 1981, which lists non-native species like grey squirrels and muntjac deer, mandating that they 'may not be released or allowed to escape into the wild unless authorised by a licence'.[92] For pheasants, the requirement for a release licence only applied in specific circumstances – if the release took place in an SAC nature reserve, or within 500 metres of one. Nevertheless, this was an historic victory: a rare admission by a Conservative government that their landowning mates couldn't just be left to their own devices.

But true to form, the government made sure that the new regulations were exceedingly light touch. Landowners wouldn't have to apply specially for a new licence – they were merely bound by its terms if the circumstances applied to them. Nor were the terms exactly onerous: the owner would have to limit pheasant numbers to 1,000 birds per hectare if releasing within half a kilometre of an SAC, or 700 birds per hectare if within the nature reserve itself. And they would have to send a short report about the number and density of gamebirds released to Natural England.[93] Even this, it turned out, would be too much of a faff for some estates.

In a quirk of history, the issue of free-roaming pheasants soon became intertwined with a battle over the public's right to roam. In January 2023, Alexander Darwall, a wealthy hedge fund manager and owner of the 4,000-acre Blachford Estate in Devon, won a court case that ended the public's right to wild camp on Dartmoor. In Scotland, you can wild camp pretty much everywhere – but England, of course, is far more uptight about these things. Up until that point, Dartmoor had been the only place in England where there was a legal right to wild camp, thanks to the Dartmoor Commons Act 1985 – everywhere else, it was against the law. Darwall argued that no such right existed. Landowners were, he argued audaciously, 'responsible for looking after the land and the environment',[94] and camping could result in litter and damage to the land. A High Court judge agreed with him, and the right to wild camp on Dartmoor came to an abrupt end.[95]

It just so happened that the Blachford Estate also boasted a major pheasant shoot.[96] Every year, it played host to the Cornwood Shoot, and the estate's woods and coombes were filled with the sounds of rich people blasting away at gamebirds. When it first came to light that Alexander Darwall was launching his legal challenge to wild camping, a group of local Devon residents, myself included, began organising protests on his estate. On our wild camping expeditions and trespasses, we stumbled across a large pheasant release pen in a woodland owned by the Blachford Estate. Pheasants were milling around on either side of the wire-mesh netting, entering and exiting the pen through numerous openings in the fencing. This release pen, it transpired, lay just 250 metres from the edge of Dendles Wood National Nature Reserve – part of the Dartmoor Special Area of Conservation. Pheasants were being released, in other words, in circumstances caught by the new licensing regime. But were the terms of the licence being adhered to?

I decided to investigate. A conservation volunteer told me that 'as a result of inevitable overspill, pheasants are one of the most common birds' in Dendles Wood. I sent an FOI request to Natural England, asking for any information they held on pheasant releases near Dendles Wood and the Dartmoor SAC: surely, I reasoned, they would have to at least hold some figures on pheasant numbers, as this was one of the conditions of the new licence. But when the response came back, I was told: 'there is no correspondence held between Natural England, Blachford Estate and/or the Darwalls concerning the release of pheasants in and around Dendles Wood NNR.'

Perturbed, I dug further. I asked Natural England to release their various reports relating to Dendles Wood and the ecological pressures it was under. One report stated that 'operations likely to damage the special interest' of Dendles Wood included 'the release into the site of any wild, feral or domestic animal'.[97] Natural England could, meanwhile, confirm that shooting rights over it were 'currently held by the Blachford Estate', and that 'the extent and scale of the shoot was undetermined at the time of writing, due to a request for its consent being uncompleted.' It listed 'overstocking with pheasants' as a factor in the wood's management. Most ominously, it noted that Dendles Wood was one of only a handful of sites in England and Wales home to the vanishingly rare Blue Ground Beetle, a species distinct to our temperate rainforests – and warned that 'high pheasant stocking rates are a threat to this species', because pheasants like to eat beetles.[98]

I later passed this information to the *Guardian*. 'The landowner who took Dartmoor National Park to court to ban wild camping may be putting a rare beetle at risk by releasing pheasants next to an ecologically important woodland,' read the ensuing news story, which noted the irony: 'This is despite him having said he pushed for a wild camping ban in order to "improve conservation of the Dartmoor commons".'[99]

I also shared what I'd found with Wild Justice, who decided to make Darwall's shooting estate a test case for whether pheasant licensing was being properly enforced by the government. They sent legal letters to Natural England and DEFRA, seeking evidence that the Blachford Estate had complied with the conditions of the licence. But when the government finally responded, they admitted they'd received 'no notification . . . of any releases of gamebirds within 500m of the Dartmoor Special Area of Conservation in either 2021 or 2022'. As Wild Justice concluded: 'We believe that such releases have taken place and failure to notify Natural England is a serious matter.' But not so serious a matter, it seemed, that the government wished to do anything about it. 'Defra does not carry out proactive compliance monitoring in relation to the general licences that it issues', Wild Justice were told.[100]

Six months later, when the Dartmoor wild camping ban was challenged on appeal, Darwall lost, and the right to wild camp on the moor was reinstated. Public protest had won the day. But the landowner's reaction was a telling one. A spokesperson for the Darwall family expressed their disappointment at the ruling, claiming: 'Our mission was to conserve this special place. It is regrettable that our role as custodians is greatly diminished.'[101]

The Darwalls have now taken their case to the Supreme Court, with a hearing scheduled for October 2024. At the time of writing, the fate of wild camping on Dartmoor still hangs in the balance. Britain's vast pheasant population, meanwhile, continues to roam free. It's one rule for the pheasants, it seems, and another for us.

7

Nature's Whistleblowers

Lately, whenever I see a KEEP OUT sign in the countryside, I wonder what it's hiding.

The countryside guards its secrets closely. Much of its architecture has been designed to exclude the public. Sometimes the exclusions are stark: a high stone wall surrounding an estate, topped with shards of broken glass; a barbed-wire fence, accompanied by menacing signs threatening trespassers with prosecution. Other times these invisible lines of power are occluded by the pleasing blur of a hedgerow. The effect is the same: you stick to the narrow footpath, and walk on by. But what's happening on the other side of the fence?

Sometimes, landowners really don't want you to know. That's what a group of us discovered when we walked in the Duke of Somerset's woods at Berry Pomeroy in Devon. The Duke owns 2,800 acres of countryside bordering the town of Totnes, including a large expanse of woodland used as a pheasant shoot. A single footpath wends its way along the northern fringe of these woods, connecting a nearby hamlet with the estate's ruined castle, but it's a permissive path – that is, the public only have permission to use it at the discretion of the landowner. During the shooting season, the path is sometimes closed. The woods beyond are off-limits to the people of Totnes and other nearby villages.

In the aftermath of the coronavirus pandemic, a group of Totnes residents – myself included – began organising monthly trespasses. After being hemmed in by repeated lockdowns, doing the same short walks day in and day out, we wanted to see more of the beautiful Devon countryside. Much of it, we knew, was out of bounds. We count ourselves lucky that we have Dartmoor nearby, where there's a public right of access over large tracts of heath and bog. But such 'open access land' covers just 8 per cent of England, mostly in remote parts of the uplands. Over the other 92 per cent, the right to roam does not apply. Forestry plantations owned by the Forestry Commission are generally accessible, but the same is not true of privately owned woods – such as those belonging to the Duke of Somerset.

To protest about this lack of access, our group decided to stage a mass trespass of the Duke's woods. We were pleasantly surprised when around two hundred people showed up on one sunny Sunday in May 2022. Gathering on the edge of the woods next to a sign proclaiming NO RIGHT OF WAY, the crowd proceeded, with trepidation, into the unknown.

By following a forestry track, edged with late bluebells and wild garlic, we made sure to minimise any impact caused by our trespass. The same could not be said for the pheasant shoot that operated in the wood, signs of which were everywhere. Large areas had been fenced off for a pheasant release pen, within which the ground flora had been worn away by the pecking and scurrying of flocks of game birds. Shooting detritus littered the wood: plastic shotgun cartridges, bits of plastic fencing, discarded plastic gamefeed bags – all breaking down and shedding their microplastics into the ecosystem. 'Please dispose of this sack carefully & keep our environment tidy', read one of the bags. 'Support the Code of Good Shooting Practice.' So much for the custodians of the countryside. We picked up all the litter we found and continued on our way.

A grassy meadow next to the wood seemed like a good place to stop for a bite to eat. Everyone got out their sandwiches and listened to my friends Chris and Kimwei play folk songs on fiddle and guitar. But perhaps we should have been singing the lyrics to the Teddy Bears' Picnic: *If you go down to the woods today, you're sure of a big surprise . . .*

'Oh. My. God . . .'

I looked up from lunch to see my pal Jules returning, ashen-faced, from the nearby hedgerow. 'I just went for a pee behind that hedge,' she said. 'But . . . you have to come and see what I found.'

Behind the hawthorns, the ground fell away into a disused quarry. Into the hole had been tipped a huge pile of wire fencing, corrugated iron sheets and old washing machines. And on top of this mound of trash were the rotting carcasses of scores of dead pheasants. We had found a mass grave of birds discarded by the shoot.

We stared down into the pit in disgust. It's one thing to shoot game for the table; quite another to kill birds and simply throw them away. Besides the senseless slaughter, there's the sheer wanton waste. Releasing 50 million pheasants a year into Britain's woods and fields already has huge environmental consequences, as we've seen. Habitats are trashed, food webs distorted, countless predators shot and trapped. All this – and then to not even eat the damn pheasants . . . I shook with anger.

The following week, I got a call from Devon police's wildlife crime officer, who had seen my post about the incident on Twitter. They promised to investigate, but I never heard back from them. In all likelihood, no laws had been broken. It was, however, a clear breach of the shooting industry's Code of Good Shooting Practice, referred to on the discarded plastic sack we'd found. The Code is unequivocal on this matter: 'All shot game must be regarded as food.'[1] Clearly, not all shoots bother to follow the Code. After all, the sheer scale of pheasant releasing these days far exceeds the appetite for roast pheasant. And what we'd found was far from unique. In 2019, *The Times* obtained video footage of a digger unloading dozens of pheasant carcasses into a pit at a game farm in Leicestershire.[2] In December 2023, over a hundred dead pheasants were found dumped in Wales.[3]

Our trespass had momentarily drawn back the veil of secrecy that cloaks much of the countryside. It's hard to shake the sense that many landowners keep the public out of their estates because they don't want them to see what goes on behind the high walls and barbed-wire fences. When we, the great unwashed, occasionally get to look behind the curtain, it threatens the myth of their benign custodial role.

Indeed, the whole narrative of stewardship is about maintaining the authority of the few who own land, and those they employ. As the former gamekeeper for the 10th Earl of Shaftesbury put it: 'Country people should be allowed to control the balance of the countryside.'[4] Such views are widespread: the slogan of the National Gamekeepers' Organisation is 'Keeping the Balance'.[5] The reality, of course, is somewhat different. Whether it's through moorland burning, exterminating predators or releasing millions of non-native pheasants into the countryside, gamekeepers and the landowners they work for have fundamentally upset the balance of nature.

But this reality is seldom seen, because of the physical and legal barriers that the masters of the countryside have erected to keep out prying eyes. And whenever the wider public dares to voice concerns about what goes on, there's a furious backlash from landed power. As the veteran environmental campaigner Chris Rose says, there is 'an ancient English cultural divide, about who has the right to determine what happens to wildlife in the countryside: landowners or the public?'[6]

This chapter is about that cultural divide: about how the public have been shut out of the countryside, and in the process denied a say over how it's managed. It's a divide with deep roots. It dates back to the violent expulsion of the public from the land.

Between the first parliamentary Enclosure Act in 1604 and the last in 1914, some 6.8 million acres of common land were enclosed – a fifth of all England.[7] The gentry driving forward the land grab grew rich off the new estates they acquired. As the historian E.P. Thompson put it, 'Enclosure (when all the sophistications are allowed for) was a plain enough case of class robbery.'[8] The dispossessed put up a stiff resistance – from the Fen Tigers to Gerrard Winstanley's Diggers – but failed to halt it. Those who had depended on the commons for their existence were pushed off the land, flocking instead to the towns and cities.

But enclosure didn't just upend livelihoods. It also dramatically changed the way many people related to the rest of the living world. To understand how enclosure disconnected the population from the rest of nature, we can turn to the Romantic poet John Clare.

Clare was the son of a farm labourer, and grew up in rural Northamptonshire at the end of the eighteenth century. He spent an idyllic childhood wandering freely about his patch of countryside, exploring every corner, revelling in nature's beauty. Clare's poetry and prose is suffused with this deep love of place. He would spend hours searching for the source of a nightingale's 'out-sobbing songs',[9] and spent his youth 'running into the woods to hunt strawberries or stealing peas in church time'. On one day's excursions, he so lost track of time that he was only prompted to turn back upon hearing 'the hedge cricket whispering the hour of waking spirits was at hand'. 'I grew so much into the quiet love of nature's presence,' Clare wrote, 'that I was never easy but when I was in the fields.'[10] But then, in 1809, an Enclosure Act was passed which would transform the landscape of his birth.

'Thus came enclosure – ruin was its guide,' wrote John Clare in a later poem, relating how the enclosers took an axe to a beautiful elm tree that he had cherished.[11] Clare lamented how 'Inclosure . . . levelled every bush and tree and levelled every hill / And hung the moles for traitors – though the brook is running still'.[12] Old common pastures and open heathlands were enclosed, ploughed up and reseeded in the name of agricultural improvement. When a patch of uncultivated land near his home was dug up for a quarry, Clare imagined himself as the land itself, torn asunder by the land-grabbers. 'And me they turned inside out,' he wrote, 'For sand and grit and stones / And turned my old green hills about / And pickt my very bones'.[13]

Enclosure not only destroyed habitats directly; it also destroyed people's access to nature. In 'The Moors' (1820), Clare recounted that before the commons were enclosed, 'Unbounded freedom ruled the wandering scene / Nor fence of ownership crept in between'. But with enclosure's advent, 'Fence now meets

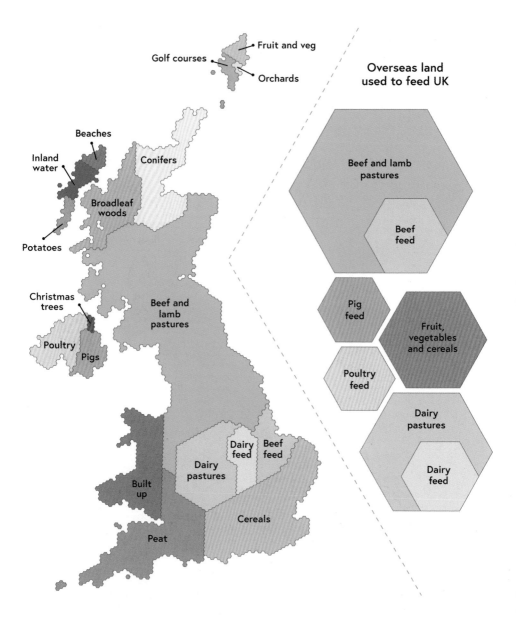

Labels on map:
Fruit and veg
Golf courses
Orchards
Beaches
Inland water
Conifers
Broadleaf woods
Potatoes
Christmas trees
Poultry
Pigs
Beef and lamb pastures
Built up
Dairy pastures
Dairy feed
Beef feed
Cereals
Peat

Overseas land used to feed UK
Beef and lamb pastures
Beef feed
Pig feed
Fruit, vegetables and cereals
Poultry feed
Dairy pastures
Dairy feed

How the UK uses its land. This graphic, produced by the National Food Strategy in 2021, shows how agriculture dominates our land use, compared to woodlands and built-up areas. Livestock farming, in particular, takes up a vast amount of land – both in the UK and overseas, to supply our imports. (The location of each land use category is not to be taken literally: Orkney, for instance, is not a giant golf course.)

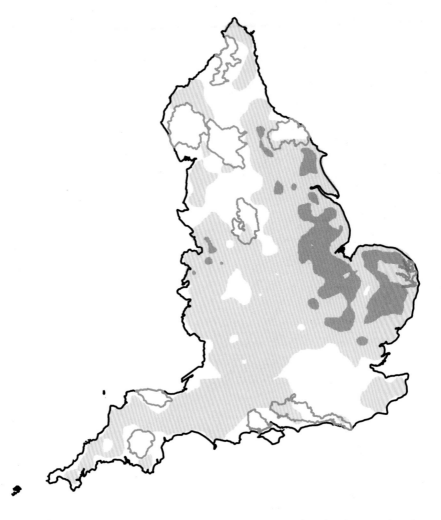

A map of England showing the most and least productive farmland, using data from the National Food Strategy 2021. In the areas coloured dark orange, we produce a third of our total calories; areas shaded light orange are medium-productivity; while in the areas left blank, we produce hardly any food. Sparing 21% of our least productive farmland for nature would mean producing only 3% fewer calories. The green lines show the locations of our national parks, which largely coincide with our least productive farmland – clearly, these places should be prioritised for nature.

Custodians of the countryside? Damage wrought to the River Lugg Site of Special Scientific Interest by one of its landowners, which resulted, unusually, in prosecution and a jail sentence.

Stewards of the land? Upland peat bogs are a vast natural carbon store. Yet every year wealthy grouse moor owners persist in the practice of moorland burning, damaging this vital national asset.

Lowland peat soils emit some 7.6 million tonnes of CO_2e per year. This field in the Fens is owned by the Church Commissioners. One of the missions of the Church of England is to 'safeguard creation'.

Each year, shooting estates release around 50 million non-native pheasants into the British countryside – weighing more than the breeding biomass of the *entire* British wild bird population.

When the Nature Conservancy Council dared to designate part of the Somerset Levels as a Site of Special Scientific Interest in the early 1980s, angry farmers made straw effigies of conservationists, strung them up from a makeshift gallows, and set them alight.

'Where landowners have failed, river guardians need to step into the gap.' Volunteers from the River Roding Trust help clear plastic waste choking a tributary of this neglected river in east London.

'Make it wild or make it ours!' Campaigners from the group Wild Card lay down the gauntlet to the royal Duchy of Cornwall, the single largest landowner in Dartmoor National Park, in a protest organised outside their offices.

In Britain, national parks are not owned by the nation. In January 2023, thousands of people protested against wealthy landowner Alexander Darwall, whose legal cases have sought to end the public's right to wild camp in Dartmoor National Park. We have a right to roam over just 8% of England.

Common land, which once covered vast swathes of the country, has mostly been enclosed by landowners. But in the Scottish town of Langholm, residents each year take part in the Common Riding, a celebration of their ancient rights of common over nearby land.

The land for the people. Local residents celebrate their purchase of the Isle of Eigg in 1997, the first Scottish community to clear a laird from his land, rather than the other way around.

'Everything you can see, from here to the horizon, is now owned by the community.' In 2021, Langholm Moor – a 10,000-acre former grouse moor belonging to the Duke of Buccleuch – was acquired by the people of Langholm in a community buyout. It is now being turned into a nature reserve.

fence in owners' little bounds . . . Each little tyrant with his little sign / Shows where man claims earth'.[14] This was Clare presciently protesting at the 'Keep Out – Private Property' signs that now cover the English countryside like a malignant fungus.

As the Victorian era dawned, Clare was committed to an asylum. His 'madness' may have resulted from a blow to the head, or even malaria. But as the environmentalist George Monbiot suggests, 'a contributing factor must have been the loss of almost all he knew and loved'.[15] Shut off from much of the landscape of his youth by the activities of the enclosers, and powerless to prevent its destruction, Clare would have felt utterly despondent. When I interviewed George for *The Land* magazine some years ago, he spoke about his admiration for John Clare's poetry, and what it revealed about life during enclosure. 'I realised that this was exactly the same process that I'd seen happening amongst indigenous people,' he told me. 'Alienation and anomie leading to psychic rupture. And then I realised that what I'd witnessed there is still with us here, in Britain today.'[16]

Clare was only the most eloquent observer of a process that affected millions. At the start of the nineteenth century, two-thirds of the population of England and Wales lived in rural areas. By its close, three-quarters of the populace lived in towns and cities.[17] Enclosure was one driver of this: the mechanisation of agriculture and craftwork was another push factor. The introduction of new-fangled threshing machines threatened to put many landless agricultural labourers out of work. For some, already immiserated by the loss of the common fields as a means of subsistence, this was the last straw. The 'Swing Riots' of 1830 saw a mass uprising of landworkers across south-east England. Gathering under the banner of a mythical folk hero, 'Captain Swing', thousands of rural labourers marched upon landowners' houses, set fire to hayricks and smashed threshing machines.[18]

Though the Swing riots were suppressed, they left a lasting folk-memory. Thomas Hardy's *Tess of the d'Urbervilles*, written later in the century, recalls the era of Captain Swing with its account of a 'despotic' threshing machine. Hardy described urbanisation as 'the process, humorously designated by statisticians as the "tendency of the rural population towards the large towns," being really the tendency of water to flow uphill when forced by machinery'.[19] And Captain Swing left another legacy: a gnawing fear amongst landowners that any large mass of people gathering in the countryside was a mob coming to get them.

Though the urban public of Victorian Britain were newly cut off from the countryside, they never lost their innate love of nature. City-dwellers no longer depended on the land for their livelihoods, but they still cared deeply about having access to it. Some yearned for the rural life they had left behind. The Labour politician Walter Southgate, born in Hackney in 1890, recalled how his mother tended a small patch of grass in their backyard because it reminded her 'of the country'.[20] In the last third of the nineteenth century, the anti-enclosure movement was rekindled in the fight to save London's last green spaces from being fenced off and despoiled. Local residents organised huge demonstrations to protest against the planned enclosure and development of Epping Forest.[21] In 1897, thousands of people gathered to rip down the fencing that had been erected around the open space of One Tree Hill near Peckham.[22] As Octavia Hill, the founder of the National Trust, wrote: 'the need of quiet, the need of air, the need of exercise, and . . . the sight of sky and of things growing seem human needs, common to all'.[23]

Urban Britons also began to demand access to the wider countryside, beyond the city limits. The early socialist movement in Britain, for instance, didn't just want fair pay: it also campaigned for workers to have more leisure time, cleaner air, and access to the outdoors. One such campaigner was the journalist Robert Blatchford, whose enormously popular book *Merrie England* sold two million copies. In the book, a collection of essays on socialism, Blatchford railed against living conditions in the industrial cities, which he decried as being 'ugly, and dirty, and smoky', and urged his readers to reach for 'pure air, bright skies, clear rivers, clean streets, and beautiful fields, woods, and gardens . . . you know that all these things are well worth having'.[24] Reminding the urban working class of the injustices done to their rural ancestors by enclosure, he argued that 'the land of England should be restored to the English people from whom it was stolen.'[25]

The millions who agreed with this vision were inspired to take action. Some formed the Clarion Cycling Clubs, distributing copies of Blatchford's *Clarion* newspaper to rural villages whilst enjoying a ride in the country on the recently invented bicycle. Others set up rambling groups and began organising weekend hikes into the countryside.[26] But many soon found that landowners' fences and trespass laws stood in their way. One of the earliest – and largest – mass trespasses in Britain was the Winter Hill Trespass of 1896, when thousands of Bolton residents marched to reclaim an ancient right of way blocked by the owner of a grouse moor.[27] The popularity of rambling exploded in the interwar period. Cheaper rail fares and a steady reduction in working hours combined with mass membership of groups like the Scouts and Woodcraft Folk to tempt many to set foot in the great outdoors. There was even a brief fad for midnight hiking: in 1932, the country writer S.P.B. Mais led a vast crowd on a moonlit walk to Chanctonbury Ring in Sussex.[28] The Kinder Scout mass trespass that same year is only the most famous of the rambling movement's direct actions, and far from being the biggest. Later that summer, 10,000 people rallied at Winnats Pass in the Peak District to demand a new Access to Mountains Bill.[29]

New laws did follow swiftly, but so did the backlash from landowners. The Rights of Way Act 1932, for instance, made it easier for a public right of way to be established through customary use. But it also contained a poison pill clause. At the last minute, the landowning Lord Strachie tabled an amendment to the Bill enabling landowners to protect their estates from future rights of way claims. A landowner need simply deposit a map of their landholdings with the local council, showing existing footpaths, and state their intention that no further rights of way be dedicated.[30] This provision was updated and strengthened in subsequent laws passed in 1980 and 2013.[31] Little known by the public, it has enabled landowners to prevent the creation of rights of way over hundreds of thousands of acres of England.[32]

The landowners also crafted a new narrative: that if the public were let into the countryside, they would mess it up. Mobs of ramblers in walking boots, clutching Ordnance Survey maps, might not be quite as threatening as Captain Swing's rioting peasants, but they still posed a challenge to the landed order. 'Townsmen seem to have the mentality of serfs,' ran one 1936 article in *Country Life*, the magazine of the landed gentry. 'They act as uneducated slaves might be expected to act when suddenly liberated. They have no sense of responsibility towards the countryside.'[33]

Landowners, by contrast, cast themselves as responsible stewards, a bulwark against rampaging hordes of townies with their litter and uncouth manners. Lord Horder, owner of the Ashford Chace Estate, set up the Anti-Noise League and suggested the urban public be shepherded into 'a national park with cheap trains and buses to and fro, where these primitive and immature citizens may be let loose, to yell and make other noises to their hearts' content'.[34] As the historian Hannah Rose Woods writes, 'rural social elites were presenting themselves as the guardians of natural beauty, casting nostalgic appeals to an older view of the countryside as their own privileged preserve as impartial environmentalism'.[35]

Yet it was urban ramblers who first proposed the idea of having a Countryside Code to guide public behaviour in rural areas. As the writer and access campaigner C.E.M. Joad observed as early as 1934, ramblers were already starting to self-police their community. 'Most walkers are reverent towards the countryside,' he wrote. 'They have a passion for the closing of gates, hunt litter like sleuths, pounce like hawks upon orange peel.' Joad suggested 'a special code of townsmen's manners in the country' to educate those not so diligent. It was unsurprising, he argued – a touch paternalistically – that some townsfolk did not know how to behave. 'You debar them, generation after generation, from every sound and sight of Nature. How can you expect them to know how to treat her?'[36]

Groups like the Ramblers Association and Council for the Protection of Rural England (CPRE) began circulating codes of conduct to their members in the 1930s, well before the government picked up the baton.[37] In 1951, the first official 'Country Code', as it was then called, was published by the new National Parks Commission. Simply worded and pleasingly illustrated, this slim volume set out ten sensible rules for responsible countryside access, including 'leave no litter', 'keep dogs under proper control' and 'fasten all gates'. But there was no mistaking that the Country Code was a one-sided contract – aimed at policing townsfolk, rather than setting out mutual responsibilities shared by landowners. 'If the simple rules of conduct laid down here are neglected by visitors to the country,' intoned the foreword sternly, '. . . the farmer will regard the holiday maker from town as his enemy.' An engraving at the end of the Code depicted a wooden sign bearing the instruction RESPECT THE LIFE OF THE COUNTRYSIDE, rather menacingly entwined with barbed wire.[38]

Despite these precautions, the 'townies will mess up the countryside' narrative returned with a vengeance in the late 1990s, during the debates over introducing a partial right to roam in England and Wales. In its 1997 election manifesto, the Labour Party had pledged to create 'greater freedom for people to explore our open countryside', whilst adding: 'We will not, however, permit any abuse of a right to greater access.'[39] Such reasonable language nevertheless provoked consternation from some landowners. At a public meeting, the Earl of Macclesfield told an astonished audience: 'The countryside cannot accommodate humans on the loose.'[40] One regional secretary of the Country Landowners' Association informed a local newspaper: 'We don't want all and sundry roaming over our land, especially not criminals, drug pushers and vandals.' Indeed, the CLA at the time seemed to think that all rural crime originated in urban areas. Another spokesperson told the *Farmers Guardian* they feared a right to roam would open the door to 'vandals, sheep stealers, badger baiters, horse slashers, illegal hare coursers, poaching gangs, birds' egg thieves and those responsible for a rising tide of crime in rural areas, many of them forced out of the towns and cities by improved policing and surveillance techniques'.[41]

The absurdity of such arguments was neatly skewered by Gordon Prentice, the Labour MP for Pendle, who had long championed responsible public access to the outdoors. 'We are told that we cannot have the right to roam because of the terrible damage that we would do,' he said during a House of Commons debate on access legislation in 1999. 'We are also told that the landowners are the true guardians of the countryside. They are holding it in trust for tomorrow, and the rest of us are all wreckers.' The reality, he argued, was rather different:

> . . . walkers and ramblers have not poisoned the countryside with pesticides. We have not polluted the water courses. We have not silenced the countryside as the birds have perished. We are not responsible for grubbing up the hedgerows and damaging biodiversity. But the landowners point an accusing finger at us and say that, if the measure goes through, we would damage or destroy the delicate ecology of the countryside that they maintain and preserve.[42]

Prentice would later find himself topping a 'Most Wanted' list produced by a group that claimed to speak for rural Britain.[43] The Countryside Alliance was formed in 1997 to contest the incoming Labour government's plans to ban fox hunting. For a while, the Countryside Alliance could reasonably claim to represent a significant section of rural opinion. Its huge 'Liberty and Livelihood' march of 2002 tapped into widespread anger in the countryside about everything from the closure of rural post offices to the government's handling of the foot and mouth disease crisis.[44] But like many populist movements of the right, it was bankrolled by the wealthy. An investigation by the *Sunday Times* in 2004 found that some of the largest donors to the Countryside Alliance were the Duke of Westminster, the Duke of Northumberland and the Duke of Bedford.[45]

Twenty years on, the Countryside Alliance appears to speak increasingly for the 1 per cent of the population who own half the land, rather than a broader segment of rural society. Nowhere is this clearer than on the issue of access to nature. When New

Labour introduced a partial right to roam through the Countryside and Rights of Way (CRoW) Act 2000, the Countryside Alliance supported the policy, recognising its popularity in the country at large.[46] But its previously sure-footed political instincts seem to have since departed.

In 2020, with my friend Nick Hayes, the author and illustrator, I co-founded the Right to Roam campaign. We began organising mass trespasses to highlight the cause, and soon the campaign team and its mailing list grew greatly. Our starting point was that the CRoW Act represented unfinished business. Whilst it was a step forward, it created a right of access over only 8 per cent of England, mainly to upland areas – mountains, moors, heaths and downs – remote from where most people lived. By contrast, for the past twenty years, people in Scotland have enjoyed a default right of public access to the majority of land and water, to be exercised responsibly and with sensible exceptions for places like private gardens and fields of crops. A Scottish Outdoor Access Code sets out the rights and responsibilities of both landowners and the public. Why not legislate for the same in England?

The current chief executive of the Countryside Alliance, Tim Bonner, has decisively opposed the idea, claiming that right to roam is a 'divisive issue' for 'rural voters'.[47] So we decided to put his contention to the test. In January 2024, we commissioned some polling from YouGov. The results were highly instructive: 68 per cent of people living in urban areas supported extending a 'right of responsible access to the rest of the countryside in England'. What about the level of support amongst people living in rural areas? It was *exactly the same*.[48] The idea that there is a 'town versus country' divide over the question of access to nature is a complete myth. Indeed, we came to learn that the Countryside Alliance had commissioned their own polling on right to roam, but had buried the findings – which had *also* found that a majority of rural voters back a greater right to roam. The *real* countryside alliance is surely the great mass of the public – both rural and urban – who care for nature and would like to spend more time in it.

None of this is to doubt that public access to the countryside *can* have negative impacts on nature. Dogs off leads are perhaps the biggest problem, disturbing nesting birds and worrying livestock. Litter is ugly, and it spreads microplastics into the environment. Careless camping brings with it the risk of wildfires.

But these problems aren't insurmountable. Dog licensing, abolished in the 1980s, could be brought back with a simple educational training course for owners. Litter could be diminished by bringing in a deposit return scheme for bottles and cans – something the previous government dithered over for years. Fire risk could be reduced by restricting the sale of disposable barbecues in the vicinity of flammable moorlands.*

The government could also properly promote the Countryside Code – something the Tories failed to do for years. Between 2010 and 2020, ministers spent the princely sum of £2,000 a year promoting the Countryside Code, according to data that I obtained from Natural England.[49] Since these shocking figures were revealed, extra money was magically found to publicise the Code, but it's still peanuts.[50] The Conservatives often claim to be the party of the countryside, but it was the last Labour government that revamped the Countryside Code and gave it a decent publicity budget.

Moreover, there's a clear double standard when it comes to the responsibilities of those accessing the countryside, versus those of its owners. Recreational access can have consequences, but it's very far down the rankings for things society is doing to screw up nature. Compared to moorland burning, fenland drainage, the release of invasive species, the agricultural pollution poured into rivers, or the mass graves of pheasants dumped by some shoots, going for a walk in the countryside isn't exactly the most ecologically reckless activity.

Yet whilst there's no shortage of hand-wringing about litter, the opinion pages of most newspapers are silent when landowners break their own codes of conduct. How many shooting estates regularly breach the Code of Good Shooting Practice, for instance? And theirs is a low bar to step over: as we've seen,

---

*And, of course, by landowners making these moors less flammable by rewetting the peat – see Chapter 2.

landowners have few defined responsibilities to abide by in the first place. How can landowners be held publicly accountable when so much land remains off-limits to the public?

Much of the access debate is fixated on the damage the public does to the countryside, and how to reduce it. But we've got things back to front. Giving people greater access to nature is not only good for people's health: it's good for the rest of the natural world, too.

This is true for several reasons. For one thing, reconnecting people with nature encourages them to care for it more. I strongly believe most of us have an innate love of the natural world, a feeling the biologist E.O. Wilson called *biophilia*. But that sense of wonder can be dulled through depriving us of any experience of it. Centuries of enclosure, urbanisation and industrialisation have severed much of the public's everyday contact with rich habitats and other species. Increased time spent in nature, however, can rekindle our sense of awe and sharpen our desire to protect it. A recent study with a sample size of 24,000 individuals looked at the relationship between people's access to green space and their adoption of green behaviours, like environmental volunteering. 'The more individuals visited nature', the study found, 'the more pro-environmental behaviour they reported.'[51]

Giving the public greater access to the countryside also means there are more eyes and ears on the ground, able to spot ecological damage and take action. Secrets lurk in the depths of rural Britain, hidden behind fences and Keep Out signs – as we found on our mass trespass into the Duke of Somerset's pheasant shoot. But by exposing them to the light of collective scrutiny, there's more chance of holding landowners and their practices to account. Even where farmers and landlords are keen to be good stewards, they may not always be aware when a problem arises – a pollution incident, for example, or the appearance of an invasive plant. In such circumstances, the public have a crucial role to play: they can act as whistleblowers for nature.

Some bold people are taking on the mantle of nature's whistleblowers already. Dave Bangs is an inveterate trespasser who's something of a legend in his home town of Brighton. Now in his seventies with a wiry frame and shock of silver hair, he's explored the downs and ghylls of Sussex for decades, coming to know many landscapes better than the local aristocrats who own vast swathes of them. 'Our Wealden countryside is not a democratic place,' Dave writes in one of his field guides to the area, a gloriously eclectic tome that combines his wealth of botanical knowledge with disquisitions on history, geology and left-wing political analysis.[52] But through his trespasses, Dave demonstrates what benefits greater rural democracy could bring. He frequently comes across instances of damage being done to nature, and alerts the authorities.

Once, on a trespass along the River Ouse, Dave found an invasive species of clam had colonised the banks, and notified the Environment Agency – who, despite the mortal danger it posed to the ecosystem, had been unaware of its presence. On another occasion, Dave discovered a tenant on a council-owned farm was shooting game despite having no licence to do so. When he reported it to the council, they took action to get the gamebird pens removed. 'It took us trespassing to get the evidence,' he told me.

Sometimes, officials disapprove of Dave's methods: he recalls bitterly a county ecologist rejecting his detailed studies of chalk grassland sites because the species lists had been obtained via trespass. But at other times, the tactic has resulted in huge victories. A mass trespass co-organised by Dave with the group Landscapes of Freedom helped save an ancient woodland from the chop by pressuring developers into abandoning their plans. As he told my Right to Roam campaign colleague Jon Moses during one trespass, Dave believes that public access is vital for protecting landscapes currently off-limits. 'Because [if] no one knows it, no one loves it, and if no one loves it no one is going to fight for it,' he said.[53]

A different sort of environmental whistleblowing is being pioneered by a group calling themselves the Rebel Botanists. During the coronavirus lockdowns, Plymouth-based teacher Liz Richmond started chalking the Latin and common names of wild plants onto the pavements where she found them growing. Later, she was joined by friends and neighbours, and 'rebel botanising' became a regular Sunday activity.[54] Cut off from nature, many of us have succumbed to 'plant blindness', a myopia towards the plant kingdom that renders us unable to distinguish between the rich diversity of species. The aim of the Rebel Botanists is to show the urban public the panoply of plants growing in cities – and alert them to the threats they face.

'Technically, we're breaking the law,' Liz told me when I joined the Rebels in Plymouth for a 'walk and chalk', her broad Westcountry twang reminding me of my Cornish relatives. 'Chalking on the pavement is illegal, like fly-postering – even though what we're doing is purely educational.' As we chatted, Liz crouched over a dandelion-like flower, spelling out its Latin name on the pavement in pink chalk: *Sanchus oleracus.* Common sowthistle. Grabbing a stick of chalk, I joined in, identifying flora with the aid of an iPhone app. Curious passers-by stopped to watch. Since they formed, the Rebel Botanists have also branched out into defending wildflower-rich verges from overzealous council mowers, and getting involved in the campaign to save Plymouth city centre's street trees from the chop. The Rebels' enthusiasm for botany seems to be catching on. When the city's ruling Conservative administration was voted out during the 2023 local elections, one Tory candidate remarked wryly: 'They've been drawing trees on the ballot papers, which makes a change from phallic symbols.'[55]

Across Britain, recent years have seen an upsurge in citizen activism on behalf of nature. On the grouse moors of northern England, a network of Moorland Monitors make use of our right to roam over moors to report illicit burning by estates flouting the law. Along the River Wye, as we saw at the beginning of this book, badly polluted by intensive agriculture but one of the few rivers in England and Wales with a clear right of navigation, 'kayaktivists' collect water samples to shame landowners into cleaning up their act. Deep in the Dorset countryside, groups of birdwatchers keep an eye out for signs of wildlife crime, in a part of the country where recent years have seen buzzards shot and a white-tailed eagle poisoned.[56] The vital work of these whistleblowers has resulted in tougher rules on moorland burning, gamekeepers being prosecuted, and river pollution becoming a national scandal, seldom out of the headlines.

Indeed, much of this activism goes beyond merely raising the alarm about environmental threats: it comprises a form of *stewardship without ownership*. In the Right to Roam campaign, we call this 'Wild Service' – an act of service to the wild.* As Nick Hayes writes in the campaign's book of essays on the subject: 'Belonging is the democratic antidote to despotic ownership . . . By being attentive to the needs of a local area, by actively setting out to improve its biodiversity, we claim a moral legitimacy to be present in that landscape that runs deeper than the legal fiction of exclusive ownership.'[57] On a cold winter's day, I headed to one of London's most neglected rivers, to meet a man putting these bold ideals into action.

Paul Powlesland loves to wear brightly coloured jumpsuits. When I meet him at his riverside mooring, he emerges from his narrowboat dressed in a bright blue number. As a boat-dwelling barrister, Paul's environmental activism straddles the worlds of both courtroom and riverbank. On previous occasions, I've seen him unzip a garish pink onesie to reveal a smart three-piece suit beneath, like a reverse Clark Kent. But whether he's in front of a judge or stood steering at the back of his boat, Paul is, in my mind, a superhero for nature.

Paul lives on the River Roding, a tributary of the Thames in Barking, East London. It's not, at first glance, a place you'd expect to find much nature. Paul's boat is overlooked by tower blocks and grey warehouses; upriver, you can see the skeletal outline of an old gasholder. Traffic roars along the North Circular, and there's the periodic rattling of tube trains along the nearby Overground line. But nestled within this built-up area is a living, flowing river. I reach Paul's mooring by following a

---

* As well as a reference to the beautiful wild service tree.

walkway of planks through a large bed of reeds, their flowery panicles sighing in the breeze.

'There's such a contrast here between the human-made world and these few wild spaces,' Paul tells me as we drink coffee, sitting in our coats in comfy old chairs on the wooden decking he's built by hand. 'You get these flashes of beauty. I've seen kingfishers darting up and down the river here.' As if on cue, our eyes are drawn to a sudden movement nearby. Poking out from beneath a gently decomposing sofa is the sleek head of a species of mustelid, its whiskers twitching as it scents the air. It disappears again before we can work out if it's weasel or mink.*

Paul is the co-founder of Lawyers for Nature, a group that uses the law to defend wildlife and habitats. In particular, it advocates for the 'rights of nature' – a concept that's alien to most western legal systems, under which nature is treated mainly as a form of private property. Paul's other passion, besides his legal activism, is the Roding. He says his dad can't quite understand why a high-powered barrister would 'dress like a hippie, live on a boat and shit in a bucket', even if that bucket's an eco-friendly compost loo. But Paul lives this way because he's fallen in love – with a river.

A few years ago, Paul set up the River Roding Trust to look after this mistreated watercourse. It's a small charity run on a shoestring budget by volunteers who organise rubbish clearance parties along the river and have planted hundreds of trees on its banks. Fastened to the railings on the riverside footpath, I see some boards bearing the Trust's name. They display photos of various religious artefacts found by the Roding: bowls of incense and small statues of Hindu gods, perhaps left by local residents of this multicultural borough as 'votive offerings' to the river.[58] If Paul has a religion, it's animism: a belief in the spirit of place. 'The Roding is sacred,' he says.[59]

Sacred, but also much profaned. The river and its banks are caked with discarded flotsam and jetsam: beer cans, coke bottles,

---

*American mink are an invasive species in Britain, but as Paul says, at least they eat rats.

polythene bags, chunks of polystyrene decomposing into white spheres ('river caviar', as Paul calls it). I've brought Paul my own offering, a single plastic bottle I picked up further down the river bank. 'I've got them coming out of my ears,' he laughs. Pretty soon, I realise that he's taken on a colossal challenge, something that certainly can't be solved through a light spot of litter picking.

The trash mostly isn't coming from people walking along the Roding: indeed, there's no right of way along large stretches of it. Rather, the waste is being washed out of storm outfalls, or carried upstream from the Thames by the tide. Litter blows in from local roads and leaches out of eroding riverside landfills. This never-ceasing flow of plastic is supplemented by industrial quantities of fly-tipping by criminal gangs, and by an enterprising thief who strips the copper from the nearby train lines and leaves behind the plastic insulation tubes. It's only thanks to Paul's efforts that footpaths have been cut through some of the bramble stands, allowing volunteers to reach the worst build-ups of rubbish. On one recent weekend, the River Roding Trust picked up around *four hundred* bags of trash. 'If you leave an urban river without access, it *will* get destroyed,' argues Paul. 'It'll get overwhelmed by plastic and sewage. You *need* people to be able to access the river to look after it.'

Much of our day together on the river is therefore spent trespassing. Paul has, in fact, walked and trespassed the entire 50-kilometre length of the Roding, from its source in Essex down to where it flows into the Thames. He documented his journey in the form of a Google Map, recording every pipe pumping sewage into the river, every field where a farmer has ploughed too close to the river's edge, every infestation of invasive Japanese knotweed ('the landowners are doing nothing about it,' he notes sadly).[60]

Paul has no formal ownership of any part of the Roding. But over his years of living here, he has found himself becoming its guardian. 'Anyone can choose to step into a relationship of guardianship,' he writes. 'The step is mental, not legal. It can be taken without permission or a name on a title deed.'[61] Meanwhile, many of those with legal title to the Roding seem to have little interest in stewarding it. Appallingly, some of these owners are public sector bodies, who clearly need reminding who it is they serve. The Port of London Authority, for instance, owns one section of the river where rubbish was piling up, but refused to do anything about it. After Paul's efforts at outreach failed, he decided to just get on with it himself. He organised a clearance day to which fifty volunteers showed up: 'they smashed it', he says, filling hundreds of bin bags with waste. 'Where the authorities and landowners have failed, river guardians need to step into that gap – regardless of whether they own that land or not,' argues Paul, adding with a defiant light in his piercingly blue eyes: 'And I'm not gonna ask for permission to care.'

Even more bizarre is the fact that much of this public land is off-limits to the public, bounded by razor-wire fencing. Were the fences to be replaced with footpaths, the Roding could be a 'green Eden' for nature-starved East Londoners. Paul is indignant. 'It's fucking wild that publicly owned land should be kept inaccessible to some of this borough's poorest and most diverse communities.'

When not clearing trash or opening up access, the River Roding Trust is trying to breathe life back into the river. The Roding's banks sport an abundance of fennel, mugwort and teasels. 'They appeared when we trimmed back some of the brambles,' Paul explains. 'We're trying to jam as much life into this narrow space as possible.' Around midwinter each year, he pilots an unpowered raft upstream to take grafts from old willows and plant them as new saplings along the denuded banks. I watch Paul grinning as we pause at one of the trees he's planted: he looks like a doting father.

Further along the river, we come to a huge storm overflow pipe. This is meant to only discharge rainwater after heavy downpours, but because it's connected to the mains sewerage system, it often exudes far worse. The metal grilles covering its entrance are jammed with a foul mess of wet wipes, face masks and used condoms. As if that weren't bad enough, Paul tells me he once discovered sewage being expelled here illegally, and reported it. If he hadn't trespassed to get here, the pollution incidents would still be happening. But Paul isn't naïvely relying on the regulators to take action. He's also taking it himself, planting willows in the mud in front of where the pipe discharges, fashioning a makeshift natural filtration bed that might help purify the water before it enters the river. 'Dunno if it'll work,' he shrugs, 'but it's worth a go.' In 2021, Paul uncovered a similar illegal sewage spill on the Aldersbrook, a tributary of the Roding, emanating from a pipe owned by Thames Water. After posting damning photos of the incident on Twitter – the waters of the Aldersbrook a very obvious shit-brown colour – Thames Water admitted its infrastructure here was broken and needed updating. The Environment Agency, however, has yet to press charges.[62]

Although the Roding has escaped the fate of many of London's lost rivers – concreted over to the point of disappearance – it is now hemmed in by hard flood defences along much of its length. That's understandable when housing has been built either side of the river. But with the climate crisis bringing heavier rains and higher tides, there's not much space for the water to go, increasing the risk of the defences being overwhelmed. Natural rivers will spill over into floodplains. Yet on the Roding, one of the few undeveloped parts of the floodplain has been turned into a golf course – and is hemmed in by flood barriers.

The Ilford golf course, Paul tells me, is one of the most wasteful uses of land along the Roding. Owned, astonishingly, by Redbridge Council, this 80-acre municipal course is off-limits to the public and caters to a diminishing number of fee-paying players. In the 1930s, the Roding was embanked, preventing the river from overtopping into this wide expanse of flat land – but in doing so, pushing the floodwaters further downstream. 'With climate change, Barking and Ilford *will* flood unless we either build ever-higher concrete flood defences,' explains Paul, 'or we restore this golf course as a floodplain.' Paul's clear preference is to free the Roding from its confinement, and turn the empty putting greens into wildlife-rich marshland, protecting the houses downstream.

Before we bring our day's adventure to a close, Paul takes me to witness what he calls 'the worst environmental crime I have encountered on the Roding'.[63] Further upstream, behind a menacing gate topped by razor wire, Paul points out a vast mound amidst the trees. In spring 2023, he trespassed this site and discovered that the landowner had illegally dumped a kilometre of construction waste along the banks of the river. With infuriating irony, the same landowner had also erected signs that read: 'Private Land – Stay Out – Do Not Drop Litter'. As Paul wrote at the time: 'I've never encountered a more perfect example of how screwed up our conversation about land access and responsibility is, and how leniently we view environmental crime by landowners.'[64]

Paul's experiences on the River Roding show that those who own land often abuse it – whilst also demonstrating that you don't need to own land to care for it deeply. His heroic work to look after this beloved river also upends the received wisdom that greater public access leads to worse outcomes for nature. On the contrary, by trespassing, he has not only picked up vast quantities of rubbish and planted hundreds of saplings: he has also uncovered flytipping by landowners and illegal sewage discharges by water companies that otherwise would have gone unnoticed. We can't clone Paul (a fact that might relieve some of his friends). But we could encourage many more people to follow the example that he and others are setting, by changing the law on access. Give the public a right to roam in the countryside, so we can all give our service to the wild.

8

A Sort of National Property

If there's anywhere in our countryside that wildness ought to be prioritised, it's surely in our national parks. Yet national parks in Britain are not owned by the nation.

That startling truth has been brought home to me by an ongoing battle over the future of Dartmoor National Park, near where I live. I've loved hiking over Dartmoor since I was a teenager, but boy, is it in a bad way. Wildlife is ebbing away from its tors and bogs. Overgrazing by sheep and repeated swaling – the Westcountry word for moorland burning – has turned vast tracts of it into a monoculture of purple moor grass. The destruction of its habitats is leading to the decline of the species they once supported. The last lapwing nested on Dartmoor in 2022; ring ouzels have also recently stopped breeding on the moor. I count myself lucky in having heard one of the moor's last curlews calling over Emsworthy Mire.[1]

After years of watching the moor's decline, I was pleased to see Dartmoor National Park Authority (DNPA), the body officially responsible for its condition, sign up to some ambitious new nature restoration targets in 2021. Amongst them was a goal to create 5,000 acres of new broadleaf woodland along Dartmoor's river valleys over the next five years. Dartmoor today is a largely treeless landscape, but it wasn't always thus. Its few remaining upland oakwoods – the temperate rainforest fragments of Wistman's Wood, Black-a-tor Beare and Piles Copse – show what once existed in far greater abundance along its river valleys and rocky hillsides.

But then, quietly and mysteriously, the target was dropped. A friend working in conservation tipped me off, so I checked the DNPA's website. The park authority's stated ambition was now just 1,200 acres of new woodland. I did a doubletake. Had I misremembered the figure? But no: there, on the Internet Archive, preserved for all to see, was an earlier version of the same webpage, showing the original target of 5,000 acres.[2] Someone had seen fit to slash the goal by three-quarters. I spoke to an officer at the national park authority, who told me the earlier target had been 'unrealistic'. But if that was the case, why had it been set in the first place?

Fundamentally, Dartmoor National Park Authority had to limit its ambitions because it doesn't actually own much of Dartmoor. Its 3,500-acre estate comprises just 1.5 per cent of the total area of the park, making its original 5,000-acre goal impossible to meet on its own. In order to achieve anything much for nature and the climate, it has to persuade the park's other landowners to step up. And those other landowners contain some very powerful people and organisations indeed, from the Ministry of Defence to the millionaire hedge fund manager Alexander Darwall, whom we met in Chapter 6.

Dartmoor's biggest landowner by far is the heir to the throne, Prince William, via his Duchy of Cornwall.[3] A recent protest aimed to apply some public pressure on the Duchy to do more for nature, stepping in to fill the gap left by the enfeebled national park authority. It was organised by the activist group Wild Card, who campaign to persuade the royal family to rewild their extensive estates.[4] In the autumn of 2023, they coordinated a 'March for a Wild Dartmoor', calling on the Duchy to rewild its landholdings.

I managed to arrive late for the protest, and found it in full swing at South Hessary Tor, not far from Princetown – a Dartmoor settlement founded by the Prince of Wales's stewards in the late 1700s. Wild Card's distinctive pink and green pennants fluttered in the wind; silhouetted against the horizon, they made the rough-hewn granite of the tor look like a medieval castle on the eve of battle. Picnicking families and kids wearing facepaint listened to local conservationists reeling off tallies of disappearing species. Folk musicians strummed guitars and a Morris side performed 'Vixana', a dance about an ancient witch of the moor. With its air of gentle rebelliousness and pageantry, it was all very English.

Then the march set off, headed for the Duchy's offices in Princetown. This grand old building, its columns and balconies topped with the crest of the Prince of Wales, is leased to the DNPA as a visitor centre: a telling sign of the landlord–tenant relationship that defines Dartmoor.[5] As the crowd of marchers gathered, a giant sculpture of a knight's armoured glove – made out of wicker and tin foil – was placed in front of the offices. Wild Card were symbolically throwing down the gauntlet to the Duchy to rewild their land. Their demand was summarised on the banner they hung from the offices: 'Make it wild or make it ours!'

'*Marxist!*' hissed the head of the Countryside Alliance, Tim Bonner, when he spotted the banner's slogan posted on Twitter.[6] But Mr Bonner's desire to see reds under the flower beds betrays his ignorance of rural history. Wild Card's words were inspired not by the writings of Karl Marx, but rather by those of a Victorian Liberal conservationist called Robert Burnard. Burnard lived in Devon in the late nineteenth century and founded the Dartmoor Preservation Association. He railed against the ongoing enclosure of the moor – something the Duchy of Cornwall had encouraged since Napoleonic times – in a powerful essay titled *Plundered Dartmoor*, published in 1895. 'The plundering of Dartmoor has been slowly going on for a long period,' he wrote. 'It is clearly only a question of time when the remnant . . . will pass away from us.' Unless, he argued, the people of Devon were to save Dartmoor 'by acquiring it for themselves'.[7]

Here was a clarion call, long before national parks existed in Britain, for taking Dartmoor into public ownership. Burnard argued that the Duchy ought to be compelled to sell its Dartmoor estate to the recently created Devon County Council. Way ahead of his time, he described the public value of what we would now call Dartmoor's 'ecosystem services'. The moor, Burnard wrote, was a 'magnificent watershed', whose peat bogs formed a 'natural reservoir'. Yet this peat was threatened through overuse and degradation. 'If the County becomes the purchasers of the Forest [of Dartmoor], the bogs will be protected from the ravages of the wholesale turf-cutter,' he proclaimed.[8]

In fact, Burnard argued, public ownership could lead not just to the protection of Dartmoor, but to its ecological restoration. 'With the Forest of Dartmoor the property of the people of Devon, the public would possess the grandest park in England. Left just as it is, with some judicious tree planting, and as a recreative region it would be perfect. With swaling under proper control, fur and feather would increase, and it might be once again made the haunt of the red deer.'[9] Or to put it another way: make it ours, and we'll make it wild.

Burnard lived in a time when liberal, centrist opinion in Britain favoured the public ownership of large tracts of land for the purpose of nature conservation. Sadly, however, the story of our national parks has turned out rather differently.

Dartmoor is not an anomaly when it comes to our national parks: nature is in freefall across virtually all of them. An analysis by the RSPB in 2018 found that Sites of Special Scientific Interest inside national parks were, on average, in a worse condition than those *outside* national parks.[10] When we dig into what the land is used for, we can see why this might be the case.

There are *eight times* as many sheep in England's national parks as there are people living in them. Admittedly, population density in our national parks is generally low – some 320,000 inhabitants across all ten – and this doesn't take into account the many millions who visit them annually. But whilst tourists sometimes leave litter, I've never seen one devour a tree sapling. The same cannot be said for the 2.8 million sheep who roam our national parks, preventing natural regeneration and mowing grasslands to a billiard-table smoothness. The English national park with the highest number of sheep is the Yorkshire Dales, and its logo – appropriately but ominously – is a Swaledale ram.[11]

Grouse moors, meanwhile, take up nearly a third of the North York Moors, a quarter of the Dales and a fifth of the Peak District.[12] Pitifully little woodland remains in England's national parks: an analysis by Friends of the Earth found that woodland cover in the Lake District (12.6 per cent) is actually lower than in the city of Sheffield (13.3 per cent).[13] Many of these woods are also, in reality, modern conifer plantations. And the stats really hit home when you look at how much land in our national parks remains dominated by agriculture. On average, 66 per cent of the land in England's ten national parks is farmed. That's barely any different than the figure for England as a whole, where 68 per cent of the land mass is used for agriculture. Only the New Forest really bucks this trend, with just a quarter of the land devoted to farming; in the Peak District, the farmed area is as high as 80 per cent.[14] Our national parks are special places, containing some spectacular landscapes and some very important sites for wildlife. But they're not *natural* parks.

Nor are national parks owned by the public. The vast majority of the land in them lies in private hands. In 1991, the Edwards Review into national parks published statistics on their ownership: the last time this was done officially. It found that 96 per cent of the Yorkshire Dales was in private ownership, 91 per cent of the Broads, 86 per cent of the Pembrokeshire Coast and 80 per cent of the North York Moors. Compared to these figures, Dartmoor looks practically progressive: a mere 57 per cent in private hands, mainly because a chunk of it belongs to the Ministry of Defence for army training purposes.[15]

Even these stark stats belie how concentrated this ownership is. It would be a mistake to assume the private owners are all small-scale farmers, the stereotypical Old Macdonald leaning on a farm gate sucking on a straw. My own investigations have found that many national parks are dominated by very large estates belonging to the aristocracy or the newly minted. A quarter of the South Downs National Park, for instance, belongs to just a dozen big landowners – amongst them the Duke of Norfolk, the

Duke of Richmond, Viscount Cowdray and Baron Leconfield.[16] In Dartmoor, fifteen landowners own almost half the land.[17] In the North York Moors, it's the same story: virtually all the land above the moorland line is held by fifteen landowners – from the Earl of Mexborough to the royal Duchy of Lancaster. Pretty much all of them devote their estates to driven grouse shooting.[18]

The amount of land in national parks actually belonging to National Park Authorities (NPAs), by contrast, is tiny. In 2021, when running a campaign for Rewilding Britain, I sourced maps and figures for the land possessed by all of Britain's NPAs. I didn't expect it to be much, but even I was staggered by how little they owned. Coming in at first place was Bannau Brycheiniog, the authority for the Brecon Beacons in south Wales, whose land takes up a whole 13.4 per cent of the national park. It only got worse from there on down. Exmoor NPA owns only 8.6 per cent of their park, the Lake District NPA just 3 per cent, Northumberland NPA a pitiful 0.2 per cent. Seven out of Britain's fifteen national park authorities own essentially no land at all,* save for the occasional car park and public toilet block.[19] No wonder they struggle to make a positive difference within their jurisdictions.

What's more, most national park authorities are now so cash-strapped, they're having to consider selling off what little land they've still got. Exmoor NPA, for instance, proposed putting around 230 acres of its estate on the market in 2022, pleading 'significant financial challenges'.[20] The next year, the Peak District NPA announced plans to sell up to a tenth of its landholdings in order to plug gaps in its budget.[21] In her report, the park's finance officer spoke of 'the disposal of surplus assets', a phrase as cold as the grave.[22] But NPAs have been given little choice about their miserly accounting. Central government has slashed their funding by 40 per cent in real terms since 2010, meaning the loss of over two hundred jobs.[23] A temporary injection of cash from DEFRA, together with a philanthropic donation, has

---

*Technically, the Broads Authority in Norfolk is not a national park, but has equivalent status.

enabled these two particular NPAs to pause their land sales. Yet without secure long-term funding, the stay of execution may not last for long.[24]

Still worse is the powerlessness of national park authorities to influence how land is used and abused. NPAs are planning authorities, meaning they do at least have control over what gets built in national parks. But – as is explored in more detail in Chapter 9 – the planning system has excluded agriculture and forestry since its inception. A national park authority can veto, say, a housing development, but has no sway over a landowner choosing to plough up an old meadow or set fire to a moorland.

This lack of power means that even authorities with good intentions can't necessarily implement them. Exmoor NPA, for example, published a brilliant plan for nature restoration in 2020, complete with a beautiful illustration showing the abundance of cuckoos, whinchat, scrub and bog plants it hoped to see returned.[25] But it was hit with a vicious backlash from Exmoor farmers and landowners, who complained their views hadn't been sought, despite an extensive consultation process. 'You've got to bring the farmers on board. It's not just the conservationists, and the greenies,' Exmoor farmer Oliver Edwards told the *Telegraph*, demanding the park's plan be 'put on the backburner'. Edwards implied the park authority's ambitious vision would see the park overrun by wealthy rewilders: 'We don't want it to turn into a rich boys' playground.'[26] What the *Telegraph* failed to mention was that Edwards' 500-acre farm also hosts a large pheasant shoot, where rich boys regularly come to play.[27]

Many national parks also have to contend with the fact that landowners and farmers are heavily represented on their governing boards. Board members are a mix of directly elected councillors and individuals appointed by the secretary of state. In 2018, I investigated this issue in depth, trawling through the registers of interests for all 195 board members of England's national park authorities. Thirty per cent of them, I found, had financial interests in land, farming or forestry, and had collectively received £1.3 million in farm subsidies in 2017.[28] Some of these members were small-scale farmers; others were baronets owning thousands of acres.

It is, of course, completely reasonable for farmers, foresters and landowners to be represented on national park boards. The question is whether they are *over*-represented, and end up exerting undue influence on decisions about how the land gets used. Given that in the UK as a whole, just 0.7 per cent of the population are employed in agriculture, and just 0.02 per cent in forestry, I would suggest they are.[29] Some might object that within national parks, farming and forestry make up a higher proportion of local jobs – although still nowhere near the levels represented. But these are meant to be *national* parks, serving the nation as a whole, for anyone who wants to visit – not just local landed interests.

Things would be a little easier for national park authorities if they at least had a say in what other public sector landowners did with their land. Public bodies overall – the MOD, Forestry Commission, Natural England and various councils, alongside NPAs themselves – own slightly over 10 per cent of Britain's national parks.[30] The proportion varies considerably from park to park: the Forestry Commission owns nearly half the New Forest, for instance, whilst there's hardly any public sector land ownership in the Yorkshire Dales. But either way, for most of their history, national park authorities have had scant control over the management of other public sector land in their jurisdictions.

All this looks even worse when you compare the situation in Britain with how national parks operate in many other countries. In the US and New Zealand, for instance, all national parks are owned by the government. Sweden set up some of the first national parks in Europe in 1909, and vested them entirely in state ownership.[31] All national parks in Ireland are owned by the Irish state; the oldest, Killarney National Park, was gifted to the government in 1932.[32] Around 85 per cent of the land in Spanish national parks is publicly owned – split between the central state, regional government and municipalities.[33] Even in Japan – which, like the UK, is a densely populated archipelago of islands with a long history of private land ownership – the situation is markedly different to ours. There, the Japanese

Ministry of the Environment notes, 'the state owns only about half the land constituting national parks.'[34] Only about half!

So what stopped Britain going down a similar route to Japan, Sweden, Spain and many other countries? To answer that, we need to go back to the founding vision for national parks in Britain, and witness the roads not taken.

It began with a poet. In his *Guide to the Lakes*, published in 1835, William Wordsworth famously wrote that the Lake District should be deemed 'a sort of national property'.[35] Its magnificent fells and glassy meres, he thought, should belong to everyone.

Less famous, but also significant, are the sentences that preceded this memorable phrase. Wordsworth, who was born and lived most of his life in the Lakes, knew full well that the Lake District's shifting patterns of ownership were altering its character and habitats. He complained about the sale of derelict farms which would 'fall into the hands of wealthy purchasers', who 'erect new mansions out of the ruins' and sweep away 'all the wild graces that grew out of them'. He expressed his wish to 'preserve the native beauty of this delightful district, because still further changes in its appearance must inevitably follow, from the change of inhabitants and owners which is rapidly taking place'.[36] Wordsworth's invocation of a national interest in the Lake District was meant as a counterpoint to the sometimes destructive behaviours of private property owners.

But how to give effect to this radical new notion of a landscape being 'national property'? The characteristically Victorian answer was to set up a charity: the National Trust. Founded in 1895, and funded by donations from the public, the Trust soon began buying up beautiful landscapes and historic buildings in order to preserve them. The Lake District was an early focus of its activities, and today it owns nearly a fifth of it, the only national park where a conservation charity owns such a large slice.[37] The National Trust's name gave it the semblance of being a public body, and it even acquired legal underpinning when an Act of Parliament made its landholdings 'inalienable', meaning they can never be sold.

But there were clear financial limits to what even the National Trust could acquire. The state, by contrast, had almost unlimited funds, whether by raising taxes or borrowing money. As the power and reach of the state grew in the late nineteenth and early twentieth centuries, so did calls for it to intervene in the preservation of land for the nation. Some, like Dartmoor's Robert Burnard, thought the county councils were the way to go. Others within the Labour movement advocated the total nationalisation of all land. Meanwhile, preservationists of all political stripes – including many Conservatives – were increasingly alarmed by the impacts of urban sprawl and industry on the British countryside. The Council for the Preservation of Rural England, founded in 1926, lobbied the government to protect landscapes from disfigurement.

It was in this context that ideas of national parks began to percolate. Yellowstone, the world's first national park, had been founded in the United States as long ago as 1872. But its vast forests, hot springs and wild mountains had seemed a world away from the tamed farmland of much of Britain. Nevertheless, by the 1920s, British visitors to Yellowstone left inspired to emulate its example back home. The national park 'provided beautiful sanctuaries for wild animals and birds', wrote Lord Bledisloe, Parliamentary Secretary to the Ministry of Agriculture, after taking a trip there in 1925.[38] In 1929, CPRE sent a briefing to the newly elected Labour Prime Minister Ramsay MacDonald, urging him to set up an inquiry into the need for national parks in Britain. MacDonald, whose election manifesto had included greater public control over land, promptly did so.[39]

The resulting National Parks Committee was chaired by the junior agriculture minister Christopher Addison, a doctor of anatomy and pioneer advocate of social housing. His remit was to 'report if it is desirable and feasible to establish one or more National Parks in Great Britain with a view to the preservation of natural characteristics including flora and fauna, and to the improvement of recreational facilities for the people'. Addison, with his medical background and concern for the poorest in society, saw national parks as being 'essential features of a "national health service"',[40] years ahead of either being established.

Even so, when the report was published in 1931, many of Addison's recommendations remained quite cautious. The committee sought to 'limit any interference with private ownership' within proposed national parks by relying mainly on new planning powers, rather than widespread state acquisition of land.[41] It recognised the need to ensure that 'rights of ownership are not exercised in a manner detrimental to the national interest', but hoped to strike deals with landowners to achieve this, adding rather naïvely: 'we should hope that it would be possible, by negotiation, to agree to many of the restrictions without payment.'[42] Mindful of the state of the public coffers, Addison's committee sought to lean on charity to do the work of government, suggesting that 'a greatly increased holding by the National Trust would probably achieve as much and cost less than a magistral policy of State purchase.'[43] Still, the committee did allow for the eventuality that 'if other methods failed, the National [Parks] Authority might acquire land'.[44]

Much of this hesitancy stemmed from the weak political position of the Labour government, battered by the Great Depression and the rightwing press. But not everyone was so reticent; even some aristocrats favoured the state acquiring land for national parks. As Lord Onslow, owner of an estate in Surrey, opined: 'people are apt to be frightened at the cost of buying a large area of land and maintaining it', but 'what is possible for a private individual should not be impossible for the public generally either under the government or by means of public subscription.'[45]

The second Labour government fell before it could make Addison's recommendations law. Economic recession, skyrocketing unemployment and the rise of Nazi Germany put the cause of national parks on the back burner for a decade and a half. But the Second World War ultimately saw it propelled back onto the political agenda. Emboldened by the state's capacity to get things done quickly and efficiently during wartime, and determined to fashion a better world once peace finally came, policymakers began contemplating all manner of ideas previously thought utopian.

It fell to a civil servant, John Dower, to produce one of the most visionary papers of the postwar period. An architect and keen walker from Yorkshire, Dower had previously done work for the CPRE and publicly advocated for national parks. During the war, whilst at the Ministry of Works, he found himself in the right place at the right time, and was asked to produce a White Paper on the prospect for national parks in England and Wales. Published in May 1945 shortly after VE Day, the Dower Report, as it's now known, was breathtakingly radical in its scope.

Dower defined the 'two dominant purposes' of national parks as being '(a) that the characteristic beauty of the landscape shall be preserved, and (b) that the visiting public shall have ample access and facilities within it for open-air recreation and for enjoyment of its beauty'.[46] As a fell-runner who went on to be president of the Ramblers Association, Dower was particularly bold in his ideas about access. He proposed that 'the public shall have the right to wander at will' over all mountains, moors and heaths within national parks, something which did not come to pass for another half-century.[47] But he also gave careful consideration to 'landscape preservation', arguing for the need to have control over both building development and wider changes in land use.[48] For Dower, 'ill-placed and ugly buildings . . . are by no means the only misuses and disfigurements which threaten the integrity of National Park areas', and he pointed to 'monotonous sharp-edged conifer plantations' and 'ill-considered felling of woodlands' as examples. 'They must be made subject to a control no less effective than that applied to ordinary building development,' Dower declared.

Most radically of all, Dower devoted a section of his report to the subject of 'Land-Ownership and National Parks'. He began it by reassuring his more conservative readers that 'The future of rural land ownership in the country . . . is a politically controversial issue on which I express no opinion' – before doing just that. '[T]he system of ownership, whatever it is, will nowhere be allowed to stand in the way of a democratically determined allocation of the land to its best use in the public interest.'[49] With this sentence, Dower comes close to being a twentieth-century equivalent of Gerrard Winstanley: not a state socialist, but rather a believer in land being subject to democratic checks and balances – a common treasury for all. And though Dower did not think that public ownership of land within national parks was essential, he argued that 'public acquisition is, however, an indispensable . . . weapon in the National Parks armoury; and it should be readily available and unhesitatingly used.'[50]

In other regards, Dower remained a man of his time. He considered modern methods of 'agricultural improvement' beneficial to landscapes within national parks, even though the destruction of downland wrought by the wartime plough-up campaign was plain to see.[51] And though he lamented the absence of 'any national policy for the conservation of wild life', Dower did not think national parks could be nature reserves in their entirety, since 'farming and recreational uses of the land are far too important . . . for strict wild life conservation to be made a first and governing consideration.'[52]

Even bolder than Dower was his counterpart, Sir J. Douglas Ramsay, who had a similar brief for national parks in Scotland. Despite having previously managed the monarch's estate at Balmoral, Ramsay clearly held views that put him at odds with Scotland's landed establishment. 'A National Park,' Ramsay declared, 'is an extensive tract of country of outstanding natural beauty, preferably also of scientific, cultural or historic interest, *owned or controlled by the Nation, accessible to all as a matter of right*' (my emphasis).[53] His committee recommended the creation of five national parks in Scotland, encompassing not only Loch Lomond and the Cairngorms but also Ben Nevis, Glen Affric and Loch Torridon. Land for these parks, Ramsay proposed, should be bought by the public sector outright – whether by agreement or by compulsion. 'Even if the acquisition of 3,000 square miles of land suitable for National Parks is not immediately practicable,' Ramsay wrote hopefully, 'yet the gradual acquisition and development of such an area in the course of the next ten or twenty years is not impossible.'[54]

Unfortunately, it *was* impossible. As the academics Ann and Malcolm MacEwen put it, Ramsay's recommendations 'came much closer to the American concept of a national park "owned or controlled by the nation"'. But in doing so, he attracted the stiff resistance of Scottish landowners.[55] Of all places in Britain, Scotland, with its small population and majestic wilderness, was perhaps best suited to a stricter form of 'national park as nature reserve'. Yet no national parks were designated in Scotland until as recently as 2002, and even then only two: Loch Lomond and the Trossachs, and the Cairngorms. Today, public bodies own just 2.7 per cent of the Cairngorms National Park. Scotland's lairds killed Ramsay's vision at birth.

In England and Wales, however, the more cautious approach meant at least a semblance of Dower's vision for national parks was to be implemented. Yet another committee was appointed by Attlee's incoming Labour government, and the resulting Hobhouse Report of 1947 mostly parroted Dower's recommendations: planning controls were favoured over public acquisitions of land, but the government would reserve the power to buy land compulsorily where there was no other option.[56]

At last, in 1949, Attlee's administration tabled its National Parks and Access to the Countryside Bill. It was to be 'the last in a series of statutes by which the postwar Labour government curtailed the rights of property',[57] following on from the creation of the planning system two years previously. The Act was a landmark achievement. Within a decade of its passage, ten national parks had been established across England and Wales, starting with the Peak District. Minister Lewis Silkin dubbed the Act a 'people's charter for the open air',[58] and public expectations were running high. An article in the *Bristol Evening Post* in 1949 breathlessly exclaimed: 'The national parks will be free to all. The great estates within their boundaries will gradually pass into public ownership as they are accepted by the Chancellor of the Exchequer in lieu of payments of death duties. So, gradually . . . the land will be returned to the people for ever.'[59]

Things did not, alas, quite turn out that way. The terms of the Act, and the way it was put into practice, led to several fundamental flaws in our system of national parks that persist to this day. First, although the legislation created a central National Parks Commission, it was a 'weak and ineffective body':[60] the day-to-day running of the parks was handed to existing county councils. Because many national parks straddled multiple council boundaries, this led to incessant bickering over jurisdictions – and even opposition to the very idea of parks. Only much later, in the 1990s, were separate national park authorities created that took over the planning powers of councils.[61]

Worse, there were no compulsory purchase powers to acquire land for the purpose of preserving natural beauty, despite this being a key recommendation of both Dower and Hobhouse.[62] The Hobhouse Report had assumed that '10 per cent of the area of National Parks may come into the [National Parks] Commission's hands during the first 10 years of their operations.'[63] Yet this never came to pass: neither the central Commission nor the county councils administering national parks were empowered to buy the land they were now responsible for. As we saw earlier, many national park authorities today own hardly any land, with only one, Bannau Brycheiniog, owning more than 10 per cent.

Second, the funding made available to national parks proved inadequate. As the *Bristol Evening Post*'s article had alluded to, Labour's Chancellor, Hugh Dalton, had created a system by which estates might pass into public ownership, called the National Land Fund. Dalton saw it as a means to 'go further on compulsory land acquisition', remarking that 'We shall have no peace around the Peak [District] until we have paid off the Dukes.'[64] But despite the Chancellor endowing the Fund with £50 million to spend, 'not a penny of it reached the national parks until 1979', when a single estate was acquired by the Lake District park authority.[65] For decades, national parks were run on a shoestring.

Third, access provisions in national parks were a disappointment. In place of the full right to roam over uncultivated land envisioned by Dower and Ramsay, councils instead merely negotiated voluntary access agreements with landowners. The trouble was, not many landowners wanted to play ball. As the pioneering right to roam campaigner Marion Shoard pointed out as late as the 1980s, 'access had been secured through the 1949 Act over only . . . 0.2 per cent of the land surface' of England and Wales.[66]

Last, and most important, was the divide the 1949 Act created between 'landscape preservation' and nature conservation. The legislation set up two parallel systems: one for preserving landscape beauty, in the form of national parks; and the other for protecting habitats and wildlife, in the form of the Nature Conservancy, National Nature Reserves and SSSIs (see Chapter 4). It meant that public sector conservationists busied themselves with managing relatively small fragments of land, whilst those responsible for the far larger areas covered by national parks had no real duty to consider the plants and animals that lived there. 'Natural beauty' might have seemed a good enough proxy to non-ecologists, but you can quite easily preserve a chocolate-box view whilst allowing it to become depleted of wildlife. Good geology hides many flaws: after all, Dartmoor retains its rugged granite grandeur despite the dire state of its peat bogs and disappearing bird life.

And, because controls over farming and forestry had been explicitly excluded from the new planning system, the councils now responsible for running national parks had little ability to rein in damaging agricultural and silvicultural practices. Ann and Malcolm MacEwen refer to this as the 'fatal contradiction', for 'it failed to anticipate the course of postwar farming and the consequences for the rural landscape'.[67] The South Downs, for example – envisaged as a national park by both Dower and Hobhouse – was so damaged by intensive ploughing that it was denied national park status at all, finally attaining the designation only in 2010.

As the historian Matthew Kelly observes, 'Britain was doing national parks on the cheap.'[68] Over the next seventy-five years, multiple attempts would be made to patch up this flawed system.

By the early 1970s, the shine had come off Britain's national parks. The limited protections afforded to these supposedly beloved landscapes had become starkly apparent through a series of site battles. On Dartmoor, private forestry firms had succeeded in felling hundreds of acres of ancient deciduous woodland, despite much opposition from the formidable campaigner Lady Sylvia Sayer.[69] In Northumberland National Park, controversy surrounded plans to flood the Kielder Valley to create a huge new reservoir.[70] And in mid-Wales, proposals for the Cambrian Mountains to become the first new national park in a decade and a half were brought crashing down after opposition from the Country Landowners' Association.[71]

It was against this unpromising backdrop that the first of three major attempts to reform the national parks system began. Lord Sandford, a Conservative peer and junior environment minister, had been appointed by Prime Minister Ted Heath to lead a review of how they worked. Reporting in 1974, Sandford's most important conclusion was his attempt to reconcile the trade-offs between the two key purposes of national parks – the preservation of natural beauty and recreational access. The 'Sandford Principle', as it became known, asserted that in cases of irreconcilable conflict between the two, nature conservation should be given greater priority. This sensible proposition was widely adopted by park authorities, although it was not actually enshrined in law for another two decades. But Sandford failed to resolve the arguably far more fundamental trade-off in national parks between conservation and other land uses, like farming and forestry. As one account puts it, his report 'shrank from recommending any controls over farming, preferring to rely on cooperation with farmers and landowners by means of voluntary management agreements'.[72] And Sandford's calls for the national parks budget to be doubled, and for councils to be given more powers to purchase land in need of protection, were roundly ignored by the incoming Labour government.

Meanwhile, a fresh controversy was erupting in Exmoor National Park. Despite being a notionally protected landscape, Exmoor remained under assault from the forces of agricultural 'improvement'. Between the end of the Second World War and the mid-1970s, some 12,000 acres of its moorland had fallen to the plough.[73] 'Exmoor as it is today will go on being eroded,' warned one ecologist, 'until one day people will wake up to the fact that it has disappeared except as a name on the map.'[74] But those warnings went unheeded by the national park's committee, whose members included several prominent Exmoor landowners. Under their watch, a number of controversial schemes to plough up moorland were waved through. This sparked an outcry which saw matters escalated upwards to central government. Something Had To Be Done, so ministers called the inevitable public inquiry. To run it, they appointed Lord Porchester, a Tory grandee with impeccable political and landowning credentials. A keen horse-breeder, known fondly as 'Porchey' by the Queen, he owned the Highclere Castle estate in Hampshire. He could easily have sided with Exmoor's landowners, but ended up being their staunchest critic.

Lord Porchester listened carefully to all sides of the debate. He heard representations from the NFU and CLA, who demanded that conservation of moorland must come with generous compensation for the farmers and landowners who spared it from the plough. But Porchester could see that relying on voluntary agreements alone wouldn't save the national park's beautiful uplands; there needed to be a backstop. He recommended Exmoor's national park authority be given powers to make Moorland Conservation Orders, legally binding in perpetuity. This would have been a big step forward, giving a national park authority some controls over agricultural land use for the first time.[75]

But Porchester's proposals were never implemented. The Labour government sat on the findings of his 1977 report, and Thatcher's victory at the next general election meant they were consigned to history. As Ann and Malcolm MacEwen, whose experience of living on Exmoor at this time shaped their critique of national parks, wrote: 'the NFU and CLA perceived [Porchester's] recommendations as a threat to the dominant political and property interests in the countryside.'[76] Some moorlands eventually got greater protection when the Wildlife and Countryside Act 1981 strengthened defences for SSSIs. But salvation had not come via the national parks.

A further attempt at reform came in 1991 with yet another review of national parks led by the biologist Professor Ron Edwards.[77] His report, *Fit for the Future*, exposed how land in national parks remained concentrated in the hands of private landowners, but proved pusillanimous in addressing this. 'National park purposes can be achieved only through sympathetic forms of land management which, in turn, are closely aligned to land ownership,' it began promisingly. But the review then chickened out, claiming it was 'simply not feasible – and probably not desirable' for national park authorities to acquire large areas of land themselves. 'Thus, our national parks must remain fundamentally different from those elsewhere in the world, where the greater proportion is in the public domain,' it concluded.[78] Perhaps Edwards felt constrained by the political context of the time, following a decade of Thatcherite privatisation; but it does rather come across as waving the white flag of surrender.

Still, Edwards' report proved much more radical in its rhetoric around nature. 'Not every hectare of our national parks has to be farmed', it boldly asserted, challenging decades of consensus that our parks are inevitably agricultural landscapes. It recommended 'a number of experimental schemes' where 'farming is withdrawn entirely and the natural succession of vegetation is allowed to take its course', referring to these as 'wilderness' areas.[79] In other words, Edwards was suggesting rewilding, decades before the idea became popular. But without a clear mechanism to achieve this within our national parks – no extension of public ownership, nor new powers over private land – there was no hope of it happening. The most lasting outcome of *Fit for the Future* came with the Environment Act 1995, which adopted Edwards' recommendation to set up national park authorities as planning bodies in their own right, separate from county councils. The primary purpose of national parks was also updated to add the word 'wildlife', alongside 'natural beauty', as something to be conserved and enhanced – an improvement, but not exactly seismic.[80]

Reading each successive review and report, I get a sense of déjà vu. Time and again, the same themes keep coming up –

and each time, the government in charge takes on board a few of the review's recommendations, whilst ignoring the more radical proposals. The same pattern holds true with the most recent government-commissioned report on national parks, the Glover Review. Chaired by Julian Glover, a journalist and former speechwriter to David Cameron, it was initiated in a context of ever more urgent scientific warnings about the depth of the climate and biodiversity crises we face. Glover's report was refreshingly honest in admitting how much has gone wrong. 'Even if we only managed to restore diminished biodiversity to levels taken for granted in 1949 when the law to create National Parks . . . was established, we would have achieved something extraordinary,' he wrote.[81] Glover proposed bringing national parks into the twenty-first century by updating their primary purpose, giving them a duty to 'recover, conserve and enhance natural beauty, biodiversity and natural capital'.[82]

Glover ducked almost entirely the question of whether national parks ought to be owned by the nation, perhaps unsurprisingly for someone who once claimed that 'social democracy is not just an unsuccessful creed; it is a positively harmful one.'[83] But he made two important recommendations. Glover echoed his predecessor Ron Edwards by calling for 'wilder areas' in national parks. Farming should be deprioritised in some places and the emphasis put instead on "'letting nature take its course"'.[84] The review pointed to some existing private and third sector rewilding projects as examples, like the National Trust's Wild Ennerdale in the Lake District. Glover, however, seems to have been unaware of the Edwards Review's strikingly similar proposal for 'wilderness areas' from twenty-eight years previously. Perhaps if he had, he might have reflected on why national park authorities – bereft of land, budgets and powers to influence private landowners – had so far decisively failed to deliver any.

Glover's other key recommendation, however, did at least offer a way to extend the powers of national park authorities over other *public* sector landowners. As we saw earlier, although NPAs own paltry areas of land, public bodies overall own around 10 per cent of Britain's national parks, so having sway over this estate would be significant. Yet, up until that point, other public sector landowners were obliged merely to 'have regard' to the statutory purposes of national parks and park management plans. 'Have regard' is a 'notoriously weak duty', in the words of Richard Benwell, head of Wildlife and Countryside Link.[85] It's the legal equivalent of saying 'have a think about this, but if you can't be arsed to act on it, don't worry'. Glover, quite rightly, called time on this parlous state of affairs. He argued that public bodies really ought to be legally obliged to help implement national park authorities' management plans.[86]

Well, it only took four years and a lot of campaigning by environmental NGOs, but eventually this proposal became law via Michael Gove's Levelling Up Act in 2023.[87] The Act deleted the weasel words 'have regard' and replaced them with a legal duty that all public bodies must 'further' the purposes and plans of national parks.* The fact that the government had to be dragged kicking and screaming into doing this – despite it being a recommendation in a report *they* had commissioned themselves – is a salutary lesson that even small changes take time, and have to be fought for every step of the way.

Given the painfully slow progress made in improving our national parks over the past seventy-five years, what hope is there for future change? The answer is that there is always hope for those who spend time campaigning for it.

If the incoming Labour government wishes to enact further reforms of national parks, there are some obvious places to start. First, for the new duties obliging *public* landowners to help recover nature in national parks to be extended to large *private* sector landowners. If you own a thousand acres, say, in a national park, surely it's right that you should treat that land in accordance with it being . . . part of a national park? Just a thought. Second, for national park authorities to be

---

*A duty that is also binding on 'statutory undertakers', such as water companies that own land in national parks.

given bigger budgets, particularly to employ more ecologists and conservationists. Third, for more of the public to have a say in the running of national parks, as a counterweight to the disproportionately high representation of landowning and farming interests on their boards. The Campaign for National Parks has proposed 'embedding deliberative democracy' in each park by setting up citizens' assemblies, and giving all local residents and visitors a voice in how they're governed.[88] Last, we really ought to be honest about how much of a global anomaly Britain is in having national parks not owned by the nation. It's bizarre that we don't encourage our national park authorities to acquire land for nature restoration, and instead treat it as some sort of taboo subject. This is a normal, accepted feature of life in liberal, capitalist democracies, from Sweden and Japan to New Zealand and the United States: it's hardly a communist plot. Treating some parts of our island as 'a sort of national property' has been a dream shared down through the ages by Romantic poets, Liberal antiquarians, green Tories and social democrats. It is a dream that will never die.

9

An Ecological Domesday

A field in England, summer 1931. Britain's second Labour government is in its dying days; a fifth of people are out of work in the wake of the Great Depression.[1] But for the group of schoolchildren walking slowly through the field, life is momentarily carefree. A crop of wheat ripens under the blazing sun; a heat haze makes the horizon shimmer. The children, however, seem curiously engrossed in what they're doing. Though it may look like it to a passing observer, they're not bunking off lessons: they're clutching maps and coloured pencils. And this is no ordinary school geography project. These schoolkids are helping compile the first Land Utilisation Survey of Great Britain.

The Land Utilisation Survey – or LUS for short – was a groundbreaking effort to map land use comprehensively across Britain. It was the brainchild of Laurence Dudley Stamp, a celebrated geographer at the London School of Economics. Stamp was the youngest of seven children, had an early interest in natural history and fought in the First World War before entering academia. Dubbed a 'new Domesday Book' by the press, the LUS was made possible in an era before satellite imagery existed thanks to thousands of volunteers who participated in surveying the land.[2] Around a quarter of a million schoolchildren took part.[3] The instructions given to them were delightfully *Blue Peter* in tone. Stamp recommended using greaseproof paper to trace parts of a local Ordnance Survey map. 'These tracings can then be taken home by the children,' he wrote, 'and observations made independently by several groups . . . [with] the results recorded on the map kept in school.'[4]

With his grey moustache, bushy eyebrows and three-piece Edwardian suit, Dudley Stamp looked like the archetypal school geography teacher. And, like all good geography teachers, he marked pupils down for poor colouring-in skills. The maps, he wrote, should 'be coloured with water colour or crayons', before adding in bold text: 'Such colouring must only be very light.'[5] There was a strict colour scheme to be followed, too: woodland was shaded dark green, grassland light green; fields of crops were coloured in brown, whilst moorland and heath were yellow. Gardens and allotments were assigned the colour purple, built-up areas were shaded red. Each land parcel was also given an index letter – A for Arable, H for heathland, and so on – so that black and white maps could also be printed.

No one had attempted to do this before for the whole country.* Ordnance Survey maps, though very detailed, somewhat sell the landscape short: the majority of an OS map is white space, giving no indication of what's growing in the fields that dominate the country. Dudley Stamp wanted to fill in the blanks. He wished to produce a clear picture of how land was being *used* in Britain in the 1930s: where the crops were being grown, where the highest concentration of market gardens was, how much land was being devoted to pasture. Holding one of the original LUS maps in my hands at the National Archives is like looking back in time: a musty-smelling yet vividly coloured snapshot from an era before we ploughed up 97 per cent of our wildflower meadows, and grubbed up most of our traditional orchards. Even with its army of volunteer cartographers, producing the Land Utilisation Survey was a vast undertaking: after the fieldwork came the creation of finished maps, work which spanned the whole of the 1930s.

---

*In 1800, the cartographer Thomas Milne had produced an extraordinary land use map of London and its environs, but did not have the resources to repeat this for the rest of Britain.

But Dudley Stamp didn't just want to monitor land use: he also wanted to see the land used better. Tellingly, for his book summarising the findings of the LUS, he chose the title *The Land of Britain: Its Use and Misuse*. Dudley Stamp argued that his survey, whilst seeking to be objective, inevitably pointed to 'some areas in which the land is either wrongly used or is not contributing as fully as it might to the national well-being'. It led, he declared, to the need for land use planning.[6] In an astonishingly prescient table, Dudley Stamp set out his vision for how Britain's land use should be optimised. The area under pasture and 'rough grazing' should be reduced dramatically, he thought, and converted to a mixture of cropland and forestry – in order to better supply Britain with food and timber.[7]

When you stop to think about it, it's remarkable that this hadn't been tried before. Britain, after all, is a relatively densely populated island: you'd have thought that the government might be interested in how we best make use of the finite and irreplaceable resource of land. All states are concerned about protecting their territory from outside threats. At what point does a state begin to get concerned about the optimal use of land *within* its territory?

In the 1930s, anyone concerned about Britain's land use was primarily focused on the loss of farmland. A long agricultural depression had caused much marginal land in the uplands – where food production had always been hardest – to be abandoned. Imports of cheap wheat from the US and Canada had led some farmers to give up growing grains and turn arable fields over to pasture. Meanwhile, Britain faced the more permanent loss of farmland through unchecked urban sprawl.[8] Building homes, roads and factories on the country's most fertile soils threatened the country's food security, argued Dudley Stamp. Between 1927 and 1939, he calculated, 60,000 acres of farmland were lost every year to development.[9]

The trend seemed to be epitomised in the construction of the new town of Slough on prime agricultural land west of London. For some interwar writers, it became a byword for mindless urban growth, undercutting food production. 'Come friendly bombs and fall on Slough!' wrote the poet John Betjeman in 1937. 'It isn't fit for humans now, / There isn't grass to graze a cow.'[10] The grassland scientist George Stapledon agreed, writing about his 'furious anger' and 'sense of despair' when visiting Slough: 'If all this had to be, was it necessary to choose land of quite such a high standard of potential fertility?'[11]

It was follies like Slough, the geographers and agronomists argued, that made land use planning vital. 'What is needed is a comprehensive *national* plan of balanced land use,' declared Dudley Stamp.[12] But there was, as yet, no comprehensive planning system in place in Britain. The previous decade had seen calls for better town planning from the newly founded Council for the Preservation of Rural England, whose founders objected to the 'octopus' of unchecked development on aesthetic grounds.[13] What gave particular urgency to land use planning in the 1930s, however, was the looming shadow of Nazi Germany. If the world was plunged back into war, could Britain feed itself?

When war finally came, the blockade of Britain's trade routes by German U-boats meant the country had little choice: it had to grow more of its own food. The most visible elements of the government's response were the 'Dig for Victory' campaign, in which householders were urged to turn their gardens into allotments, and the formation of War Agricultural Committees, which oversaw a massive plough-up of pasture for crops. But the necessity of survival, wrote Dudley Stamp, also meant 'the Government awoke to the very rapid loss of good agricultural land.'[14] In 1942, Lord Reith, Minister of Works and Buildings, announced that the government would 'seek to avoid the diversion of productive agricultural land to other purposes'.[15] Around the same time, a Committee on Land Utilisation in Rural Areas was set up, with Dudley Stamp its vice-chair. One of Dudley Stamp's key tasks on the committee was to work out a way of grading land according to how fertile it was.

To do this, he drew upon the wealth of maps produced by the Land Utilisation Survey. First, Dudley Stamp classified the land, from 'good quality land' through to 'poor quality'. Then, using the data gathered by the LUS, he mapped the distribution of each land grade across the country.[16] The best quality farmland was found in places like the Fens; the poorest quality in the uplands. Here, at last, was a guide for making decisions about land use. The country needed housing; it also needed food. If the government wanted both, it made sense to at least protect the best-quality farmland, and build on lower-quality land instead. Dudley Stamp's Land Classification scheme formed a key part of the new post-war planning system.* Maps showing the broad locations of land, from good quality to poor, were printed by the Ordnance Survey, and distributed to councils to inform their reconstruction efforts.[17]

The creation of the national planning system was a momentous event. Up until that point, landowners had counted the right to construct buildings on their land as part of the 'bundle of property rights' that came with freehold ownership. The Town and Country Planning Act of 1947 essentially nationalised development rights over land, giving local government the power to decide whether landowners should be permitted to build. This also had the effect of democratising decisions about the use of land for development, because the public was able to take part in the planning process, expressing their support for schemes or raising objections to their local council.

Nowadays, we're constantly being told that the planning system is throttling housebuilding. But in the thirty years after the Act was passed, Britain built more homes than ever before.[18] It did so whilst *also* protecting large swathes of land from development, through the creation of Green Belts around large cities, and concentrating house building in a series of New Towns.

But there was a catch. From the outset, agriculture and forestry were explicitly excluded. The Town and Country Planning Act declared that they 'shall not be deemed . . . to involve development of the land'.[19] So, even as the planning system protected the countryside from built development and urban sprawl, it had

---

*A version of the Agricultural Land Classification (ALC) scheme is still in use today – though, of course, it's not always followed by councils heavily lobbied by developers.

no real control over what farming and forestry operations did to the land. After all, neither farming nor forestry were seen as causing serious damage to landscapes. Farmers and landowners could be left to their own devices, the trusted custodians of the countryside.

Yet it was the intensification of agriculture and forestry that really drove nature's decline in the three decades after the war. Hedgerows ripped up, ancient woods chopped down, chalk downland lost: such dramatic land use changes all took place outside the control of the new land use planners. This was the flipside of Dudley Stamp's desire to see land improved for food production; of the agronomist George Stapledon's work to tame the uplands with higher-yielding breeds of grass; and of the wartime plough-up campaign that grew more wheat, but sacrificed so many wildflower meadows.

The land use planners of the 1930s and 40s had rightly seen unchecked urban sprawl as the biggest threat to the integrity of the countryside at that time. What they had failed to foresee was how industrialised agriculture, forestry and shooting would become even greater threats. Moreover, Dudley Stamp and his colleagues had seen land use decisions as mainly a trade-off between food and housing, rather than a three-way split with nature as the third part of the equation. The government had hived off responsibility for protecting species and habitats to the new Nature Conservancy, and landscape aesthetics were largely the preserve of the new national parks. But these bodies, too, had very limited powers when it came to influencing land use decisions beyond the built environment.

For the next three decades, nature conservationists struggled to control the 'engine of destruction' unleashed on Britain's habitats by intensive farming, forestry and shooting interests. But with these sectors excluded from the land use planning system, something had to give. The crisis point came in the late 1970s, with a cry for help from the government's own nature watchdog.

Thirty years after the end of the Second World War, nature conservation in Britain was in crisis. The scale of habitat loss wrought over the past few decades was now becoming starkly apparent. Ecologists despaired at their powerlessness to change things. Then in 1977, the government's official conservation body, the Nature Conservancy Council, published a startling report, titled *Nature Conservation and Agriculture*.

The time had come, the NCC said, for a rural land use strategy. Wildlife and habitats in Britain faced huge and growing pressures from agriculture's impact on the land, the report argued; simply creating small-scale nature reserves wouldn't cut it any more. The report proposed creating a 'rural land use strategy that takes account of nature conservation' for the first time.[20] The report's author, Norman Moore – a brilliant entomologist and expert on dragonflies – was keen to avoid accusations of Soviet-style central planning. 'Such a strategy', he emphasised, 'would not infer a system of detailed centralised direction and planning, but would take the form of a statement of intent', making national priorities clear.[21] Land use planning in Britain to date had arbitrated between food and housing: now nature needed a voice too.

Other conservationists agreed. The NCC's chief scientist, the legendary botanist Derek Ratcliffe, wrote independently in 1977: 'Planning is in the ascendant, but has virtually no control over the two forms of land use – agriculture and forestry – affecting the greatest part of this country.' Competing demands for land, he wrote, were 'often in head-on collision . . . the sectional character of these interests thus proves a major obstacle to any coordinated approach to land use'.[22] And Max Nicholson, the former boss of the Nature Conservancy in the 1950s, accused the government of 'having dodged since the mid-century the issue of national land use planning'. Whilst much of the public were interested in conservation by the 1970s, Nicholson warned that this 'does not yet include most of the key people whose activities are punishing the environment'. He added, in typically pungent prose: 'It is as if we were trying to extinguish and prevent fires amid a community of mad arsonists.'[23]

The land use debate hit the mainstream with the publication of Marion Shoard's bestselling book *The Theft of the Countryside*, published in 1980. It laid bare the scale of devastation being wrought on Britain's wildlife and habitats by intensive agriculture, puncturing the myth of landowners as custodians. Shoard had read science at Oxford before training to be a planner and then working for CPRE. A softly spoken churchgoer, she did not fit the easy stereotype of an environmentalist firebrand. But as one reviewer noted, Shoard wrote with a 'surprising edge of passion that comes from a sense of shock'.[24] *The Theft of the Countryside* declared that 'the planning system is the means our society has chosen for reconciling the private pursuit of gain through land-use change with the public interest.' But, Shoard argued, the system was incomplete. 'It was always anomalous that most activity in the countryside should have been beyond the reach of the town *and country* planning system. Agriculture was exempted only because its impact on the countryside was relatively small at the time when the planning system was crystallising.'[25]

The answer, Shoard reasoned, was to extend the planning system to the 90 per cent of the country that was not built on.[26] She proposed a new Act of Parliament to do so, and that in future farmers and landowners would have to seek planning permission if they wanted to remove hedgerows, chop down trees or woods, drain marshes and ponds, or do anything that might damage moorland, downland and heath. 'Many (but not all) farmers would undoubtedly resent any such encroachment on their existing freedom to do whatever they like with their land,' wrote Shoard. But as she pointed out, homeowners in towns already had to live within the constraints of the planning system. 'There would be nothing peculiar in imposing a similar constraint on rural freeholders,' she argued.[27]

But though Shoard, the NCC and other ecologists had jointly reignited the debate about land use planning, they disagreed about the right solution. It was one thing to draw up a high-level strategy, like Norman Moore's desired 'statement of intent', setting broad guidelines for rural land use. It was quite another to subordinate every major decision that a farmer or landowner might make to planning controls. An assessment by the countryside writer Christopher Hall in the pages of *New Scientist* distinguished between 'weak' and 'strong' approaches to land use planning. 'The NCC appears to have a *weak* form in mind,' wrote Hall. Yet without a means to influence specific land use decisions, he argued, 'at best the weak-form strategy can be no more than a set of guidelines possessing perhaps some propaganda value, although even this is doubtful.'[28] But did the stronger approach, of looping farming and forestry into the planning system, stand any chance of becoming a political reality?

There were, in fact, two attempts made by politicians to legislate for greater land use planning around this time. In the dying days of Jim Callaghan's Labour administration, the government published a Countryside Bill. It contained a clause that would have granted local authorities the power to make management agreements with landowners, obliging them to preserve or enhance the 'natural beauty' of their land.[29] The historian Matthew Kelly argues this would have been a 'significant break with established practice by increasing the power of the nature state at the expense of rural property rights'.[30] But the Bill never made it onto the statute book, as a general election was called and Labour booted out of office. The incoming Conservative government did, however, introduce its own Wildlife and Countryside Bill, which attracted much debate and numerous amendments in the House of Lords. One such amendment aimed 'to bring agriculture and forestry under planning control', but was swiftly voted down.[31] The measures passed in the Wildlife and Countryside Act 1981 did significantly strengthen protections for SSSIs, as discussed in previous chapters. But these covered less than 10 per cent of England: more radical measures to protect nature from farming, forestry and shooting over the wider countryside were left by the wayside.

The problem was that imposing such a far-reaching system of land use planning came up against powerful landed interests and their friends in government. As Charlie Pye-Smith, a conservation writer, and Chris Rose, Friends of the Earth's countryside campaigner, wrote in 1984: 'Since the Second World War the belief that the fate of rural land should be determined by market forces and the whims of those who own it has been reinforced by governments which have left agriculture and forestry outside the framework of democratic planning controls.' Extending democratic say over land use, they argued, could act as a 'palliative to the evident inequity consequent on less than 1 per cent of the population owning land in Britain'. But as Pye-Smith and Rose readily acknowledged, 'opposition to planning controls over farming and forestry' was being driven precisely by 'the power of landowners and vested interests'.[32]

Seven years after the publication of *Nature Conservation and Agriculture*, with its bold plan to prioritise nature, the NCC issued a new report, with a deeply gloomy prognosis. In a chapter starkly titled 'Failures', the NCC admitted that conservationists had underestimated the 'powerful entrenched interests . . . such as agriculture and forestry' who saw conservation bodies seeking a say in land use as 'territorial intrusions'. 'This helps to explain why there has been considerable recent resistance to the concept of a national land-use strategy,' bemoaned the NCC, 'or indeed to any proposals which could be interpreted as involving a significant change to the *status quo* in control of land-use.'[33] The report concluded that 'the earlier concept of a National Land-Use Strategy has attracted little support and will not be pursued further.'[34] The conservationists had admitted defeat; the 'powerful entrenched interests' had won.

Writing in his memoirs at the end of the 1980s, Norman Moore lamented the fact that 'there is still no national strategy for land use in Britain. As a result, each contentious case is taken on its local "merits", without reference to a national plan because no such plan exists . . . there are no simple guidelines on land-use priorities.'[35] When Moore died in 2015, his *Telegraph* obituary praised his far-reaching impact on nature conservation, but noted that 'the Conservative Government jibbed at his proposal for a national land use strategy.'[36] Given the historically close relationship between landowners and successive Conservative governments, this was not surprising.[37] As the rural policy expert Michael Winter wrote after a decade of Margaret Thatcher being in power, 'the absence of a national land use strategy in the UK is partly a result of the poorly developed notion of the state in England and partly a consequence of the ideological and political composition of modern Conservatism.'[38]

Such a diagnosis did not bode well for how another Conservative government would view proposals for a land use strategy when they resurfaced in the second decade of the twenty-first century.

The urgency of the climate and biodiversity crisis has pushed land use back on to the political agenda today. It even forced Rishi Sunak's Tory administration to promise to publish a Land Use Framework for England.* But as we will see, it has been repeatedly delayed, and hamstrung through deference to landowners. It will fall to the incoming government to take the tough decisions needed on how we prioritise land use in a time of ecological emergency.

We have green groups like Friends of the Earth and Climate Camp to thank for first pushing the climate emergency into the political mainstream during the final years of New Labour. In 2008, the then newly established Committee on Climate Change (CCC) issued its first assessment of how the UK should decarbonise. The landmark Climate Change Act had only just become law; the UK's carbon targets still only aimed for an 80 per cent reduction in greenhouse gas emissions by mid-century – it would be another decade before the goal was strengthened to 'net zero'. Yet even at this early stage, it was obvious that a major change in approach to British land would be needed to help restore natural carbon sinks and draw down CO_2 from the air. The CCC recommended that the UK government get to work on this by developing a 'broader forestry and land use strategy'.[39]

A report with similarly far-reaching implications for land use was the Lawton Review of 2010. Chaired by the acclaimed ecologist Sir John Lawton, it called for a root-and-branch change to how we conserve and restore nature in England. Lawton's recommendations for policy were pithily summarised as being

---

*Whilst a 'land use framework' perhaps implies something a bit looser than a 'land use strategy', the differences seem more presentational than substantial.

'more, bigger, better, and joined'.[40] We need more land protected for nature; these nature reserves need to be bigger, and better managed; and, crucially, they have to be better joined up. Lawton is widely credited with crystallising a shift in British conservation away from focusing mainly on discrete sites like SSSIs, and towards landscape-scale ecological connectivity.

The third report of note was a review of land use published in 2010 by the Government Office for Science, an advisory body. It had been sparked by a speech given three years earlier to the CPRE by New Labour's policy wonk supremo David Miliband, entitled 'A land fit for the future?'. 'I want to ask "what is land for?" and why do we value land?' said Miliband, who at the time was environment secretary. 'We need a new consensus and a new vision for Britain and how it makes the most out of its land.' The future, he added, could see 'major changes in agricultural land', with land repurposed for habitat restoration, carbon sinks and afforestation.[41] The resulting report, called Foresight *Land Use Futures*, attempted to map the array of factors influencing UK land use, and how these might need to change over the next fifty years to tackle challenges like climate change, biodiversity loss and public health. Dense, sprawling, and filled with 'systems maps' of baffling complexity,[42] it nevertheless made a clear recommendation, like the CCC before it: the UK needed a 'strategic land use framework'.

These three reports all urged government to take land use seriously – but Westminster was predictably slow to react. It probably didn't help that the warnings had been sounded on the cusp of a change in government; talk of targets and strategies smacked rather too much of New Labour for the incoming Coalition government. It certainly didn't help that David Cameron and George Osborne were rather more interested in promising to cut 'red tape' and axe 'green quangos' than they were in coming up with serious solutions to complex environmental problems. So it would be another decade and three Tory prime ministers later before land use finally returned to the policy agenda.

In the meantime, various civil society groups put in a huge amount of effort to get land use discussed again. Environmental charities like CPRE, the RSPB and Green Alliance all advocated for a land use strategy.[43] Most significant of all has been the work of the Food, Farming and Countryside Commission (FFCC), helmed by the redoubtable Sue Pritchard, who has experience on both sides of the debate, from running action research programmes to managing an organic farm in Wales. The FFCC began as a project of the Royal Society of Arts, convening discussions between scores of groups and individuals, before being spun off as an independent charity. At an early stage, it identified that the key policy innovation needed was a 'land use framework for England'.[44] I was fortunate to take part in a couple of the FFCC's early roundtables on land use, one of which was held in the grand setting of the College of St George at Windsor Castle. It felt quite subversive to be debating radical changes to land use in such an establishment setting, with the assembled great and good: civil servants, academics, farming groups, environmental NGOs. Perhaps I had just been overawed by the medieval architecture, but I left the discussions feeling that if anyone could make demands for a land use framework go mainstream, it would be these folks.

For a time, things seemed to be going their way. In 2021, the government-commissioned National Food Strategy – chaired by Henry Dimbleby, co-founder of the Leon chain of restaurants – issued its final report. Amongst its recommendations was, yet again, a 'rural land use framework' for England.[45] In its response, Boris Johnson's government ended up junking nearly all of Dimbleby's suggestions to improve public health and the environment – *except* for his proposal of a land use framework.[46] A team of civil servants in DEFRA was established to take the idea forward. It was all quite exciting: might the government finally be taking land seriously?

But then, political inertia set in. Deadlines for publication of the long-awaited land use framework were delayed, and then delayed again. The CCC urged ministers to deliver their land use framework by the first quarter of 2023, but the first quarter of 2023 came and went.[47] The Tory party was too busy swapping bad prime ministers for worse ones to care about the trifling issue of how England uses its most finite resource. Behind the scenes, DEFRA officials were hard at work untangling the knotty issue of how to make a land use framework operate. But they were up against a constantly shifting set of ministers, none of whom seemed at all keen on the idea.

'I don't think communism works here,' bleated farming minister Mark Spencer, when asked for his clearly carefully considered views on the government's forthcoming land use framework. 'The freedom-loving economist in me doesn't want to be too prescriptive . . . dictating to landowners and managers what they can and can't do with their land.'[48] At a DEFRA roundtable on the land use framework, environment secretary Thérèse Coffey informed participants: 'Whitehall's not going to tell each farmer exactly what they're going to do' – as if that were ever on the cards. According to one read-out from the meeting, the Secretary of State wasn't even keen on publishing any maps of future land use, for fear of upsetting landowners. Not offending the CLA and NFU seemed to be the overriding concern. When I spoke to my contacts in DEFRA, they were gloomy about the prospects for being able to get anything meaningful past recalcitrant ministers. The government's land use framework remained unpublished when the 2024 general election was called.

Given these delays, the real decisions about how to enact a land use framework will now fall to the incoming Labour government. If it's to work well – and not just be another report gathering dust on a shelf, its findings forgotten and repeated by another report in a few years' time – there are several key things a new framework must do.

First, a land use framework must be an ongoing process, not a single event. If it's just a report that gets set aside and never updated, it's dead in the water. The genius of the Climate Change Act was that it created a *process* for decarbonising the UK, playing out to the drumbeat of five-yearly carbon budgets, and subject to regular chivvying from the Committee on Climate Change. We need to set a similar process in train for land use change. A 2022 inquiry by the House of Lords into land use in England recommended that alongside a land use framework, the government should create an English Land Use Commission to implement and update it over time.[49] This is an absolutely essential idea.

Second, effective planning must be democratic. One of the best parts of the FFCC's project on land use is that it has involved lots of people, who sometimes disagree, in co-designing a framework. But policy processes like these are always vulnerable to 'stakeholder capture'. When DEFRA runs consultations, they invariably end up being dominated by the powerful landowning and farming groups – who already have outsize sway over land use decisions. If we're to seriously change the way land is used, we know the current owners don't have all the answers. So we need the wider public to be involved and exert democratic pressure. That aspiration can be found in Scotland's first Land Use Strategy, published in 2011. It emphasised the need for greater democracy: 'People should have opportunities to contribute to debates and decisions about land use.'[50]

Third, an effective land use framework needs to entail tough decisions. If I have a criticism of the recommendations made by the FFCC and House of Lords inquiry, it's that they set too much store by the concept of 'multifunctional land use'.[51] This means using the same piece of land for multiple different things – for instance, to produce food at the same time as storing carbon. Obviously, almost all land is multifunctional in some respects: for instance, orchards produce food, are good for pollinators and provide joy for anyone going apple-picking in them. But when we look at the country as a whole, it's clear that certain land is better suited for some functions than others. In other words: we need to prioritise.

The need to have different priorities for different sorts of land was clearly recognised by Henry Dimbleby's National Food Strategy. It points out that some land is highly productive for growing food, whilst other areas are very poor: the soils are too low quality, it's too wet to grow crops, the terrain is too exposed even for the hardiest livestock. This is an insight that takes us back to the 1940s and Dudley Stamp's land classification maps. We have long known that it's hard to eke food from the uplands, whilst fertile East Anglia is the breadbasket of England. Broadly speaking, the land that's least productive for food is also the land with the most potential for restoring carbon sinks and nature: our upland peat bogs, heathlands and some downland areas. The one part of England where the value of the land for growing food comes into major conflict with storing carbon is the Fens – a challenge explored in detail in Chapter 5.

The National Food Strategy puts numbers to this, and shows that the least productive 21 per cent of England's land produces just 3 per cent of our calories. As their evidence report states, this land 'could – in theory – not be farmed at all if we reduced waste in the system' – such as by eating less meat and cutting food waste. We could then reprioritise such land for other ends.[52] Doing so would be a trade-off – prioritising nature over food – but as these numbers show, it would be a very sensible trade-off. The influential FFCC shies away from talking about how to best prioritise land use, but unfortunately, you can't always have your land and eat it too.

Fourth, any land use framework worth its salt needs a map to go with it. It must take a 'spatial approach' – to recognise that geography matters. Decisions about the best use of land obviously need to take into account the natural constraints and opportunities presented by topography, ecology and climate. Our peat bogs, huge natural carbon sinks, are fixed in location and, because they take thousands of years to accumulate, cannot simply be 'recreated' elsewhere in the country in any meaningful human timescale. Taking these natural constraints into account should help us prioritise certain land for nature and carbon, as opposed to producing food or building houses. Amongst the National Food Strategy's recommendations was for a 'National Rural Land Map . . . which would supply detailed assessments of the uses to which any given area of land would be best suited'.[53]

And if the government needs a hand working this out, it's in luck: over the past decade numerous studies have been done to map future land use scenarios for England (and the wider UK). The Committee on Climate Change, National Food Strategy, Centre for Alternative Technology, Friends of the

Earth and Green Alliance have all carried out spatial modelling that would help optimise land use to meet food and housing needs, net zero targets and nature recovery.[54] Nowadays, we don't need to call on schoolchildren to map land use field by field with colouring pencils: we can draw on decades of satellite imagery instead. Perhaps the most detailed and impressive land use mapping has been conducted by the RSPB. It modelled nine scenarios for future UK land use, four of which reduced emissions from land to net zero. The report's authors then took a further step to model what these scenarios could mean for biodiversity and food production. They found there were some definite trade-offs – the need to reduce livestock numbers and meat consumption to free up land for nature, for example – but that there are also win-wins. The scenarios that drew down most carbon also saw the biggest restoration of natural habitats, benefiting breeding birds.[55]

But to achieve these optimal outcomes, the RSPB concluded, 'requires strategic land-use planning'.[56] As the lead author Tom Finch said: 'The assumptions we made . . . were aimed at minimising negative impacts. We didn't model an unregulated "Wild West" free-for-all scenario, but this would probably be . . . bad.'[57] Unfortunately, an unregulated free-for-all is the scenario most recent governments have been set on.

The last and most important element of a successful land use framework is a mechanism for it to influence real-world decisions. It's one thing to map an ideal scenario for land use – quite another for that to drive changes on the ground. The elephant in the room is land ownership. Funnily enough, this wasn't something the House of Lords inquiry on land use grappled with; the fact that the chair of the inquiry was a significant landowner must be coincidental.[58] But as the earlier Foresight *Land Use Futures* report acknowledged, 'For the most part, land is privately owned . . . [and] private property rights are well entrenched in law'; therefore, 'changing the way land is used requires careful thought'.[59]

Careful thinking was, alas, in short supply amongst DEFRA ministers under the previous Tory government. When farming minister Mark Spencer was asked about the levers government can pull to deliver changes in land use, he responded, predictably: 'We can do that through carrots or sticks. I personally believe carrots work a lot better at motivating people.' Well, we've been offering landowners and farmers a veritable feast of carrots for decades, in the form of Environmental Stewardship payments – and we're still up shit creek. True, a land use framework *could* help direct where future payments are targeted. But this would hardly be innovative: spatial criteria already influence the distribution of farm payments, such as whether the land is protected as an SSSI. If a land use framework is to have real added value, it's as a form of regulatory underpinning. It's to help government say to the most regressive landowners, 'the land you own is essential to the national interest, and needs to be cared for.'

The most obvious yet far-reaching solution to this would be to finally bring agriculture and forestry within the planning system, as Marion Shoard advocated in the 1980s. The benefits are plain. It would clearly impact on real-world decisions. It would mean expanding the remit of the existing planning permission system, but one that many people are already familiar with – offering a local, democratic, participatory way to decide how land is best used. In this context, a land use framework would operate as a kind of national guidance, with decision-making over land use delegated to local authorities.

But it would also be a formidable challenge to implement. You would first have to define the sort of changes to land that would qualify as 'development' and be subject to an expanded planning system. It's one thing to have to get planning permission to put in a loft extension; but how would farmers react to having a council officer sign off on their plans to plough up a meadow? Existing piecemeal protections, like Tree Preservation Orders and hedgerow regulations, would probably need to be folded into the new system to avoid confusion. Councils would need to be much better resourced, and employ more ecologists to deal with the added caseload. Most of all, the political resistance from landowners, farmers and their lobby groups would be enormous. As a DEFRA civil servant once told me, 'we have to have rural planning . . . but at present, that's just not politically achievable.'

So, until a government is brave enough to pick this up, what could be more easily put in place in the meantime? I think there are two key policies. And, to allay some politicians' paranoid fears about rural communism, both of my proposals draw deeply on English history and tradition.

The first takes inspiration from Dudley Stamp's pioneering land utilisation survey, and in particular his Agricultural Land Classification maps. A version of these maps is still used by planning authorities today, in order to protect high-quality farmland – grades 1, 2 and 3a – from being built on. This remains a vital function; but it also needs an update for the twenty-first century. The land classification maps published by Natural England today make no reference to land's value for nature, carbon capture and flood mitigation. The land least suitable for producing food – grades 4 and 5 – is also the land where much of our carbon is stored, in upland peat. And because this land is invariably too steep, wet and exposed to grow much food, it's where the natural regeneration of native woodlands make most sense. What's more, these areas are generally remote from where most built development would occur. So grades 4 and 5 land should be reclassified as being protected from *both* agriculture and housebuilding, and prioritised instead for nature restoration.

It's true that central and local government would be limited in how they could enforce this, unless and until the planning system were extended to include wider land use decisions. But they could still use the updated land classification maps to better direct public funding towards areas prioritised for nature restoration. They could also choose to buy such land directly – whether on the open market or via compulsory purchase. And such a map would inform councils' forthcoming Local Nature Recovery Strategies. By showing graphically that some parts of the country should be prioritised for nature, some for food production and others for housing, the government would also be sending a powerful signal to landowners and farmers that these are all nationally important land uses.

My second proposal reaches back even further into English history for its inspiration: the government should enact an Ecological Domesday Survey. The original Domesday Book of 1086 surveyed who owned land; Dudley Stamp's 'new Domesday' of the 1930s surveyed how land was being used. An Ecological Domesday Survey would go one step further: it would be an account of what landowners are doing to steward the land.

It would mandate all landowners possessing 1,000 acres or more to tell us how they will be helping the country sequester carbon, restore habitats, and aid the recovery of wildlife. Let's be clear: if you're lucky enough to own 1,000 acres, you're a very big landowner – in England, three-quarters of all farmers own or rent landholdings that are smaller than 250 acres.[60] Each major landowner would be asked to supply three things. First, a digitised map of their estate boundaries. Second, a baseline survey of habitats, species and carbon stocks on their landholdings. And third, a plan for what they intend to do to help meet national targets for carbon reduction, 30x30 and species recovery over the next five years.

Every map, survey and plan would be made publicly available online, compiled by an English Land Use Commission. A single digital map showing all estates over 1,000 acres would be published: click on each landholding, and you would be able to read that landowner's plans for nature recovery and carbon sequestration. To avoid landowners wriggling out of this reporting obligation by trying to split their estates into units smaller than the 1,000-acre threshold, the government would verify estate boundaries and their ultimate owners against records held by the Land Registry and Companies House.[61] The Land Use Commission would then contact landowners meeting the threshold, informing them of their new reporting duties. Because land ownership in England is so concentrated in the hands of a few, I calculate that this will mean at the very most 25,000 landowners producing reports, and probably far fewer, covering around 50 per cent of England's land.[62]

Landowners could hardly complain that this new duty would be onerous: most large estates are run like businesses and already have management plans. They just aren't usually made public, and they won't all be good for nature or the climate. Pioneering landowners already doing great work to rewild their land or practise regenerative farming will find this an easy ask. Recalcitrant landowners who couldn't care less will moan and do the bare minimum to comply, but because it will all be published, the public will be able to judge whether what an estate says is credible and ambitious.

A second round of reporting after five years could introduce tougher rules, ratcheting up action like the five-yearly carbon budgets that bind the UK government. Indeed, the Climate Change Act already mandates that large companies must report on their greenhouse gas emissions; this is merely establishing an ecological reporting duty for large estates.[63] And if you think this sounds politically impossible, the Scottish government is currently consulting on a similar proposal for inclusion in its third Land Reform Bill; why not do this in England, too?[64]

If landowners baulk at this new public duty, perhaps they should be reminded of what stewardship truly means. It means looking after the land on behalf of someone else. To the seventeenth-century lawyer Matthew Hale, whom we met at the start of this book, everyone would ultimately have to give an account of their stewardship to God – explaining how they had made prudent use of the Earth's resources entrusted to them. That was why Hale entitled his seminal essay *The Great Audit, with the Account of the Good Steward.*[65] And King William's original Domesday Survey got its name because it was compared to the Last Judgement: God's audit of humanity at the end of time. Nowadays, we need landowners to be accountable not to gods or kings, but to the wider public. And we need a twenty-first-century Domesday Survey for a very pressing Earthly reason: in order to help ward off an ecological doomsday.

Conclusion: A Common Treasury for All

Let me close with the parable of the nature-friendly farmers let down by the landowning establishment.

Over the past twenty years, a small group of heroic farmers and landowners have battled to bring beavers back to Britain. The beaver is a native British species, but it was wiped out some four centuries ago by hunting and habitat destruction. These furry, toothy mammals are ecosystem engineers, whose presence in the environment gives a massive boost to biodiversity. The leaky dams they build across streams, constructed out of small trees they've gnawed down, generate pools and swamps teeming with dragonflies, newts and frogs. Ponds created by beavers have been found to support a third more plant species and a quarter more beetles than other wetlands.[1] Even better, by slowing the flow of water downstream, beavers help to reduce flood risk: pretty handy when the climate crisis is bringing increasingly torrential rainfall. What's not to like?

That's been the view of the maverick farmers who've pioneered the return of the beaver. In Cornwall, the person leading the charge has been Chris Jones, an organic beef farmer.[2] Some years ago, he witnessed flooding in the village near his farm, and wondered whether beavers could help fix the problem. He set aside five acres of his land for a beaver enclosure, in a boggy area next to a stream.

A few summers back, I visited Chris's farm and witnessed the extraordinary transformation he'd allowed the animals to work on his land. A vast, almost primeval swamp had been created by the beavers behind their network of dams fashioned from felled willow saplings. The air was heavy with the scent of water mint growing in the still pools. Beavers are most active around dusk; and, sure enough, as the sun began to set in the west, we saw movement in the dark waters. In the fading twilight, Chris scampered about the banks of the ponds with childlike glee, using an infrared torch to illuminate beaver activity for me without disturbing them. Monitoring work on the stream has shown the beavers' dams have already reduced peak flows downstream, lowering flood risk[3] – all whilst Chris continues to produce food on the rest of his farm.

In Scotland, beaver reintroduction was spearheaded by Paul and Louise Ramsay, owners of the Bamff Estate on the edge of the Cairngorms. Their son Adam, an environmental journalist, once took me on a tour of the incredible habitat generated by the estate's beaver families. Venturing out by moonlight, we squelched through a vast wet marshland, peppered with occasional conifer stumps that bore the unmistakable signs of beavers' teeth-marks.

Another pioneer is Derek Gow, a gruff and sweary ex-sheep farmer from Scotland who, with his whiskery beard, bears some resemblance to a beaver himself. Derek gave up his flock some years ago, bought a farm in Devon and began populating it with beavers, water voles and wildcats. He's enraged by the ongoing collapse in wildlife and impatient to reverse it. 'If we keep on course with this we'll be left living on a planet full of pigeons and dogs on the beaten-down crust of our own excrement,' he says, with characteristic vigour.[4]

These farmers, and others like them, have the public on their side. Beaver reintroduction is backed by 62 per cent of Brits, according to a poll conducted by YouGov in 2020.[5] Beavers are, in some ways, the least controversial symbol of rewilding. If Britain can't bring back the harmless beaver, what hope does it have of reintroducing lost predators like lynx and wolves?

Yet these pioneers have been opposed by a reactionary coalition of farming unions and regressive landowners. Sometimes the rewilding movement is accused of being a pastime of toffs, who have no financial need to farm, and it certainly has its supporters amongst the aristocracy. But the *anti*-rewilding movement comprises a far more influential section of landed power.

Opposition to bringing back the beaver has come from the very top. King Charles, when he was Prince of Wales and owner of the Duchy of Cornwall, was widely rumoured to be against beaver reintroductions. When Naomi Oakley, a Duchy tenant farmer on Dartmoor, applied for permission to release a pair of beavers, she was refused by her landlord. For all his environmental credentials, it seems that Charles retains a traditionalist view of the British landscape: one kept tidy and managed, rather than wild. Whether the policy has changed since Prince William took charge of the Duchy remains unclear.

The return of the beaver is also vehemently opposed by newly wealthy landowners. James Dyson, the inventor who was named the richest man in Britain in 2020 and owns some 33,000 acres of land via his farming companies, appears to hate beavers.[6] When asked whether he would release beavers on his estates, he told *The Times*: 'No, I don't want them, or otters. They kill everything. They killed all last year's and this year's cygnets in Gloucestershire. At my house in Singapore they killed all my fish; bit their heads off . . . It's nice to be romantic but, as farmers know, a lot of these things are pests.' The fact that beavers don't eat birds or fish – they're herbivores – does not seem to have crossed Dyson's mind. He is, after all, an engineer, not an ecologist. But why, then, do we rely on such landowners to be good stewards of nature? When the *Times* journalist asked Dyson if he would rather be paid to be a 'custodian of the countryside', he replied: 'Why on earth would you want to do that?'[7]

Our landowning politicians are little better. The Tory MP Richard Drax, owner of a 14,000-acre estate – one of the biggest in Dorset – shared his wisdom on the beaver during two parliamentary debates in 2022.[8] Attacking what he termed 'reckless rewilding', Drax argued that returning beavers to Dorset would 'create havoc to river flows and banks and lead to flooding'.[9] Drax failed to mention, of course, that allowing some boggy fields to flood might be preferable to flooding his constituents downstream. On a later occasion, he observed that beavers couldn't be trusted to stay on one side of a fence: 'Scotland experimented with it, and once beavers had bred, they did not keep to the allocated space. They went all over the place. They are not appropriate for small rivers in Dorset.'[10] But then Drax, whose estate is bounded by one of the longest walls in England, and whose speeches often attack immigration, is not a fan of freedom of movement.

Some of the most vociferous campaigns to stop beaver releases have come from the lobby groups that claim to speak for all farmers. 'Beavers should not be a protected species,' thundered the NFU in 2021, demanding compensation for farm businesses impacted by beavers building ponds.[11] When the UK government unusually ignored the farming union's wishes by swiftly granting legal protection to beavers, the NFU's then-president Minette Batters slammed the decision as 'unacceptable'.[12] The chair of the NFU's environmental forum, arable farmer Richard Bramley, argues that flood mitigation is better done without the beaver. 'You can't control what it does or how it does it,' he says. But this line betrays what's really at stake here: control.[13]

The epicentre of beaver derangement syndrome, however, appears to be Scotland. In an interview with the *Sunday Times* in 2022, NFU Scotland president Martin Kennedy claimed that some Scottish farmers 'considered the threat posed by beavers as "bigger than Brexit"'.[14] Leaving the world's largest trading bloc, it seems, has nothing on the existential challenge posed by a few furry mammals. But speak to farmers in European countries where beavers have co-existed with people for decades, and you encounter a rather more sensible attitude. When he was setting up the Cornwall Beaver Project, Chris Jones visited Bavaria, where beavers were reintroduced fifty years ago. 'How big is the problem of beavers . . . in the whole sphere of farming?' he asked one bemused Bavarian farmer. 'Well . . . 2 to 3 per cent,' shrugged the farmer, with characteristic German precision.

But any hopes that British farmers and landowners might get some perspective on the beaver situation were dented in January 2024, when an anti-beaver protest took place in Scotland. The previous month, the Cairngorms National Park Authority had announced that, following extensive consultations, it would be releasing two pairs of beavers into the national park, which covers over a million acres.[15] This, however, was two pairs too many for a group of local farmers, who drove their tractors en masse to protest outside the park authority's offices. 'NO TO SLATER'S BEAVERS', read one of the spray-painted signs, referring – with all the subtlety of a sniggering *Viz* comic strip – to Scottish environment minister Lorna Slater, who held responsibility for species reintroductions. 'You Cannot Eat Trees', read another placard – seemingly oblivious to the fact that beavers, of course, can.[16]

The moral of this tale is twofold. It demonstrates that *yes*, some farmers and landowners *are* brilliant stewards of nature: actively pioneering the return of a native species to their farms, and doing so to delight and benefit the wider public. A handful of mavericks can inspire a lot of good; and in the case of beaver releases, they have the majority of the public on their side.

But Britain's ongoing beaver wars also demonstrate the deeper challenge this country faces if we're to repair our impoverished ecosystems. We face an uphill struggle against a landed establishment that is reactionary, jealously wants to maintain control, and is often ecologically illiterate. Reading through the litany of nonsense spouted about beavers by landowners ranging from billionaires to royals to farming union officials, you wonder how any of them still have the temerity to proclaim themselves 'custodians of the countryside'. Yet because they *own* most of the land, this small elite holds most of the cards. The view of farmer-turned-rewilder Derek Gow is typically blunt, but true: 'They have no mandate to have it their way only.'[17] Their mandate, such as it is, comes from their money. That's why, to save nature in Britain, we need new ways of democratising decision-making over land.

Who really cares for the countryside? For centuries, landowners have claimed to be the trusted stewards of Britain's landscapes. Private property ownership, they argue, has guaranteed the preservation of our green and pleasant land.

Stewardship is a noble enough idea, in theory. As we've seen, its origins lie in the efforts of Stuart-era biblical scholars to preach parsimony: the Earth was made by God, they argued, so humans ought to steward it carefully. In the final judgement, everyone would have to give an account of their stewardship; and God was unlikely to be pleased with those who had failed to look after their share of creation. Some of the first proponents of stewardship were early environmentalists, like John Evelyn, who encouraged large landowners to plant trees in the face of a growing timber crisis. There are, to this day, shining examples of individual farmers and landowners who live up to such public-spirited ideals.

The problem is, claims of stewardship by landowners increasingly ring hollow. In recent decades, there has been a concerted campaign to convince us that *all* landowners and farmers are good stewards, 'custodians of the countryside', and shouldn't be troubled with pesky environmental regulations or taxes. Politicians have fallen for this hook, line and sinker, parroting the phrase each time they make a speech about rural affairs. This genuflection is usually accompanied by promises of more public money and fewer burdensome regulations; more carrot, and less stick. Yet since this mantra was first uttered, Britain's ecosystems have only declined further. Once-common farmland birds like turtle doves and tree sparrows have seen their numbers collapse by over 90 per cent since the 1970s.[18] Despite decades of governments paying landowners and farmers to nurse nature back to health, just 39 per cent of England's Sites of Special Scientific Interest are in favourable condition.[19]

And claims of custodianship or stewardship are not merely disingenuous: they're also conceptually flawed. The role of a steward is to look after land on someone else's behalf. But who are landowners and farmers stewarding our countryside *for*? To whom are they accountable, if they fail to be good stewards? To seventeenth-century proponents of stewardship, it was God; to modern advocates, it might be future generations. Yet conveniently, neither can pass judgement on you in the present. For claims of stewardship to be meaningful, landowners have to be accountable to the public now. As the sociologist Howard

Newby wrote in 1979, 'the public has a legitimate right to be interested in the land which it entrusts to its custodians.'[20]

The reality is that private property ownership *doesn't* inevitably breed respect for nature. If it did, why do so many landowners still trash habitats, persecute wildlife, release invasive plants and animals, and oppose the reintroduction of native species like the beaver? On the contrary, love of place seems unrelated to legal ownership. This book is replete with examples of people who care for land without it belonging to them, from trespassing botanists uncovering evidence of wildlife crimes, to community groups clearing plastic waste from neglected streams. As the Scottish poet Norman MacCaig once wrote: 'Who possesses this landscape? / The man who bought it or I who am possessed by it?'[21]

In fact, a small number of landowners have had an outsize impact on Britain's countryside, bearing responsibility for destroying some of our most important habitats and carbon sinks. It took just thirteen landowning venture capitalists to initiate the draining of the Fens, laying waste to what was once one of the largest wetlands in western Europe. We have Queen Victoria and Prince Albert to thank for sparking the aristocratic fashion for driven grouse shooting – leading to the transformation of Britain's upland peat bogs, and the release of perhaps half a billion tonnes of carbon, in service to this elite sport. A handful of landowners with more money than sense are nowadays responsible for releasing 50 million non-native pheasants into the British countryside every year – weighing more than the total breeding biomass of the *entire* British wild bird population.[22] One or two individuals have made outstanding contributions in the field of ecological disruption. The 11th Duke of Bedford, who introduced invasive grey squirrels and muntjac deer to these shores, has perhaps had more impact on Britain's ecosystems than any other single organism in this island's history.[23]

But, to quote Winston Churchill in his now-forgotten book on land reform, 'It is not the individual I attack, it is the system.'[24] The seeds of ecological destruction are contained within the framework of property rights which grant legal title over land. Private land ownership comprises a 'bundle of rights', one of which is the *jus abutendi*: the right to waste and destroy. Yet there is no corresponding legal duty on landowners to be the good stewards they often claim to be.

Enormous amounts of time and money have been spent in recent decades trying to tip-toe around this inconvenient truth. Successive Tory governments, wedded to small-state ideologies and bankrolled by landed power, have placed great emphasis on voluntary environmental initiatives by landowners and farmers. Where these have failed to achieve the desired results, ministers have opted to grease the wheels with cash.

Some £9.2 billion of taxpayers' money has been spent over the last thirty years on agri-environment subsidies in England, often badged as 'Countryside Stewardship' schemes. Some of these schemes have undoubtedly done much good. But many have been a waste of money, handing out millions to landowners for little discernible improvement in the state of a habitat. In some situations, it would have been better value for money for the government to simply buy the land outright and manage it themselves. There is, after all, a limit to what incentives alone can do. No landowner or farmer is under any obligation to take the money. Plenty of farmers are motivated by tradition and peer pressure, not just economics. And if you're trying to persuade a billionaire to change their shooting habits, you're going to need a big chequebook.

Nature conservation, therefore, ultimately has to confront private property rights. Wildlife and habitats require legal protections that can override the right of the landowner to destroy them. And if we're to repair the ecosystems that have already been lost – the fens that have been drained, the moorlands burned – we need new policies that compel landowners to do so, or otherwise force them to sell. The public needs to be able to assert that some parts of our land – our most important carbon stores, our most precious ecosystems – have to be managed for the common good, rather than trashed for private gain.

We should all have a say in how land is best used. This may sound radical, but it used to be lived experience for many communities before the enclosure of the commons. Common land covered around 30 per cent of England at the time of Shakespeare, and was governed by locally run organisations – from Fen Reeves to Forest Verderers – that regulated its sustainable use. But, as John Clare reminds us, 'Inclosure came and trampled on the grave / Of labour's rights and left the poor a slave'.[25] With just 3 per cent of England today remaining commons, the enclosures enacted by the landed gentry were not just a land grab: they also robbed the public of their say in how the countryside was run.

The earliest movements for democracy in Britain were bound up with a yearning to democratise the governance of land, from the Levellers to Gerrard Winstanley's Diggers. Democracy in land, for Winstanley, was the only way to make 'the earth . . . a common treasury for all'.[26] Over three centuries later, we all now have a vote and get to elect our governments. But we still haven't democratised the way we make decisions over land.

To those who would dismiss this as some sort of pinko communism, it's worth recalling again the words of Winston Churchill, who in 1909 wrote: 'Land, I say, differs from all other forms of property.' Land, he argued, is 'a necessity of human existence' and 'the original source of all wealth'[27] – what we might today call 'natural capital'. Classical nineteenth-century liberals understood perfectly that land ought to be treated differently to personal possessions and the fruits of human labours. 'No man made the land,' wrote John Stuart Mill. 'It is the original inheritance of the whole species.' The public had a clear stake in how land was used, he argued: 'a man whom . . . the law permits to hold thousands of acres as his single share, is not entitled to think that all this is given to him to use and abuse, and deal with as if it concerned nobody but himself.' Even to an arch-liberal like Mill, it was perfectly reasonable that a landowner 'be legally compelled to make his interest and pleasure consistent with the public good.'[28]

During the twentieth century, it was recognised that conserving land was a public good, and that democratic governments had a mandate to curb private property rights over land to protect it. Escalating ecological damage – urban sprawl, the loss of fertile soils – drove the creation of 'the Nature State'.[29] Pre-eminent ecologists and geographers like Arthur Tansley and Max Nicholson were convinced of the need for state involvement in nature conservation, and persuaded the post-war Labour government to pass a slew of far-reaching laws to this effect. The new planning system amended the bundle of property rights, removing the landowner's automatic right to develop land and making it subject to democratic oversight. The new system of SSSIs and National Nature Reserves, overseen by the Nature Conservancy, began to constrain the *jus abutendi* in some of the country's most precious remaining habitats. The creation of national parks at last gave expression to William Wordsworth's dream, that our most beautiful landscapes be treated as 'a sort of national property'.

But these reforms, far-sighted though they were, remain unfinished business. The planning system, by excluding farming and forestry decisions from its scope, failed to anticipate how industrialised agriculture, commercial plantations and intensive shoots would reshape the countryside in the post-war decades. National parks, set up 'on the cheap', fell far short of early visionaries' hopes that they would be 'owned or controlled by the Nation'.[30] The Nature Conservancy and its successors found themselves locked in battle with landowners and farmers who ploughed up and hacked down habitats, despite them being designated as SSSIs.

The debate about who gets a say over the use of land resurfaced in the 1970s and 80s, prompted by alarming evidence of the quickening decline of nature. This period saw a set of remarkable proposals put forward to improve the governance of land, now largely forgotten. The planner Marion Shoard argued forcefully for the extension of the planning system to include agriculture and forestry; ecologists at the Nature Conservancy Council called for a new land use strategy; geographers Ann and Malcolm MacEwen pushed for the reform of national parks so that they better served nature. But although fresh legislation in the early 1980s gave stronger legal protections to SSSIs, these more radical solutions were ignored. And the Nature State was further undermined by the deregulatory ideology of successive Tory governments – from Nicholas Ridley's attacks on the Nature Conservancy Council, to David Cameron's later attempted sell-off of National Nature Reserves and the public forest estate.

Landed interests also successfully staged a fightback around this time by reviving the language of stewardship, and by claiming to be the voice of rural Britain. Older organisations like the NFU and CLA were joined by new lobby groups such as the Moorland Association and the Countryside Alliance. These lobbyists still claim to speak for the countryside, despite most of them representing tiny numbers of people with huge power and wealth: the 27,000 members of the CLA who own around a third of the land of England and Wales; the 150 or so grouse moor estates that own at least half a million acres of the English uplands.[31] Even the 45,000 members of the NFU and the 100,000 who belong to the Countryside Alliance comprise but a small fraction of the rural population.[32] By shouting loudly, they have occluded the fact that farming, forestry and fishing make up just 7 per cent of employment even in *rural* areas of England.[33] Across the UK as a whole, agriculture generates just 0.5 per cent of GDP and employs only 1.5 per cent of the workforce, yet takes up 71 per cent of the land.[34] Land use decisions remain disproportionately dominated, therefore, by a small number of people.

In recent years, with the climate and nature crises deepening, the use and abuse of land has again risen up the political agenda. The Committee on Climate Change warns that farming and land use accounts for 11 per cent of UK greenhouse gases.[35] In fact, emissions from agriculture are now likely larger than those from the UK's electricity sector, following a collapse in coal power and surging installations of renewable energy.[36] Yet there's been no similar progress in cutting emissions from the land use sector; to meet carbon targets, land must rapidly become a net carbon sink by the mid-2030s.[37] The 2023 State of Nature report warned that the UK is now one of the most nature-depleted countries on Earth, and that 'significant and ongoing changes in the way we manage our land for agriculture' is a key cause.[38] The UK government has pledged to protect 30 per cent of England for nature by 2030 – the '30x30' goal – yet currently only around 3 per cent of England makes the cut.[39] There is, in other words, a mountain to climb, and very little time left to do it.

The good news is that changing land use to this extent is technically possible.

The National Food Strategy calculated that sparing 21 per cent of England's least productive land for nature would only lead to a 3 per cent loss in food production, which could be readily made up for as Brits continue to eat less meat and dairy.[40] Our least productive land mainly comprises upland areas, which happily coincide with the location of our most important carbon sink – moorland peat – and where there's greatest potential for allowing the natural regeneration of trees, along hillsides and steep-sided valleys. Most of these areas are contained within our National Parks and National Landscapes,* which together cover around 26 per cent of England: so managing these areas for nature would get us close to the 30x30 goal. The drained peat of the Fens poses a trickier problem to resolve, as it remains vital for growing fresh vegetables. Yet even here, novel methods of 'swamp-farming' in rewetted soils, alongside some restoration of wild fenland habitat, could reduce the vast amounts of carbon being emitted from this degraded landscape.

The bad news is, many landowners and agribusiness interests are dead set against such changes. Most upland peat belongs to a handful of vast grouse moor estates, who appear utterly unwilling to give up their damaging practices. In the subsiding Fens, even the Church Commissioners – supposedly motivated by the moral imperative of 'safeguarding creation' – seem in no hurry to alter the intensive farming methods that make this drained landscape a vast source of carbon emissions. When the NFU published its much-heralded plan for how the farming sector could meet net zero, it couldn't bring itself to contemplate shifts in diet or significant land use change. Instead, it relied overwhelmingly on the unproven technofix of bioenergy carbon capture and storage to offset emissions from agriculture.[41]

In the face of such opposition, current government policies on land use won't cut it.

---

*National Landscapes in England were until recently called Areas of Outstanding Natural Beauty (AONBs).

To save nature in Britain – to weave back together the fraying fabric of life – we need new policies that go further.

How land is used is everyone's concern. This truth was recognised even by Rishi Sunak's Conservative government. As a consultation on land ownership transparency issued by the Department for Levelling Up recently stated: 'Although land may be owned by individuals, companies, trusts or other entities, all citizens have a collective interest in ensuring that land is used properly and for the benefit of society.'[42]

I couldn't agree more. It's time to democratise the governance of land, and make landowners accountable for their claims of stewardship. So here are my ten proposals to make this happen. Most of these asks are directed towards politicians in Westminster, so apply mainly to England; some of them take inspiration from policies pioneered in Scotland over the past twenty years. Where the Welsh and Scottish governments could also take further action, I make this clear.

1. Take back control of our most important carbon store: ban moorland burning and outlaw driven grouse shooting

Peat soils are Britain's most important carbon store, containing some 3 billion tonnes of carbon.[43] Yet upland peat bogs currently emit some 3.4 million tonnes of CO_2e annually,[44] as a result of being drained, burned and intensively managed for driven grouse shooting – an elite sport practised by a tiny percentage of the population. What's more, by damaging the natural sponge-like qualities of blanket bog through such mismanagement, grouse moors threaten communities downstream with worse flooding. And by transforming the uplands of Britain into a giant grouse farm, where everything is designed to maximise the number of birds to be shot, grouse moor owners and their gamekeepers have waged a war on wildlife. Hundreds of thousands of foxes, stoats, weasels, polecats, mountain hares and crows have been trapped and killed to sustain this sport. That's not to mention the endemic wildlife crime that props up grouse shooting, with countless hen harriers, goshawks and other birds of prey illegally shot and poisoned on grouse moors across Britain.

Today, there are around 150 grouse moor estates in England, and another 300 in Scotland, owned by a wealthy elite of aristocrats, oligarchs and hedge fund managers. These landowners regard their grouse moors as the 'ultimate trophy asset', and appear utterly unwilling to give up their Victorian fad. Enough. It's time to bring an end to the archaic practices that have wrecked some 3 million acres of our uplands, worsened the climate crisis, choked communities with the smoke from moorland burning and left them at the mercy of worsening floods. The UK government must ban moorland burning outright, removing the many loopholes that bedevil the current partial ban, and outlaw driven grouse shooting. After enacting this in England, it should work with the Scottish government to achieve the same outcomes in the Highlands.

Such legislation would likely spark a wave of sales of grouse moor estates. To avoid these estates being bought up by carbon-offsetting cowboys or forestry plantation firms, we should also put in place new policies to allow communities and the public sector to acquire this land instead. Through their reckless failure to steward this land, grouse moor owners have forfeited their right to own it. The huge carbon store they possess should no longer be treated as a 'trophy asset', trashed for private sport – it's a crucial *national* asset, and this land should be returned to the people.

2. Democratise land ownership: create a Community Right to Buy in England

Since the 1990s, there has been a revolution in land ownership in Scotland. Communities have risen up to reclaim control of land from which their ancestors were forcibly ejected two centuries ago. Inspired by a wave of buyouts, the Scottish government has since supported communities to acquire land by providing public funding, and legislating for a Community Right to Buy. Now, half a million acres of Scotland belongs to communities.[45]

Democratic participation and sustainable development are baked into the legal frameworks that community buyouts have to abide by: they are publicly accountable in ways that private landowners simply aren't. The example of the Langholm Moor buyout shows the scale of what's possible: a 10,000-acre former grouse moor once owned by the Duke of Buccleuch, the largest individual landowner in Britain, now being transformed into a nature reserve belonging to the community.

Predictably, England has lagged far behind Scotland in this regard. Weak community ownership laws introduced by David Cameron's government offer only a pale imitation of the rights enjoyed by communities north of the border. England should introduce a Community Right to Buy that follows Scotland's example, giving communities the ability to not only designate land and property as Assets of Community Value, but also get right of first refusal on them when they come up for sale. The ordinary sales process should be paused for twelve months to allow communities the time to raise funds and draw up business plans, and the existing Community Ownership Fund should offer to cover up to 80 per cent of the capital costs of a buyout, as is the case with the Scottish Land Fund.[46] The official criteria under which land can be listed as an Asset of Community Value must be broadened to include environmental and economic benefits, alongside social ones – as a recent report commissioned by the Labour Party recommended.[47]

Doing so would allow communities in England to not only acquire pubs and village halls, but also woods, rivers and green spaces. Imagine if a community living downstream from a grouse moor, plagued by flooding, were able to buy the moorland and rewild it: turning it back into a natural flood defence, active carbon sink and wildlife-rich nature reserve. Communities in Scotland don't need to imagine: they're already doing so. The public in England, and in Wales, deserve such a right too.

3. Use public money to buy land for nature: set up a Public Nature Estate

The public sector, despite bouts of privatisation and austerity, still owns 8.5 per cent of England (and significant chunks of Scotland and Wales), spanning millions of acres. Though some of this land is built on, vast swathes of it comprise moorlands, forests and farmland – all of which could be doing more to aid nature's recovery. The Forestry Commission in England, for example, should be compelled to rapidly restore the 105,000 acres of Plantations on Ancient Woodland Sites that it possesses – turning them from conifer monocultures back into species-rich broadleaved woods. Old weapons testing sites belonging to the Ministry of Defence need to be decontaminated, whilst the 200,000 acres of County Farms owned by English councils ought to be saved from being flogged off, and instead rejuvenated as beacons of regenerative agriculture. All publicly owned land should become part of a new Public Nature Estate, dedicated to maximising nature recovery and carbon storage.

A bold government would also empower the public sector to acquire more land and add to this Public Nature Estate over time – using powers of compulsory purchase where necessary. As the historian Matthew Kelly argues, there is a long history in Britain of taking 'natural habitat into state ownership when landowners fail in their custodial duties'.[48] Indeed, that was the original strategy of Britain's first official conservation body, the Nature Conservancy, when it was set up in 1949. But four decades of neoliberalism have dampened our faith in the power of government to do good. It's time to rediscover the potential power of the Nature State, whose functions have been allowed to wither and atrophy.

This book is packed with examples of habitats crying out to be rescued by the public sector from their careless private owners. And in some circumstances, public acquisition of land may be the most effective use of public funds. Rather than spend millions of pounds of taxpayers' money paying a private landowner for environmental outcomes that may never be delivered, why not simply buy the land outright and have it managed by a public body like Natural England? Even if compulsory purchase powers were used only sparingly, the threat that they might be deployed as a backstop would encourage landowners to be better stewards of nature. After all, when councils fail, they're taken over by central government; why not follow the same principle with failing landowners?

4. Make polluting landowners pay: levy a carbon land tax
Drained in the 1700s, the Fens today is a devastated landscape, leaking vast quantities of carbon to the air and rapidly leaching

its fertility into the sea. The ongoing collapse of the fenland peat is not only an ecological disaster: it also poses a threat to Britain's food security, with the country reliant on these fertile soils for a third of its fresh vegetables. The current owners of the Fens comprise a set of wealthy institutional investors, from pension funds to the Church Commissioners, whose mismanagement of this landscape sits at odds with their professed environmental ethics and supposed long-term investment decisions.

There are good ways to start fixing the Fens: from restoring parts of it to semi-natural wetlands, to pioneering 'swamp-farming' of crops that can grow in rewetted peat soils. Yet progress is slow, and there's a lot of money bound up in maintaining the status quo. New Countryside Stewardship payments for raising the water table in lowland peat might help nudge things along. But to save the Fens before its peat soils are exhausted, we shouldn't just be talking about carrots: we also need to deploy some sticks.

The UK government should levy a carbon land tax on the owners of fenland peat, proportionate to the millions of tonnes of carbon pollution pouring off their lands. Those landowners that switch to paludiculture or opt to restore wetlands – supported in either case by stewardship payments – would be exempt from the tax. Those who stick with the extractive systems of agriculture so damaging the Fens would be taxed: it's fair, after all, that the polluter pays. Money raised through the carbon land tax should be spent by the Treasury on boosting British horticulture outside of the Fens. A carbon land tax would send a clear signal: if you keep draining the Fens, we'll drain your wallets.

5. Stop letting landowners unleash their plague of pheasants on Britain

It's absurd that we allow landowners to release 50 million pheasants a year into the British countryside, without any serious checks. Our governments profess concern about the impact of invasive species on our ecosystems, yet offer a free pass to shooting estates to deluge the landscape with a non-native gamebird. The sheer weight of pheasants now strutting about our woods and fields is having a profound environmental impact: degrading habitats, adding to the pressures on endangered species like adders, and upending food webs. I'm not against shooting in itself. But there's a world of difference between low-intensity shoots where you eat what you kill, and the grotesque waste of industrialised bloodsports – littering the countryside with plastic, and leading to mass graves of discarded pheasants.

Pheasant releases have increased ten-fold since Roald Dahl wrote *Danny the Champion of the World*, easily the most famous portrayal of a pheasant shoot in English literature. The UK government should set out a strategy to return pheasant numbers to what they were in Danny's day: a 'pheasant phase-down', if you will. To achieve this reduction, ministers must reform the ridiculous tax breaks that prop up some shooting estates – HMRC's 'tax-exempt heritage assets' scheme, in particular – and properly enforce the pheasant licensing regime, so that releases in and around nature reserves are strictly controlled. Scotland and Wales are putting in place more extensive licensing regimes for pheasant shoots; England should learn from these and follow suit, to restore the balance of the countryside.

6. Let the public become whistleblowers for nature: create a right of responsible access across the English countryside

In England, the public has a right to roam over just 8 per cent of the country. Those who want to keep it this way often claim that letting the public roam more widely would mess up the countryside. Yet hidden from sight behind barbed-wire fences and Keep Out signs, secrets lurk. Those who dare to trespass into the wider countryside often uncover evidence of wildlife crimes, habitat destruction and river pollution. Motivated by a love of place, rather than through dint of ownership, groups of citizens are trying to hold landowners to account for the damage they're doing: from moorland monitors raising the alarm about raptor persecution, to river guardian groups testing for agricultural pollutants.

If we extend access rights in England, the public can take on the role of nature's whistleblowers, its last and best line of defence against ecological harms. Taking inspiration from Scotland's example, the government should extend the public's right of responsible access across the rest of the English countryside, with sensible exemptions for private gardens, fields in which crops are growing and sensitive nature sites. The Countryside Code, meanwhile, was neglected for years by the Conservative government: between 2010 and 2020, ministers spent less than £2,000 per year promoting it.[49] The incoming government should draw up a new English Outdoor Access Code that outlines the responsibilities of both access users and landowners, and properly fund its promotion, including by teaching it in schools. Let's cultivate a new land ethic – that when exploring nature we don't just 'leave no trace', but proactively care for the environment through acts of wild service.

7. Make national parks serve the interests of nature and the nation
National parks are meant to be the pinnacle of our landscapes, yet instead they are 'places where wildlife goes to die', in the pithy phrase of beaver-wrangler Derek Gow.[50] Encompassing many of Britain's SSSIs, a large proportion of our peat bogs and ancient woodlands, and some of our least productive farmland, national parks ought to be hotspots for ecological recovery. Yet our national parks are not, contrary to popular belief, owned by the nation: the vast majority of the land in them lies in private hands. This makes it hard for national park authorities to influence land use within their boundaries.

Eighty-three per cent of the public support the idea of making Britain's national parks wilder.[51] So let's give NPAs the means to do so. In England, ministers should finally adopt the recommendation of the Glover Review to update the official purpose of NPAs to include nature recovery.* Recent changes to the law have belatedly placed an obligation on other public sector landowners to help NPAs in their efforts: this should be extended to large private landowners, too. Having suffered from an eye-watering 40 per cent cut in their budgets during austerity, our national parks desperately need better resourcing,

---

*This would carry greater weight than the general public sector biodiversity duty contained in the Environment Act 2021.

so that they can employ more ecologists and rangers. To counter the disproportionate influence of landowners and farmers on decision-making in national parks, each park could set up citizens' assemblies with representation from the wider public, embedding deliberative democracy at their heart. Lastly, national park authorities should be encouraged to acquire more land outright, especially where doing so would protect habitats neglected by their current owners. It is, after all, commonplace around the world for national parks to be largely owned by the public; Britain is the woeful exception.

8. Put in place a land use framework for England and open up data on land

Land is a strictly finite resource; as Mark Twain once quipped, 'they're not making it anymore.' So it's remarkable that there is no comprehensive strategy for how we use land in England.

Far-sighted thinkers in the twentieth century understood the need for greater land use planning. The geographer Laurence Dudley Stamp, who oversaw the first-ever Land Utilisation Survey of Britain, sought to rationalise how the country prioritised its land. His system of Agricultural Land Classification, drawn up during the Second World War, has helped protect top-quality land from development ever since. Understandably missing from Dudley Stamp's 1940s prospectus, however, was the need to prioritise certain landscapes for nature and carbon, and the need to place limits on industrial farming and forestry.

With both Conservatives and Labour now agreed on the need for a land use framework for England, the real challenge is putting one in place that actually bites on decision-making – rather than being yet another report gathering dust on a shelf in Whitehall. An effective land use framework, therefore, must be spatial in nature – with the government publishing a map to help guide land use decisions. It should update Dudley Stamp's classification maps so that the least-productive land – Grades 4 and 5 – is prioritised for nature, carbon and flood mitigation. And to guide land use change over the long term, a land use framework must be a process, not a single event. To this end, the government should set up an England Land Use Commission, to review the framework over time and monitor progress.

Coupled to this, ministers need to open up data about land. Because so much about how we use land is bound up with who owns it, the Land Registry must finally be completed and made freely accessible to the public. And to improve transparency and accountability, we should extend the Freedom of Information Act to cover large establishment landowners currently exempt from FOI requests, such as water companies, the Church Commissioners, and the Duchies of Cornwall and Lancaster.

9. Carry out an Ecological Domesday Survey: require large landowners to give an account of their stewardship
The original Domesday Book of 1086 surveyed who owned land, and how much tax they owed to William the Conqueror. Today, we need an Ecological Domesday Survey: an audit of what the country's largest landowners are doing to steward the land in their care.

All landowners possessing 1,000 acres or more should be mandated to tell us how they will be helping the country sequester carbon, restore habitats, and aid the recovery of wildlife over the next five years. Such plans would be published on a government website, along with a digitised map of each estate, so that the public can see what each landowner is doing. Because land ownership in England is so concentrated in the hands of a few, I calculate this will mean at the very most around 25,000 landowners producing reports, covering around 50 per cent of England's land.[52]

Large landowners could hardly complain that this new duty would be onerous: most big estates are run like businesses and already have management plans – just not ones that are made public, or are necessarily good for nature and the climate. Pioneering landowners already doing good work will find this an easy task. Recalcitrant estate owners should be reminded that the meaning of stewardship is to look after land on behalf of someone else: that 'someone else' is the public.

10. Join campaigns to hold landowners to account and change the laws of the land

My last proposal isn't a policy, but rather a plea to everyone reading this book. It is that you put this book down, and campaign like hell to fix the problems it discusses.

Join campaigns that hold large landowners to account for their claims of stewardship: from Wild Card's campaign to persuade the royal family to rewild their estates; to Wild Justice's heroic work to rein in pheasant shoots; to Operation Noah's efforts to get the Church Commissioners to be better stewards of their fenland peat. Join campaigns that seek to change the laws of the land: from River Action's work to better regulate the agribusinesses polluting the River Wye; to the Right to Roam campaign's mass trespasses, aimed at winning the public a right of responsible access to England's countryside. For inspiration, look to what past campaigns have achieved – like the extraordinary success of Scotland's wave of community buyouts, from the Isle of Eigg to Langholm Moor. And if there's a part of the land debate that doesn't yet have a campaign – start one.

Democracy is about so much more than putting a cross in a box every few years. It's about having a say in the running of things, from your local area to the country you live in. It's about being able to participate, using all the tools we still have available to us as citizens: from interrogating government departments through submitting Freedom of Information requests, to engaging in civil disobedience. How land is used and abused contributes to so many of the urgent crises we face, yet it is rarely subject to democratic oversight. So don't just get angry, get involved. The fate of our land is too important to be left only to those few who own it.

For too long, we've been told a lie – that you need to own land in order to care for it. Let's replace the lie of the land with a profound truth: that anyone can develop a deep love of nature, place and land, regardless of whether you own it.

Acknowledgements

I began the journey of writing this book some years ago, and along the way have become indebted to the wisdom of many expert guides.

Firstly, huge thanks to my agent James Lockhart, and to everyone at William Collins who has brought this book to fruition: to publishing director Arabella Pike; to my editor Eva Hodgkin, for an inspired subtitle, and whose judicious edits have improved this book no end; to Lizzie Rowles, Matt Clacher, and Alex Gingell; and to my former editor Sho Rokadiya, who got the whole ball rolling.

Thanks to the many farmers and landowners who live up to the ideal of stewardship (but are too often let down by the lobby groups that claim to speak for the countryside); and in particular to Naomi Oakley, Mark Owen, Merlin Hanbury-Tenison, John Howell and Chris Jones, whose work is inspirational.

Equally inspirational has been the work of various thinkers and practitioners within the Scottish land reform movement. Andy Wightman and Alastair McIntosh, pioneering authors and campaigners, lit a fire that continues to spread south of the border. My thanks also goes to Jenny Barlow, Kat Mayer and Margaret Pool, for their generosity in showing me around Langholm and opening my eyes to the possibilities of community ownership. And I'm grateful to Tom Chance at the Community Land Trust Network, and Will Brett at the campaign group We're Right Here, for their tireless advocacy on this issue in England.

Whenever I've got depressed thinking about the state of nature in Britain, I've been re-energised by seeing the dedication of people who are trying to turn things around. To mention just a few of these 'whistleblowers for nature': my thanks to Liz Richmond and the Rebel Botanists, for opening the public's eyes to the plants whose names we have unforgivably forgotten; to Paul Powlesland and the River Roding Trust, for their extraordinary work to clean up this neglected waterway; to Dave Bangs, trespassing botanist, for his courage and determination; and to all the river guardian groups that have sprung up in recent years, blowing the whistle on river pollution from the Dart to the Wye.

Many, many people have given generously of their time in helping me research this book. Big thanks to Tom Lancaster for his policy expertise *par excellence* and number-crunching of agri-environment payments. Thanks to Patrick Thompson, Luke Steele and Andy Baird for discussions and correspondence about peat, moorland burning and grouse moors; and to Mark Avery, Ruth Tingay and Chris Packham for chatting about raptor persecutions and pheasants (and for being champions of nature). Thanks to historians Matthew Kelly, Nick Kirsop-Taylor, Glen O'Hara and Tom Breen, for discussing the history of Britain's 'nature state', the Nature Conservancy, and right to roam. I'm grateful to Miles King for sharing his expertise on the SSSI system (whilst roaming through some glorious Dorset chalk grassland), and to Chris Rose for words of wisdom drawn from a lifetime campaigning. Thanks to Rosie Wood, for insights from her time at Natural England; to Sue Pritchard at the Food, Farming and Countryside Commission, for inviting me to take part in various roundtable discussions about a Land Use Framework; and to Kate Jennings and David Hampson at RSPB for discussing the Glover Review and how to fix our failing national parks. A big thanks also to Richard Benwell and Matt Browne at Wildlife and Countryside Link, for inviting me to work on proposals for a Public Nature Estate – and for being all-round campaigning legends.

London likes to think of itself as the centre of the world, but in reality, that accolade belongs to Devon. It's heaving with expert ecologists and environmental campaigners, many of whom I've been lucky to befriend since moving here four years ago. Especial thanks to Kevin and Donna Cox, Tony Whitehead and Lisa Schneidau, and George Monbiot and Rebecca Wrigley, for many late-night chats about sheep, curlews, commons, and how to fix a problem like Dartmoor. My thanks also to Joel Scott-Halkes, Elena Grice and the Wild Card team, for injecting energy into nature campaigning; and to everyone who dances in MAYDAY Morris - for proving that a) Morris dancing is cool, actually, and b) that every protest needs a Morris side.

As a campaigning author on the 'outside' of government, I get to speak my mind freely – but I have huge respect for anyone trying to change the system from within. My thanks go to those working within the Labour party on environmental policies – to Steve Reed MP, Adam Dyster, Eleanor Salter, Hugh Greenwood, Muneera Lula, Isabel Abbs and others – for many conversations, and in hope that the new government will take bold action on the nature crisis. And a big thankyou to the civil servants and public officials who've spoken to me anonymously: you know who are – keep up the good work on the inside!

Three final words of thanks. Firstly, to my wonderful partner Louisa Casson, oceans campaigner extraordinaire – for enduring endless chats about pheasants, fens and furious landowners. Secondly, to Mum and Dad, and to Louisa's parents, Jonathan Casson and Alison Boardman – for putting up with us, and putting us up!

And lastly, thankyou to the Right to Roam campaign crew – to whom this book is dedicated: to Amy-Jane Beer, Dan Grimston, Harry Jenkinson, Jess Day, Jon Moses, Lewis Winks, Maria Fernandez, Nadia Shaikh, Nick Hayes and Paul Powlesland. You're all amazing, and you're the best team I've ever been part of.

List of Illustrations

Page 1:
Land use in Britain (National Food Strategy, 2021)

Page 2:
Farmland productivity in England (National Food Strategy, 2021), overlaid with national park boundaries (© Natural England copyright. Contains Ordnance Survey data © Crown copyright and database right 2024)

Page 3:
Damage to the River Lugg (© Environment Agency copyright and/or database right 2024. All rights reserved)

Grouse moor burning (Alamy)

Page 4:
Fenland peat soils (author photo)

Pheasant grave (Independent Digital News & Media Ltd)

Page 5:
Farmers burning effigies of conservationists (Roger Hutchings)

Page 6:
River Roding Trust trespassing to pick up litter (Paul Powlesland)

Wild Card Duchy protest (Felix Prater)

Page 7:

Old Crockern wild camping protest on Stall Moor (Getty Images)

Langholm Common Riding (Getty Images)

Page 8:

Eigg islanders celebrate community buyout (Murdo MacLeod)

Langholm's regenerating moorland (author photo)

Endnotes

Epigraph

1 Matthew Parris, 'Trespass and the Right to Roam' – interview with Nick Hayes, BBC Radio 4, 10 Jan 2023, www.bbc.co.uk/sounds/play/m001gwyk

2 Gerrard Winstanley, *A Watch-Word to the City of London and the Army* (1649) reproduced in Christopher Hill (ed.), *Winstanley: 'The Law of Freedom' and Other Writings*, 1972, p. 128.

Introduction

1 Etymology of Lugg: from Eilert Ekwall, *The Concise Dictionary of English Place Names*, p. 338, archive.org/details/in.ernet.dli.2015.184064/page/n337/mode/2up

2 Herefordshire Wildlife Trust quoted in Katie Feehan, 'Farmer, 67, who bulldozed riverside Herefordshire beauty spot to protect homes from flooding faces criminal charges brought by Natural England and the Environment Agency', *Daily Mail*, 10 Mar 2022, www.dailymail.co.uk/news/article-10597835/Farmer-John-Price-bulldozed-River-Lugg-beauty-spot-help-flooding-faces-criminal-charges.html

3 Herefordshire Wildlife Trust statement, 'Justice for the River Lugg', 20 Apr 2023, www.wildlifetrusts.org/news/justice-river-lugg

4 Feehan, 'Farmer, 67, who bulldozed riverside Herefordshire beauty spot to protect homes from flooding faces criminal charges'.

5 Nicola Goodwin and Caroline Gall, 'Farmer who damaged River Lugg has sentence cut after appeal', BBC News, 17 May 2023, www.bbc.co.uk/news/uk-england-hereford-worcester-65625272

6 Feehan, 'Farmer, 67, who bulldozed riverside Herefordshire beauty spot to protect homes from flooding faces criminal charges'.

7 'Very good farmer': letter from Terry Hall to the *Hereford Times*, 2 July 2023, www.herefordtimes.com/news/23624877.jailed-farmer-john-price-tried-improve-river-lugg/. 'Freed immediately and compensated': letter from Will Fenn to the *Ledbury Reporter*, 5 June 2023, www.ledburyreporter.co.uk/news/letters/23569208.river-lugg-farmer-john-price-freed-immediately/

8   Emma Gatten, 'Farmer jailed for dredging river "was looking after land like his father and grandfather"', *Telegraph,* 21 Apr 2023, www.telegraph.co.uk/ environment/2023/04/21/farmer-jailed-dredging-river-looking-after-land-like-father/

9   Tweet by Ben Goldsmith, 22 Apr 2023, twitter.com/bengoldsmith/ status/1649678121396781056?s=46&t=gKpdna_au6zdzT6Ls7sKFQ

10   George Monbiot, 'At last, England's dying rivers are an election issue – and the danger isn't just sewage', *Guardian,* 3 May 2023, www.theguardian. com/commentisfree/2023/may/03/england-rivers-election-sewage-water-pollution?CMP=Share_iOSApp_Other

11   John G. Sprankling, 'The Right to Destroy', chapter in Sprankling, *The International Law of Property,* 2014, academic.oup.com/book/5438/chapter-ab stract/148323903?redirectedFrom=fulltext

12   William Blackstone, *Commentaries on the Laws of England,* Book III, ch. 14; see also Book III, ch. 18. For a discussion of the history of *jus abutendi,* see Edward J. McCaffery, 'Must We Have the Right to Waste?', USC Olin Research Paper No. 00-16 (no date), mylaw2.usc.edu/centers/class/class-workshops/usc-legal-studies-working-papers/documents/00_16_paper.pdf

13   Wildlife & Countryside Link, 'Nature 2030: five urgent reforms to meet natural environment targets in the next Parliament', July 2023, p. 9. For a list of all Natural England's enforcement actions, see www.gov.uk/government/ publications/register-of-enforcement-action-taken-by-natural-england. At the time of writing, the total number of prosecutions brought by Natural England over damage to SSSIs since 2006 totalled just 18.

14   At the time of writing, 39% of England's 4,127 SSSIs were deemed by Natural England to be in 'favourable' condition: designatedsites.naturalengland.org.uk/ ReportFeatureConditionSummary.aspx?SiteType=ALL

15   Wildlife & Countryside Link, 'Achieving 30x30 in England on land and at sea', Sep 2021, p. 9.

16   Christopher Rodgers, 'Property Rights, Land Use and the Rural Environment: A Case for Reform', *Land Use Policy* 26, Supplement 1, 2009, pp. S134–S141, eprints.ncl.ac.uk/file_store/production/157055/76164E8B-57A7-495F-9821-8604D6670C3A.pdf

17   William Gilpin, *Observations on the River Wye,* 1770, p. 76, quod.lib.umich. edu/e/ecco/004863361.0001.000/1:7?rgn=div1;view=fulltext

18   Wye Salmon Association, 'River Wye Salmon Action Plan', Dec 2019, p. 3, www.wyesalmon.com/wp-content/uploads/2019/12/Bold-and-Urgent-Action-Full-Report-v18-FINAL.pdf

19   Helena Horton, 'River Wye health status downgraded by Natural England after wildlife review', *Guardian,* 30 May 2023, www.theguardian.com/ environment/2023/may/30/river-wye-has-health-status-downgraded-by-natural-england-after-wildlife-assessment

20   Hywel Griffith, 'River Wye: Pollution not caused by farming, says NFU', BBC News, 14 Aug 2023, www.bbc.co.uk/news/uk-wales-66440390

21   Save the Wye campaign website, 'About us', savethewye.org/about-us/

22 Friends of the River Wye campaign website, 'About us', www.fouw.org.uk/aboutus

23 Lottie Limb, 'River Cam becomes first UK river to have its rights declared', 22 June 2021, www.cambridge-news.co.uk/news/cambridge-news/river-cam-becomes-first-uk-20876969

24 Patrick Barkham, '"The Roding is sacred and has rights": the hammer-wielding barrister fighting for London's forgotten river', *Guardian*, 5 Dec 2022, www.theguardian.com/environment/2022/dec/05/river-roding-barrister-paul-powlesland-london-polluters-footpaths

25 Billy Stockwell, 'The rights of rivers', *The Ecologist*, 9 Aug 2022, theecologist.org/2022/aug/09/rights-rivers

26 British Canoeing, 'Clear Access, Clear Waters' campaign, clearaccessclearwaters.org.uk/about-clear-access-clear-water-campaign/

27 UK river access map, accessmap.riveraccessforall.co.uk/map

28 Amy-Jane Beer, *The Flow: Rivers, Water and Wildness*, 2022, p. 226.

29 Isabella Tree and Charlie Burrell's Knepp Estate is 3,500 acres; see Knepp Estate website, knepp.co.uk/rewilding/background/. The Holkham Estate, for which Jake Fiennes is land manager, is 25,000 acres: see 'Who Owns Norfolk: Holkham Estate map', www.whoownsnorfolk.org/post/holkham-estate-map. James Rebanks farms 185 acres: see '"Don't give up on us": James Rebanks on the future of farming and how he saved his land', Penguin website, 2 Sep 2020, www.penguin.co.uk/articles/2020/09/james-rebanks-interview-english-pastoral-shepherds-life. England is 32m acres, so 28,685 acres is 0.09% of the country.

30 Half of farmland birds: DEFRA, 'National statistics: Wild bird populations in the UK, 1970 to 2021', 13 Apr 2023, www.gov.uk/government/statistics/wild-bird-populations-in-the-uk/wild-bird-populations-in-the-uk-1970-to-2021; the farmland bird index cited shows a 58% decline between 1970 and 2020. Lowland hay meadows destroyed: Miles King, 'Nature's Tapestry: The story of England's grasslands and why not all grass is green', report for the Grasslands Trust, 2011, www.magnificentmeadows.org.uk/assets/pdfs/Natures_Tapestry.pdf. Ancient woodland cut down: this figure relates to Britain, and is from Oliver Rackham, *Trees and Woodland in the British Landscape*, 1976, p. 174. Hedgerows grubbed up: People's Trust for Endangered Species, 'A History of Hedgerows', suggests half of all UK hedgerows were lost between 1950 and 2007: ptes.org/hedgerow/a-history-of-hedgerows/. Hedgehog numbers: Natural History Museum, 'Britain's rural hedgehogs see dramatic population decline', 22 Feb 2022, www.nhm.ac.uk/discover/news/2022/february/britains-rural-hedgehogs-see-dramatic-population-decline.html. Insect decline: BugLife, 'Bugs Matter survey finds that UK flying insects have declined by nearly 60% in less than 20 years', 5 May 2022, www.buglife.org.uk/news/bugs-matter-survey-finds-that-uk-flying-insects-have-declined-by-nearly-60-in-less-than-20-years/. Earthworm decline: Damian Carrington, 'Earthworms may have declined by a third in UK, study reveals', *Guardian*, 19 Dec 2022, www.theguardian.com/environment/2022/dec/19/earthworms-may-have-declined-by-a-third-in-uk-study-reveals

31   See, for example, how the Conservative MSP Murdo Fraser accused the Scottish Government in 2015 of 'pursuing an ideologically-driven class war in our countryside, driven by the politics of envy', after its introduction of legislation to extend a Community Right to Buy. 'SNP accused over land reform plans', *Herald,* 20 Feb 2015, www.heraldscotland.com/news/13202476.snp-accused-land-reform-plans/

32   Chris Rose, 'Revolution in Taliban Alley', 5 Sep 2022, threeworlds. campaignstrategy.org/?p=2982, and accompanying essay, 'Chapter 4: Where To Go Now?', threeworlds.campaignstrategy.org/wp-content/uploads/2022/09/Chapter-4-Where-To-Go-Now.pdf

33   John McNeill, *Something New Under the Sun: An environmental history of the twentieth century,* 2000, p. 111.

34   Mark Easton, 'How much of your area is built on?', BBC News, 9 Nov 2017, www.bbc.co.uk/news/uk-41901294. The analysis was carried out by Dr Alasdair Rae using CORINE land cover data.

35   'Intensive management of agricultural land, largely driven by policies and incentives since WW2, has been identified as the most significant factor driving species' population change in the UK.' State of Nature Partnership, 'State of Nature 2019', p. 67, nbn.org.uk/wp-content/uploads/2019/09/State-of-Nature-2019-UK-full-report.pdf

36   'This country is full': Richard Drax MP, House of Commons immigration debate, 6 Sep 2012, hansard.parliament.uk/commons/2012-09-06/debates/12090626000001/Immigration. Drax owns the 14,000-acre Charborough Estate: for the stats and maps, see Guy Shrubsole, 'The ten landowners who own one-sixth of Dorset', 4 Jan 2020, whoownsengland.org/2020/01/04/the-ten-landowners-who-own-one-sixth-of-dorset/

37   Alasdair Rae, 'Think your country is crowded? These maps reveal the truth about population density across Europe', The Conversation, 23 Jan 2018, theconversation.com/think-your-country-is-crowded-these-maps-reveal-the-truth-about-population-density-across-europe-90345

38   Keith Mellanby, 'Can Britain Feed Itself?', 1975; the thought experiment was repeated and updated by Simon Fairlie for *The Land* magazine in 2007: www.thelandmagazine.org.uk/sites/default/files/can_britain_feed_itself.pdf

39   'Giving 21% of the least productive farmland to nature would mean we produce 3% less calories.' Henry Dimbleby et al., *The National Food Strategy: The Evidence,* p. 41, www.nationalfoodstrategy.org/wp-content/uploads/2021/08/NFS_Evidence-Pack.pdf

40   In 1086, some 190 barons owned around 54% of England. See Thomas Hinde (ed.), *The Domesday Book: England's Heritage, Then and Now,* 1985, p. 14.

41   See, for instance, Peter Chappell, 'Dartmoor farming couple seek veto on wild camping', *The Times,* 14 Dec 2022, www.thetimes.co.uk/article/dartmoor-farming-couple-seek-veto-on-wild-camping-h0s827dt6

42   See whoownsengland.org/2021/03/22/who-owns-dartmoor/. The websites of the Blachford Estate and Cornwood Shoot were taken down in Jan 2023.

43 Climate Change Committee, June 2023 progress report, p. 241, www.theccc.
org.uk/wp-content/uploads/2023/06/Progress-in-reducing-UK-emissions-
2023-Report-to-Parliament.pdf

44 Climate Change Committee, June 2022 progress report, p. 304, www.theccc.
org.uk/wp-content/uploads/2022/06/Progress-in-reducing-emissions-2022-
Report-to-Parliament.pdf

45 CCC, June 2023 progress report, www.theccc.org.uk/publication/2023-progress-
report-to-parliament/#key-messages; CCC, June 2022 progress report, p. 285.

46 Tom Lancaster, 'Analysis of progress against Carbon Budget Delivery Plan
targets for farming and land use', 27 June 2023, eciu.net/analysis/reports/2023/
analysis-of-progress-against-carbon-budget-delivery-plan-targets-for-farming-
and-land-use

47 Forestry Commission Key Performance Indicators: Report for 2022–23, p. 45:
second graph on page shows just 1 hectare (2.5 acres) of PAWS were restored
by private landowners in 2022–3. assets.publishing.service.gov.uk/government/
uploads/system/uploads/attachment_data/file/1162830/Forestry-Commission-
Key-Performance-Indicators-Report-2022-23.pdf

48 Dustin Benton, 'The Sustainable Farming Incentive is spending public money
but for what public good?', 6 July 2023, greenallianceblog.org.uk/2023/07/06/
the-sustainable-farming-incentive-is-spending-public-money-but-for-what-
public-good/

49 Originally, ELMs was intended to be evenly split between its three tiers – the
Sustainable Farm Incentive (SFI), Local Nature Recovery and Landscape Recovery.
Each would have been allocated a third of the £2.4bn annual ELMs budget, or
around £800m per year. But in 2022, following concerted lobbying from the
NFU and others, the government U-turned on this, allocating just £50m over
three years to finance Landscape Recovery. See Ben Spencer and Harry Yorke,
'Boris Johnson turns his back on green agenda with rewilding rethink', *Sunday
Times,* 12 June 2022, www.thetimes.co.uk/article/boris-johnson-turns-his-back-
on-green-agenda-with-rewilding-rethink-p2q8hhbgs.

50 Phil MacDonald, Uni Lee and Ali Candlin, 'The UK's coal to clean journey', Ember,
24 Mar 2023, ember-climate.org/insights/research/the-uks-coal-to-clean-journey/

1 Stewards of the Earth

1 'Stewardship': Merriam-Webster Dictionary, www.merriam-webster.com/dictionary/
stewardship

2 'Custodian': Merriam-Webster Dictionary, www.merriam-webster.com/dictionary/
custodian

3 CLA press release, 'Education course has potential to shed light on UK food
production, says CLA', 21 Apr 2022, www.cla.org.uk/news/education-course-
will-shed-light-on-uk-food-production-says-cla/

4 CLA consultation response, 'Environmental Targets', 27 June 2022, www.cla.org.
uk/documents/535/CLA_Consultation_Response_on_Environmental_Targets.
pdf: 'the CLA's 27,000 members operate 250 different types of business located
in the rural area, covering over 10 million acres across England and Wales'.

England and Wales are 37m acres in extent, so 10m acres is 27% of England and Wales, roughly a third of the land area. In another recent CLA consultation response, 'England Tree Strategy', 11 Sep 2020, www.cla.org.uk/documents/50/ Tree_strategy_Consultation_Response_CLA_Accompanying_Doc_-_final_11_ Sept_2020.pdf, they state: 'Our 30,000 members own or manage around half the rural land in England and Wales – over 10 million acres.' Rural land here clearly excludes urban land, hence the higher proportion stated.

5   The Moorland Association, 'Moorland Association response to Committee for Climate Change report', 23 Jan 2020, www.moorlandassociation.org/2020/01/ moorland-association-response-to-committee-for-climate-change-report/

6   See my book *Who Owns England?*, 2019, p. 86.

7   I found references to stewardship on the websites of twelve out of twenty-two ducal estates: the Duchy of Cornwall (duchyofcornwall.org/sustainable-stewardship/); the Duke of Northumberland's Northumberland Estates (northumberlandestates.co.uk/the-estate/agriculture/); the Duke of Devonshire's Bolton Abbey Estate (boltonabbey.com/a-greener-bolton-abbey/); the Duke of Buccleuch's Buccleuch Estates (www.buccleuch.com/wp-content/uploads/ sites/8/2022/05/Buccleuch-community-engagement-strategy-web-1.pdf);   the Duke of Westminster's Grosvenor Estates (www.grosvenor.com/rural-estates); the Duke of Marlborough's Blenheim Palace (www.blenheimpalace.com/ worldheritagesite/downloads/Full%20PMP%202014%20(R).pdf);   the Duke of Rutland's Belvoir Castle Estate (www.belvoircastle.com/conservation/); the Duke of Richmond's Goodwood Estate (www.goodwood.com/careers/about-goodwood/the-goodwood-legacy/); the Duke of Bedford's Bedford Estates (www.bedfordestates.com/about-us/); the Duke of Atholl's Atholl Estates (atholl-estates.co.uk/estate/about/life-on-atholl-estates/); the Duke of Roxburghe's Floors Castle (www.floorscastle.com/environment/farming/); and the Duke of Fife's Kinnaird Castle (kinnairdcastle.co.uk/estate/).

8   Northumberland Estates website, webpage on 'Agriculture', northumberlandestates.co.uk/the-estate/agriculture/

9   Belvoir Castle website, 'Conservation', www.belvoircastle.com/conservation/

10   Environment Secretary Thérèse Coffey, speech to NFU conference, 22 Feb 2023, www.gov.uk/government/speeches/secretary-of-state-therese-coffey-addresses-nfu-conference

11   Owen Paterson, 'Private owners can be trusted to look after our land', *Sunday Telegraph*, 5 May 2019, www.telegraph.co.uk/books/what-to-read/rewilding-fashionable-nonsense-private-owners-can-trusted/

12   Tweet by James Rebanks (@herdysheperd1), 6 Jan 2021, twitter.com/ herdyshepherd1/status/1346815715941216257

13   Genesis 1:26. The Bible, King James Version, 1611, www.kingjamesbibleonline. org/Genesis-1-26/

14   Genesis 2:15. The Bible, King James Version, 1611, www.kingjamesbibleonline. org/Genesis-2-15/

15   Lynn White, Jnr., 'The Historical Roots of Our Ecological Crisis', *Science* 155, 1967, pp. 1203–7, www.cmu.ca/faculty/gmatties/lynnwhiterootsofcrisis.pdf

Endnotes

16 Matthew Hale, 'The Great Audit, with the Account of the Good Steward', in *Contemplations Moral and Divine,* 1679 (published posthumously), p. 293.

17 Psalms 24:1. The Bible, King James Version, 1611, www.kingjamesbibleonline. org/Psalms-Chapter-24/

18 Michael Drayton, *Poly-Olbion,* 1612, the Second Song, p. 25, poly-olbion. exeter.ac.uk/the-text/full-text/song-2/

19 For a fuller discussion of the early environmentalism of this period, see John U. Nef, 'An Early Energy Crisis and Its Consequences', *Scientific American* 237:5, Nov 1977, pp. 140–51; Andrew McRae, 'Tree-felling in Early Modern England: Michael Drayton's environmentalism', *The Review of English Studies,* New Series, 63:260, June 2012, pp. 410–30; and Felicity Stout, 'Before Evelyn: trees, tree planting and tree management in sixteenth- and early seventeenth-century England,' *Arboricultural Journal* 37:3, 2015, pp. 150–65.

20 Arthur Standish, *New Directions of Experience to the Commons Complaint,* 1613, online at wellcomecollection.org/works/nvny486z/items?canvas=9

21 John Evelyn, *Sylva,* Vol. 2, 1664, p. 166. Available online at archive.org/details/ sylvaordiscourse02evelrich/page/164/mode/2up.

22 Evelyn, *Sylva,* Vol. 2, p. 164. 'Nemorum' is Latin for woodlands or groves; 'vindix', protector or defender; 'instaurator magnus', great restorer or renewer.

23 Evelyn, *Sylva,* Vol. 2, p. 170.

24 Forestry England, 'Celebrating England's woodlands as the Forestry Commission turns 100 on 1st September', 2019, www.forestryengland.uk/news/celebrating-englands-woodlands-the-forestry-commission-turns-100-1st-september; DEFRA, 'Government Forestry and Woodlands Policy Statement', 2013, p. 21 (graph showing woodland as a percentage of land area in England), assets. publishing.service.gov.uk/government/uploads/system/uploads/attachment_ data/file/221023/pb13871-forestry-policy-statement.pdf

25 Thirty per cent of England was common land in 1600: see Gregory Clark and Anthony Clark, 'Common Rights to Land in England, 1475–1839', *Journal of Economic History* 61:4, Dec 2001, pp. 1009–36.

26 Thomas More, *Utopia,* 1516, Book One.

27 Christopher Hill, *The World Turned Upside Down,* 1972, ch. 3, 'Masterless Men'.

28 Colonel Nathaniel Rich and General Ireton quoted in Paul Foot, *The Vote,* 2005, pp. 29–30.

29 Quoted in Hill, *The World Turned Upside Down,* p. 132.

30 Gerrard Winstanley, *A Watch-Word to the City of London and the Army* (1649) reproduced in Christopher Hill (ed.), *Winstanley: 'The Law of Freedom' and Other Writings,* 1972, p. 128.

31 See Frank McLynn, *The Road Not Taken,* 2013, p. 178.

32 H.T. Dickinson, *Liberty and Property: Political Ideology in Eighteenth-Century Britain,* 1977, p. 51.

33 Tom Williamson and Liz Bellamy, *Property and Landscape,* 1987, p. 124: 'The great landowner was mythologized as a wise and powerful figure . . . the landowner's wealth was in the nation, and his interest was thus the national good.'

34   John Phibbs, *Place-Making: The Art of Capability Brown*, English Heritage, 2017.

35   William Cowper, *The Task*, 1785, Book I.

36   Edmund Burke, *Reflections on the Revolution in France*, 1790, p. 117.

37   Burke, *Reflections on the Revolution in France*, p. 144.

38   Howard Newby, Colin Bell, David Rose and Peter Saunders, *Property, Paternalism and Power*, 1978, p. 23.

39   Howard Newby, *Green and Pleasant Land? Social Change in Rural England*, 1979, p. 69.

40   BBC documentary presented by Dan and Peter Snow, *Whose Britain Is It Anyway?*, 2006, available online at www.youtube.com/watch?v=VMUkgRzRhik&ab_channel=TheLandGeeks

41   Rackham, *Trees and Woodland in the British Landscape*, p. 174.

42   Hedgerow loss: the People's Trust for Endangered Species (PTES) states: 'In 1950, a Forestry Commission assessment concluded that we had 1 million km of hedgerow. By 2007, this reduced to 477,000km, a loss of approximately 52%', ptes.org/hedgerow/a-history-of-hedgerows/. Ninety-seven per cent of wildflower meadows were lost between 1930 and 1984: see R.A. Fuller, 'The changing extent and conservation interest of lowland grasslands in England and Wales: A review of grassland surveys 1930–1984', *Biological Conservation* 40:4, 1987, pp. 281–300.

43   Marion Shoard, *The Theft of the Countryside*, 1980, p. 9.

44   Michael Winter, *Rural Politics: Policies for Agriculture, Forestry and the Environment*, 1996, p. 203.

45   Robert J.F. Burton, 'The role of farmer self-identity in agricultural decision making in the Marston Vale Community Forest', PhD thesis, 1998, www.researchgate.net/profile/Rob-Burton/publication/35721494_The_Role_of_Farmer_Self-identity_in_Agricultural_Decision-making_in_the_Marston_Vale_Community_Forest/links/5abacbe445851563660ae812/The-Role-of-Farmer-Self-identity-in-Agricultural-Decision-making-in-the-Marston-Vale-Community-Forest.pdf. See also C. McEachern, 'Farmers and conservation: conflict and accommodation in farming politics', *Journal of Rural Studies* 8:2, 1992, pp. 159–71.

46   Speech by NFU President Henry Plumb at the City of Birmingham Show 1971, reported in the *Burton Observer and Chronicle*, 'Understanding between town and country', 16 Sep 1971.

47   NFU press release, 'Farmers to become wildlife watchers', 29 Aug 1998, Countrylife On-line, www.countrylife.org.uk/news/NFU29898dd.asp

48   Farming UK, 'NFU contributes to improved state of the environment 2005', 9 June 2005, www.farminguk.com/news/nfu-contributes-to-improved-state-of-the-environment-2005_1494.html; Isabel Davies, 'NFU to tell public how farmers nurture nature', *Farmers Weekly*, 1 Apr 2005, www.fwi.co.uk/news/environment/nfu-to-tell-public-how-farmers-nurture-nature

49   Andrew Watts, 'Peter Kendall on how the NFU is handling the disease crisis', *Farmers Weekly*, 13 Oct 2007, www.fwi.co.uk/business/peter-kendall-on-how-the-nfu-is-handling-the-disease-crisis

50   NFU press release, 'Net zero – NFU President tackles *Guardian* on diet claims', 23 Aug 2022, www.nfuonline.com/updates-and-information/net-

zero-nfu-president-tackles-guardian-on-diet-claims/. In November 2023, Tom Bradshaw – then NFU deputy president – similarly attacked a carbon footprint calculator that purportedly encouraged users to go vegetarian, and 'added that livestock farmers are custodians of large swathes of iconic landscapes'. See Philip Clarke, 'NatWest to correct misleading claims about livestock emissions', *Farmers Weekly,* 24 Nov 2023, www.fwi.co.uk/news/environment/carbon/natwest-to-correct-misleading-claims-about-livestock-emissions. In Feb 2024, Bradshaw was elected NFU President.

51   Farmland bird populations declined by 58% between 1970 and 2020. See DEFRA National Statistics, 'Wild Bird Populations in the UK, 1970 to 2021', updated 13 Apr 2023, www.gov.uk/government/statistics/wild-bird-populations-in-the-uk/wild-bird-populations-in-the-uk-1970-to-2021#breeding-farmland-bird-populations-in-the-uka-name--2-breeding-farmland-bird-populations-in-the-uka

52   Margaret Thatcher, speech to Conservative Party Conference, 14 Oct 1988, www.margaretthatcher.org/document/107352

53   Cited in Dominic Sandbrook, *Who Dares Wins: Britain, 1979–1982*, 2019, p. 236.

54   HM Government, White Paper on the Environment, *This Common Inheritance,* Sep 1990, p. 10. The White Paper was published two months before Thatcher was deposed from office by her own party.

55   *This Common Inheritance*, ch. 7, 'Countryside and Wildlife', p. 96.

56   Michael Winter, 'Agriculture and Environment: The Integration of Policy?', *Journal of Law and Society* 18:1, Law, Policy and the Environment, Spring 1991, pp. 48–63.

57   *This Common Inheritance*, pp.13–14.

58   England's first Countryside Stewardship scheme ran from 1991 to 2004, before being replaced by Environmental Stewardship in 2005–14; the name Countryside Stewardship was then revived again in 2015 for the current scheme. With the transition to a new post-Brexit system of Environmental Land Management Schemes, there was briefly talk of calling one of the three tiers of payment schemes 'Local Nature Recovery'. But in 2022, it was decided that it would once again be called Countryside Stewardship: testament to the enduring strength of this narrative framing. The other two tiers of ELMS are called the Sustainable Farming Incentive (SFI) and Landscape Recovery (LR).

59   New Zealand Ministry for the Environment briefing, 'Legally protected conservation land in New Zealand', Apr 2010, www.tiakitamakimakaurau.nz/media/zmvh0uzv/legally-protected-conservation-land-snapshot.pdf. It states: 'Legally protected public land (managed by the Department of Conservation and regional councils) accounted for 8,525,000 hectares.' New Zealand is 26,771,00ha in extent, so legally protected public land covers 32% of the country.

60   See Shrubsole, *Who Owns England?*, Table 2, p. 297.

61   This figure was calculated by combining figures from the following sources; my huge thanks to Tom Lancaster for digging these out and for his assistance in

the calculation. 1) For the period 1992–2000 – DEFRA, 'Annex II impacts of the previous programming period: EAGGF resources deployed to support rural development', webarchive.nationalarchives.gov.uk/ukgwa/20040119120419/ http:/www.defra.gov.uk/erdp/docs/national/annexes/annexii.htm. For 2000–2007: DEFRA, 'The rural development programme for England 2007–2013', Annex to Chapter 3.4, which details spend 2000–07, assets.publishing.service. gov.uk/government/uploads/system/uploads/attachment_data/file/350781/ CH3.4_-_Annex.pdf. For 2007–2013: DEFRA, '7: Indicative breakdown by measure', assets.publishing.service.gov.uk/media/5a74853f40f0b616bcb17247/ CH7__final_adjusted_for_11th_Mod_.pdf. For 2014–2020: DEFRA, 'United Kingdom – Rural Development Programme (Regional) – England', assets.publishing.service.gov.uk/media/63369ebee90e0772e400e682/ United_Kingdom_-_Rural_Development_Programme_England.pdf. For 2021 and 2022 figures, see DEFRA, 'Future Farming and Countryside Programme annual report', 2021, assets.publishing.service.gov.uk/ media/635fb279d3bf7f04e834e0f7/ffcp-annual-rpt2021-2022.pdf; 2022, assets.publishing.service.gov.uk/media/6537e4011bf90d000dd8452e/FCP-annual-accounts2223.pdf

62 Patrick Barkham, 'Natural England to get 47% funding increase amid "green recovery" plans', *Guardian*, 20 May 2021, www.theguardian.com/ environment/2021/may/20/natural-england-to-get-47-funding-increase-amid-green-recovery-plans

63 Samuel Lovett, 'Environment Agency funding cut by 50% over past decade as sewage spills rise, analysis shows', *Independent*, 29 Aug 2022, www.independent. co.uk/climate-change/news/water-pollution-sewage-environment-agency-funding-b2154848.html

64 Newby, *Green and Pleasant Land?*, p. 69.

2 The Ultimate Trophy Asset

1 Dominic Prince, 'The ultimate trophy asset for the new-money elite', *Spectator*, 15 Mar 2008, www.spectator.co.uk/article/the-ultimate-trophy-asset-for-the-new-money-elite/

2 *Sunday Times* Rich List, 19 May 2023, www.thetimes.co.uk/article/duke-of-westminster-net-worth-sunday-times-rich-list-bqbqpjlqf

3 Cited in Sam Roberts, 'Gerald Grosvenor, British Duke and Billionaire, Dies at 64', *New York Times*, 15 Aug 2016.

4 'New estate – but Duke stays put', *Chester Observer*, 19 Sep 1980; 'Duke refutes move rumour', *Chester Chronicle*, 19 Sep 1980. The £2.5m price tag appears to have been first reported in the *Daily Mail* on 18 Sep, although the Duke's estate disputed the figure.

5 Mark Avery, 'Poor Old Duke', 29 Aug 2019, markavery.info/2019/08/29/poor-old-duke/

6 Natural England, Designated Sites View website (designatedsites.naturalengland. org.uk), entry for Bowland Fells SSSI. The West Bowland Fells SSSI was first designated in 1951; it was re-notified as the Bowland Fells SSSI in 1988.

See Natural England summary note on Bowland Fells SSSI: designatedsites. naturalengland.org.uk/PDFsForWeb/Citation/1005542.pdf

7   Grosvenor Estate website, 'Rural Estates', www.grosvenor.com/rural-estates

8   Natural England, site checks and condition assessments for Bowland Fells SSSI, Unit 15 (last site check 28 Feb 2022), designatedsites.naturalengland.org.uk/UnitDetail. aspx?UnitId=1011798&SiteCode=S1005542&SiteName=bowland%20 fells&countyCode=25&responsiblePerson=; Bowland Fells SSSI, Unit 50 (last site check 25 Mar 2021), designatedsites.naturalengland.org.uk/UnitDetail. aspx?UnitId=1030227&SiteCode=S1005542&SiteName=bowland%20 fells&countyCode=25&responsiblePerson=

9   Wild Justice report, 'Meddling on the Moors', 8 Aug 2023, p. 13, wildjustice. org.uk/hen-harriers/meddling-on-the-moors-a-wild-justice-report/. See also Avery, 'Poor Old Duke'. Hen harriers clearly *used* to breed on the Abbeystead Estate: a newspaper article from 1982 states there were three pairs nesting in the area back then. 'Whirlybirds protect the feathered type on shoot land', *Liverpool Daily Post*, 9 Aug 1982, via British Newspaper Archive. Subsequent references to old newspaper articles come from the British Newspaper Archive unless otherwise stated.

10 Wild Justice, 'Meddling on the Moors'; Shosha Adie, 'Water company to end grouse shooting on its land by 2027', ENDS Report, www.endsreport.com/ article/1831036/water-company-end-grouse-shooting-its-land-2027

11 For example, the Forest of Bowland AONB lists some peat restoration work as having taken place in the Bowland Fells SSSI in Mar 2018, jointly funded by the AONB, Grosvenor Estate, Environment Agency and DEFRA: www. forestofbowland.com/node/4981.

12 The figure of £5.5m was calculated as follows. I downloaded the maps of Environmental Stewardship agreements published by Natural England here: naturalengland-defra.opendata.arcgis.com/datasets/ ca68c90958c342a285d6370ddd7edd66. I then cropped this using a digitised map of the Abbeystead Estate published by Lancashire County Council under the Highways Act 1980 section 31.6 landowner deposits scheme. This allowed me to isolate the Environmental Stewardship payments that went to the trustees of the 4th Duke of Westminster's 1964 Settlement and the other tenant farmers and graziers on the Abbeystead Estate, and add up the total amount.

13 Analysis of area of grouse moors in England carried out by the author: for the map and methodology, see 'Who owns England's grouse moors?', 28 Oct 2016, whoownsengland.org/2016/10/28/who-owns-englands-grouse-moors/. The figure of 550,000 acres is a conservative one: the Moorland Association, which represents the grouse moor industry, says its members manage 860,000 acres of moorland in England and Wales. See the website front page of the Moorland Association: www.moorlandassociation.org/

14 Oliver Gilbert, *Lichens*, Collins New Naturalist Guide, 2000, p. 77.

15 David Hey, *A History of the Peak District Moors*, 2014, pp. 142–4. Sir William Spencer-Stanhope started shooting grouse on his moor at Dunford Bridge in the Peak District in 1836, the year before Queen Victoria took the throne; he began

intensifying management practices there in the 1840s. The moor is now owned by Yorkshire Water, who continue to lease it for grouse shooting.

16   Queen Victoria, *Leaves from the Journal of Our Life in the Highlands*, 1868, p. 18. The entry describes Victoria and Albert's first visit to Scotland in Sep 1842.

17   David Cannadine, *The Decline and Fall of the British Aristocracy*, 1990, p. 364.

18   Tom Williamson, *An Environmental History of Wildlife in England, 1650–1950*, 2013, pp. 124–5.

19   Benedict Macdonald, *Rebirding: Rewilding Britain and its birds*, 2020 (revised and updated edition), pp. 195–6.

20   Williamson, *An Environmental History of Wildlife in England*, p. 122.

21   Hey, *A History of the Peak District Moors*, p. 15.

22   This account draws upon Hey, *A History of the Peak District Moors*, ch. 6. Maps of common land can be viewed online via the government's MAGIC Map, magic. defra.gov.uk/.

23   Williamson, *An Environmental History of Wildlife in England*, p. 123.

24   A.S. Leslie (ed.), *The Grouse in Health and Disease: Being the popular edition of the report of the Committee of Inquiry on Grouse Disease*, 1912, p. 346. Available online at www.biodiversitylibrary.org/item/63540#page/11/mode/1up

25   Leslie, *The Grouse in Health and Disease*, pp. 356–7.

26   The UK National Ecosystem Assessment 2011 states there are 450 grouse shooting moors in the UK, with 296 in Scotland and 10 in Wales, meaning that England has *c.* 144. See ch. 5, p. 25: uknea.unep-wcmc.org/LinkClick. aspx?fileticket=CZHaB2%2FJKlo%3D&tabid=82. An earlier study puts the total slightly higher, at 153 grouse moor estates in England: see P.J. Hudson, *Grouse in Space and Time* (Game Conservancy Trust, 1992). On the area of grouse moors in England: 550,000 acres is the author's calculation, using a methodology explained in detail at 'Who owns England's grouse moors?', 28 Oct 2016, whoownsengland.org/2016/10/28/who-owns-englands-grouse-moors/. That figure is a conservative one: the Moorland Association says its members manage 860,000 acres of moorland in England and Wales; see www.moorlandassociation.org/. On the area of grouse moors in Scotland: 'There is uncertainty about the extent of grouse moors in Scotland, but they are estimated to cover somewhere between 1 and 1.5m hectares [2.47m–3.7m acres], amounting to 12–18% of the country's landmass'. Dr Ruth Tingay and Andy Wightman, 'The Case for Reforming Scotland's Grouse Moors', report for Revive, 2018, p. 4, revive.scot/wp-content/uploads/ReviveReport.pdf. I have gone for the lower end of this estimated area, 2.5m acres.

27   Countryside Alliance briefing note, 'Grouse Shooting – 10 Key Questions Answered', July 2018, www.countryside-alliance.org/resources/news/countryside-alliance-briefing-note-grouse-shooti.

28   F. Worrall, P. Chapman, J. Holden, C. Evans, R. Artz, P. Smith and R. Grayson, 'Peatlands and climate change: Report to IUCN UK Peatland Programme', 2010. See also IUCN UK Commission of Inquiry on Peatlands, 2011, p. 38, www.iucn-uk-peatlandprogramme.org/sites/default/files/2019-07/IUCN%20

UK%20Commission%20of%20Inquiry%20on%20Peatlands%20Full%20
Report%20spv%20web_0.pdf

29 For example, see the GWCT website, 'Rewetting moorland', www.gwct.org.uk/
policy/briefings/driven-grouse-shooting/rewetting-moorland/. Here they state
that moorland drainage was done for 'the primary aim of improving the land
for livestock', and that 'it is often incorrectly stated that moor owners drained
the moors for grouse shooting'. The evidence presented in my chapter suggests
otherwise.

30 On sheep as tick mops, see the GWCT website, 'Disease control on grouse
moors', Q&A for 'How can tick numbers be controlled on moorland?', www.
gwct.org.uk/policy/briefings/driven-grouse-shooting/disease-control-on-grouse-
moors/

31 Williamson, *An Environmental History of Wildlife in England*, p.123.

32 Hey, *A History of the Peak District Moors*, p. 144.

33 *The Field*, Saturday 10 Sep 1904, via British Newspaper Archive.

34 *Country Life*, 'The Management of Grouse Moors', 10 Sep 1904, p. 387.

35 Leslie, *The Grouse in Health and Disease*, pp. 368–9.

36 Richard Waddington, 'Grouse Shooting and Management', 1958, p. 47.

37 J. Phillips and R. Moss, 'Effects of subsoil draining on heather moors in
Scotland', *Journal of Range Management* 30:1, 1977, pp. 27–9.

38 Cited in P. J. Hudson, 'Some effects of sheep management on heather moorlands
in northern England', in D. Jenkins (ed.), *Agriculture and the Environment*,
Institute of Terrestrial Ecology, Cambridge, 1984.

39 Heritage Landscape Management Plan for the Bolton Abbey Estate, July 1993,
p.13, drawn up as part of the estate's agreement with HMRC for tax breaks
under the tax-exempt heritage assets scheme. The full plan is included in this
document produced by the Chatsworth Settlement Trustees, on pp. 107–224:
www.cravendc.gov.uk/media/3043/50635_badoas_incl_appendices_07-04-17_
reduced.pdf. When the author corresponded with the Bolton Abbey Estate in
2020, they confirmed that this 1993 plan was still in force.

40 Tweet by Kevin Walker, 14 Aug 2023, twitter.com/bsbiscience/
status/1690978531134619648?s=46&t=gKpdna_au6zdzT6Ls7sKFQ

41 Tweet by Bob Berzins, 9 Oct 2023, twitter.com/BerzinsBob/
status/1711368079505007091

42 L.E. Brown, J. Holden and S.M. Palmer, 'Effects of moorland burning on the
ecohydrology of river basins. Key findings from the EMBER project', University
of Leeds, 2014, water.leeds.ac.uk/wp-content/uploads/sites/36/2017/06/
EMBER_full-report.pdf

43 Glaves et al., *Natural England Review of Upland Evidence 2012 – The effects of
managed burning on upland peatland biodiversity, carbon and water*. Natural
England Evidence Review 004, 2013, p. vii, publications.naturalengland.org.
uk/publication/5978072

44 There are lots of studies of the effects of moorland burning on peat. Here is a
selection: M.H. Garnett, P. Ineson, A.C. Stevenson, 'Effects of burning and
grazing on carbon sequestration in a Pennine blanket bog, UK', *The Holocene*

10:6, 2000, pp. 729–36; S.E. Ward, R.D. Bardgett, N.P. McNamara, J.K. Adamson, N.J. Ostle, 'Long-term consequences of grazing and burning on northern peatland carbon dynamics', *Ecosystems* 10:7, 2007, pp. 1069–83; Bain et al., 'IUCN UK Commission on Peatlands', 2011, section 5.1 'Burning on peatlands', pp. 60–2; Murray C. Grant, John Mallord, Leigh Stephen and Patrick S. Thompson, RSPB Research Report 43, 'The costs and benefits of grouse moor management to biodiversity and aspects of the wider environment: a review', 2012, section 4.3.2 'Effects of rotational muirburn on carbon store and water quality', citeseerx.ist.psu.edu/document?repid=rep1&type=pdf&doi=b25fd-077954c9b4b078b563ad4d1541c491cfc87; Brown et al., 'Effects of fire on the hydrology, biogeochemistry, and ecology of peatland river systems', *Freshwater Science* 34:4, Dec 2015, www.journals.uchicago.edu/doi/10.1086/683426; Ashleigh R. Harper et al., 'Prescribed fire and its impacts on ecosystem services in the UK', *Science of the Total Environment* 624, May 2018, pp. 691–703, www.sciencedirect.com/science/article/pii/S0048969717335878?via%3Dihub#bb0040

45   See, for instance, the Moorland Association's webpage on 'Wildfire Mitigation', which claims that 'With red grouse moor management, comes vegetation management through mowing and rotational burning and the risk of a severe wildfire is lower due to a reduced amount of vegetation available to burn ("fuel load")', www.moorlandassociation.org/wildfire/

46   '1,213,000 ha (41%) of the UK peat area remains under some form of semi-natural peatland vegetation, but has been affected to varying degrees by human activities including drainage, burn-management, and livestock grazing. This has led to drying of the peat, loss of peat-forming species and erosion, converting these areas into net GHG sources. Although the emissions per unit area of modified peatland are relatively low, their great extent makes them significant contributors to overall UK peatland GHG emissions (3,400 kt CO_2e yr^{-1}, 15% of total emissions).' Evans et al., 'Implementation of an emission inventory for UK peatlands', Report to the Department for Business, Energy and Industrial Strategy, Centre for Ecology and Hydrology, 2017, p. 1, uk-air.defra.gov.uk/assets/documents/reports/cat07/1904111135_UK_peatland_GHG_emissions.pdf. See also Table 4.6 on p. 46 of the CEH report: adding the CO_2e totals for 'Eroded Modified Bog', 'Heather-dominated Modified Bog' and 'Grass-dominated Modified Bog' also gives a total of 3.4mt CO_2e per year. 1.2m ha = c.3m acres, which happens to correspond with the approximate area of grouse moors in England and Scotland.

47   The precise figures are 523,753 tonnes of CO_2e per year from English grouse moors, over an area of 282,000 ha (696,837 acres) of grouse moors on peat. GWCT, 'Peatland Report 2020', p. 27, www.gwct.org.uk/media/1157594/GWCT-Peatland-Report-2020-lr.pdf

48   I calculated this as follows. Evans et al. 2017 states that modified peat bogs are responsible for 3.4mt CO_2e per year. I multiplied this by 173 years (1850 to 2023) = 588mt CO_2e. I refined the figures slightly by ramping up from an assumed zero emissions in 1850 to 3.4mt CO_2e by 1900, following a simple

linear trajectory to reflect the development of grouse shooting, and then maintaining that level to 2023 = 504mt CO_2e.

49 Adam Watson and Jeremy D. Wilson, 'Seven decades of mountain hare counts show severe declines where high-yield recreational game bird hunting is practised', *Journal of Applied Ecology* 55:6, Nov 2018, pp. 2663–72. See also Patrick Barkham, 'Scotland's mountain hare population is at just 1% of 1950s level', *Guardian*, 14 Aug 2018, www.theguardian.com/environment/2018/aug/14/scotlands-mountain-hare-population-severe-decline; and RSPB Scotland website, 'Myth-busting mountain hare management claims', 10 July 2019, community.rspb.org.uk/ourwork/b/scotland/posts/myth-busting-mountain-hare-management-claims

50 The League Against Cruel Sports estimates that a quarter of a million animals are killed each year in Scotland alone to support grouse moors. LACS, 'Calculating Cruelty', Aug 2020, raptorpersecutionscotland.files.wordpress.com/2020/08/calculating-cruelty.pdf

51 Rod Liddle, 'Red kites are glorious. Murdering them in aid of a shoot-'em-up for spivs is grotesque', *Sunday Times,* 20 Aug 2023, www.thetimes.co.uk/article/red-kites-are-glorious-murdering-them-in-aid-of-a-shoot-em-up-for-spivs-is-grotesque-gkcdbrtsx

52 Raptor Persecution UK, 'Gamekeeper convicted of raptor persecution on Moy – a notorious Scottish grouse-shooting estate', 31 Mar 2023, raptorpersecutionuk.org/2023/03/31/gamekeeper-convicted-of-raptor-persecution-on-moy-a-notorious-scottish-grouse-shooting-estate/: 'He is the 56th gamekeeper to be convicted of raptor persecution offences in Scotland since 1990.'

53 Raptor Persecution UK, '101 hen harriers confirmed "missing" or illegally killed in UK since 2018, most of them on or close to grouse moors', 18 Aug 2023, raptorpersecutionuk.org/2023/08/18/101-hen-harriers-confirmed-missing-or-illegally-killed-in-uk-since-2018-most-of-them-on-or-close-to-grouse-moors/. See also Ewing et al., 'Illegal killing associated with gamebird management accounts for up to three-quarters of annual mortality in Hen Harriers *Circus cyaneus*', *Biological Conservation* 283, July 2023, 110072, doi.org/10.1016/j.biocon.2023.110072

54 Emma Yeomans, '"Killing" of rare bird of prey filmed on Queen's grouse moor in North Yorkshire', 20 July 2020, www.thetimes.co.uk/article/killing-of-rare-bird-of-prey-filmed-on-one-of-queen-s-grouse-moors-in-north-yorkshire-pf6l2vr0j. See also Alex Thomson, Channel 4 News, 'Undercover in the UK's grouse shooting industry', 2 Sep 2020, www.youtube.com/watch?v=aLCr2CBZd5c&ab_channel=Channel4News

55 Disraeli: 'During her reign Queen Victoria regularly dragged attendant politicians northwards to the Balmoral estate and presented a Scottish itinerary which invariably involved hunting, the shooting of grouse and deer and the catching of salmon. Disraeli counted himself fortunate to escape with two visits'. P. Higgins, L. Jackson, L. and G. Jarvie, 'Deer Forests, Sporting Estates and the Aristocracy: Some Preliminary Observations', Scottish Centre Research Papers in Sport, Leisure and Society 2, 1997, pp. 32–52, www.docs.hss.ed.ac.uk/education/

outdoored/higgins_jackson_jarvie_deer_forests.pdf. Chamberlain: 'Millden Estate . . . was where George VI and his prime minister, Neville Chamberlain, enjoyed some sport just before the onset of the Second World War.' David Leask, '"Holy Grail" for grouse shooters divides opinion', *Herald,* 17 Oct 2019, www.heraldscotland.com/news/17973720.holy-grail-grouse-shooters-divides-opinion/. Churchill: 'he thoroughly enjoyed game shooting in Britain, too, being especially keen on driven grouse and pheasants', and accompanying photo of Churchill shooting in North Wales as a guest of the Duke of Westminster. *The Field,* 'Churchill's guns: the personal armoury of Sir Winston Churchill', 5 Aug 2020, www.thefield.co.uk/shooting/churchills-guns-the-personal-armoury-of-sir-winston-churchill-44492

56   'Premier on Grouse Shoot', *Civil & Military Gazette (Lahore)*, 20 Aug 1957, via British Newspaper Archive.

57   For example, Macmillan was again snapped shooting grouse on the Swinton Estate in 1961: 'Mr Macmillan Goes Grouse Shooting', *Liverpool Echo*, 15 Aug 1961, via British Newspaper Archive. In 1958, Macmillan went shooting on the Bolton Abbey grouse moor, where he was 'the guest of his nephew, the Duke of Devonshire': 'Premier enjoys himself at grouse-shoot', *The Scotsman*, 25 Aug 1958, via British Newspaper Archive.

58   Harold Wilson, speech 19 Jan 1964, quoted in Dominic Sandbrook, *White Heat: A History of Britain in the Swinging Sixties*, 2006, p. 8.

59   The former conservation director of the RSPB, Mark Avery, writes: 'Sir Anthony was the first Chair of the Moorland Association at a time when it was much more highly respected than it is now, and that was very largely because we all knew Sir Anthony to be a real gentleman who was torn at times, it seemed, between his love of grouse shooting as a sport and his abhorrence of wildlife crime.' Mark Avery, 'Sunday book review – A Wild Life by Anthony Milbank', 28 Jan 2018, markavery.info/2018/01/28/sunday-book-review-wild-life-anthony-milbank/

60   'Bid to protect the purple belt', *Derby Daily Telegraph*, 15 Dec 1987, via British Newspaper Archive. See also Moorland Association website, 'Who We Are', www.moorlandassociation.org/who-we-are/

61   Chris Lloyd, 'Obituary: Sir Anthony Milbank: Recalling a life of adventure around the world', *Darlington and Stockton Times*, 10 Aug 2016, www.darlingtonandstocktontimes.co.uk/news/14673660.sir-anthony-milbank-recalling-a-life-of-adventure-around-the-world/

62   In its May 1986 final report, the Common Land Forum called for a new law that would, amongst other things, 'grant a right of access to persons on foot' to all commons. (The report is available online at publications.naturalengland.org.uk/publication/216081.) The forum represented not just access groups like the Ramblers and the Open Spaces Society, but also the CLA, NFU and various large institutional landowners like the Crown Estate. The Moorland Association wasn't represented because it hadn't been founded yet, but the forum did take evidence on grouse moors from Earl Peel, who co-founded the MA with Sir Anthony Milbank. Responding to the forum's proposals, the 1987 Conservative manifesto pledged to 'legislate to safeguard common land on the basis of the Common

Land Forum, and continue to protect public access to the countryside through footpaths'. Conservative Party 1987 Manifesto, www.conservativemanifesto.com/1987/1987-conservative-manifesto.shtml

63 Sir Anthony Milbank, 'Moorland tension unwanted', letters page of the *Newcastle Journal,* 1 Oct 1990, via British Newspaper Archive.

64 Mr M. Griffiths, 'No More Moor Access', letters page of the *Rossendale Free Press,* 29 Sep 1990, via British Newspaper Archive.

65 The Environmentally Sensitive Areas (ESAs) scheme, which started in 1987, followed by the Countryside Stewardship Scheme from 1991.

66 Guy Shrubsole, 'Revealed: English grouse moor estates got £10 million in subsidies last year', 12 Aug 2019, whoownsengland.org/2019/08/12/revealed-english-grouse-moor-estates-got-10million-in-subsidies-last-year/

67 'Natural England data supplied to the RSPB indicated that over a 10 year period more than £105 million of agri-environmental funding supported management systems that carry out burning of blanket bog habitat on grouse moors [in] a Special Area of Conservation or Special Protection Area.' RSPB written evidence to Parliament Petitions Committee, debate on driven grouse shooting, Oct 2016: committees.parliament.uk/writtenevidence/72968/html/

68 Matt Ridley, 'Don't grouse about grouse', *Spectator,* 12 Aug 2016, www.spectator.co.uk/article/don-t-grouse-about-grouse/

69 Matt Ridley, 'More cash subsidies for hill farmers', *Newcastle Journal,* 28 Feb 1994, p. 44.

70 Matt Ridley assumed the hereditary title of Viscount Ridley in 2012, acquired a grouse moor in the Pennines in 2018 (see my blog, 'The climate sceptic's grouse moor', Who Owns England, 4 Jan 2021, whoownsengland.org/2021/01/04/the-climate-sceptics-grouse-moor/), and became President of the Moorland Association in 2020.

71 Harry Cockburn, 'Burning moorland for grouse shooting and grazing "biggest threat to most important wildlife sites", says RSPB', *Independent,* 8 Dec 2020, www.independent.co.uk/climate-change/news/burning-moorland-heather-grouse-shooting-rspb-b1768016.html

72 Sholto Byrnes, 'Who's posher: Clegg or Cameron?', *Guardian,* 20 Apr 2010, www.theguardian.com/commentisfree/2010/apr/20/clegg-cameron-posher. David Cameron reportedly gave up pheasant shooting when he became Tory leader, but returned to it after stepping down as Prime Minister a decade later. See John Stevens, 'He's game for anything! David Cameron "has gone back to pheasant shooting" since resigning as PM', *Daily Mail,* 16 Dec 2016, www.dailymail.co.uk/news/article-4042592/David-Cameron-gone-pheasant-shooting-resigning-PM.html

73 For a blow-by-blow account of the Walshaw Moor affair, see Mark Avery's 'Wuthering Moors' blogposts: markavery.info/category/wuthering-moors/. Quote here taken from Mark Avery, 'Wuthering Moors 28', 15 Oct 2012, markavery.info/2012/10/15/wuthering-moors-28/. Emails between Lord Benyon and the Moorland Association profiled in 'Wuthering Moors 20', 1 July 2012, markavery.info/2012/07/01/wuthering-moors-20/. On the £2.5m

environmental stewardship scheme subsequently signed between Natural England and the Walshaw Moor Estate, see George Monbiot, 'This flood was not only foretold – it was publicly subsidised', *Guardian,* 29 Dec 2015, www.theguardian.com/commentisfree/2015/dec/29/deluge-farmers-flood-grouse-moor-drain-land

74   'Londoners diary: A tale of Boris Johnson and the grouse that got away', *Evening Standard,* 29 Sep 2014, www.standard.co.uk/news/londoners-diary/londoners-diary-a-tale-of-boris-johnson-and-the-grouse-that-got-away-9762362.html

75   'Another item up for auction was a 'fantastic grouse shoot for 8' at the Westerdale and Rosedale Estate in North Yorkshire'. Westerdale and Rosedale is owned by David Ross. Ben Riley-Smith, 'Private cabaret, grouse shooting and a weekend at a mansion modelled on Buckingham Palace auctioned to Tory donors at Black and White Ball', *Telegraph,* 6 Feb 2017, www.telegraph.co.uk/news/2017/02/06/private-cabaret-grouse-shooting-weekend-mansion-modelled-buckingham/

76   Dan Bloom, 'Boris Johnson exempts shooting from "rule of six" – months after freebie from moor owner', *Mirror,* 16 Sep 2020, www.mirror.co.uk/news/politics/boris-johnson-exempts-shooting-rule-22693020

77   You can see a map of the fifteen grouse moor estates in Rishi Sunak's constituency in my tweet here: twitter.com/guyshrubsole/status/1228302526430294017

78   Rishi Sunak in House of Commons debate on driven grouse shooting, Hansard Vol. 616, 31 Oct 2016, hansard.parliament.uk/commons/2016-10-31/debates/06472E95-10EC-49A0-BF93-84CAD2BE4191/DrivenGrouse-Shooting

79   Tweet by the Moorland Association, 17 July 2018, twitter.com/MoorlandAssoc/status/1019220149293940736: 'Delighted to recently join Rishi Sunak MP at Bolton Castle to show the many benefits of moorland mgmt for grouse.'

80   Matt Cross, 'Massive blow for antis as Sunak takes Number 10', *Shooting Times,* 28 Oct 2022, secure.shootinguk.co.uk/news/massive-blow-for-antis-as-sunak-takes-number-10-136993

81   Helena Horton, 'Kemi Badenoch backs net zero in Tory leadership climate U-turn', *Guardian,* 18 July 2022, www.theguardian.com/environment/2022/jul/18/kemi-badenoch-backs-net-zero-tory-leadership-climate-u-turn

82   'Unpublished data for 2022 and 2023 released to ECIU shows that Defra are well off course to meet the target of 35,000ha of peatland restored in this Parliament.' ECIU, 'Analysis of progress against carbon budget delivery plan targets for farming and land use', 27 June 2023, eciu.net/analysis/reports/2023/analysis-of-progress-against-carbon-budget-delivery-plan-targets-for-farming-and-land-use

83   The FOI'd meeting minutes can be seen here: whoownsengland.files.wordpress.com/2018/08/annex-c-180206_blanket_bog_round_table_note_of_meeting-final_redactedv2-1_redacted.pdf. The original document released had been incorrectly redacted, so the names of the landowners in attendance could be revealed by copying and pasting the text. More information on my investigations can be found at whoownsengland.org/2018/08/12/revealed-the-aristocrats-and-city-bankers-who-own-englands-grouse-moors/. The FOI'd documents

were covered by Rob Evans, 'Michael Gove accused of letting wealthy grouse moor owners off the hook', *Guardian,* 12 Aug 2018, www.theguardian.com/environment/2018/aug/12/michael-gove-accused-of-letting-wealthy-grouse-moor-owners-off-the-hook.

84 The FOI'd emails from the Moorland Association to Michael Gove can be seen online at cdn.friendsoftheearth.uk/sites/default/files/downloads/FOI-response-Moorland-Assoc-to-Gove.pdf

85 The footage can be viewed on the Friends of the Earth website, 'Friends of the Earth sparks moorland burning investigation': friendsoftheearth.uk/climate/friends-earth-sparks-moorland-burning-investigation

86 Emma Howard and Crispin Dowler, 'Satellites reveal widespread burning on England's protected peatlands, despite government ban', *Greenpeace Unearthed,* 30 May 2022, unearthed.greenpeace.org/2022/05/30/satellites-fires-burning-england-peatland-grouse-shooting/

87 Raptor Persecution UK, 'Moorland Association Director Ben Ramsden convicted for burning on deep peat on Middlesmoor Estate grouse moor, Nidderdale', 20 Oct 2023, raptorpersecutionuk.org/2023/10/20/moorland-association-director-ben-ramsden-convicted-for-burning-on-deep-peat-on-middlesmoor-estate-grouse-moor-nidderdale/

88 Tellus Natural Capital Limited was incorporated in Feb 2021 – see Companies House website entry: find-and-update.company-information.service.gov.uk/company/13233554/filing-history

89 Tellus Natural Capital website frontpage: www.tellusnatcap.com/

90 Richard Benyon meeting with Tellus Natural Capital 31 Jan 2022, 'to discuss landowner access to natural capital projects': DEFRA Ministerial meetings transparency data, Jan to Mar 2022, assets.publishing.service.gov.uk/media/6318b4048fa8f5020ac90fd6/Defra_mins_trans_mtgs_Q4_Jan_Mar_2022.csv/preview; meeting with Rishi Sunak: see tweet by Tellus Natural Capital, 27 May 2022, 'Attended Farming Forum in @RishiSunak constituency with Defra Minister @VictoriaPrentis today to raise a technical IHT point with the Chancellor', twitter.com/TellusNatCap/status/1530230171541848064

91 The four directors and three Persons with Significant Control for Tellus Natural Capital Limited are listed on Companies House here: find-and-update.company-information.service.gov.uk/company/13233554/officers. Michael Stone owned the Weardale Estate and Andrew Stone is his son: see 'Michael Stone obituary', *The Times,* 20 Apr 2019, www.thetimes.co.uk/article/michael-stone-obituary-0vvzklghc. Andrew Stone's biography for Tellus Natural Capital also includes the line that he 'enjoys field sports': www.tellusnatcap.com/andrew-stone. The other registered directors of Tellus Natural Capital are Sebastian Green, who 'manages some of the most prestigious sporting estates in the country' (www.tellusnatcap.com/sebastian-green), and Natasha Lucas, whose work includes 'management of one of the largest and most successful grouse moors in the UK' (www.tellusnatcap.com/natasha-lucas).

92 In the Confirmation Statement for Tellus Natural Capital made on 26 Feb 2023 with updates, Richard Bannister is listed as holding 8 ordinary shares in

the company. Document available for download at find-and-update.company-information.service.gov.uk/company/13233554/filing-history

93   Video from launch event embedded on frontpage of Tellus Natural Capital website. Ian Coghill speaks 2 mins 54 seconds in.

94   Benedict Macdonald, *Rebirding: Rewilding Britain and its birds,* 2020 (revised and updated edition), pp. 196–7.

95   A summary of recent moves by corporate and charitable landowners in England to move away from grouse shooting is given in Wild Justice's report 'Meddling on the Moors', Aug 2023, p. 19, wildjustice.org.uk/wp-content/uploads/2023/08/Meddling_On_Moors_WJ_Final_compressed.pdf. Other recent developments have been tracked by the organisation Wild Moors; see their News page: www.wildmoors.org.uk/category/news/

96   Sandra Dick, 'Highland Scotland's greatest missed opportunity?', *The Herald,* 22 Nov 2020, www.heraldscotland.com/news/18889287.highland-scotlands-greatest-missed-opportunity/?ref=rss

97   Rebecca English, 'Like father, like gun! Prince George, 7, watches dad Prince William on grouse shoot at Balmoral', 31 Aug 2020, www.dailymail.co.uk/news/article-8683065/Youre-real-son-gun-Prince-George-watches-dad-Prince-William-grouse-shoot-Balmoral.html

98   Of course, this risk is sometimes cited by defenders of the grouse shooting industry as reason to stick with the status quo. But getting rid of one destructive land use need not inevitably lead to another: see Crowle et al. 'Alternative future land use options in the British uplands', *Ibis* 164:3, Jan 2022, pp. 825–34, doi.org/10.1111/ibi.13041

3 The Land for the People

1   For a detailed discussion of the history of this, see Andy Wightman, 'The Vassalage of Langholm', 7 Jan 2014, www.andywightman.com/archives/3354

2   Langholm Common Riding guidebook 2023. The history of the Common Riding is also recounted online at www.langholmcommonriding.com/about/history-of-the-common-riding/

3   See Wightman, 'The Vassalage of Langholm'.

4   See, for example, the Langholm Moor Demonstration Project website, www.langholmproject.com/, and the RSPB's write-up of the Langholm Moor Demonstration Project, 3 Dec 2019, community.rspb.org.uk/ourwork/b/scotland/posts/langholm-moor-demonstration-project.

5   A map of the Tarras Valley Nature Reserve can be seen online at www.google.com/maps/d/u/0/viewer?ll=55.182168512293465%2C-2.9216899553309594&z=12&mid=1Lz-NgydGjR67yd01PmY5DJ1jRiKG9Hw

6   John Muir Trust pamphlet, 'Langholm Moor Community Appeal 2020', p.4. The author holds a copy.

7   John Muir Trust, 'Langholm Moor Community Appeal 2020', p.3.

8   In 2015, Margaret received a national award from the Scottish Environment Minister in recognition of her work. Sharon Liptrott, 'A Langholm woman picked up her town award for keeping Muckle Toon tidy for 23 years', *Daily*

Record, 10 Mar 2015, www.dailyrecord.co.uk/news/langholm-woman-picked-up-town-5304786

9   John Muir Trust, 'Langholm Moor Community Appeal 2020', p. 6. See also Ali Mitib, 'Wild future offers fresh hope for a community in decline', *The Times*, 17 Mar 2022, www.thetimes.co.uk/article/wild-future-offers-fresh-hope-for-a-community-in-decline-nwj6066kh

10 Richard Bunting, 'Beacon of Hope', Green Adventures blog, Nov 2023, www.greenadventurestravel.com/langholm.html

11 Press release by the Langholm Initiative, 'South of Scotland's biggest community buyout completes', 26 Mar 2021, www.langholminitiative.org.uk/news/south-of-scotland's-biggest-community-buyout-completes--

12 Scottish Government, 'Community ownership in Scotland 2021', 27 Sep 2022, www.gov.scot/publications/community-ownership-scotland-2021/. This states that 211,998ha (523,858 acres) of land is owned by communities. Community Land Scotland's latest figures are slightly higher, stating 563,000 acres of land is currently owned by communities: www.communitylandscotland.org.uk/

13 James Hunter, *From the Low Tide of the Sea to the Highest Mountain Tops*, 2012, cited in Wightman, *The Poor Had No Lawyers*, p. 205.

14 Wightman, *The Poor Had No Lawyers*, pp. 201–2.

15 Wightman, *The Poor Had No Lawyers*, p. 193.

16 Fergus Campbell, 'Irish popular politics and the making of the Wyndham Land Act, 1901–1903', *Historical Journal* 45:4, 2002, pp.755–73.

17 This draws on the account by Wightman, *The Poor Had No Lawyers*, ch. 15, pp. 197–9.

18 Alastair McIntosh, *Soil and Soul*, 2002, p. 267.

19 Jamie Wilson, 'Laird who deluded himself with an action for libel', *Guardian*, 20 May 1999, www.theguardian.com/uk/1999/may/20/jamiewilson1; Helen Carter, 'Eigg not overrun by guests', *Guardian*, 27 Apr 1999, www.theguardian.com/uk/1999/apr/27/helencarter

20 McIntosh, *Soil and Soul*, p. 192.

21 McIntosh, *Soil and Soul*, p. 194.

22 McIntosh, *Soil and Soul*, p. 187.

23 McIntosh, *Soil and Soul*, p. 139.

24 McIntosh, *Soil and Soul*, p. 263.

25 McIntosh, *Soil and Soul*, p. 268.

26 McIntosh, *Soil and Soul*, p. 266.

27 McIntosh, *Soil and Soul*, p. 269.

28 McIntosh, *Soil and Soul*, p. 270.

29 McIntosh, *Soil and Soul*, p.165.

30 See for example McIntosh, *Soil and Soul*, p.188: 'it looked as though market spoiling was working'.

31 McIntosh, *Soil and Soul*, p. 264; *The Herald*, 'Island's owner in fraud probe', 29 Nov 1995, www.heraldscotland.com/news/12061875.islands-owner-in-fraud-probe/

32 McIntosh, *Soil and Soul*, 2002, p.271.

33 In the year 2000, there were 144,000 acres of land in Scotland in community

ownership; by 2010, that had risen to 420,000 acres. See Wightman, *The Poor Had No Lawyers*, p. 199.

34 See the Land Reform (Scotland) Act 2003, Part 3, Section 34: Community Bodies, www.legislation.gov.uk/asp/2003/2/section/34. The 2003 Act originally stipulated that 'community bodies' must be limited companies, but the Community Empowerment Act 2015 amended this so that registered charities and community benefit societies could also qualify.

35 Scottish Government website, 'Policy: Land Reform: Community Right to Buy', section on 'Right to Buy process', www.gov.scot/policies/land-reform/community-right-to-buy/#right%20to%20buy%20process

36 This summary of the legislative provisions draws upon Malcolm M. Combe, Jayne Glass and Annie Tindley (eds), *Land Reform in Scotland: History, Law and Policy*, 2020, in particular chapters 7–10 covering Community Right to Buy.

37 Scottish *Daily Mail*, 24 Jan 2003. Reproduced in Wightman, *The Poor Had No Lawyers*, plates section.

38 See the discussion by Frankie McCarthy in 'Property Rights and Human Rights in Scottish Land Reform', in Malcolm M. Combe, Jayne Glass and Annie Tindley (eds), *Land Reform in Scotland: History, Law and Policy*, 2020, ch. 9.

39 See for example the Scottish Land Fund's Guidance Notes, July 2021, p. 6: 'As part of your stage 1 application, we expect you to demonstrate some community support for your project'; and p. 8: 'We will assess . . . the extent to which local people are engaged in and supportive of your project', www.tnlcommunityfund. org.uk/media/documents/scottish-land-fund/Scottish-Land-Fund-guidance-notes.pdf

40 Andrea Ross, 'The Evolution of Sustainable Development in Scotland: A Case Study of Community Right to Buy Law and Policy, 2003–18', in Combe, Glass and Tindley (eds), *Land Reform in Scotland*, p. 244.

41 Ross, 'The Evolution of Sustainable Development in Scotland', pp. 239, 245.

42 In June 2013, Scotland's then First Minister, Alex Salmond, announced a target of 1m acres of land in community ownership by 2020. See Scottish Government, 'One Million Acres by 2020', Dec 2015, www.gov.scot/publications/one-million-acres-2020-strategy-report-recommendations-1-million-acre/

43 Wightman, *The Poor Had No Lawyers*, pp. 200–1, 347–8.

44 Jamie Mann, 'Just two communities bid for right to buy neglected land in five years', *The Ferret*, 20 Aug 2023, theferret.scot/communities-bid-right-to-buy-neglected-land-5-years/

45 Sale of Tayvallich Estate: see Paul Drury, '"Once in a lifetime" opportunity as £10.5m island estate goes up for sale', *The Times*, 6 Sep 2022, www.thetimes. co.uk/article/once-in-a-lifetime-opportunity-as-10-5m-island-estate-goes-up-for-sale-70v885rf7. Scottish Land Fund's budget of £10m a year: see question asked by Rhoda Grant MSP in Scottish Parliament and answer by Minister Mairi McAllan, 22 July 2021, www.parliament.scot/chamber-and-committees/questions-and-answers/question?ref=s6w-01794

46 Severin Carrell, 'Ministers need to be bolder over Scotland's land reforms, say campaigners', *Guardian*, 27 July 2023, www.theguardian.com/uk-news/2023/

jul/27/ministers-need-to-be-bolder-over-scotlands-land-reforms-say-campaigners. Alastair McIntosh also anticipated the need for a Land Value Tax to help bring down land prices and provide a revenue stream to fund community buyouts in *Soil and Soul*, p. 269.

47 England is roughly 32m acres, so 250 acres is around 0.0007% of the country.

48 The Community Ownership Fund was launched in 2021 with a budget of £150m spread over four years (i.e. £37.5m a year). See DLUHC, 'Community Ownership Fund: prospectus', www.gov.uk/government/publications/community-ownership-fund-prospectus. For its first two rounds, applicants had to match-fund all the public funding they received – in other words, bid for 'a maximum of 50% of the capital funding that they seek for a project': see House of Commons Library briefing, 'Assets of Community Value', 10 Mar 2022, p.10, researchbriefings.files.parliament.uk/documents/SN06366/SN06366.pdf. In May 2023, the Community Ownership Fund reduced its match-funding requirements, offering up to 80% of the capital funding sought by an applicant. See UK Parliament, 'Launch of Community Ownership Fund Round 3 Prospectus', 15 May 2023, Hansard Vol. 732, hansard.parliament.uk/commons/2023-05-15/debates/2305154000010/LaunchOfCommunityOwnershipFundRound3Prospectus. The Scottish Land Fund states that they 'anticipate that over the life of the Fund, the average contribution to eligible project costs will be 80%', and that they 'can fund up to 95% of eligible project costs'; see Scottish Land Fund Guidance Notes, July 2021, www.tnlcommunityfund.org.uk/media/documents/scottish-land-fund/Scottish-Land-Fund-guidance-notes.pdf

49 George Monbiot, 'England's right-to-build laws are tokenistic and feeble – just ask the people of Totnes', *Guardian*, 15 Sep 2021, www.theguardian.com/commentisfree/2021/sep/15/england-right-to-build-laws-totnes-devon-housing. See also the project website, with details of the nature reserve that would serve as a natural flood defence: www.totnescommunity.org.uk/

50 See middlemarchescommunitylandtrust.org.uk/ and www.orecommunitylandtrust.org.uk/.

51 Zoe Williams, 'Mine's a peak: pub customers rally to buy £1.75m Blencathra', *Guardian*, 9 May 2014, www.theguardian.com/theguardian/2014/may/09/pub-customers-rally-buy-175m-blencathra; Patrick Sawer, 'Lake District's Blencathra Mountain withdrawn from sale – to local relief', *Telegraph*, 20 May 2016, www.telegraph.co.uk/news/2016/05/20/lake-districts-blencathra-mountain-withdrawn-from-sale---to-loca/; Helen Pidd, 'Crowdfunding campaign to buy Lake District mountain admits defeat', *Guardian*, 5 Sep 2016, www.theguardian.com/uk-news/2016/sep/05/blencathra-crowdfunding-lake-district-mountain

52 James Robinson, '"We have got to try": Ambitious plan for community purchase of £35m Rothbury Estate launched', *Chronicle*, 13 July 2023, www.chroniclelive.co.uk/news/north-east-news/rothbury-estate-for-sale-duke-27317159

53 Katie Neame, 'The Conservative Party commitment to levelling up is "dead", Nandy declares', *LabourList*, 18 July 2022, labourlist.org/2022/07/nandy-declares-the-conservative-party-commitment-to-levelling-up-dead/. The article

includes a full transcript of Nandy's speech, including its pledges on Community Right to Buy.

54 In January 2024, Angela Rayner stated: 'Labour will strengthen the powers available to local communities to regenerate their high streets and town centres, through a strengthened Community Right to Buy. A Labour Government will provide communities with first refusal on a wider range of assets of community value, review the definition of community assets in existing legislation, and double the time period for communities to raise finance to buy assets of community value from six months to twelve.' Lizzy Buchan, 'Majority of bids to save libraries, pubs and village halls rejected by Tory scheme', *Mirror,* 10 Jan 2024, www.mirror.co.uk/news/politics/majority-bids-save-libraries-pubs-31867319.amp. In a document summarising its five missions for Britain, the Labour Party states: 'Labour will strengthen the powers available to local communities to regenerate their high streets and town centres, through a strengthened Community Right to Buy': Labour, 'Let's Get Britain's Future Back', April 2024, labour.org.uk/wp-content/uploads/2024/04/Lets-Get-Britains-Future-Back.pdf.

55 Report of the Community Ownership Commission, 'Unleashing Community Ownership', Jan 2024, party.coop/wp-content/blogs.dir/5/files/2024/01/20240104-community-ownership-report-final-compress.pdf

56 Winston Churchill, 11 Nov 1947, winstonchurchill.org/resources/quotes/the-worst-form-of-government/

4 A Public Nature Estate

1 'Father of British ecology' is an accolade that many have given to Tansley, including in this potted biography by the New Phytologist Foundation: www.newphytologist.org/trust/tansley/about. Tansley's words taken from Arthur Tansley, *Our Heritage of Wild Nature: A Plea for Organized Nature Conservation,* 1945, p. 40.

2 Tansley introduced the concept of the ecosystem in his 1935 paper, 'The use and abuse of vegetational concepts and terms', *Ecology* 16, pp. 284–307. See also his books *The British Islands and their Vegetation,* 1939, and *Britain's Green Mantle,* 1949.

3 Tansley, *Our Heritage of Wild Nature,* p. 40.

4 Nature Reserves Investigation Committee, *Nature Conservation in Great Britain,* Jan 1943. The SPNR had overseen the creation of the Committee, following a conference in 1941.

5 British Ecological Society, 'Memorandum on Wild Life Conservation and Ecological Research from the National Standpoint', 6 June 1945. A copy is in the National Archives within folder FT 3/1, 'Origin, history and general information on the Nature Conservancy', discovery.nationalarchives.gov.uk/details/r/C1260149

6 For more on the interwar history of councils buying land for preservation and public amenity, see my blog post 'What land is owned by councils?', 4 May 2020, whoownsengland.org/2020/05/04/what-land-is-owned-by-councils/

7 Paul Addison, *The Road to 1945,* 1975, p.14.

8   Gov.uk, 'Past Prime Ministers: Clement Attlee', www.gov.uk/government/history/past-prime-ministers/clement-attlee

9   *Conservation of Nature in England and Wales: Report of the Wild Life Conservation Special Committee*, chaired by Dr J. S. Huxley, July 1947 (Cmd 7122), p. 52.

10   The National Parks and Access to the Countryside Act 1949.

11   Matthew Kelly, 'Habitat Protection, Ideology and the British Nature State: The Politics of the Wildlife and Countryside Act 1981', *The English Historical Review* 137:586, June 2022, pp. 847–83, doi.org/10.1093/ehr/ceac112. See also Matthew Kelly, 'Conventional thinking and the fragile birth of the nature state in post-war Britain', in Wilko Graf von Hardenberg et al. (eds), *The Nature State: Rethinking the History of Conservation,* 2017, pp. 114–34.

12   National Parks and Access to the Countryside Act 1949, section 17, www.legislation.gov.uk/ukpga/1949/97/pdfs/ukpga_19490097_en.pdf

13   *Conservation of Nature in England and Wales*, p. 43.

14   Such as, for example, Dendles Wood NNR in Devon, examined in more detail in Chapter 6.

15   John Sheail, *Nature Conservation in Britain: The formative years*, 1998, p. 50.

16   Letter 2 Jan 1951 from unnamed official at the Nature Conservancy to M.F. Clapp at the Treasury informing him of the purchase of Yarner Wood. National Archives, T 223/352, 'Acquisition of land', discovery.nationalarchives.gov.uk/details/r/C187727

17   See, for example, my account of the post-war felling of Atlantic oakwoods in *The Lost Rainforests of Britain,* ch. 7.

18   Sheail, *Nature Conservation in Britain*, p. 34.

19   Sheail, *Nature Conservation in Britain*, p. 37.

20   Minute of meeting between Sir James Crombie of the Treasury and Max Nicholson, 29 Oct 1953, National Archives, T 223/352, 'Acquisition of land'.

21   Andrew Roth, 'Obituary: The Marquess of Salisbury', *Guardian*, 15 July 2003, www.theguardian.com/news/2003/jul/15/guardianobituaries.conservatives. See also whoownsengland.org/2017/07/10/the-marquess-of-salisburys-offshore-estates/

22   Letter from E. W. Playfair of the Treasury to Sir E. Bridges, 7 Dec 1955, National Archives, T 223/352, 'Acquisition of land'. John Morrison MP later became the 1st Baron Margadale; the 9,000-acre Fonthill Estate in Wiltshire is still in his family's ownership.

23   Letter from E.W. Playfair to Sir E. Bridges, 7 Dec 1955.

24   Sheail, *Nature Conservation in Britain*, p. 36.

25   Letter from E.W. Playfair to Sir E. Bridges, 7 Dec 1955.

26   Max Nicholson, *The Environmental Revolution,* 1970, pp. 184–5.

27   Nicholson, *The Environmental Revolution*, p.33.

28   This precis of the Ribble Estuary debacle draws on the accounts in Kelly, 'Habitat Protection, Ideology and the British Nature State', and Sheail, *Nature Conservation in Britain*, pp. 212–13.

29   'Over three-quarters of the members of Mrs Thatcher's 1981 Cabinet were owners of rural land': Charlie Pye-Smith and Chris Rose, *Crisis and Conservation: Conflict in the British Countryside*, 1984, p. 15.

30   See Peter Marren, *Nature Conservation* (Collins New Naturalist series), 2002, p. 89.

31   Marren, *Nature Conservation*, Collins New Naturalist series, 2002, p. 92.

32   Jeremy Purseglove, *Taming the Flood: Rivers, Wetlands and the Centuries-Old Battle Against Flooding* (2nd edn), 2015, p. 305.

33   Marren, *England's National Nature Reserves*, 1994, p. 264.

34   Nicholas Ridley MP, House of Commons debate on Nature Reserves, 17 Feb 1988, api.parliament.uk/historic-hansard/commons/1988/feb/17/nature-reserves#S6CV0127P0_19880217_HOC_12

35   Sheail, *Nature Conservation in Britain*, p. 247; Marren, *England's National Nature Reserves*, p. 264. See also Nicholas Ridley MP, House of Commons debate on the Nature Conservancy Council/ Countryside Commission, 11 July 1989, api.parliament.uk/historic-hansard/written-answers/1989/jul/11/nature-conservancy-councilcountryside#S6CV0156P0_19890711_CWA_380

36   Brett Christophers, *The New Enclosure: the Appropriation of Public Land in Neoliberal Britain,* 2018. See also Brett Christophers, 'The biggest privatisation you've never heard of: land', *Guardian,* 8 Feb 2018, www.theguardian.com/commentisfree/2018/feb/08/biggest-privatisation-land-margaret-thatcher-britain-housing-crisis

37   Marren, *England's National Nature Reserves*, p. 264. Ridley's view was that the NCC should 'keep their land holdings to the minimum necessary for their functions' and 'consider also the size of the NNR network'. See House of Commons debate, 'Nature Reserves', 13 Jan 1988, api.parliament.uk/historic-hansard/written-answers/1988/jan/13/nature-reserves-1#S6CV0125P0_19880113_CWA_132

38   See also Jonathan Leake, 'U turn on sale of nature reserves', *Sunday Times,* 6 Feb 2011, www.thetimes.co.uk/article/u-turn-on-sale-of-nature-reserves-c6wlrd8gmvt

39   Natural England, Annual Report and Accounts, 1 Apr 2019 to 31 Mar 2020, chair's foreword, p. 2, assets.publishing.service.gov.uk/government/uploads/system/uploads/attachment_data/file/957981/natural-england-annual-report-and-accounts-2019-to-2020.pdf

40   Natural England data, obtained by the author through correspondence with officials.

41   Emma Howard, 'Nearly half of England's "most important wildlife sites" at risk after not being monitored for years', Greenpeace Unearthed, 7 Sep 2018, unearthed.greenpeace.org/2018/09/07/half-england-sssi-sites-not-monitored/

42   Statistic calculated by measuring maps of land owned and leased by Natural England, released to the author via an FOI request. See my blog post 'Unnatural England', 9 Feb 2023, whoownsengland.org/2023/02/09/unnatural-england/

43   Mark Avery, *Reflections: what wildlife needs and how to provide it,* 2023, pp. 175–6.

44   Congressional Research Service, 'Federal Land Ownership: Overview and Data', updated 21 Feb 2021, sgp.fas.org/crs/misc/R42346.pdf

45   New Zealand Ministry for the Environment briefing, 'Legally protected conservation land in New Zealand'. New Zealand is 26,771,000ha in extent, so legally protected public land covers 32% of the country.

46 Marc Koch and Carolin Maier, 'Forest Land Ownership Change in Germany', COST Action FP1201 FACESMAP Country Report, 2015, p. 8, facesmap. boku.ac.at/library/FP1201_Country%20Report_GERMANY.pdf

47 Japanese Ministry of the Environment, 'Natural Park Systems in Japan', undated briefing, p. 2, www.env.go.jp/en/nature/nps/park/doc/files/parksystem.pdf

48 Another way of giving Natural England greater sway over the management of public and quasi-public landholdings would be to reinvigorate the Major Landowners' Group (MLG), a forum set up in 2003 and still operating in 2024. Its members comprise large public, third sector and private landowners (such as the major water companies), and it has been chaired variously by DEFRA and Natural England. Its remit is focused, however, on the better management of SSSIs, rather limiting its scope. A bold government would replace the MLG with a Public Nature Estate group; broaden its remit to encompass nature recovery over *all* land owned by its members; task the group with delivering 30x30 and Environment Act 2021 targets; and give Natural England final sign-off powers over the land management plans of public sector landowners and water utilities.

49 Author's calculations. See Guy Shrubsole, *Who Owns England?*, 2019, p. 297 and *passim*.

50 HM Government, Environmental Improvement Plan, Jan 2023, p. 49: 'Forestry England will continue to deliver its commitment to restore all 42,814 hectares of its PAWS'. 42,814ha = *c.* 105,000 acres. assets.publishing.service. gov.uk/government/uploads/system/uploads/attachment_data/file/1133967/ environmental-improvement-plan-2023.pdf

51 Forestry Commission, Key Performance Indicators, Report for 2022–23, p.45, second graph down – shows that in England, 1,948ha (4,813 acres) of PAWS sites owned by FE were restored in England in 2022–3. assets.publishing.service. gov.uk/government/uploads/system/uploads/attachment_data/file/1162830/ Forestry-Commission-Key-Performance-Indicators-Report-2022-23.pdf

52 Forestry England, Biodiversity Plan 2022–26, 'Forest Wilding', p. 9, www. forestryengland.uk/sites/default/files/documents/Forestry%20England_ Biodiversity%20Plan%202022-26_0.pdf

53 Author's calculations. See Shrubsole, *Who Owns England?*, p. 297 and *passim*.

54 Miles King, 'Victory at Lodge Hill raises questions about brownfield first and sale of public land', A New Nature Blog, 25 June 2013, anewnatureblog. com/2013/06/25/victory-at-lodge-hill-raises-questions-about-brownfield-first- and-sale-of-public-land/

55 Author's calculations. See Shrubsole, *Who Owns England?*, p. 297, and blog post 'What land is owned by councils?', 4 May 2020, whoownsengland. org/2020/05/04/what-land-is-owned-by-councils/

56 CPRE, 'Reviving County Farms', 2019, www.cpre.org.uk/wp-content/ uploads/2019/12/December-2019_Reviving-county-farms.pdf

57 See for instance Enfield Council, 'London's first beaver project gets new dam dwellers', 27 Mar 2023, www.enfield.gov.uk/news-and-events/2023/03/ londons-first-beaver-project-gets-new-dam-dwellers

58 Kiran Stacey and Fiona Harvey, 'Labour cuts £28bn green investment pledge

by half', *Guardian,* 8 Feb 2024, www.theguardian.com/politics/2024/feb/08/labour-cuts-28bn-green-investment-pledge-by-half

59   Tweet by Matthew Kelly, 12 Feb 2023, twitter.com/Scorhill/status/1624715088065183751

5 The Great Draining

1   The figure of 330,000 acres is the area of the peat soils in the Fens, derived by the author by measuring Natural England's map of peat soils. For the methodology, data sources and maps behind this figure, see Guy Shrubsole, 'Who owns our carbon?', Nov 2021, whoownsengland.files.wordpress.com/2021/11/who-owns-our-carbon-nov-2021.pdf. A third of England's fresh veg: Environment Agency, 'The Fens – preserving the "breadbasket of Britain"', 17 July 2023, environmentagency.blog.gov.uk/2023/07/17/the-fens-preserving-the-breadbasket-of-britain/

2   Evans et al., 'Implementation of an emission inventory for UK peatlands', Report to the Department for Business, Energy and Industrial Strategy, Centre for Ecology and Hydrology, 2017, p. 1, uk-air.defra.gov.uk/assets/documents/reports/cat07/1904111135_UK_peatland_GHG_emissions.pdf. This is a figure for the UK as a whole, comprising 518,700 acres of peat on which crops are grown, including places like the Somerset Levels and parts of Lancashire; but clearly the Fens, with 330,000 acres of lowland peat, comprises the bulk of this. See also the map of wasted peat in England on p. 22, and Table 4.6 on p. 46, which shows that crops grown on 'wasted' peat alone emit slightly over 5m tonnes of CO_2e annually. Crops grown on deep peat (some of which still remains in the Fens and other lowland areas) takes the total to the 7.6mt CO_2e cited.

3   Church of England, 'The Five Marks of Mission', Nov 2017, www.churchofengland.org/sites/default/files/2017-11/mtag-the-5-marks-of-mission.pdf. The Marks of Mission were developed in the 1980s and adopted by the C of E's General Synod in 1996; this is their latest iteration.

4   Albini et al., 'Early detection and environmental drivers of sewage fungus outbreaks in rivers', *Ecological Solutions and Evidence* 4:3, July–Sep 2023, besjournals.onlinelibrary.wiley.com/doi/10.1002/2688-8319.12277

5   See, for instance, BBC News, 'Fen Blow phenomenon: High winds and loose soil halt traffic', 18 Apr 2013, www.bbc.co.uk/news/uk-england-22201168; and Facebook post by BBC Radio Cambridgeshire, 5 May 2015, showing footage of the Fen Blow taking place near Mepal, just south of Church Commissioners' estate: www.facebook.com/bbcradiocambridgeshire/videos/fen-blow-captured-at-mepal-this-eveningthis-fenland-phenomenon-occurs-when-stron/1087832721245808/.

6   BBC News, 'UK's lowest spot is getting lower', 29 Nov 2002, news.bbc.co.uk/1/hi/england/2529365.stm

7   Benedict Macdonald, *Rebirding,* 2019, p. 24.

8   Oliver Rackham, *The History of the Countryside,* 1986, p. 383.

9   These descriptions also draw upon the accounts of fenland wildlife given in

Macdonald, *Rebirding*, pp. 24–5, and Williamson, *An Environmental History of Wildlife in England*, pp. 33–4.

10   *Felix's Life of St Guthlac*, quoted in Rackham, *The History of the Countryside*, p. 374. An alternative but very similar translation is quoted in H. C. Darby, *The Medieval Fenland*, 1940, p.8.

11   William of Malmesbury, writing in the twelfth century AD, cited in James Boyce, *Imperial Mud: The Fight for the Fens*, 2020, pp. 21–2.

12   Bede, writing in 731 AD, quoted in Darby, *The Medieval Fenland*, p. 7.

13   Leah Hamilton, 'To Pay Rent in Medieval England, Catch Some Eels', *Atlas Obscura,* 18 May 2023, www.atlasobscura.com/articles/medieval-eel-rent-map-england. For the original source of Ely's eel-rent figure, see Rory Naismith, 'The Ely Memoranda and the Economy of the Late Anglo-Saxon Fenland', *Anglo-Saxon England* 45, 2017, pp. 333–77, www.jstor.org/stable/26332322.

14   Boyce, *Imperial Mud*, p. 23.

15   Darby, *The Medieval Fenland*, p. 16.

16   Joan Thirsk, cited in Boyce, *Imperial Mud*, p. 23.

17   William Dugdale, *The History of Inbanking and Drayning Diverse Fens and Marshes,* 1662, p. ix, cited in Williamson, *An Environmental History of Wildlife in England*, p. 33.

18   Lieutenant Hammond, writing in 1635; cited in Boyce, *Imperial Mud*, p. 149.

19   Lord Macaulay, *History of England,* ed. C. H. Firth, iii, pp. 1349, 1914; cited in Darby, *The Medieval Fenland*, p. 42.

20   Rackham, *The History of the Countryside*, p. 390.

21   Along with former monastic lands elsewhere at Woburn and Tavistock.

22   For a list of the nineteen original investors in the Company of Adventurers, see the table on the Ouse Washes website, 'The Company of Adventurers and the Bedford Level Corporation', www.ousewashes.info/drainage-authorities/adventurers-and-blc.htm

23   Lord Willoughby, writing in 1597–8 in response to an earlier plan to drain the Fens: quoted in Boyce, *Imperial Mud*, p. 38.

24   Quoted in Boyce, *Imperial Mud*, p. 46.

25   Boyce, *Imperial Mud*, p. 46.

26   Quoted in Lee Raye, 'Wildlife wonders of Britain and Ireland before the industrial revolution – my research reveals all the biodiversity we've lost', The Conversation, 17 July 2023, theconversation.com/wildlife-wonders-of-britain-and-ireland-before-the-industrial-revolution-my-research-reveals-all-the-biodiversity-weve-lost-208721

27   Eric H. Ash, *The Draining of the Fens,* 2022.

28   Boyce, *Imperial Mud*, p. 160.

29   D. A. Ratcliffe, 'Nature Conservation: Aims, Methods and Achievements', *Proceedings of the Royal Society of London*, Series B: *Biological Sciences*, cxcvii, no. 1126, 1977, p. 27, royalsocietypublishing.org/doi/pdf/10.1098/rspb.1977.0054

30   Butterfly Conservation, 'Large Copper', butterfly-conservation.org/butterflies/large-copper. 'First discovered from Dozen's Bank near Spalding in Lincolnshire in 1749, the Large Copper became extinct in the British Isles just short of 100

years later in 1851 . . . Its decline was the result of changing fenland management and, in particular, the draining of the fens.'

31 Nature Conservancy Council, 'Nature Conservation in Great Britain', 1984, p. 105; the bar chart on p. 57 also makes the scale of this loss abundantly clear.

32 Jan Jansson, 'A general Plott and description of the Fennes and surrounded grounds', dated 1640, which was 'a later state of a map of the same name first published by Henricus Hondius sometime around 1632'. A copy can be seen online at www.raremaps.com/gallery/detail/83442/the-fens-and-the-isle-of-ely-a-general-plott-and-descripti-jansson

33 Sir Jonas Moore, 'A Mapp of ye Great Levell of ye Fenns…', 1658. A copy can be seen online at: antiqueprintmaproom.com/product/a-mapp-of-ye-great-levell-of-ye-fenns-extending-in-sir-jonas-moore/

34 'The Fens produces more than 7% of England's total agricultural production, worth a staggering £1.23 billion.' NFU brochure, 'Delivering for Britain: Food and farming in the Fens', Apr 2019, p. 4, www.fensforthefuture.org.uk/admin/resources/downloads/food-farming-in-the-fensweb.pdf

35 The acreages listed here, and in the following paragraph, were calculated by the author by mapping land ownership in the Fens in detail. See Guy Shrubsole, 'Who owns our carbon?', Nov 2021, whoownsengland.files.wordpress.com/2021/11/who-owns-our-carbon-nov-2021.pdf

36 The £37bn figure comes from the Wellcome Trust's website, 'Investments', wellcome.org/who-we-are/investments

37 Much of the Mormon Church's farmland in Britain is owned via the UK-registered company Farmland Reserve UK Limited. The Companies House entry for Farmland Reserve UK Limited shows its Person with Significant Control to be Farmland Reserve Inc., based in Salt Lake City, Utah. See find-and-update.company-information.service.gov.uk/company/01332670/persons-with-significant-control. The figure of 7,600 acres that the Mormons own in the Fens is my calculation; in East Anglia more widely, they are thought to own more like 14,000 acres. See Emma Cook, 'How the Mormons brought Salt Lake City to East Anglia', *Independent*, 2 Jan 1999, www.independent.co.uk/arts-entertainment/how-the-mormons-brought-salt-lake-city-to-east-anglia-1044463.html.

38 Cook, 'How the Mormons brought Salt Lake City to East Anglia'.

39 Hope William-Smith, 'South Yorkshire Pensions Authority sets 2030 carbon neutral goal', www.businessgreen.com/news/4021344/south-yorkshire-pensions-authority-sets-2030-carbon-neutral-goal

40 For a study of the potential impact of increased coastal flooding on soil salinity in Lincolnshire, see Iain J. Gould et al., 'The impact of coastal flooding on agriculture: A case-study of Lincolnshire, United Kingdom', *Land Degradation & Development* 31:12, July 2020, pp. 1545–59, onlinelibrary.wiley.com/doi/10.1002/ldr.3551

41 Natural England, 'Restoration of Lowland Peatland in England and Impacts on Food Production and Security', Oct 2010, p. 15, www.fensforthefuture.org.uk/admin/resources/downloads/lowland-peatland-restoration-study.pdf

42 Natural England, 'Restoration of Lowland Peatland in England and Impacts on Food Production and Security'.

43 Church of England, 'The Environment and The Five Marks of Mission', Oct 2019, p. 2, www.churchofengland.org/sites/default/files/2023-06/five-marks-of-mission-final-oct-2019.pdf

44 For more on the Church's lands, see my book *Who Owns England?*, pp. 64–73.

45 You can see the (incomplete) map I've made of Church Commissioner landholdings in my blog post '"God's acres": the land owned by the Church Commissioners', 4 Nov 2019, whoownsengland.org/2019/11/04/gods-acres-the-land-owned-by-the-church-commissioners/

46 Andrew Selous MP, Church Commissioner Questions, 17 June 2021, churchinparliament.org/2021/06/17/church-commissioner-questions-worship-choral-singing-bereavement-support-marriage-rewilding-tree-planting-net-zero-targets-regenerative-agriculture-westminster-abbey/. A clip of the exchange can also be viewed on my Twitter feed at twitter.com/guyshrubsole/status/1405556737659244547?s=20

47 Church Commissioners press release, 'Church Commissioners develop net zero carbon strategy for its land investments', 11 Aug 2021, www.churchofengland.org/media-and-news/press-releases/church-commissioners-develop-net-zero-carbon-strategy-its-land

48 General Synod, Nov 2021, Questions, Q77, pp. 45–6, www.churchofengland.org/sites/default/files/2021-11/questions-notice-paper-november-2021.pdf

49 Joe Ware, 'Commissioners on course to be net zero 20 years after the rest of the C of E', *Church Times,* 22 Apr 2021, www.churchtimes.co.uk/articles/2021/23-april/news/uk/commissioners-on-course-to-be-net-zero-20-years-after-the-rest-of-the-c-of-e

50 Operation Noah, 'Church Land and the Climate Crisis', Sep 2022, brightnow.org.uk/wp-content/uploads/2022/09/Church-Land-and-the-Climate-Crisis.pdf

51 Church Commissioners, 'Our approach to sustainability for real assets', July 2023, p. 8, www.churchofengland.org/sites/default/files/2023-07/6346_1_cc_rasr_full_300623_lr2.pdf

52 Besides Wicken Fen, Woodwalton Fen and Holme Fen (all discussed here), there's the Nene Washes, owned by the RSPB.

53 Michael McCarthy, 'Charles Rothschild: The banker who changed the world for good', *Independent,* 12 May 2012, www.independent.co.uk/climate-change/news/charles-rothschild-the-banker-who-changed-the-world-for-good-7737977.html

54 For more on Charles Rothschild, the SPNR, and the early history of Wicken and Woodwalton Fens, see Jennifer Jenkins and Patrick James, *From Acorn to Oak Tree: The growth of the National Trust 1895–1994,* 1994, pp. 36–7; and John Sheail, *Nature in Trust: The History of Nature Conservation in Britain,* 1976, *passim.*

55 Wildlife Trusts, 'About the Great Fen', www.greatfen.org.uk/about-great-fen, and see also www.wildlifebcn.org/nature-reserves/great-fen

56 The UK imported 42 per cent of its food in 2022. See DEFRA, 'Food statistics

in your pocket', 15 Feb 2024, Section 3.1: Origins of food consumed in the UK, 2022, www.gov.uk/government/statistics/food-statistics-pocketbook/food-statistics-in-your-pocket

57   Olly Watts, 'Swamp farming comes to Britain?', RSPB blog, 1 Dec 2017, community.rspb.org.uk/ourwork/b/climatechange/posts/swamp-farming-comes-to-britain

58   Mulholland et al., 'An assessment of the potential for paludiculture in England and Wales', Literature Review: DEFRA Project SP1218, Apr 2020, p. 32, fensforthefuture.org.uk/admin/resources/downloads/defra-lp2-paludiculture-report-april-2020-1.pdf

59   See Fens for the Future's web pages on bulrush: fensforthefuture.org.uk/creating-the-future/wetland-crop-typha, reeds: fensforthefuture.org.uk/creating-the-future/wetland-crop-reed, and sphagnum: fensforthefuture.org.uk/creating-the-future/wetland-crop-sphagnum-moss

60   Mulholland et al., 'An assessment of the potential for paludiculture in England and Wales', Literature Review: DEFRA Project SP1218, Apr 2020, p. 33, fensforthefuture.org.uk/admin/resources/downloads/defra-lp2-paludiculture-report-april-2020-1.pdf

61   The Lancashire Wildlife Trust, for instance, is trialling growing celery in a rewetted peatland field. See Jenny Bennion, 'Could celery help fight climate change?', 20 June 2022, www.lancswt.org.uk/blog/jenny-bennion/could-celery-help-fight-climate-change

62   See Fens for the Future's webpage on *Glyceria*: fensforthefuture.org.uk/creating-the-future/wetland-crop-glyceria

63   Lowland Agricultural Peat Task Force – Chair's Report, 2023, pp. 61, 52, assets.publishing.service.gov.uk/media/649d6fe1bb13dc0012b2e349/lowland-agricultural-peat-task-force-chairs-report.pdf

64   For more on County Farms, and statistics charting their rise and decline, see my blog post 'How the extent of County Farms has halved in 40 years', 8 June 2018, whoownsengland.org/2018/06/08/how-the-extent-of-county-farms-has-halved-in-40-years/, and CPRE, 'Reviving County Farms', Dec 2019, www.cpre.org.uk/resources/reviving-county-farms/

65   Stephen Briggs video interview for the Woodland Trust, 'Strengthen soils for improved farm productivity' (no date), www.woodlandtrust.org.uk/plant-trees/stephen-briggs/

66   Lowland Agricultural Peat Task Force – Chair's Report, 2023, p. 50, assets.publishing.service.gov.uk/media/649d6fe1bb13dc0012b2e349/lowland-agricultural-peat-task-force-chairs-report.pdf

67   Lydia Collas, 'The carbon footprint of crops grown on English peatlands', Green Alliance briefing, June 2023, green-alliance.org.uk/briefing/the-carbon-footprint-of-crops-grown-on-english-peatlands/

68   'In 1951 there were 445 hectares [1,099 acres] of glass in the Lea Valley. Currently there are 75 ha [185 acres], a decline of over 80% in 60 years'. Epping Forest District Council, 'Local Plan Evidence Base report – The Lea Valley Glasshouse Industry: Planning for the Future', 16 July 2012, p. 4, rds.eppingforestdc.

gov.uk/documents/s43150/PLA-006%20report%20on%20Glasshouse%20
Industry%20study%20May%202012%20Edited.pdf

69 DEFRA Minister Mark Spencer, reply to parliamentary question tabled by
    Kerry McCarthy MP, 2 May 2023, questions-statements.parliament.uk/written-
    questions/detail/2023-04-26/182809

70 Lowland Agricultural Peat Task Force – Chair's Report, 2023, p. 37.

71 DEFRA, 'Agricultural Transition Plan update January 2024', Annex 4: Premium
    payments, www.gov.uk/government/publications/agricultural-transition-plan-
    2021-to-2024/agricultural-transition-plan-update-january-2024#annex-4-
    premium-payments

72 The Church Commissioners own around 5,350 acres in the Fens, which is
    2,165ha. With payments for rewetting lowland peat rated at £1,409 per hectare,
    rewetting all of this land could bring in £3,050,485, i.e. £3m, per year.

73 The South Yorkshire Pension Authority owns some 12,187 acres in the Fens,
    which is 4,932ha, x £1,409 per hectare = £6,949,188, ie £7m per year.

74 There are *c.* 333,000 acres of fenland peat, which is 133,546ha. Multiplying this
    by £1,409 per hectare = £188m of tax revenues annually.

75 A similar proposal has been made recently in Scotland. See John Muir Trust press
    release, 'Support for Carbon Emissions Land Tax grows', 10 Aug 2023, www.
    johnmuirtrust.org/whats-new/news/1521-support-for-carbon-emissions-land-
    tax-grows

6 A Plague upon the Land

1   Dan Eatherley, *Invasive Aliens: The Plants and Animals from Over There That Are
    Over Here*, 2019, p. 104.

2   R.S.R. Fitter, *The Ark in our Midst*, 1959, p. 38.

3   Eatherley, *Invasive Aliens*, pp. 102–5.

4   Eatherley, *Invasive Aliens*, p. 102.

5   Eatherley, *Invasive Aliens*, p. 102.

6   *Lisburn Standard*, 1 July 1905, via British Newspaper Archive.

7   Eatherley, *Invasive Aliens*, p. 118.

8   BBC News, 'Bedford duke blamed for spread of grey squirrel in UK', 27 Jan
    2016, www.bbc.co.uk/news/uk-england-beds-bucks-herts-35417747

9   *Leighton Buzzard Observer and Linslade Gazette*, 19 Jan 1904, via British
    Newspaper Archive.

10 *Luton Times and Advertiser*, 5 July 1907, via British Newspaper Archive.

11 *Luton Reporter*, 20 Oct 1910, via British Newspaper Archive.

12 Fitter, *The Ark in our Midst*, p. 93.

13 *Ross Gazette*, 4 Oct 1906, via British Newspaper Archive.

14 'Squirrels Let Loose: A London Park Experiment', *Northern Daily Telegraph*, 27
    Sep 1906, via British Newspaper Archive.

15 'Squirrels in London Parks', *Northern Daily Telegraph*, 8 Dec 1906, via British
    Newspaper Archive.

16 Fitter, *The Ark in our Midst*, p. 94.

17 *Luton Times and Advertiser*, 19 June 1908.

18 Eatherley, *Invasive Aliens*, p. 118.

19 Entry for the Duke of Bedford, *Burke's Peerage, Baronetage and Knightage*, 1956, p. 181.

20 *Luton Times and Advertiser*, 5 Nov 1910.

21 Fitter, *The Ark in our Midst*, p. 94.

22 'Grey Squirrels: Their Rapid Spread and Menace', *Devon and Exeter Gazette*, 22 May 1930, via British Newspaper Archive.

23 The Grey Squirrels (Prohibition of Importation and Keeping) Order 1937, an amendment to the Destructive Imported Animals Act 1932. See Hansard, Vol 105, 29 June 1937, hansard.parliament.uk/lords/1937-06-29/debates/9f9a10bd-c780-474a-ae29-7ef515905aeb/GreySquirrels(ProhibitionOfImportationAndKeeping) Order1937.

24 'Pests' and 'little grey killers' from 'Pests we imported', *Advertiser and Times*, 29 Dec 1933, via British Newspaper Archive. 'North American invaders' from 'Heralds of the Spring', *The Sphere*, 26 Mar 1932, via British Newspaper Archive. 'Public enemies' from Arthur Nettleton, 'Grey Squirrels are Public Enemies: Exterminate them – or Britain may go hungry', *Weekly Telegraph*, 11 Feb 1950, via British Newspaper Archive.

25 'The Grey Squirrel and Bird Sanctuaries', *Northern Whig*, 2 Sep 1922, via British Newspaper Archive.

26 'Grey Squirrel Menace', *Buckinghamshire Examiner*, 24 Apr 1936, via British Newspaper Archive.

27 For more on the 'ring-barking' habits of grey squirrels, and their impacts on trees and forestry plantations, see Forest Research, 'Management of grey squirrels', www.forestresearch.gov.uk/research/management-of-grey-squirrels/.

28 National Archives, MAF 130/82, 'The grey squirrel campaign' – containing various documents pertaining to the grey squirrel bounty up to its conclusion in 1958.

29 Red squirrels are still present in Scotland and Wales. Within England, small populations are found in a few places like the Isles of Scilly (greys haven't yet boarded the *Scillonian*) and the Wirral. The figure of 2.7m grey squirrels comes from Natural England, 'A Review of the Population and Conservation Status of British Mammals: Technical Summary', June 2018, p. 18, www.mammal.org.uk/wp-content/uploads/2021/06/MAMMALS-Technical-Summary-FINALNE-Verision-FM3290621.pdf.

30 House of Commons Environmental Audit Committee, 'Invasive Species', Oct 2019, p. 5, publications.parliament.uk/pa/cm201919/cmselect/cmenvaud/88/88.pdf. See also GB Non-Native Species Secretariat website, 'Non-native species', www.nonnativespecies.org/non-native-species/.

31 Sarah J. Manchester and James M. Bullock, 'The impacts of non-native species on UK biodiversity and the effectiveness of control', *Journal of Applied Ecology* 37:5, Oct 2000, besjournals.onlinelibrary.wiley.com/doi/full/10.1046/j.1365-2664.2000.00538.x

32 Using the results of the government's 1873 Return of Owners of Land, the Victorian writer John Bateman was able to calculate that around 4,000 members

of the aristocracy and gentry owned around half of England. See John Bateman, *The Acre-ocracy of England*, 1876.

33   Forestry Commission, 'NFI Preliminary Estimates of the Presence and Extent of Rhododendron in British Woodlands', 2016, www.forestresearch.gov.uk/documents/2715/Presence_of_Rhododendron_in_British_Woodlands.pdf. The report estimates that rhododendron covers 37,600 ha of England, 53,300 ha of Scotland and 7,900 ha of Wales: 98,800 ha in total, or 244,000 acres. Birmingham is around 268 km^2 (Encyclopaedia Britannica: www.britannica.com/place/Birmingham-England), or 66,000 acres (x4 = 264,000 acres).

34   Samantha Subramanian, 'The war on Japanese knotweed', *Guardian*, 16 May 2023, www.theguardian.com/environment/2023/may/16/the-war-on-japanese-knotweed

35   J.P. Bailey and A.P. Conolly, 'Prize-winners to pariahs – A history of Japanese Knotweed *s.l.* (Polygonaceae) in the British Isles', *Watsonia* 23, 2000, pp. 93–110, archive.bsbi.org.uk/Wats23p93.pdf

36   Eatherley, *Invasive Aliens*, pp. 107–10.

37   The People's Trust for Endangered Species puts the total number of Reeves' muntjac in Britain at 52,000: ptes.org/get-informed/facts-figures/reeves-chinese-muntjac/. The Game and Wildlife Conservation Trust cites an older study from 1995, putting the total at 40,300 individuals: www.gwct.org.uk/research/long-term-monitoring/national-gamebag-census/mammal-bags-comprehensive-overviews/muntjac/.

38   Caroline Davies, 'Japanese knotweed and other invasive species may be costing UK £4bn a year', *Guardian*, 6 July 2023, www.theguardian.com/environment/2023/jul/06/japanese-knotweed-invasive-non-native-species-costing-uk-4bn-a-year-ash-dieback

39   Alex Keeble, 'The origins of driven shooting', *Shooting Times*, 4 Oct 2019, www.shootinguk.co.uk/popular-reads/driven-shooting-108347. See also David S.D. Jones, 'Pheasant shooting: a short history', *Fieldsports Journal* (no date), fieldsports-journal.com/fieldsports/shoot/pheasant-shooting-a-short-history

40   'The Game and Wildlife Conservation Trust calculate, based on their long-running National Game Bag Census, that the numbers released in the UK in 2018 were . . . 49.5 million pheasants.' DEFRA witness statement in legal case brought by Wild Justice, Exhibit EB2, 6 Oct 2020, p. 113, para 1.3, assets.publishing.service.gov.uk/government/uploads/system/uploads/attachment_data/file/931394/defra-witness-statement-gamebird-release-exhibit2.pdf. Prior to this, a 2019 study had calculated that 47m pheasants are released annually in Britain, plus 10m non-native red-legged partridges: see N.J. Aebischer, 'Fifty-year trends in UK hunting bags of birds and mammals, and calibrated estimation of national bag size, using GWCT's National Gamebag Census', *European Journal of Wildlife Research* 65:64, 2019, doi.org/10.1007/s10344–019–1299–x. See also GWCT, What the Science Says website, 'How many gamebirds are released in the UK per year?', www.whatthesciencesays.org/how-many-gamebirds-are-released-in-the-uk-per-year/

41   RSPB website, bird A–Z, entry for blackbird: www.rspb.org.uk/birds-and-wildlife/wildlife-guides/bird-a-z/blackbird/

42 'In September, just before the beginning of the shooting season, total pheasant biomass is about 1.6–1.7 times the total biomass of the British breeding bird population estimate for spring.' GWCT, What the Science Says website, 'Estimating the number and biomass of pheasants in Britain', 14 July 2020, www.whatthesciencesays.org/estimating-the-number-and-biomass-of-pheasants-in-britain/. See also T.M. Blackburn and K.J. Gaston, 'Abundance, biomass and energy use of native and alien breeding birds in Britain', *Biological Invasions* 20, 2018, pp. 3563–73, link.springer.com/article/10.1007/s10530-018-1795-z

43 See the definition of 'invasive' used by the GB Non-Native Species Secretariat in its FAQs: 'Invasive non-native species are species that have been introduced (deliberately or accidentally) by people, which are having a detrimental impact on the economy, wildlife or habitats of Britain.' www.nonnativespecies.org/resources-and-projects/faqs/. See also the definition referred to by the House of Commons Environmental Audit Committee, 'Invasive Species', Oct 2019, p. 5, publications.parliament.uk/pa/cm201919/cmselect/cmenvaud/88/88.pdf.

44 GWCT website, 'Game cover: top of the crops', www.gwct.org.uk/game/advice/game-cover-top-of-the-crops/

45 R.B. Sage, C. Ludolf and P.A. Robertson, 'The ground flora of ancient semi-natural woodlands in pheasant release pens in England', *Biological Conservation* 122:2, Mar 2005, pp. 243–52, www.researchgate.net/publication/248200175_The_ground_flora_of_ancient_semi-natural_woodlands_in_pheasant_release_pens_in_England

46 Sage, Ludolf and Robertson, 'The ground flora of ancient semi-natural woodlands in pheasant release pens in England'.

47 Capstick et al., 'Ground flora recovery in disused pheasant pens is limited and affected by pheasant release density', *Biological Conservation* 231, Mar 2019, pp. 181–8, www.sciencedirect.com/science/article/abs/pii/S0006320718311339?via%3Dihub. See also GWCT press release, 'Shoots urged to pay more attention to release pen locations, says new GWCT study', 21 Jan 2019, www.gwct.org.uk/news/news/2019/january/shoots-urged-to-pay-more-attention-to-release-pen-locations,-says-new-gwct-study/

48 Sage et al., 'The flora and structure of farmland hedges and hedgebanks near to pheasant release pens compared with other hedges', *Biological Conservation* 142, 2009, pp. 1362–9, www.gwct.org.uk/research/scientific-publications/2000-09/2009/sage2009/

49 GWCT, 'The impact of pheasant release at Exmoor shooting estates' (no date or author details given), www.gwct.org.uk/game/research/species/pheasant/the-impact-of-pheasant-release-at-exmoor-shooting-estates/

50 This list of pheasants' diets comes from Brian Vesey-Fitzgerald, *British Game*, Collins New Naturalist Guide, 1946, p. 54.

51 Neumann et al., 'Releasing of pheasants for shooting in the UK alters woodland invertebrate communities', *Biological Conservation* 191, Nov 2015, pp. 50–9, www.researchgate.net/publication/279446032_Releasing_of_pheasants_for_shooting_in_the_UK_alters_woodland_invertebrate_communities

52 Nicholas Milton, 'Game birds "could wipe out adders in most of Britain within

12 years"', *Guardian*, 1 Oct 2020, www.theguardian.com/environment/2020/oct/01/adder-extinct-across-britain-snake-threat-game-birds-release. The GWCT's What the Science Says website says that this claim is unsupported, but adds: 'This is an important area of research for the future'. See www.whatthesciencesays.org/are-released-pheasants-driving-adders-to-extinction/.

53   'Feeders were visited by gamebirds and songbirds in early and late winter, but rodents, columbids [pigeons], corvids [crows, rooks, etc.], lagomorphs [rabbits and hares], predators (mammals and raptors), waterbirds, and other species accounted for 54% of visits and consumed 67% of grain provided.' Sanchez-Garcia et al., 'Supplementary winter food for gamebirds through feeders: Which species actually benefit?', *Journal of Wildlife Management* 28:5, July 2015, pp. 832–45, wildlife.onlinelibrary.wiley.com/doi/abs/10.1002/jwmg.889.

54   Professor Stephen Harris, 'A review of the animal welfare, public health, and environmental, ecological and conservation implications of rearing, releasing and shooting non-native gamebirds in Britain', report to the Labour Animal Welfare Society, May 2021, p. 37, www.labouranimalwelfaresociety.org.uk/wp-content/uploads/2021/07/MASTER-GAMEBIRD-REPORT-MAY-2021_V2_SPREADS-1.pdf. The calculation is reproduced in full here: 'As a rule of thumb, eight tons of feed are required per 1000 pheasants released to support them from release to the end of the shooting season. This is about 2 tons of grower's pellets to take the birds to 12 to 14 weeks of age, followed by about 6 tons of wheat. So the estimated 47 million pheasants released each year require 376,000 tons of feed, of which 94,000 tons is grower's pellets and 282,000 tons is wheat. To put this into perspective, the five-year average for wheat production in the UK is 15.1 million tonnes, and so the shooting industry uses nearly 2% of the UK's annual wheat production to rear pheasants for shooting.'

55   See for example George Davis, 'Game farmers' diary: February', 17 Feb 2023, shoothub.gunsonpegs.com/articles/rearing/game-farmers-diary-february, in which Tom Welham, a spokesperson for game feed supplier Marsdens, discusses how soya is an 'important source of protein in game diets', how it is 'procured from soya producing nations such as Brazil, Argentina and the USA', and how it is 'imperative therefore that all our soya in Marsdens feed is responsibly sourced and certified to guarantee it doesn't contribute to negative practices such as de-forestation'.

56   GWCT, 'How many birds are shot in the UK?', *Game and Wildlife Review* 2017, p. 43.

57   Mark Avery, 'The Common Pheasant: its status in the UK and the potential impacts of an abundant non-native', *British Birds* 112, July 2019, pp. 372–89.

58   Avery, 'The Common Pheasant'.

59   Avery, 'The Common Pheasant'.

60   Henrietta Pringle et al., 'Associations between gamebird releases and generalist predators', *Journal of Applied Ecology* 56:8, Aug 2019, pp. 2102–13, besjournals.onlinelibrary.wiley.com/doi/10.1111/1365-2664.13451

61   'At least 70 released pheasants tested positive for avian influenza during 2022.' RSPB website, 'Avian Flu (bird flu)', FAQ on 'What is the RSPB doing about

gamebird releases?', www.rspb.org.uk/birds-and-wildlife/advice/how-you-can-help-birds/disease-and-garden-wildlife/avian-influenza-updates/

62   DEFRA, 'Risk Assessment on the spread of High Pathogenicity Avian Influenza (HPAI) H5N1 to wild birds from released, formerly captive gamebirds in Great Britain: Pheasants', Oct 2022, assets.publishing.service.gov.uk/government/uploads/system/uploads/attachment_data/file/1124975/Risk_Assessment_on_the_spread_of_High_Pathogenicity_Avian_Influenza__HPAI__H5N1_to_wild_birds_from_released__formerly_captive_gamebirds_in_Great_Britain_Pheasants.pdf

63   Sandra Laville, 'RSPB calls for suspension of game-bird releases over avian flu fears', *Guardian*, 18 May 2023, www.theguardian.com/world/2023/may/18/rspb-calls-for-suspension-of-game-bird-releases-over-avian-flu-fears

64   Roald Dahl, *Danny the Champion of the World*, 1975, pp. 29, 63.

65   Roald Dahl Museum, Great Missenden, 'Countryside Trail' leaflet.

66   Jonathan Young, 'The 20 best pheasant shoots in Britain', 18 Nov 2015, www.thefield.co.uk/shooting/the-20-best-pheasant-shoots-in-britain-30528

67   Area of the Hampden Estate calculated from Buckinghamshire Council's digitised estate maps deposited under the Highways Act 1980, section 31.6.

68   Dahl, *Danny the Champion of the World*, p. 26.

69   Chilterns local historian Tony Marshall writes about the Davis family's game farm business in his history of the parish of Prestwood. 'One farm business that continued to thrive . . . was the rearing of pheasants on Denner Hill, expanded by Dudley Davis's son Derek and currently managed by his son George . . . By the 1980s, the Arthur Davis Game Farm was the oldest in the country'. Online at www.thehomeofcricket.com/prestwood/chapter11.html#11intro

70   Davis, 'Game Farmers' Diary: February'.

71   'The "wild" population of Pheasants has nearly doubled in 45 years, the number shot has increased five-fold and the number released has increased ten-fold.' Avery, 'The Common Pheasant'. See also the GWCT's index of pheasant bags and releases, www.gwct.org.uk/research/long-term-monitoring/national-gamebag-census/bird-bags-summary-trends/common-pheasant/, and the results of the BTO's Breeding Birds Survey for pheasants, summarised at www.bto.org/understanding-birds/birdfacts/pheasant.

72   George Monbiot, 'The Shooting Party', *Guardian*/Monbiot.com, 29 Apr 2014, www.monbiot.com/2014/04/28/the-shooting-party/

73   To view the FOI'd data, see Guy Shrubsole, 'The English shooting estates that rear 20 million pheasants a year', Who Owns England blog, 2 Apr 2019, whoownsengland.org/2019/04/02/the-english-shooting-estates-that-rear-20-million-pheasants-a-year/

74   Natural England, 'Ecological consequences of gamebird releasing and management on lowland shoots in England', p. 69, publications.naturalengland.org.uk/publication/5078605686374400. NE cites more recent 2019 APHA data than the figures I received under FOI, and was able to view statistics broken down into pheasants kept for rearing (11m) and releasing (10m). Given estimates of *c.* 50m pheasants released annually across Britain, this suggests, as NE says, registration compliance rates of less than 25%.

75   George Davis, 'Game Farmers' Diary: March', 17 Mar 2023, ShootHub/ GunsOnPegs, shoothub.gunsonpegs.com/articles/rearing/game-farmers-diary-march

76   Shrubsole, 'The English shooting estates that rear 20 million pheasants a year'.

77   Sage et al. estimate '9,000 ha of release pen enclosing about 1% of the total woodland area' of England. Sage, Ludolf and Robertson, 'The ground flora of ancient semi-natural woodlands in pheasant release pens in England'.

78   The Google map I've made of Exmoor's pheasant shoots can be viewed here: www.google.com/maps/d/u/0/edit?hl=en&mid=18tnkcHqbdACIM48xQ5JRol otGqD7j7A&ll=51.13666410555876%2C-3.780367145455201&z=12

79   GWCT, grant application form to Exmoor National Park Authority for project on 'Released pheasants and their impacts on woodland and farmland habitats on Exmoor', 2015, statistics cited on p. 15: www.exmoor-nationalpark.gov.uk/__data/assets/pdf_file/0033/289392/ar-dbsc-21.07.15-Item-6.1.pdf

80   Exmoor Society, 'Game Shooting in Exmoor – Exmoor Society Perspectives', 4 Dec 2018, www.exmoorsociety.com/assets/uploads/exmoorsocietyperspectivesongameshootingdec2018-65245.pdf

81   GIS mapping files produced by Exmoor National Park Authority for their 'Landscape Monitoring Project: Landscape monitoring case studies', 2022, released to the author following an FOI request.

82   Exmoor National Park Authority, 'Landscape Monitoring Project: Landscape monitoring case studies', 2022, pp. 13–17, www.exmoor-nationalpark.gov.uk/__data/assets/pdf_file/0022/432094/Landscape-Monitoring-Project-Final.pdf

83   The boast is made on the front page of the website of the Mornacott Shoot: mornacott-shoot.co.uk/

84   On Elizabeth Clare McLaren Throckmorton and her younger sister Felicity, see en.wikipedia.org/wiki/Clare_McLaren-Throckmorton. On the area of the Throckmorton Estate, see the website for the Molland Shoot, www.mollandhouse.com/the-molland-shoot, corroborated by the author by measuring digitised Highways Act s31.6 maps deposited by the estate with Devon County Council.

85   Website for the Molland Shoot: www.mollandhouse.com/the-molland-shoot

86   The entry for the Molland Estate can be found on the HMRC 'Tax-exempt heritage assets' scheme website at www.hmrc.gov.uk/gds/heritage/lbsearch.htm.

87   HMRC, 'Guidance: Tax relief for national heritage assets', www.gov.uk/guidance/tax-relief-for-national-heritage-assets

88   Entries for the Hampden Estate and Newburgh Priory Estate can be found on the HMRC 'Tax-exempt heritage assets' scheme website at www.hmrc.gov.uk/gds/heritage/lbsearch.htm. For more on Newburgh Priory's pheasant shoots, see www.newburghpriory.co.uk/Estate/Shooting. For the English grouse moors benefiting from the tax break, I count the Nawton Tower Estate, Bilsdale Estate, Bolton Abbey Estate, Bolton Castle Estate and Hawnby Estate in Yorkshire, the Helbeck Estate in Cumbria and the Crag Estate in the Peak District – seven in total; there may be others.

89   Institute for Fiscal Studies (IFS), 'Reforming Inheritance Tax', 27 Sep 2023, ifs.

org.uk/publications/reforming-inheritance-tax. As the IFS state, 'Exemption thresholds, which allow many couples to pass on up to £1 million tax-free, mean that the share of deaths resulting in inheritance tax is small, at around 4% in 2020–21.'

90   Wild Justice press release, 'Wild Justice challenges gamebird releases', 18 July 2019, wildjustice.org.uk/gamebird-releases/wild-justice-challenges-gamebird-releases/

91   Wild Justice press release, 'Impacts of non-native gamebird releases need to be assessed – another success for Wild Justice', 12 Sep 2019, wildjustice.org.uk/general/impacts-of-non-native-gamebird-releases-need-to-be-assessed-another-success-for-wild-justice/; and 'Wild justice statement on gamebird licensing', 30 Oct 2020, wildjustice.org.uk/gamebird-releases/wild-justice-statement-on-gamebird-licensing/. See also DEFRA publication, 'Decision: Review of gamebird releases on and around European protected sites', 30 Oct 2020, www.gov.uk/government/publications/review-of-gamebird-releases-on-and-around-european-protected-sites

92   Wildlife and Countryside Act 1981, Schedule 9: www.legislation.gov.uk/ukpga/1981/69/schedule/9. The Statutory Instrument passed to include pheasants and red-legged partridges on Schedule 9 was 'The Wildlife and Countryside Act 1981 (Variation of Schedule 9) (England) (No.2) Order 2021', and can be viewed at www.legislation.gov.uk/uksi/2021/548/made

93   DEFRA, 'Statutory guidance: GL43: licence to release common pheasants or red-legged partridges on certain European sites or within 500m of their boundary', www.gov.uk/government/publications/gamebirds-licence-to-release-common-pheasants-or-red-legged-partridges-on-certain-european-sites-or-within-500m-of-their-boundary-gl43/gl43-licence-to-release-common-pheasants-or-red-legged-partridges-on-certain-european-sites-or-within-500m-of-their-boundary

94   'A spokesperson for the Darwalls said they were not challenging the park's existing bylaws but "just asking the Dartmoor National Park Authority to cooperate with those who are responsible for looking after the land and the environment".' Tom Wall, 'National park authority defends wild camping rights on Dartmoor', *Guardian*, 13 June 2022, www.theguardian.com/environment/2022/jun/13/national-park-authority-defends-wild-camping-rights-on-dartmoor

95   For more coverage of the Darwalls' wild camping court case, see Helena Horton and Tom Wall, 'Legal right to wild camp on Dartmoor never existed, court hears', *Guardian*, 13 Dec 2022, www.theguardian.com/uk-news/2022/dec/13/landowners-lawyer-says-there-has-never-been-legal-right-to-wild-camp-on-dartmoor; Helena Horton, 'Right to wild camp in England lost in Dartmoor court case', *Guardian*, 13 Jan 2023, www.theguardian.com/environment/2023/jan/13/dartmoor-estate-landowner-alexander-darwall-court-case-right-to-camp

96   As the Blachford Estate's website (blachfordestate.com) stated, 'The estate forms part of the much sought after Cornwood Shoot.' The website has been taken offline since early 2023, but the most recent version of it can still be seen on the Wayback Machine at web.archive.org/web/20221219061709/blachfordestate.com/

97 Natural England, 'Operations likely to damage the special interest – site name: Dendles Wood' (no date), designatedsites.naturalengland.org.uk/PDFsForWeb/Consent/1003586.pdf

98 Natural England, 'Dendles Wood Management Plan 2015–2020', released to the author under FOI laws, July 2022. For more about the habitats of the rare Blue Ground Beetle, found at just fifteen sites in the UK, see BBC News, 'New populations of rare beetle found on Dartmoor', 22 Nov 2022, www.bbc.co.uk/news/uk-england-devon-63717559

99 Helena Horton, 'Dartmoor landowner who won wild camping ban may be putting rare beetle at risk', *Guardian*, 21 Jan 2023, www.theguardian.com/environment/2023/jan/21/dartmoor-landowner-who-won-wild-camping-ban-may-be-putting-rare-beetle-at-risk

100 Wild Justice, 'Pheasants camping out in Dartmoor woods', 8 Feb 2023, wildjustice.org.uk/gamebird-releases/pheasants-camping-out-in-dartmoor-woods/; 'Dendles wood – a sorry tale', 17 Mar 2023, wildjustice.org.uk/gamebird-releases/dendles-wood-a-sorry-tale/; and 'Wild Justice starts new legal challenge of gamebird release regulations', 8 June 2023, wildjustice.org.uk/gamebird-releases/wild-justice-starts-new-legal-challenge-of-gamebird-release-regulations/.

101 Helena Horton, 'Wild camping allowed on Dartmoor again after court appeal succeeds', *Guardian*, 31 July 2023, www.theguardian.com/environment/2023/jul/31/wild-camping-dartmoor-court-appeal

7 Nature's Whistleblowers

1 BASC, CLA, Countryside Alliance, GWCT, National Gamekeepers' Organisation et al., 'Code of Good Shooting Practice', p. 10, www.codeofgoodshootingpractice.org.uk/pdf/COGSP.pdf

2 Jerome Starkey and Emma Yeomans, '"Abomination" of pheasants dumped into pit by digger', *The Times,* 17 Jan 2019, www.thetimes.co.uk/article/abomination-of-pheasants-dumped-into-pit-by-digger-whrw935fb

3 Raptor Persecution UK, '"In excess of 100 dead pheasants" dumped in Wales', 29 Dec 2023, raptorpersecutionuk.org/2023/12/29/in-excess-of-100-dead-pheasants-dumped-in-wales/

4 Don Ford, formerly employed by the 10th Earl of Shaftesbury as head gamekeeper for the St Giles Estate, based on Wimborne St Giles, Dorset. www.dorsetlife.co.uk/2011/06/dorset-lives-his-own-man/

5 See, for example, the National Gamekeepers' Organisation Official Blog, which has 'Keeping the Balance' as the slogan on its title page: gamekeepersblog.com/. *Keeping the Balance* is also the name of the the NGO's membership magazine.

6 Chris Rose, 'TB, Badgers and Cattle in The UK: A Campaign Ripe For A Reboot', 5 Dec 2020, threeworlds.campaignstrategy.org/?p=2701

7 UK Parliament website, 'Enclosing the land', www.parliament.uk/about/living-heritage/transformingsociety/towncountry/landscape/overview/enclosingland/

8 E.P. Thompson, *The Making of the English Working Class*, 1963, p. 237.

9 John Clare, 'The Nightingale's Nest', 1832, in Geoffrey Summerfield (ed.), *John Clare: Selected Poems*, 1990, p. 108.

10 Prose passages from Eric Robinson and David Powell (eds.), *John Clare By Himself*, 1996, pp. 39–41. Quoted in 'Toby Jones reads John Clare', Oxford Brookes University website, www.brookes.ac.uk/research/units/hss/projects/the-meeting/toby-jones-reads-john-clare.

11 Clare, 'The Fallen Elm', 1821, in *Selected Poems*, p. 167.

12 Clare, 'Remembrances', 1832, in *Selected Poems*, p.195.

13 Clare, 'The Lament of Swordy Well', 1830s, in *Selected Poems*, p. 172. See also Alan Franks, blog post, 'John Clare – The Lament of Swordy Well', 28 May 2022, alanfranks.org/2022/05/28/john-clare-the-lament-of-swordy-well/

14 Clare, 'The Moors', 1820, in *Selected Poems*, p. 169.

15 George Monbiot, 'John Clare, the poet of the environmental crisis – 200 years ago', *Guardian*, 9 July 2012, www.theguardian.com/commentisfree/2012/jul/09/john-clare-poetry

16 'Reclaiming the Commons', *The Land* 22, 2018, www.thelandmagazine.org.uk/articles/reclaiming-commons.

17 R. Lawton, 'Rural depopulation in Nineteenth Century England', in Dennis R. Mills (ed.), *English Rural Communities: The Impact of a Specialised Economy*, 1973, p. 195, Table 9.1: Urban and rural populations in England and Wales, 1801–1971.

18 See for instance Eric Hobsbawm and George Rudé, *Captain Swing*, 1969.

19 Thomas Hardy, *Tess of the d'Urbervilles*, 1891, ch. 47 (despotic threshing machine), ch. 51 (account of urbanisation). I am grateful to Alastair McIntosh for alerting me to Hardy's account of urbanisation.

20 Quoted in Mark Gorman, *Saving the People's Forest: Open spaces, enclosure and popular protest in mid-Victorian London*, 2021, pp. 23–4.

21 Gorman, *Saving the People's Forest*.

22 See the Past Tense blog post (no author given), 'Today in London History: Riot against enclosure of One Tree Hill, 1897', 17 Oct 2017, pasttense.co.uk/2017/10/17/demo-against-enclosure-of-one-tree-hill-honor-oak-erupts-into-rioting-1897/

23 Gillian Darley, *Octavia Hill: A Life*, 1990, p. 310.

24 Robert Blatchford, *Merrie England*, 1895, p. 21.

25 Blatchford, *Merrie England*, p. 61.

26 Some of these, such as the Sheffield Clarion Ramblers, were also directly inspired by Blatchford's writings. See David Hey, *A History of the Peak District Moors*, 2014, p. 167.

27 See Lancashire Past website, 'The Winter Hill Trespass 1896', lancashirepast.com/2022/12/03/the-winter-hill-trespass-1896/; Paul Salveson, *Will Yo' Come O' Sunday Mornin'?: The 1896 Battle for Winter Hill*, 1996. I was pleased to attend a memorial event for the 125th anniversary of the Winter Hill trespass in 2021, organised by Chris Chilton and the Bolton Socialist Club.

28 Frank Trentmann, 'Civilization and Its Discontents: English Neo-Romanticism and the Transformation of Anti-Modernism in Twentieth-Century Western Culture', *Journal of Contemporary History* 29:4, Oct 1994, p. 587.

29 Marion Shoard, *A Right to Roam: Should we open up Britain's countryside?*, 1999, p. 181.

30 Rights of Way Act 1932, section 1, subsection (4). For Lord Strachie's tabling of this amendment, see Hansard, House of Lords debate (Committee Stage of Rights of Way Bill 1932), 21 June 1932, vol. 85, column 26, api.parliament.uk/historic-hansard/lords/1932/jun/21/rights-of-way-bill#S5LV0085P0_19320621_HOL_106. As the Open Spaces Society has said, 'The Rights of Way Act 1932 also benefited landowners, by introducing a provision (against the wish of the society) whereby landowners could rebut the presumption that a route had been dedicated as a public highway': see OSS website, 'Eightieth anniversary of milestone law for walkers and riders', 1 Jan 2014, www.oss.org.uk/eightieth-anniversary-of-milestone-law-for-walkers-and-riders/

31 This provision was updated in the Highways Act 1980, section 31, subsection (6). To this day, Highways Authorities (councils with jurisdiction over highways) must maintain a public register of s31(6) landowner deposits and maps made under this section of the Act. Unwittingly, this makes for a very useful source of information on the extent of estates. The provision was strengthened in the Growth and Infrastructure Act 2013, extending the period for which a deposit is valid from ten to twenty years.

32 A conservative estimate based on the author's provisional measurement of the area of the s31(6) landowner deposits digitised by thirty-four English councils.

33 Cited in Hannah Rose Woods, *Rule, Nostalgia: A Backwards History of Britain*, 2022, p. 121.

34 Anti-Noise League 1935 Noise Abatement Exhibition handbook written by Lord Horder, quoted in James Mansell, '"A Chamber of Noise Horrors": sound, technology and the museum', *Science Museum Group Journal*, Special Issue: Sound and Vision, Spring 2017, journal.sciencemuseum.ac.uk/article/sound-technology-and-the-museum/. The Horder family acquired the 300-acre Ashford Chace Estate in Hampshire in the 1920s; see History of Steep website, historyofsteep.co.uk/portfolio/ashford-chace/

35 Hannah Rose Woods, *Rule, Nostalgia: A Backwards History of Britain*, 2022, p.121.

36 C.E.M. Joad, *A Charter for Ramblers,* 1934, pp. 176, 178.

37 Gavin Parker, 'Country Code', Museum of English Rural Life publication, May 2021, p. 4, merl.reading.ac.uk/wp-content/uploads/sites/20/2021/05/Object_21_-_Country_Code_-_The_MERL-51_Voices-1.pdf

38 National Parks Commission, 'Country Code', 1951.

39 Labour Party general election manifesto 1997. All past Labour manifestos can be viewed online at www.labour-party.org.uk/manifestos/

40 As related by Gordon Prentice MP, who told the Commons on 26 Mar 1999: 'A few weeks ago, in the Grand Committee Room on 10 March [1999], at a meeting called by the Socialist Environmental Resources Association – SERA – to discuss the right to roam, the Earl of Macclesfield told the astonished audience, "The countryside cannot accommodate humans on the loose." That is what he said; I jotted it down.' Speech during House of Commons debate on Right to Roam Private Members Bill, 26 Mar 1999, Hansard vol. 328, cc629–648, api.parliament.uk/historic-hansard/commons/1999/mar/26/right-to-roam-bill

41 As related by Gordon Prentice MP, speech during House of Commons debate on Land (Public Access), 30 Jan 1998, Hansard vol. 305 cc696–700, api. parliament.uk/historic-hansard/commons/1998/jan/30/land-public-access

42 Gordon Prentice MP, speech during House of Commons debate on Right to Roam Private Members Bill, 26 Mar 1999.

43 *Lancashire Telegraph*, 'MP tops hunters' "most wanted" list', 18 Dec 2003, www.lancashiretelegraph.co.uk/news/5866278.mp-tops-hunters-most-wanted-list/

44 BBC News, 'Huge turnout for countryside march', 22 Sep 2002, news.bbc.co.uk/1/hi/uk/2274129.stm

45 Jonathon Carr-Brown, 'Aristocrats and tycoons bankroll foxhunt lobby', *Sunday Times*, 19 Sep 2004, www.thetimes.co.uk/article/aristocrats-and-tycoons-bankroll-foxhunt-lobby-vj3fjrcfdzc

46 'The Countryside Alliance has always encouraged people to visit the countryside and supported the CROW Act': Tim Bonner, 'Playing politics in the countryside', 3 Nov 2022, www.countryside-alliance.org/resources/news/tim-bonner-playing-politics-in-the-countryside

47 Tim Bonner, 'Labour turns its back on "Right to Roam" campaigners', 26 Oct 2023, www.countryside-alliance.org/resources/news/tim-bonner-labour-turns-its-back-on-right-to-roam-campaigners

48 YouGov polling for the Right to Roam campaign, 8–9 Jan 2024. Full results online at ygo-assets-websites-editorial-emea.yougov.net/documents/WyldService_OpenCountry_240109_W.pdf. The poll was covered by Adam Vaughan, 'Country dwellers just as keen as townies on better nature access', *The Times*, 23 Jan 2024.

49 Patrick Barkham, 'Littering epidemic in England as government spends just £2k promoting Countryside Code', *Guardian*, 26 Aug 2020, www.theguardian.com/uk-news/2020/aug/26/littering-epidemic-england-countryside-code

50 In 2021, following Right to Roam's campaigning, the promotional budget for the Countryside Code was increased to around £50k for the 2021–22 financial year. Patrick Barkham, '"Make a memory": campaigners fear revised Countryside Code lacks bite', *Guardian*, 1 Apr 2021, www.theguardian.com/uk-news/2021/apr/01/make-a-memory-campaigners-fear-revised-countryside-code-lacks-bite. A subsequent FOI request I made to Natural England revealed that the promotional budget increased to *c.* £160k in 2022–23 and *c.* £170k in 2023–24. Whilst any increase is an improvement, this remains peanuts compared to many public information campaigns: for instance, the UK Government spent £46m on its 'Get Ready for Brexit' advertising.

51 Ian Alcock et al., 'Associations between pro-environmental behaviour and neighbourhood nature, nature visit frequency and nature appreciation: Evidence from a nationally representative survey in England', *Environment International* 136, Mar 2020, www.sciencedirect.com/science/article/pii/S0160412019313492?via%3Dihub

52 Dave Bangs, *The Land of the Brighton Line: A field guide to the Middle Sussex and South East Surrey Weald*, 2018, p. 63.

53 Jonathan Moses, 'The need to trespass: let people in to protect nature, says guerrilla

botanist', *Guardian*, 26 Nov 2021, www.theguardian.com/environment/2021/nov/26/david-bangs-sussex-guerrilla-botanist-trespass-protecting-nature-aoe

54 Jonathan Morris, '"Rebel botanists" in Plymouth identify urban plants', BBC News Devon, 8 Sep 2020, www.bbc.co.uk/news/av/uk-england-devon-54012372

55 Tweet by Martyn Oates, Political Editor at BBC South West, 5 May 2023, twitter.com/bbcmartynoates/status/1654309632980967424

56 See, for instance, Raptor Persecution UK, 'The estate that Dorset Police refused to search after discovery of poisoned eagle is the same location where gamekeeper was today convicted of multiple raptor persecution crimes', 4 Jan 2023, raptorpersecutionuk.org/2023/01/04/the-estate-that-dorset-police-refused-to-search-after-discovery-of-poisoned-eagle-is-the-same-location-where-gamekeeper-was-today-convicted-of-multiple-raptor-persecution-crimes/.

57 Nick Hayes, *Wild Service: Why Nature Needs You*, 2024, prologue, p. xv.

58 See 'River Roding Artefacts', a photo collection by Andrew Brown, with text by Paul Powlesland, 2020, www.andrewjohnbrown.com/artefacts

59 Patrick Barkham, '"The Roding is sacred and has rights": the hammer-wielding barrister fighting for London's forgotten river', *Guardian*, 5 Dec 2022, www.theguardian.com/environment/2022/dec/05/river-roding-barrister-paul-powlesland-london-polluters-footpaths

60 You can see Paul's remarkable map of the Roding at www.google.com/maps/d/u/0/viewer?mid=1sRlultQxEvAO1e_PLlRBx-JRtJRhyrg&ll=51.7072236730857%2C0.17641155000003295&z=10

61 Paul Powlesland, 'Guardianship', in Hayes, *Wild Service*, p. 69.

62 Twitter thread by Paul Powlesland, 21 Nov 2022, twitter.com/paulpowlesland/status/1594703825495117831

63 Paul's description of the dumping of construction waste on the Roding's banks is recorded on his Google Map: www.google.com/maps/d/u/0/viewer?mid=1sRlultQxEvAO1e_PLlRBx-JRtJRhyrg&ll=51.622639784186795%2C0.051450390645553234&z=20

64 Twitter thread by Paul Powlesland, 23 Apr 2023, twitter.com/paulpowlesland/status/1651570781275471873. As BBC Radio London reported, the dump comprises approximately 10,000 tonnes of construction waste: twitter.com/BBCRadioLondon/status/1655827468635209729

8 A Sort of National Property

1 *Devon Birds* 76:3, Jan 2024: entries for lapwing and ring ouzel. My thanks to Kevin Cox and Tony Whitehead for sharing this data with me, and for discussing the decline of curlew and other birds on Dartmoor. See also Mary Colwell's tweet about lapwings no longer breeding on Dartmoor, 27 June 2023: twitter.com/curlewcalls/status/1673646619609145350.

2 The revised target of 500 ha (1,200 acres) can be seen in the Dartmoor National Park Authority management plan 2021–26, www.yourdartmoor.org/the-plan/better-for-nature/conserve-and-enhance-natural-beauty. The original target of 2,000 ha (5,000 acres) can be seen via the Internet Archive's Wayback Machine,

in this snapshot of the same DNPA webpage from 30 June 2021: web.archive. org/web/20210630140913/www.yourdartmoor.org/the-plan/better-for-nature/ conserve-and-enhance-natural-beauty

3   For a map of Dartmoor's largest landowners, see my blog 'Who owns Dartmoor?', 22 Mar 2021, whoownsengland.org/2021/03/22/who-owns-dartmoor/

4   See the Wild Card website, www.wildcard.land/

5   GIS map of land owned and leased by Dartmoor National Park Authority, obtained by the author via FOI request. The entry for the Princetown visitor centre shows it is leased by the Duchy to DNPA.

6   Tweet by Tim Bonner, 1 Oct 2023, twitter.com/CA_TimB/ status/1708469864376029638

7   Robert Burnard, *Plundered Dartmoor*, 20 Dec 1895. My thanks to Kate Ashbrook of the Open Spaces Society for sending me a copy of Burnard's map and pamphlet. For more on Burnard (and a photo of his map of Dartmoor's enclosures), see Kate Ashbrook, 'Dartmoor's Burnard', 15 Apr 2020, campaignerkate.wordpress. com/2020/04/15/dartmoors-burnard/

8   Burnard, *Plundered Dartmoor*.

9   Burnard, *Plundered Dartmoor*.

10   Kevin Cox, Alice Groom, Kate Jennings and Isobel Mercer (RSPB), 'National Parks or Natural Parks: how can we have both?', *British Wildlife*, Dec 2018, pp. 87–96.

11   Data on the number of sheep in England's national parks comes from DEFRA, 'Structure of the agricultural industry in England and the UK at June', 2021 data, spreadsheet for national parks: www.gov.uk/government/ statistical-data-sets/structure-of-the-agricultural-industry-in-england-and-the-uk-at-june. Data on the number of people living in England's national parks comes from the Office for National Statistics (ONS), 'National park residents, England and Wales: Census 2021', 9 June 2023, www. ons.gov.uk/peoplepopulationandcommunity/populationandmigration/ populationestimates/bulletins/nationalparkresidentsenglandandwales/ census2021. The precise figures are: sheep – 2,858,694; people – 320,571. In other words, more than eight times as many sheep as people.

12   My analysis for Rewilding Britain: '20% of National Park Land is Nature-Impoverished Grouse Moor', 5 Aug 2021, www.rewildingbritain.org.uk/press-hub/20-per-cent-of-national-park-land-is-nature-impoverished-grouse-moor

13   Danny Gross, 'Missing in action: natural climate solutions in England's national parks', Friends of the Earth, 29 Sep 2020, policy.friendsoftheearth.uk/insight/ missing-action-natural-climate-solutions-englands-national-parks

14   DEFRA, 'Structure of the agricultural industry in England and the UK at June'. The figure of 68% of England being used for agriculture comes from the same source, in the spreadsheet labelled 'England annual time series (1983 to 2023)'. For consistency with the national parks data, I have used the 2021 figure.

15   Professor Ron Edwards (chair), 'Fit for the Future. Report of the National Parks Review Panel', Countryside Commission, 1991. I have republished the report's table of national park ownership statistics in my blog post, 'Are landed

interests over-represented on England's national park authorities?', 24 June 2019, whoownsengland.org/2019/06/24/are-landed-interests-over-represented-on-englands-national-park-authorities/. When Edwards carried out his review, there were still no national parks in Scotland (the first was created in 2002), and the South Downs and New Forest had not yet been designated as national parks in England.

16   Guy Shrubsole, 'Who owns the South Downs?', 16 Feb 2018, whoownsengland.org/2018/02/16/who-owns-the-south-downs/

17   Guy Shrubsole, 'Who owns Dartmoor?', 22 Mar 2021, whoownsengland.org/2021/03/22/who-owns-dartmoor/

18   My map of grouse moor owners, including those in the North York Moors, can be seen at grousemoors.whoownsengland.org/. A full list of the fifteen landowners who dominate the land above the moorland line in the North York Moors is given in Shrubsole, *Who Owns England?*, pp. 248–9.

19   Analysis conducted by the author for Rewilding Britain, 2021. My Google Map of land in national parks owned by public bodies and water firms can be seen at www.google.com/maps/d/u/0/edit?mid=11OyJM2kP9socbf6k_aBiI6-TNCjBecwr&ll=51.284626459132824%2C-3.153762640625004&z=7

20   Exmoor National Park Authority website, 'FAQs on land sales and disposals', www.exmoor-nationalpark.gov.uk/about-us/open-data/land-and-assets/disposals; Zoe Tidman, 'National park could be forced to sell off public woodland because of funding cuts', *Independent*, 16 Nov 2022, www.independent.co.uk/climate-change/news/exmoor-national-park-budget-cuts-b2225391.html.

21   Christina Massey, 'Peak District chiefs plan to sell off part of national park', *Derbyshire Live*, 31 Mar 2023, www.derbytelegraph.co.uk/news/local-news/peak-district-chiefs-plan-sell-8311460

22   Peak District National Park Authority, 'Capital Strategy 2023/23 to 2027/28', 8 Mar 2023, democracy.peakdistrict.gov.uk/documents/s50777/Capital%20Strategy%20March%202023.pdf

23   Campaign for National Parks blog, 'Severe funding cuts threaten the future of our National Parks' (no date, but embedded links suggest 2022), www.cnp.org.uk/news/severe-funding-cuts-threaten-future-our-national-parks; see also Campaign for National Parks briefing, 'Impact of grant cuts on English national park authorities', July 2015, www.cnp.org.uk/sites/default/files/uploadsfiles/Final%20national%20Stop%20the%20Cuts%20briefing%20July%202015.pdf

24   I am grateful to Rose O'Neill, chief executive of the Campaign for National Parks, for sharing the latest intelligence with me on these land sales proposals.

25   Exmoor NPA, 'Exmoor Nature Recovery Vision', 3 Nov 2020, www.exmoor-nationalpark.gov.uk/about-us/meetings-agendas-reports/exmoor-national-park-authority/03-nov-2020/ar-enpa-03.11.20-Item-13.pdf, and Exmoor NPA press release, 'Our vision to restore nature on Exmoor', 4 Nov 2020, www.exmoor-nationalpark.gov.uk/about-us/press-room/press-room/news-2020/our-shared-vision-to-restore-nature-on-exmoor.

26   Emma Gatten, 'Rewilding will turn Exmoor into a "rich boys' playground",

say fearful farmers', *The Telegraph*, 6 Nov 2020, www.telegraph.co.uk/environment/2020/11/06/rewilding-will-turn-exmoor-rich-boys-playground-say-fearful/

27 The Westermill shoot is shown on Exmoor NPA's map of pheasant shoots in Exmoor – GIS map obtained by the author under FOI (and see Chapter 6 for more details). See also tweet by Oliver Edwards (@Exmoorfarmer) on 17 Dec 2017, 'Shoot day at Westermill syndicate', twitter.com/exmoor_farmer/status/942320313920049152 and accompanying post on Instagram, www.instagram.com/p/BczDg6QHp99/. For acreage and location, see the farm's website, www.westermill.com/contact_us.html

28 The full results can be found in my blog post, 'Are landed interests over-represented on England's national park authorities?', 24 June 2019, whoownsengland.org/2019/06/24/are-landed-interests-over-represented-on-englands-national-park-authorities/

29 Agricultural employment figures: as of 2022 (the latest year available), 471,000 people were employed on commercial farm holdings in the UK; that's 0.7% of the UK population of 67m. DEFRA, DAERA, Welsh Government and Scottish Government, 'Agriculture in the UK 2022', assets.publishing.service.gov.uk/media/6548e4bc59b9f5000d85a2cc/auk-2022-13jul23ii.pdf. Forestry employment figures: as of 2023, 20,000 people were employed in forestry in the UK, 0.02% of the UK population of 67m. Forest Research, 'Forestry Statistics 2023', Sep 2023, list of key findings: www.forestresearch.gov.uk/tools-and-resources/statistics/forestry-statistics/

30 GIS mapping analysis by the author for Rewilding Britain in 2021. The total area of land owned by public bodies (the MOD, Forestry Commission and its devolved equivalents, Natural England, NPAs and councils) across all fifteen of Britain's national parks sums to 594,897 acres. The total area of the national parks is 5,719,128 acres. So public bodies own 10.4% of Britain's national parks.

31 Swedish Environmental Protection Agency, 'Sweden's 30 National Parks: A Guide to our Finest Landscapes', 2020, p. 6, www.naturvardsverket.se/4ac63f/globalassets/media/publikationer-pdf/8800/978-91-620-8815-6.pdf

32 'All National Parks in Ireland are fully owned and managed by the State through the National Parks and Wildlife Service' – Malcolm Noonan, Minister of State at the Department of Housing, Local Government and Heritage, during Dáil Éireann debate on national parks, 19 Jan 2022, www.oireachtas.ie/en/debates/question/2022-01-19/449/. See also Irish Government's webpage for Killarney National Park, www.nationalparks.ie/killarney/

33 Spanish Ministry for the Ecological Transition, 'The National Parks Network', 14 Mar 2019, table on pp. 6–7 (note that the table shows total percentage of public land in national park to be 85%, whereas the preceding sentence erroneously states it to be 82%): www.miteco.gob.es/content/dam/miteco/es/red-parques-nacionales/divulgacion/red-parques-ingles-2019_tcm30-67600.pdf

34 Japanese Ministry of the Environment, 'Natural Park Systems in Japan', undated briefing, p. 2, www.env.go.jp/en/nature/nps/park/doc/files/parksystem.pdf. See also MoE webpage, 'Definition of National Parks: Purpose and Function',

www.env.go.jp/en/nature/nps/park/about/index.html, where under the section 'Characteristics of Japan's National Parks' there is a pie chart showing that, as of 2017, state-owned land comprised 60.2% of the land in national parks, with other public land comprising a further 12.8%.

35   William Wordsworth, *Guide to the Lakes*, 1835 edition, p. 70.

36   Wordsworth, *Guide to the Lakes*, pp. 68–70.

37   The Lake District National Park is 583,747 acres, according to the Lake District National Park Authority's website: www.lakedistrict.gov.uk/learning/factsandfigures. Measuring GIS maps of land owned by the National Trust within the Lake District NP gives an area of 110,124 acres, or around 18% of the Lake District.

38   Quoted in Sheail, *Nature in Trust*, p. 71.

39   Virtually every Labour manifesto between 1918 and 1945 pledged land nationalisation and the taxation of land values. Its 1929 manifesto attacked private landlords for 'starving the land of capital and the countryside of cultivation and people', and proposed that 'the land must therefore pass under public control.' See www.labour-party.org.uk/manifestos/1929/1929-labour-manifesto.shtml

40   Sheail, *Nature in Trust*, p. 73.

41   Report of the National Parks Committee ('Addison Report'), 1931, p. 13.

42   Addison Report, pp. 13, 16.

43   Addison Report, p. 56.

44   Addison Report, p. 1.

45   Quoted in Sheail, *Nature in Trust*, p. 76.

46   John Dower, Ministry of Town and Country Planning, 'National Parks in England and Wales' (the 'Dower Report'), May 1945, p. 15.

47   Dower Report, p. 28.

48   Dower Report, p. 15.

49   Dower Report, p. 45.

50   Dower Report, pp. 45–6.

51   See, for instance, Dower's enthusiasm for Sir George Stapledon and agricultural 'improvement' on p. 21 of the Dower Report.

52   Dower Report, pp. 42–3.

53   Report by the Scottish National Parks Survey Committee, 'National Parks: A Scottish Survey' (the 'Ramsay Report'), 1945, p. 5.

54   Ramsay Report, p. 10.

55   Ann and Malcolm MacEwen, *Greenprints for the Countryside? The Story of Britain's National Parks*, 1987, p. 10.

56   Report of the National Parks Committee (England and Wales), ('Hobhouse Report'), 1947; see also MacEwen and MacEwen, *Greenprints for the Countryside?*, p. 12.

57   MacEwen and MacEwen, *Greenprints for the Countryside?*, pp. 6–7.

58   Lewis Silkin, Minister of Town and Country Planning, second reading of the National Parks and Access to the Countryside Bill, 31 Mar 1949, Hansard, col 1486, hansard.parliament.uk/Commons/1949-03-31/debates/acd6cf72-b57e-430b-8f4f-1bf73665c540/NationalParksAndAccessToTheCountrysideBill

59   Stanley Clark, *Bristol Evening Post,* 6 June 1949, via British Newspaper Archive.

60   Ann and Malcolm MacEwen, *National Parks: conservation or cosmetics?,* 1982, p. 18.

61   For more on the administrative flaws of the 1949 Act, see MacEwen and MacEwen, *Greenprints for the Countryside?,* pp. 12–14. National Park Authorities were eventually set up through the 1995 Environment Act.

62   MacEwen and MacEwen, *Greenprints for the Countryside?,* p.12.

63   Hobhouse Report, p. 40.

64   Jennifer Jenkins and Patrick James, *From Acorn to Oak Tree: The growth of the National Trust, 1895–1994,* 1994, p. 140. Dalton's remark is probably a reference to the conflicts between the Kinder Scout trespassers and the Duke of Devonshire over access in the Peak District.

65   MacEwen and MacEwen, *Greenprints for the Countryside?,* p.12; MacEwen and MacEwen, *National Parks,* p. 12.

66   Marion Shoard, *This Land Is Our Land: The Struggle for Britain's Countryside,* 1987, p. 313. Shoard was citing a study of access agreements done in 1973, but as she stated, 'the situation has not changed significantly since then.'

67   MacEwen and MacEwen, *Greenprints for the Countryside?,* p. 7.

68   Kelly, 'Conventional thinking and the fragile birth of the nature state in post-war Britain', p. 116.

69   For example, 300 acres of oak and beech at Buckland Woods along the River Webburn were clear-felled in 1959, despite the best efforts of Sylvia Sayer and the Dartmoor Preservation Association. See Matthew Kelly, *The Women who Saved the English Countryside,* 2022, pp. 291–2.

70   Kielder Water was conceived in the late 1960s and given the go-ahead by Parliament in 1974. See C.S. McCulloch, 'The Kielder Water Scheme: the last of its kind?', 2006 conference paper to the British Dams Society, britishdams. org/2006conf/papers/Paper%2010%20Mcculloch.PDF

71   Kate Ashbrook, 'Cambrian Mountains: the park that never was', 17 July 2023, campaignerkate.wordpress.com/2023/07/17/cambrian-mountains-the-park-that-never-was/

72   MacEwen and MacEwen, *Greenprints for the Countryside?,* p. 19.

73   This was the conclusion of the Porchester Review, which found that between 1947 and 1976, the area of moorland on Exmoor had fallen by 4,900ha (12,000a.). See Matt Lobley and Michael Winter, 'Born out of crisis': Assessing the Legacy of the Exmoor Moorland Management Agreements', *Rural History* 20:2, 2009, pp. 229–47, ore.exeter.ac.uk/repository/bitstream/handle/10036/4118/Lobley_78435_Born%20out%20of%20crisis.pdf

74   The words of John Phillips, an expert on heather management, in his 1977 report 'Certain aspects of Exmoor', cited in MacEwen, *National Parks,* p. 178.

75   This account draws on Lobley and Winter, 'Born out of crisis'.

76   MacEwen, *National Parks: conservation or cosmetics?,* p. 193.

77   For more on Ron Edwards, see Steve Ormerod's obituary in the *Independent,* 11 Aug 2007, republished on the website of Cardiff University: www.cardiff.ac.uk/obituaries/obituary/ron-edwards

78   Report of the National Parks Review Panel, 'Fit for the Future' (the 'Edwards Review'), Jan 1991, p. 29.

79   Edwards Review, pp. 58–9, 61; p. 20.

80   HM Government, Environment Act 1995, Part III: National Parks.

81   DEFRA, 'Landscapes Review: Final Report' (the 'Glover Report'), Sep 2019, p. 12, assets.publishing.service.gov.uk/media/5d8a19a3e5274a083d3b78bd/landscapes-review-final-report.pdf

82   Glover Report, p. 38.

83   Julian Glover, 'Tories must tackle the failure of the state, not abolish it', *Guardian*, 3 Oct 2010, www.theguardian.com/commentisfree/2010/oct/03/conservatives-state-smaller-effective-government. Glover's report touched upon land ownership when he made the obvious point that NPAs must 'work in partnership with others, since they are not significant landowners' (p. 13). But it contained no deeper analysis of why this has ended up being the case, and how anomalous it is internationally.

84   Glover Report, p. 44.

85   Richard Benwell, 'Will the Environment Bill weaken legal protection for sites and species?', May 2021, www.wcl.org.uk/habitats-regs-at-risk.asp. The discussion here concerns a clause in the then Environment Bill (now Environment Act 2021), but the same form of words exists in the National Parks Act 1949 and Environment Act 1995.

86   Glover Report, p. 50.

87   Levelling Up and Regeneration Act 2023, section 245, p.295, www.legislation.gov.uk/ukpga/2023/55/pdfs/ukpga_20230055_en.pdf. Section 11A of the National Parks & Access to the Countryside Act 1949 defines 'relevant authority' as encompassing public bodies and 'statutory undertakers', which includes water companies that own land in national parks: www.legislation.gov.uk/ukpga/Geo6/12-13-14/97/section/11A

88   Campaign for National Parks, 'National Parks Health Check Report: Nature Recovery', April 2024, p.28, https://www.cnp.org.uk/wp-content/uploads/2024/04/National-Parks-Health-Check-Report-Nature-Recovery-2024.pdf

9 An Ecological Domesday

1   Meredith Paker, 'Industrial, regional, and gender divides in British unemployment between the wars', Oct 2020, p. 2, www.economics.ox.ac.uk/files/jobmarketpaper-meredithpakerpdf

2   'New "Domesday" Book', *Tamworth Herald*, 11 Apr 1931; 'Modern Domesday', *Daily News* (London), 6 Apr 1936, via British Newspaper Archive.

3   L. Dudley Stamp, *Man and the Land*, 1955, p. 242.

4   Land Utilisation Survey of Britain, 'Instruction Leaflet for Schools', 4th edn June 1932, reproduced in Humphrey Southall and Paula Aucott, 'The Records of the Land Utilisation Surveys of Britain: A Report for the Frederick Soddy Trust', Jan 2007, pp. 14–17, pure.port.ac.uk/ws/portalfiles/portal/178033/Soddy_Report_Land_Use_Surveys.pdf

5   Land Utilisation Survey of Britain, 'Instruction Leaflet for Schools'.

6   L. Dudley Stamp, 'The Land of Britain: Its Use and Misuse', 1948, p. 425.

7   L. Dudley Stamp, 'Nationalism and Land Utilization in Britain', *Geographical Review* 27:1, Jan 1937, p. 14. Also reproduced in Stamp, 'The Land of Britain', p. 438, and preceding discussion, pp. 435–7.

8   For more on this period's history and the development of town planning and rural preservation movements, see David Matless, *Landscape and Englishness*, 2016 (second edition), especially Chapter 1: Ordering England.

9   L. Dudley Stamp, *Man and the Land*, 1955, p. 240.

10   John Betjeman, 'Slough', 1937.

11   R.G. Stapledon, *The Land, now and to-morrow*, 1935, pp. 50–1.

12   L. Dudley Stamp, *The Land of Britain and How It Is Used*, 1946, p. 79.

13   The CPRE was founded 1926. In 1928 one of its founding members, the architect Clough Williams-Ellis, published *England and the Octopus*, about the 'octopus' of unbridled development.

14   Dudley Stamp, *Man and the Land*, p. 242.

15   Lord Reith, in Lords debate on a Central Planning Authority, *Hansard*, vol 121, cc751–96, 11 Feb 1942, api.parliament.uk/historic-hansard/lords/1942/feb/11/central-planning-authority#S5LV0121P0_19420211_HOL_10. In two of his books, Dudley Stamp states that around this time the Government told both Houses of Parliament that it would 'seek to avoid the use of good agricultural land for housing development where other and less valued land could be appropriately used' (*The Land of Britain*, p. 441; *Man and the Land*, p. 242). I cannot, however, find this exact sentence in the Hansard archive, so assume he is paraphrasing Lord Reith's statement.

16   For Dudley Stamp's account, see *Man and the Land*, pp. 244–8. A black and white version of his map is shown on p. 243. A 'small outline map' was published in the 'Scott Report' – the Report of the Committee on Land Utilisation in Rural Areas (Cmd. 6378), 1942.

17   The Land Classification map published in 1945 by Ordnance Survey, based on Dudley Stamp's LUS and work by the Ministry of Town and Country Planning, can be viewed on the National Library of Scotland's maps website: maps.nls.uk/view/91546453

18   Chart by Full Fact, 'House building: at its lowest level since the 1920s?', 29 Sep 2016, fullfact.org/economy/house-building-lowest-level-1920s/. As their chart shows, house building did surge in the 1930s, but reached neither the same peak nor the sustained growth of 1945–75.

19   Town and Country Planning Act 1947, s12(2)(e), www.legislation.gov.uk/ukpga/1947/51/pdfs/ukpga_19470051_en.pdf

20   NCC, *Nature Conservation and Agriculture*, 1977, back cover text.

21   NCC, *Nature Conservation and Agriculture*, p. 28. The proposals for a national rural land use strategy was also discussed on pp. 30–1.

22   D.A. Ratcliffe, 'Nature Conservation: Aims, Methods and Achievements', *Proceedings of the Royal Society of London*, Series B: *Biological Sciences*, cxcvii, no. 1126 (1977), p. 26, royalsocietypublishing.org/doi/pdf/10.1098/rspb.1977.0054

23   Max Nicholson, 'Rallying to the call of the wild', *Guardian*, 5 Mar 1981.

24   Caroline Moorhead, 'Landscape Villains' (review of *The Theft of the Countryside*), *The Times*, 29 Oct 1980, marionshoard.co.uk/Books/The-Theft-Of-The-Countryside/Reviews.php#landscapevillains

25   Shoard, *The Theft of the Countryside*, pp. 204–5.

26   Even in 2023, only 8.8% of England is built on. That figure falls to just 5.9% when looking at the whole of the UK. Mark Easton, 'How much of your area is built on?', BBC News, 9 Nov 2017, www.bbc.co.uk/news/uk-41901294. The analysis was done by Dr Alasdair Rae using CORINE data.

27   Shoard, *The Theft of the Countryside*, p. 205.

28   Christopher Hall, 'Who needs a national land use strategy?', *New Scientist* 90, 1981, pp. 10–12.

29   House of Commons debates, 'Countryside Bill', Hansard, Vol 961, 30 Jan 1979, hansard.parliament.uk/commons/1979-01-30/debates/145175dc-a1b9-42da-9244-8e0fa02a269f/CountrysideBill. The relevant section of the Bill was clause 6(1).

30   Matthew Kelly, 'Habitat Protection, Ideology and the British Nature State: The Politics of the Wildlife and Countryside Act 1981', *The English Historical Review* 137:586, June 2022, pp. 847–83, doi.org/10.1093/ehr/ceac112

31   Kelly, 'Habitat Protection, Ideology and the British Nature State'. For the relevant debate, see Hansard, 'Wildlife and Countryside Bill', House of Lords, 12 Feb 1981, vol. 417, cols 285–340, api.parliament.uk/historic-hansard/lords/1981/feb/12/wildlife-and-countryside-bill-hl#column_285.

32   Charlie Pye-Smith and Chris Rose, *Crisis and Conservation: Conflict in the British Countryside*, 1984, pp. 11, 49, 134.

33   NCC, *Nature Conservation in Great Britain*, p. 49.

34   NCC, *Nature Conservation in Great Britain*, p. 88.

35   N.W. Moore, *The Bird of Time: the science and politics of nature conservation*, 1987, p. 117.

36   'Norman Moore, conservationist – obituary', *Telegraph*, 22 Oct 2015, www.telegraph.co.uk/news/obituaries/11948316/Norman-Moore-conservationist-obituary.html

37   In their 1987 general election manifesto, the Labour Party pledged to 'extend the planning system to cover agricultural forestry and water developments requiring them, and industry, to take account of environmental considerations'. But Labour once again lost to Thatcher's Conservatives in a landslide.

38   Michael Winter, 'Land use policy in the UK: The politics of control', *Land Development Studies* 7:1, 1990, pp. 3–14.

39   Committee on Climate Change, 'Building a low-carbon economy – the UK's contribution to tackling climate change', 2008, p. 351, www.theccc.org.uk/wp-content/uploads/2008/12/Building-a-low-carbon-economy-Committtee-on-Climate-Change-2008.pdf

40   Professor Sir John Lawton (chair), 'Making Space for Nature: A review of England's Wildlife Sites and Ecological Network' (The 'Lawton Review'), Sep 2010, p. viii.

41   David Miliband, 'A land fit for the future?', speech to CPRE, 9 Mar 2007. The

full text of Miliband's speech seems to have disappeared from the internet (the DEFRA archived webpage for it no longer works), but a summary can be found on this CPRE blog site, from which these quotes have been taken: cpredebates. wordpress.com/2007/03/09/david-milibands-vision-for-the-future-of-the-land/

42 Some of the flow diagrams in the Foresight report are just out of control: yes, land use systems are complicated, but when faced with these wonkish powerpoint slides it's perhaps not surprising that some politicians baulked at the challenge. Government Office for Science, Foresight *Land Use Futures* project, 2010, accompanying Systems Maps: assets.publishing.service.gov.uk/media/5a7 cb744e5274a38e57564fd/10-632-land-use-futures-systems-maps.pdf

43 CPRE, 'Landlines: Why we need a strategic approach to land', 2017, www. cpre.org.uk/wp-content/uploads/2019/11/CPREZLandlinesZ-ZwhyZweZneed ZaZstrategicZapproachZtoZland.pdf. In 2016, the RSPB's then Conservation Director Martin Harper advocated for a national land use strategy in his blog post 'The 2016 challenge: managing land for life', 4 Jan 2016, community.rspb. org.uk/ourwork/b/martinharper/posts/managing-land-for-life. Green Alliance have written numerous briefings and reports on the need for a land use strategy or framework; for example, 'Back to the land', report for FFCC, 2 May 2019, ffcc.co.uk/publications/paper-back-to-the-land; 'Land of opportunity: a new land use framework to restore nature and level up Britain', 13 Aug 2022, green-alliance.org.uk/publication/land-of-opportunity-a-new-land-use-framework-to-restore-nature-and-level-up-britain/

44 RSA FFCC final report, 'Our future in the land', 2019, pp. 54–5, www.thersa. org/globalassets/reports/rsa-ffcc-our-future-in-the-land.pdf

45 'National Food Strategy: An independent review for government – The Plan', 2021, pp. 156, 232–3, www.nationalfoodstrategy.org/

46 'We will publish a land use framework in 2023 to ensure we meet our net zero and biodiversity targets, and help our farmers adapt to a changing climate, whilst continuing to produce high quality, affordable produce that supports a healthier diet.' DEFRA, Government Food Strategy, June 2022, p. 11, assets. publishing.service.gov.uk/government/uploads/system/uploads/attachment_ data/file/1082026/government-food-strategy.pdf.

47 Committee on Climate Change, 2022 Progress Report to Parliament, June 2022, p. 41, entry in table for 'Agriculture and Land Use Strategy', www.theccc.org.uk/ wp-content/uploads/2022/06/Progress-in-reducing-emissions-2022-Report-to-Parliament.pdf

48 Abi Kay, 'Land Use Framework won't be "communist", says Defra minister', *Farmers Weekly*, 13 July 2023, www.fwi.co.uk/news/land-use-framework-wont-be-communist-says-defra-minister

49 House of Lords Land Use in England Committee, 'Making the most out of England's land', Report of Session 2022–23, 13 Dec 2022, Chapter 5: A land use framework and a Land Use Commission, publications.parliament.uk/pa/ ld5803/ldselect/ldland/105/10502.htm

50 Scottish Government, 'Getting the best from our land: land use strategy for Scotland', 17 Mar 2011, section 1.1, Principles for Sustainable Land Use

(principle (i)), www.gov.scot/publications/getting-best-land-land-use-strategy-scotland/pages/2/

51 'Land is too often seen as doing one thing or another . . . Yet land can and should deliver multiple benefits . . . A framework for land use in England would manage competing pressures on land and encourage multifunctionality.' RSA FFCC final report, 'Our future in the land', 2019, pp. 54–5, www.thersa.org/globalassets/reports/rsa-ffcc-our-future-in-the-land.pdf. See also House of Lords Land Use in England Committee, 'Making the most out of England's land', Chapter 4: The future of land use: multifunctionality and integration of priorities, publications.parliament.uk/pa/ld5803/ldselect/ldland/105/10507.htm

52 'National Food Strategy: An independent review for government – The Evidence', 2021, p. 41, www.nationalfoodstrategy.org/

53 'National Food Strategy: An independent review for government – The Plan', pp. 156, 232–3

54 CCC, 'Land use: Policies for a Net Zero UK', Jan 2020, www.theccc.org.uk/publication/land-use-policies-for-a-net-zero-uk/, and underpinning spatial modelling analysis commissioned from Environment System Ltd (Envsys), 'Tree Suitability Modelling – Planting Opportunities for Sessile Oak and Sitka Spruce in Wales in a Changing Climate', Jan 2020, www.theccc.org.uk/wp-content/uploads/2020/01/Environment-Systems-Ltd-2020-Tree-Suitability-Modelling-%E2%80%93-Planting-Opportunities-for-Sessile-Oak-and-Sitka-Spruce-in-Wales-in-a-Changing-Climate.pdf; 'National Food Strategy: An independent review for government – The Plan', 2021, maps shown on pp. 234–5, www.nationalfoodstrategy.org/; Centre for Alternative Technology, 'Zero Carbon Britain – Rethinking the Future', 2013, pp. 81–98 on land use, cat.org.uk/info-resources/zero-carbon-britain/research-reports/zero-carbon-rethinking-the-future/; Friends of the Earth, 'Balancing UK Land Use: A Guide to Friends of the Earth's UK Land Calculator', Nov 2016, policy.friendsoftheearth.uk/sites/default/files/documents/2019-11/uk-land-use-calculator-guide-99953.pdf, and 'Finding the land to double tree cover', Mar 2020, policy.friendsoftheearth.uk/insight/finding-land-double-tree-cover; Lydia Collas and Dustin Benton, Green Alliance, 'Shaping UK land use: priorities for food, nature and climate', Jan 2023, green-alliance.org.uk/wp-content/uploads/2023/02/Shaping-UK-land-use.pdf

55 Finch et al., 'Spatially targeted nature-based solutions can mitigate climate change and nature loss but require a systems approach', *One Earth* 6:10, 20 Oct 2023, pp. 1350–74, www.sciencedirect.com/science/article/pii/S259033222300444X. See also Vanessa Amaral-Rogers, 'Challenges and benefits of a net zero UK land sector', RSPB website, 20 Oct 2023, community.rspb.org.uk/ourwork/b/science/posts/challenges-and-benefits-of-a-net-zero-uk-land-sector.

56 Finch et al., 'Spatially targeted nature-based solutions can mitigate climate change and nature loss but require a systems approach'.

57 Twitter thread by Tom Finch, 20 Oct 2023, x.com/tomfinch89/status/1715275330066305078?s=20

58 The chair of the House of Lords Land Use in England Committee was Lord

Cameron of Dillington, who owns a 3,000-acre estate in Somerset. See Lord Cameron's register of interests, members.parliament.uk/member/3705/registeredinterests, and website for the Dillington Estate, www.dillingtonestate.co.uk/.

59   Government Office for Science, Foresight *Land Use Futures* project, final report, 2010, p. 80, assets.publishing.service.gov.uk/media/5a7c30bfe5274a1f5cc76631/10-631-land-use-futures.pdf

60   See DEFRA, 'Structure of the agricultural industry in England and the UK at June' (last updated Oct 2023), www.gov.uk/government/statistical-data-sets/structure-of-the-agricultural-industry-in-england-and-the-uk-at-june. Under the England heading, select 'results by type of farm' and within the spreadsheet select the tab named 'Farm sizes (area and holdings)'; see the columns for numbers of farms less than 100ha (*c.* 250 acres) and the total farmed area under farms of this size. There are 104,476 farms in England as of 2022; 79,518 of these – or 76% – are below *c.* 250 acres in size.

61   For example, if a landowner chose to split their landholdings between multiple companies (as some already do), a Land Use Commission could see from Companies House data on 'Persons with Significant Control' that all of these companies have the same ultimate owner. The Land Registry records for these companies' landholdings would then be combined and, if the 1,000-acre+ threshold is reached, the reporting duty would be invoked.

62   DEFRA publish annual farm statistics which enumerate the number of farm holdings in England and the area of land covered by farms of different sizes. Counting the number of farm holdings isn't quite the same as counting the number of landowners: many farms are tenanted. But in the absence of an opened-up Land Registry, it's our best available proxy dataset, and one that I discussed in my earlier book *Who Owns England?*. Using DEFRA's latest 2022 dataset as a proxy for land ownership shows that around 25,000 landowners own 16.8m acres, or 52% of England. We know from DEFRA's data that each of these owners' landholdings is larger than 250 acres (100 ha), but it's not possible to say exactly how many landholdings are larger than, say, 1,000 acres. For the data, see DEFRA, 'Structure of the agricultural industry in England and the UK at June' (last updated October 2023), www.gov.uk/government/statistical-data-sets/structure-of-the-agricultural-industry-in-england-and-the-uk-at-june. Under the England heading, select 'results by type of farm' and within the spreadsheet select the tab named 'Farm sizes (area and holdings)'; see the columns for numbers of farms >=100ha and the total farmed area under farms of this size.

63   Following provisions laid down in section 85 of the Climate Change Act 2008, the Companies Act 2006 (Strategic Report and Directors' Reports) Regulations 2013 laid a requirement on large and medium-sized companies to report information on greenhouse gas emissions in their Directors' Reports. The relevant section of the Regulations can be read at www.legislation.gov.uk/uksi/2013/1970/regulation/7/made

64   The Scottish Government is proposing the publication of 'compulsory Land Management Plans' for all estates over 3,000ha (a threshold that seems

unnecessarily high, particularly if applied to England where estates tend to be smaller than in Scotland). See Scottish Government, 'Land Reform in a Net Zero Nation: Consultation Paper', Part 6, pp.14–17: www.gov.scot/binaries/content/documents/govscot/publications/consultation-paper/2022/07/land-reform-net-zero-nation-consultation-paper/documents/land-reform-net-zero-nation-consultation-paper/land-reform-net-zero-nation-consultation-paper/govscot%3Adocument/land-reform-net-zero-nation-consultation-paper.pdf

65 Hale, 'The Great Audit', p. 293.

Conclusion: A Common Treasury for All

1   Nigel Willby et al., 'Rewilding wetlands: beaver as agents of within-habitat heterogeneity and the responses of contrasting biota', *Phil. Trans. R. Soc. B* 373:1761, Dec 2018, 20170444-20170444, royalsocietypublishing.org/doi/10.1098/rstb.2017.0444

2   For more on Chris Jones' Cornwall Beaver Project and his organic farm, see woodlandvalley.co.uk/beavers/

3   Video by Cornwall Wildlife Trust, Jan 2018, youtu.be/LeOmBbLwPm4

4   Phoebe Weston, '"It's going to be our way now": the guerrilla rewilder shaking up British farming', *Guardian*, 4 Sep 2020, www.theguardian.com/environment/2020/sep/04/its-going-to-be-our-way-now-the-guerrilla-rewilder-shaking-up-british-farming-aoe

5   YouGov poll, 28 Jan 2020 – press release: yougov.co.uk/politics/articles/27455-third-brits-would-reintroduce-wolves-and-lynxes-uk and full results: d3nkl3psvxxpe9.cloudfront.net/documents/Rewilding_survey.pdf

6   On the amount of land owned by Dyson, see Philip Case, 'Brexiter Dyson warns government not to cut farm subsidies', *Farmers Weekly*, 28 July 2017, www.fwi.co.uk/news/brexiteer-dyson-warns-government-not-cut-farm-subsidies, and my blog, 'Why is James Dyson hoovering up land?', 19 Sep 2017, whoownsengland.org/2017/09/19/why-is-james-dyson-hoovering-up-land/. On Dyson being named the richest man in Britain in 2020, see the *Sunday Times* Rich List 2020, www.thetimes.co.uk/article/rich-list-2020-profiles-1-20-featuring-roman-abramovich-and-jim-ratcliffe-50m6h3xdf

7   Alice Thomson, 'James Dyson talks the future of farming, Brexit and why rewilding is a waste of good land', *The Times*, 19 Sep 2020, www.thetimes.co.uk/article/james-dyson-talks-the-future-of-farming-brexit-and-why-rewilding-is-a-waste-of-good-land-jksbzmbn8

8   Richard Drax's Charborough Estate in Dorset covers some 13,800 acres: see my blog post 'The ten landowners who own one-sixth of Dorset', 4 Jan 2020, whoownsengland.org/2020/01/04/the-ten-landowners-who-own-one-sixth-of-dorset/

9   Richard Drax, speech to Parliament, 1 Feb 2022, video and transcript on Drax's website: www.richarddrax.com/news/westminster-hall-debate-environment-land-management-scheme

10 Richard Drax MP, speech to Parliament, 23 Nov 2022, video and transcript on Drax's website: www.richarddrax.com/news/speech-support-british-farming.

11 NFU website, 'Long-term plans needed before beavers are reintroduced', 19 Nov 2021, mid-way down webpage at www.nfuonline.com/updates-and-information/defra-consultation-on-beaver-management/

12 NFU website, 'NFU responds to beavers being given legal protection by government', 21 July 2022, partway down webpage at www.nfuonline.com/updates-and-information/defra-consultation-on-beaver-management/

13 Patrick Barkham, '"You can't control what beavers do or how they do it!" Could rewilding help England fight droughts?', *Guardian*, 24 Aug 2022, www.theguardian.com/environment/2022/aug/24/you-cant-control-what-beavers-do-or-how-they-do-it-could-rewilding-help-england-fight-droughts

14 Katie Tarrant, 'Farmers say tree-felling beavers pose bigger threat in Scotland than Brexit', *Sunday Times*, 2 Oct 2022, www.thetimes.co.uk/article/farmers-say-tree-felling-beavers-pose-bigger-threat-in-scotland-than-brexit-k5xnqhc23

15 The Cairngorms National Park covers some 4,528km², or around 1.1m acres.

16 Mairi Riddoch and Jennifer Bowey, 'Crofters and farmers in Cairngorms park protest', BBC News, 16 Jan 2024, www.bbc.co.uk/news/articles/c892vvwr2gpo. More video footage of the tractors bearing aloft protest signs can be seen on this Facebook post from 15 Jan 2024: www.facebook.com/share/v/gBDqibbedSBFsRSF/?mibextid=WC7FNe

17 Comment on Facebook by Derek Gow, posted at 21.03 on 15 Jan 2024, in response to the anti-beaver protest by Cairngorms farmers: www.facebook.com/share/v/gBDqibbedSBFsRSF/?mibextid=WC7FNe

18 British Trust for Ornithology (BTO), 'BirdTrends 2022' report, section on declining species: www.bto.org/our-science/publications/birdtrends/2022/declining-species

19 Natural England SSSI condition dashboard, figure correct at time of writing: designatedsites.naturalengland.org.uk/ReportFeatureConditionSummary.aspx?SiteType=ALL

20 Newby, *Green and Pleasant Land?*, p. 71.

21 Norman MacCaig, 'A Man in Assynt', in *A Man In My Position*, 1969.

22 GWCT, 'What the Science Says' website, 'Estimating the number and biomass of pheasants in Britain', 14 July 2020, www.whatthesciencesays.org/estimating-the-number-and-biomass-of-pheasants-in-britain/. See also T.M. Blackburn and K.J. Gaston, 'Abundance, biomass and energy use of native and alien breeding birds in Britain' *Biological Invasions*, 2018, 20:3563–3573, link.springer.com/article/10.1007/s10530-018-1795-z

23 An adaptation of a phrase used by the historian John McNeill about Thomas Midgley, the American inventor of CFCs and leaded petrol. See John McNeill, *Something New Under the Sun: An environmental history of the twentieth century*, 2000, p. 111.

24 Winston Churchill, *The People's Rights*, 1909, p. 125.

25 Clare, 'The Moors'.

26 Gerrard Winstanley, *A Watch-Word to the City of London and the Army* (1649), reproduced in Christopher Hill (ed.), *Winstanley: 'The Law of Freedom' and Other Writings*, 1972, p. 128.

27 Winston Churchill, *The People's Rights*, 1909, p. 117.

28 John Stuart Mill, *Principles of Political Economy*, 1866, Book II, Ch. I, § 6, pp. 202–3.

29 Matthew Kelly, 'Habitat Protection, Ideology and the British Nature State'. See also Kelly, 'Conventional thinking and the fragile birth of the nature state in post-war Britain'.

30 Ramsay Report, p. 5.

31 CLA consultation response, 'Environmental Targets', 27 June 2022, www.cla. org.uk/documents/535/CLA_Consultation_Response_on_Environmental_ Targets.pdf: 'the CLA's 27,000 members operate 250 different types of business located in the rural area, covering over 10 million acres across England and Wales'. Grouse moors cover some 550,000 acres of England, using a methodology explained in detail at 'Who owns England's grouse moors?', 28 Oct 2016, whoownsengland.org/2016/10/28/who-owns-englands-grouse-moors/. That figure is a conservative one: the Moorland Association says its members manage 860,000 acres of moorland in England and Wales; see www. moorlandassociation.org/

32 NFU website, 'About us': 'The NFU represents more than 45,000 farming and growing businesses', www.nfuonline.com/about-us/. The Countryside Alliance claims to have 100,000 members; see for instance this job advert for a press officer, 8 May 2017: www.countryside-alliance.org/resources/news/job-opportunity-press-officer-at-the-countryside

33 DEFRA, 'Statistical Digest of Rural England: Businesses', May 2022, p. 8, assets. publishing.service.gov.uk/media/628e8ccb8fa8f5561cd9b2db/Businesses_ May_2022_final.pdf

34 DEFRA, 'The Future Farming and Environment Evidence Compendium', Sep 2019, p. 3, assets.publishing.service.gov.uk/media/5d8b8a1d40f0b609978eee7e/ evidence-compendium-26sep19.pdf

35 CCC, June 2023 progress report, p. 241 (11% of GHGs), www.theccc.org. uk/wp-content/uploads/2023/06/Progress-in-reducing-UK-emissions-2023-Report-to-Parliament.pdf

36 'The electricity sector likely dropped below agriculture for the first time.' Carbon Brief, 'Analysis: UK emissions fell to lowest level since 1879', 11 Mar 2024, www. carbonbrief.org/analysis-uk-emissions-in-2023-fell-to-lowest-level-since-1879/.

37 Emissions from land use and agriculture virtually unchanged over past decade: CCC, June 2023 progress report, p. 17; land use must become net carbon sink by mid-2030s: CCC, June 2022 progress report, p. 285.

38 State of Nature Partnership, 'State of Nature report 2023', p. 3, stateofnature. org.uk/wp-content/uploads/2023/09/TP25999-State-of-Nature-main-report_2023_FULL-DOC-v12.pdf

39 Wildlife & Countryside Link, '2022 Progress Report on 30x30 in England', Oct 2022, /www.wcl.org.uk/assets/uploads/img/files/WCL_2022_Progress_Report_ on_30x30_in_England.pdf

40 'Giving 21% of the least productive farmland to nature would mean we produce 3% less calories.' Henry Dimbleby et al., *The National Food Strategy: The*

Evidence, p. 41, www.nationalfoodstrategy.org/wp-content/uploads/2021/08/NFS_Evidence-Pack.pdf

41 NFU, 'Achieving Net Zero: Farming's 2040 goal', Sep 2019, www.nfuonline.com/media/jq1b2nx5/achieving-net-zero-farming-s-2040-goal.pdf

42 Department for Levelling Up, Housing and Communities (DLUHC), consultation, 'Transparency of land ownership involving trusts', 27 Dec 2023, Executive Summary, www.gov.uk/government/consultations/transparency-of-land-ownership-involving-trusts-consultation/transparency-of-land-ownership-involving-trusts

43 Worrall et al., 'Peatlands and climate change'. See also IUCN UK Commission of Inquiry on Peatlands, 2011, p. 38, www.iucn-uk-peatlandprogramme.org/sites/default/files/2019-07/IUCN%20UK%20Commission%20of%20Inquiry%20on%20Peatlands%20Full%20Report%20spv%20web_0.pdf

44 Evans et al., 'Implementation of an emission inventory for UK peatlands', Report to the Department for Business, Energy and Industrial Strategy, Centre for Ecology and Hydrology, 2017, p. 1, uk-air.defra.gov.uk/assets/documents/reports/cat07/1904111135_UK_peatland_GHG_emissions.pdf

45 Scottish Government, 'Community ownership in Scotland 2021', 27 Sep 2022, www.gov.scot/publications/community-ownership-scotland-2021/. This states that 211,998ha (523,858 acres) of land is owned by communities. Community Land Scotland's latest figures are slightly higher, stating 563,000 acres of land is currently owned by communities: www.communitylandscotland.org.uk/

46 A twelve-month pause in the ordinary sales process is the recommendation of the 'Gregory Review' into community ownership that reported to the Labour Party in early 2024. See the report of the Community Ownership Commission, 'Unleashing Community Ownership', Jan 2024, p. 6, party.coop/wp-content/blogs.dir/5/files/2024/01/20240104-community-ownership-report-final-compress.pdf

47 Report of the Community Ownership Commission, 'Unleashing Community Ownership', Jan 2024, p.7, party.coop/wp-content/blogs.dir/5/files/2024/01/20240104-community-ownership-report-final-compress.pdf

48 Tweet by Matthew Kelly, 12 Feb 2023, twitter.com/Scorhill/status/1624715088065183751

49 Patrick Barkham, 'Littering epidemic in England as government spends just £2k promoting Countryside Code', *Guardian*, 26 Aug 2020, www.theguardian.com/uk-news/2020/aug/26/littering-epidemic-england-countryside-code

50 Jonathan Leake, 'RSPB chief: UK national parks risk losing UN nature reserve status over wildlife losses', *Sunday Times*, 24 Mar 2019, www.thetimes.co.uk/article/rspb-chief-uk-national-parks-risk-losing-un-nature-reserve-status-over-wildlife-losses-kp9zvll0z

51 YouGov polling commissioned by Rewilding Britain, 'Four in five Britons support rewilding, poll finds', 19 Jan 2022, www.rewildingbritain.org.uk/press-hub/four-in-five-britons-support-rewilding-poll-finds

52 See Chapter 9, 'An Ecological Domesday', for the source of these figures.

Index